Studies in Economic Transition

General Editors: **Jens Hölscher**, Professor of Economics, Bournemouth University and Horst Tomann, Professor of Economics, Free University Berlin

This series has been established in response to a growing demand for a greater understanding of the transformation of economic systems. It brings together theoretical and empirical studies on economic transition and economic development. The post-communist transition from planned to market economies is one of the main areas of applied theory because in this field the most dramatic examples of change and economic dynamics can be found. The series aims to contribute to the understanding of specific major economic changes as well as to advance the theory of economic development. The implications of economic policy will be a major point of focus.

Titles include:

Arkadiusz Mironko
DETERMINANTS OF FDI FLOWS WITHIN EMERGING ECONOMIES
A Case Study of Poland

Johannes Stephan (*editor*)
THE TECHNOLOGICAL ROLE OF INWARD FOREIGN DIRECT INVESTMENT IN CENTRAL EAST EUROPE

Vera Trappmann
FALLEN HEROES IN GLOBAL CAPITALISM
Workers and the Restructuring of the Polish Steel Industry

Christopher Hartwell
INSTITUTIONAL BARRIERS IN THE TRANSITION TO MARKET
Examining Performance and Divergence in Transition Economies

Will Bartlett, Sanja Maleković, and Vassilis Monastiriotis (*editors*)
DECENTRALISATION AND LOCAL DEVELOPMENT IN SOUTH-EAST EUROPE

Sönke Maatsch
CENTRAL AND EAST EUROPEAN MIGRANTS' CONTRIBUTIONS TO SOCIAL PROTECTION

Tilman Bruk and Hartmut Lehmann (*editors*)
IN THE GRIP OF TRANSITION
Economic and Social Consequences of Restructuring in Russia and Ukraine

Björn Jindra
INTERNATIONALISATION THEORY AND TECHNOLOGICAL ACCUMULATION
An Investigation of Multinational Affiliates in East Germany

Pasquale Tridico
INSTITUTIONS, HUMAN DEVELOPMENT AND ECONOMIC GROWTH IN TRANSITION ECONOMIES

Daniela Gabor
CENTRAL BANKING AND FINANCIALIZATION
A Romanian Account of How Eastern Europe became Subprime

Tomasz Mickiewicz
ECONOMICS OF INSTITUTIONAL CHANGE
Central and Eastern Europe Revisited

Milica Uvalic
SERBIA'S TRANSITION
Towards a Better Future

Enrico Marelli and Marcello Signorelli (*editors*)
ECONOMIC GROWTH AND STRUCTURAL FEATURES OF TRANSITION

Jens Lowitzsch
FINANCIAL PARTICIPATION OF EMPLOYEES IN THE EU-27

Hans van Zon
RUSSIA'S DEVELOPMENT PROBLEM
The Cult of Power

Horst Tomann
MONETARY INTEGRATION IN EUROPE

Iraj Hoshi, Paul J. J. Welfens, and Anna Wziatek-Kubiak (*editors*)
INDUSTRIAL COMPETITIVENESS AND RESTRUCTURING IN ENLARGED EUROPE
How Accession Countries Catch Up and Integrate in the European Union

David Lane (*editor*)
THE TRANSFORMATION OF STATE SOCIALISM
System Change, Capitalism, or Something Else?

Saul Estrin, Grzegorz W. Kolodko, and Milica Uvalic (*editors*)
TRANSITION AND BEYOND

Studies in Economic Transition
Series Standing Order ISBN 978–0–333–73353–0
(*Outside North America only*)

You can receive future titles in this series as they are published by placing a standing order. Please contact your bookseller or, in case of difficulty, write to us at the address below with your name and address, the title of the series and the ISBN quoted above.

Customer Services Department, Macmillan Distribution Ltd, Houndmills, Basingstoke, Hampshire RG21 6XS, England

Determinants of FDI Flows within Emerging Economies

A Case Study of Poland

Arkadiusz Mironko
The A. Gary Anderson Graduate School of Management, University of California Riverside and Rotterdam School of Management Erasmus University, The Netherlands

palgrave
macmillan

First published 2014 by
PALGRAVE MACMILLAN

Palgrave Macmillan in the UK is an imprint of Macmillan Publishers Limited, registered in England, company number 785998, of Houndmills, Basingstoke, Hampshire RG21 6XS.

Palgrave Macmillan in the US is a division of St Martin's Press LLC, 175 Fifth Avenue, New York, NY 10010.

Palgrave Macmillan is the global academic imprint of the above companies and has companies and representatives throughout the world.

Palgrave® and Macmillan® are registered trademarks in the United States, the United Kingdom, Europe and other countries

ISBN: 978–1–137–37215–4

This book is printed on paper suitable for recycling and made from fully managed and sustained forest sources. Logging, pulping and manufacturing processes are expected to conform to the environmental regulations of the country of origin.

A catalogue record for this book is available from the British Library.

A catalog record for this book is available from the Library of Congress.

To Nella

Contents

List of Figures

List of Tables

Foreword

This book makes an important contribution to the recent revitalization of interest in the drivers and effects of the location of foreign direct investment (FDI) in sub-national regional areas or clusters within countries. The renewed attention being paid to this research topic returns the international business (IB) field to one of the areas in which it began. In some of his early work in the 1950s and 1960s, for example, John Dunning examined issues connected with the location of firms in cities or local areas. However, as the focus of attention in the IB field gradually shifted from the host location – in which FDI was sited to the multinational corporation (MNC) as the actor responsible for such investment – IB researchers came to interact much more with scholars working on industrial organization or business strategy, and less with those in economic geography or regional science. The MNC was itself defined as an organization which conducts business across national borders, which required a cross-national perspective, and therefore lent itself most naturally to treatments of the host location as a country. This approach was reinforced by the greater availability of data at a country level than at a sub-national, regional level, especially in a comparable form across different countries or parts of the world. As a consequence, the subject of FDI in sub-national regions was, for a time, addressed mainly by economic geographers and regional scientists, and in a specialist literature. Thankfully, this research topic has moved back to center stage for the wider IB field once more, and it is gradually being reintegrated with the mainstream IB literature. This book helps to achieve just such a reintegration of key ideas and concepts, and provides a framework for doing so.

One factor behind the revival of interest among IB scholars in a more nuanced analysis of location has been the rediscovery of the role of clusters and localized knowledge spillovers (LKS) in the business strategy literature. This rediscovery began with the principle that the location may become a source of competitive advantage or capabilities for the firm and, hence, must be recognized as part of its strategic configuration. Inevitably, this gave rise before long to various strands of work that have emphasized the heterogeneity of firms when considering the nature of their interaction with the locations in which their activities are sited. That is, not all firms can benefit to the same extent from locating in a given cluster, and firms are likely to make very different location choices according to their own distinctive profile of potential gains and losses from being situated in a range of possible alternative locations. The story becomes further complicated once we acknowledge that such firm location decisions may well not be independent of one another, so firms are likely to respond over time to the location decisions made by other firms in their industry, or from the same country-of-origin. Indeed, certain strands of this literature have argued that some firms may lose from LKS, where others gain (so the spillover principle that a rising tide of knowledge lifts all boats is not the only principle in play) and, therefore, location decisions are based in part on strategic calculations. Given this backdrop, it is highly appropriate that in examining the regional location of foreign MNCs in Poland, Arkadiusz Mironko takes a strategic approach and distinguishes between the leading firms in an industry and others.

The findings reported here are very interesting in this respect. The existing presence of leading MNCs in a region can deter smaller followers from locating there, as the resources and networking opportunities available in the location are disproportionately drawn to the dominant player. In a recent paper, Ram Mudambi and I discussed a similar effect that we had observed in a UK context, one which we termed the physical attraction exercised by the dominant firms in an industry (Cantwell and Mudambi, 2011). Yet, this is not a uniform effect since, as suggested in our paper, it depends on the extent of the dispersion of large firms that are active in a local industry, rather than on the presence of large incumbent firms in the industry. Thus, where a region is large and munificent enough to allow for the co-presence of multiple leading firms, the firms compete with one another to bring greater vibrancy, and in so doing provide an increased variety of potential networking opportunities for other actors in the local industry. While large established firms are present, they share the market, and industrial concentration remains lower than in a situation in which there is a single dominant firm operating in a location – which single major channel tends to be associated with dependency on the part of other actors in that place, and a lack of entrepreneurial networking opportunities for independent smaller firms of a more innovative kind. Therefore, the findings of Arkadiusz Mironko's valuable research show us that, when explaining different FDI locational strategies, we have to take into account the heterogeneity of regions or locations, as well as the heterogeneity of firms in an industry. Regions that attract few leading foreign firms may deter the entry of other companies and, so, never really take off, whereas regions that attract a diversity of leading foreign firms may enter into a virtuous cycle of favorable cumulative causation, in which the strategic interaction between firms helps to promote further local resource development and thereby sustains growth.

For further exploration of the analysis of regions and FDI, the investigation of the Polish case, in itself, is interesting, since by definition it has not, until recently, been feasible to conduct such studies in emerging market economies in transition. The sudden shock to the structure of the Polish economy constituted by the institutional reform process provides a useful test bed for just such a study as the one documented in this volume, since we can assess the relevant relationships in a relatively pure early-stage form. Some social statisticians claim that this kind of policy-induced shock to a system constitutes the closest one can come, in the social sciences, to a natural experiment of the kind used in the natural sciences – one in which we can isolate the effect we are most concerned with from other complicating factors associated with the complex or systemic heritage carried forward from the past For this study, the relevant institutional shock was provided by the opening up of Poland to the investments of foreign MNCs.

With all this in mind, I am very happy to commend this work to anyone with an interest in the related themes of the location of FDI and of international business strategy.

John Cantwell
Rutgers Business School
Newark/New Brunswick, New Jersey

Preface and Acknowledgments

This book is the product of a research interest that became a passion. In 2004, Poland, my country-of-origin, was at an interesting crossroads when (along with a number of other developing nations of Central and Eastern Europe) it joined the European Union. Poland had an aspirational goal, one which was burdened with a solid risk.

The most obvious task in Poland's endeavor was to attract foreign investment to help the country prosper and develop its economy. This goal is easier to devise than to deliver and, like most developing countries, Poland faced numerous challenges. The members of transition governments do not always see eye-to-eye and, hence, Poland's factions were undoing each other's policies. Initially, during the first phase of privatization, which took place in the early 1990s, it was relatively easy to attract investment. For foreign investors it must have felt like being at a yard sale, where they could buy outdated factories on the cheap and gain access to new developing markets. Not a bad deal.

In turn, the expectation of the Polish government and citizenry was that employment levels would be maintained and that – in addition to capital – new technology, know-how, and skills would be brought in. The hope in such cases is that existing indigenous capabilities will be developed based on increasing knowledge, delivering, in due course, planned or sometimes spontaneously occurring specializations. Such capability and specialization developments often follow a pattern of industrial specialization or country-of-origin commonality, often creating a spontaneous or predetermined collaborative effect in developing networks of firms. The participants in these networks, when they develop, are generally set in geographic proximity to each other due to an existing access to needed knowledge – skills, resources, or markets, which enable efficient and complementary operations.

This book presents empirical evidence generally taken into consideration in the decision-making process of foreign investors setting up operations in Poland and other developing economies – and by national and regional policy makers in an attempt to attract foreign direct investment. Such decisions are often driven by exogenous strengths that specific investors bring with them, and by national and regional economic factors generally represented in the form of the host regions' existing resources, skills, and capabilities.

The majority of studies on the subject focus on developed economies, while a limited number of studies are dedicated to developing economies. The aim of the present work is (in the Polish context) to shed some light on the methods of analysis of the capabilities of host economies and of the relationships between those economies and foreign investors – not only at a national level, but also at regional and, possibly, subregional levels to determine the strengths of developing nations. The focus on the transitional period of Poland's accession to the European Union offers a specific dimension as to the influence, proximity, and openness of the neighboring markets as the economy enters a vastly larger and more affluent free-trade market.

Especially close links promoting development of capabilities in select Polish regions are explored here, with a close view on how MNCs develop relationships in new areas of economic interest by creating collaborative economies similar to those described by Adam Smith in 1776, some of which reach sustainable scales, while some are simply exploited by investors for short-term gain.

In the case of some regions in Poland, a detailed review of the results presented here should give the methodology and an in-depth picture as to the location patterns and integration of foreign investment, results applicable not only to the Polish economy, but also to other developing economies.

Most importantly, I must express my gratitude to Professor John Cantwell, who has offered his advice and guidance to me over the years when I was researching the subject. I appreciate his sharing of ideas and criticisms throughout the process. His wisdom and candor are certainly very much appreciated.

Finally, I want to express particular thanks to the Central Statistical Office of Poland (GUS) for allowing me the use of their materials and data.

List of Abbreviations

CE	Central Europe
CSO	Central Statistical Office – (Główny Urząd Statystyczny – GUS)
EU	European Union
FDI	foreign direct investment
IMF	International Monetary Fund
ITO	International Trade Organization
NUTS	European Nomenclature of Territorial Units of Statistics
NTS	Nomenclature of Territorial Statistics
PAIIZ	Polish Information and Foreign Investment Agency (Polska Agencja Infirmacji i Inwestycji Zagranicznych)
PKD	Polish Classification of Activity (Polska Klasyfikacja Dzialalnosci)
RDB	Regional Data Bank
RLAco	Revealed Location Advantage for a country-of-origin
RLA	Revealed Location Advantage for industrial specialization
RTA	Revealed Technological Advantage
SME	small and medium enterprises
WB	World Bank

1
Location Choice and Clustering of Foreign Subsidiaries on the Economic Sustainability and Competitiveness of the Host Regions

1.1 Background and problem setting

In the last two decades many countries in Central and Eastern Europe have ventured onto the road of economic development via privatization, economic reorganization and opening their doors to foreign investors while adopting the rules of the free market economy. For most countries of Central Europe (CE), this journey has by now culminated in their joining the free economic trade and movement of people in different zones of the European Union (EU). Included in that group is Poland, the country whose economic environment and attractiveness to foreign investors is the subject of this study.

As the result of this economic and governance change, Poland's developing economy is successfully searching for, and accepting a relatively significant amount of, foreign direct investment (FDI) as compared to its neighbors.[1] The relationship between foreign investors, domestic investors, and policymakers is often one that contributes to, or prevents, local economies from benefiting from such investment.

Researchers recognize a number of issues arising from both a lack of, and the presence of, foreign investment in a country. Equally important and researched are patterns of distribution of foreign direct investment within recipient countries (Blomstrom and Kokko, 1997). Potential benefits to both an investor and the local economy may depend on the existing local economic factors required for success of the investment. Obviously, short-term and long-term considerations are taken into account by researchers considering these matters.

The central issue addressed in this research will be the relationship between clustering of foreign firms across regions in Poland, and the country's future ability to attract further foreign investment into them based on: the regional industry and country-of-origin concentration levels; regional economic drivers; and type of foreign investors. While most studies of FDI location choice concentrate on cross-national decision-making, and few of the studies look into location determinants across regions within a country, this present study will attempt to explain the reasons for concentration of foreign firms in Poland by testing whether foreign firms investing there follow particular industry-based trajectory patterns and, also, whether they locate in the proximity of the leading firms in their industries.

The importance of industrial cluster formation and how foreign investors choose locations in which to establish their operations are important and difficult questions that many researchers have attempted to answer (Marshall, 1920; Porter, 1998b; and Krugman, 1991, among others). Such a choice as whether to locate in an established agglomeration or away from one – therefore independently – is influenced by a number of locational factors and by whether an investor is a leader or follower in an industry (Knickerbocker, 1973).

Besides the locational decisions of foreign investors, national and regional policy issues and local economic factors are significant determinants in the development of an agglomeration of foreign investment patterns and development of local regions. In addition, the influence of industry-leading firms (identified as Fortune 500 companies, along with industry leaders[2]) and followers (small and medium size foreign firms) will be studied to determine existing interaction effects between both types of firms.

The literature shows mixed positive and negative effects of FDI on host economic developments (Borensztein et al., 1993; Kogut, 1983), especially in the long-term. Therefore, the importance of regional economic factors, the presence of established industrial centers, and the nature of local policies is quite substantial on such an effect. As such, national and local policies further influence the location choices of foreign investors within a country and, in turn, contribute to the recipient regions' success.

This present work should offer an analysis and reveal location choices of foreign investors establishing their subsidiaries in Poland, with specific determination of the existence and development of industrial trajectories across regions. Also the review of local economic factors and the relationship between them and the existing concentration of foreign firms (based on industrial classification across regions) will be made. In addition, degree of collocation between various types of firms – industry leaders and followers – will be explored to determine its effect on location choices of future investors. Finally, based on the results of this research, national and regional policy considerations will be offered with additional observations as to before and after the European Union accession effect in the flow and location choices of FDI into Poland.

1.2 Outline of the book

This book analyzes the determinants and the impact of foreign direct investment in Poland. The research offered here is based on panel data and on the impact the results have on the location choice of foreign firms across Poland. The organization of this book is as follows:
Chapter 1 introduces the subject of flow of foreign direct investment into developing economies and its determinants.

Chapter 2 sets out the problem and reviews relevant literature by discussing location choice theory and reasons behind clustering of firms.

Chapter 3 develops a model and reviews research design, data and the methodology used to analyze possible relationships between foreign investors and local strengths.

Chapter 4 analyzes the results and outcomes by exploring, at the level of regions in Poland, concentration of foreign firms – an analysis based on industrial specialization and country-of-origin criteria.

Chapter 5 discusses the results of hypotheses testing and offers analysis of location choices by industry-leading firms investing in Poland on the decisions of small and medium size foreign investors. The existence of such relationships is important to both foreign investors as well as to indigenous businesses and regional policy.

Chapter 6 offers conclusions and a final analysis of FDI patterns across regions in Poland and presents policy recommendations. This chapter identifies and reveals the existing preferred location choices for FDI within Poland and determines specific geographic advantages and heterogeneity of its regions. By addressing the questions raised, this research also provides a framework for the analysis of location decisions of multinational firms in regions within developing economies.

2
Heterogeneity of Economic Space: Introduction of the Problem

2.1 Regional location choices and clustering of firms

Although there is a common understanding that almost all industries are somewhat localized, a number of studies measure the localization levels of FDI and its influence on host economies. That relationship between collocating firms and the formation of centers of economic activity within a country influence the location choices of future entrants into that country (von Thünen, 1826, trans. of 1966; Marshall, 1920; Krugman, 1991). Also, so-called "Marshallian factor" market externalities (David and Rosenbloom, 1990), which include capital stock and size of the labor force and markets, strongly contribute to the growth and competitiveness of urban-industrial agglomerations, thereby enhancing the attractiveness of a region to potential foreign investors. Even earlier than Marshall, Adam Smith (1776) spoke of trade impacts on location decisions, suggesting that trade and location are interrelated and have a significant role in regional economic geography.

More recently, Ellison, and Glaeser (1997) developed an empirical test to confirm the same premise, using examples of geographic concentration of industries in some U.S. regions. The researchers also considered the presence of corporate networks emerging as a result of upstream–downstream inter-firm supplier relations (Porter and Stern, 2001). Those specialized inter-industry and intra-industry networks already present in an area were the engines behind the gravitation of new firms to that locale.

As subsidiaries of foreign corporations establish their firms in host economic regions where, according to Ellison and Glaeser (1997), the possibility of cluster formations increases in accord with the strengths of the existing operations and expanding demands of upstream–downstream production networks that, in turn, bring new subsidiaries of multinational corporations (MNCs) into the regions and around them, *the neighboring regions* (also earlier, von Thünen, 1826, trans. 1966; Marshall, 1920; Krugman, 1991). According to Marshall (1920) regions containing agglomerations of economic activity (termed by the author as clusters, districts, and milieus) become hubs of tacit knowledge accumulation and growth, where physical proximity is an initial prerequisite for the generation of a regional-specific competitive advantage. As it is not easy to determine it concretely, even an assumption of the existence of this tacit capability of the cluster can attract new investors.

As new entrants decide to establish operations in the developing countries, many economic factors play an important role in determining optimal location strategy. This strategy engages crucial factors of economic activity, such as: level of presence of foreign firms in a region, size of the local market, distance to foreign markets, cost and availability of the workforce, availability of a skilled workforce, and the level of R&D investment needed to attract FDI into a region.

The key question related to the one presented in this research is whether the presence of the existing clusters attracts and benefits new entrants. This question was researched by Shaver (1998b), who reviewed the influence of labor and wages and the presence of other firms in the region selected for the location of new subsidiaries. Shaver's research determined that, when done right, collocation is an essential part of an investment strategy due to its potential intrinsic advantages, which improves the rate of success for investment in the location. Such obvious examples are the Michigan automobile industry, California's Silicon Valley, and the IT and biotech R&D found along Route 128 in Massachusetts (Saxenian, 1994). Necessary for success is an understanding of the strategic choice of location as an integral element driven by the motives behind cluster formation.

2.2 Nature of cluster formation

2.2.1 Understanding of clusters and their development

While clusters may be viewed and defined from a variety of perspectives, this study will follow close to Porter's definition of a cluster as a geographically proximate group of interconnected companies and associated institutions in a particular field, linked by commonalities and complementarities (Porter, 2000). Further, we include Marshall's (1920) understanding of clusters as concentric circles, spheres of various distances, and surrounding towns. These understandings of agglomerations see clusters not limited to a particular industrial class, but inclusive of interaction between various industrial and economic activities.

This study will view clusters as a regionally proximate group of interrelated foreign companies. The analysis of clusters will have dual focus: on industry classification and country-of-origin. Additionally, clusters will be viewed from the perspective of the types of firms, leaders, and small and medium enterprises they are hosting and attracting (Porter, 1998a) to form sustainable agglomerations of economic activity.

Even as former reasons for clustering have diminished in importance with economic globalization, new influences of clusters on competition have a growing importance in an increasingly complex, knowledge-based, and dynamic economy. Understood as such, clusters represent a new way of thinking about national, state, and local economies, and they necessitate new roles for companies, governments, and other institutions for enhancing their competitiveness (Porter, 2000).

That point is supported by Jaffe and colleagues (1993), presenting one obvious explanation why innovative activity in some industries tends to cluster geographically more than the same activity in other industries: the location of production is more concentrated spatially. Marshall (1920) and later Krugman (1991), argue that there may be geographic boundaries to information flows or knowledge spillovers (particularly tacit knowledge) among the firms in an industry, citing localization of economic activity as well, since innovation occurs within a particular area only when other salient conditions, such as agglomeration and interaction of firms, occur first.

For foreign investors, geography is a salient determinant in choosing the optimal location for establishing new subsidiaries (Marshall, 1920; Krugman, 1991; Porter, 2000). In making those choices, (MNCs examine a number of locational conditions which motivate the investment. Choosing an optimally desirable location may be a complicated process, taking into account the correlation of the location's economic factors which are necessary for a successful investment (Dunning, 1993; and Blomstrom, 1991). These studies determine that regions with developed internal networks use the advantages of flexibility and specialization as a key to technological learning. Lowering the costs of production while retaining flexibility of production are highlighted by Storper (1992) in a study of French, Italian, and American production networks.

Also, Porter (2000) cited "the prevalence of clusters which reveals important insights about the microeconomics of competition and the role of location in developing a competitive advantage." It is widely recognized that changes in technology and competition have diminished many of the traditional roles of location. Yet, clusters (geographic concentrations of interconnected companies) are a striking feature of virtually every national, regional, state, and even metropolitan economy, especially in more advanced nations (Porter, 2000). This indicates that while the economic development of a nation or a region increases, so does the role of agglomerations of economic activity.

By measuring the relationship between specified economic factors and the regional industrial specialization of foreign firms, this study will point out specific competitive advantages where industrial clusters of foreign investors are identified as being strong.

2.2.2 Development of a regional industrial trajectory and competitiveness

Fundamentally, clustering of multinational corporations within a foreign country develops incrementally over time (Cantwell, 2000), and with accumulation of a particular technological capability in the area. As a result of continuous aggregation and cumulative agglomeration of forces, the cooperation of the foreign firms often develops across industries or according to a particular industrial specialization (Nelson, 1993; Cantwell, Iammarino, and Noonan, 2000). Since the necessary advantages of the host regions are exploited first, the subsequent step (not studied here) would be knowledge transfer between foreign and host firms, and knowledge creation, making those clusters potentially more competitive and sustainable.

This evolutionary path, which as a result of regional industrial specialization is often narrowing, cannot always be promoted effectively by indigenous firms but requires knowledge and processes available from the outside via attraction of foreign investors to supply them (Mutinelli and Piscitello, 1998). Subsequently, the development trajectory of foreign firms indicates the strength of a particular location for a specific type of investment (Cantwell, 2000). A rising trajectory is generally developed over time and is difficult, often nearly impossible, to achieve by a new (Cantwell, 2000) or through national or local economic policy influence.

Where enabled, knowledge transfers derived from foreign investment are expected to augment the existing stock of knowledge in the recipient economy through the introduction of alternative management practices, organizational arrangements, labor training and skill acquisition and implementation (de Mello Jr, 1997).

Earlier, Marshall (1920) emphasized permanence of numerous localized manufacturing industries at sites that had been fixed by "accidents of history" in what were geographically unstructured and newly developing conditions in contemporary (to him) America. This approach might be derived from earlier writings of von Thünen (1826) and was subsequently developed in the early writings of Weber (1929), which depicted industry location as "more-or-less foreordained by invariant geographical and technological considerations" (also, Arthur, 1989; David and Rosenbloom, 1990).

Further, technological trajectories of development within a national and regional economic structure are closely linked to industrial success (Cantwell, 2000) of regions. Continuity in technological specialization within a location may lead to advantages in attracting FDI within a particular industry. Linking agglomeration of economic activity to FDI in itself is not a new idea. Cantwell (1991a), for example, shows that there are significant benefits to both domestic and foreign firms from agglomeration (also, Shaver, 1998b). Therefore, firms generally follow industrial development trajectory (Cantwell and Piscitello, 1997). Further location advantages could be a self-perpetuating local development path whereby additional growth of the local industry makes the location even more attractive for doing business (Head et al., 1995; Krugman, 1991; Wheeler and Mody, 1992; De Propris et al., 2005) and draw additional investors into the region.

In discussing eclectic paradigm Dunning (1981) argues that three conditions must be satisfied simultaneously for foreign investment to take place successfully. The firm must have both an ownership (O) advantage and an internalization (I) advantage, while the foreign market must offer a locational (L) advantage. Here the location aspect is viewed from a market-access perspective alone, possibly limiting locational consideration to the just the market factor.

Following the same line, Bevan and Estrin's (2004) research on multinational firms determined that they need an internalization advantage, since "the benefits accrue to the enterprise from exploiting the ownership advantage from choosing to produce abroad internally, rather than through the market by franchising or licensing the product or process internationally." Obviously, location advantages are relevant in determining where the firm chooses to manufacture its products. These advantages appear due to factor prices, access to customers, government trade regulations, capital flows, and institutional and political stability in the country (ibid).

In examining the significance of the knowledge strength of firms investing in foreign economies, Berry (2006) concluded that a firm's prior possession of relevant knowledge and skill is crucial for success of the investment venture in the new location. These firms bring their expertise with them. However, in the early stages they generally engage in low value-added activities (Dunning, 1997). The development of existing activity from the basic to the higher grade is a desired outcome, not only for the investors, but also for local policy makers and governments. Governments, at both national and local levels, desire to attract foreign investment as well as to improve both long-term and short-term national and regional growth. While foreign companies investing in specific locales mainly want to maximize their profits, some foreign firms increasingly seek to source local knowledge and know-how (Jaffe et al., 1993; Audretsch and Feldman, 1994; Audretsch and Stephan, 1996; Cantwell and Piscitello 1997; Acs et al., 1997; Zhao, 2009).

A number of earlier studies also suggest that, in practice, foreign investment in transition economies begins with low value-added activity (i.e., car manufacturing and assembly plants, food processing, basic chemistry). When successful, they then move towards higher value-added activity. The proximity to large markets and a region's own market size may help the participating firms move toward those high value-added activities within the region (e.g., Florida, 1995; Dunning, 1997; Ambos, 2005), a transition that helps to develop and sustain a successful industrial development trajectory. That finding indicates that agglomeration of firms, over time, should lead to a higher concentration of firms and also to a sharpening of local industrial specialization (Cantwell, 1994; Cantwell and Iammarino, 2000).

Soete (1987), following Arthur (1986) and Kaldor (1955), indicates that the growth of small regions and countries can be more "path dependent" due to a higher propensity for technological "lock-in." As such, smaller economies are more specialized in their exports than are larger ones (Lundvall, 1986). To further affirm this, Schumpeter (1954) points out that a focus on a certain economic activity in a region is most beneficial in the long-term, rather than pursuing an array of economic objectives – often not complementary with one another – which puts a strain on resources of a region.

In the 1960s, scholars such as Vernon (1966, 1974) and Wells (1972), working on the determinants of FDI, gave priority to place with regard to location variables, particularly those determining locations for U.S. firms seeking FDI from U.S. firms in advanced industrial countries (also, Bandera and White, 1968; Scaperlanda and Mauer, 1969). The geography of international business activity is not independent of its entry mode nor, indeed, of the competitive advantages of the investing firms. This interdependence is particularly apparent when one examines the dynamics of knowledge-intensive, higher grade, Multinational enterprise (MNE) activity (Dunning, 1998a, 2002; Javorcik, 2004; Athreye and Cantwell, 2007). In their study of technology-generation, Athreye and Cantwell (2007), using data on patents, find that knowledge-generation increases with the rise of FDI levels by countries considered to be new recipients of FDI. Also, Barro and Martin (1995) have encouraged research into the channels through which FDI can be expected to promote growth in the long run. Similarly, according to the findings of de Mello Jr (1997), FDI is determined to be a very important contributor to "human capital augmentation and technological change in developing economies," as it in general promotes the use of more advanced technologies by domestic firms and offers specific productivity-increasing labor training and skills gain.

Further, foreign firms may choose a location based on regional industrial strength and in proximity to firms that have common origins in a national system of innovation and are likely to cluster in certain industries and technologies, rather than with groups of firms that, instead, originated in other countries (Knickerbocker, 1973; Cantwell, 2000: p. 6; Kojima, 2000). Cantwell and Iammarino (2000) also studied the importance of regional concentration of firms in the location hierarchy of FDI in the UK and its role in innovative activities. They concluded that the technological specialization of foreign-owned affiliates in various regional locations is determined by the position of the region in the hierarchy, which suggests the importance of the early economic development phase, the clustering of firms, for the successful development of subsidiaries within a chosen location.

In addition to these points, other studies look at the spillover effects foreign investment has on domestic firms in horizontally and vertically related industries, and the impact of a host region's policies on the attractiveness of the right type of investment (Javorcik, 2004; Javorcik and Spatareanu, 2008). These studies also indicate that the host country's own companies participating in the trade or collaboration with foreign operations may not benefit equally, as local firms may lack knowledge-absorption capacity and may be disadvantaged in such a relationship. In such cases weaker industries may be in need of support or protection by local or regional policy makers to develop and strengthen their capabilities to be able to compete more effectively.

Also, according to the findings of de Mello Jr (1997) policy makers in the developing world (before making efforts in attracting foreign investment) may want to consider potential limitations associated with FDI-led growth. Creation of a better environment for domestic investment is indispensable in order to increase the country's or the region's ability to successfully host foreign investment. If such conditions for domestic investors are not created first, the success of policies designed to attract FDI may be limited in the long-term.

One of the objectives of this present study is to determine the conditions supporting the trajectories of the collocation of foreign firms and the probability of future location choices of foreign firms across Polish regions – voivodships and *powiats.*[1]

2.2.3 "Follow my leader" – the principle of the leader's effect on the rest

While many firms choose to locate within, or near, the center of the industrial activity they participate in, leading firms are most likely to choose locations independent of popular trends and do so purposefully to protect their tacit capability. Those firms would locate apart from obvious industrial agglomerations (Kojima, 2000; Berry, 2006). The location choices for foreign investment by multinational corporations have long-term consequences for the investor and the chosen location. Such choices, combined with an increasing number of possible locations due to changes in the global and regional economic and political landscapes, present the increased significance of decision making while considering all economic factors offered by a specific location.

Regardless of the planned entry mode, foreign firms at first move their production operations in order to substitute for exports and to explore locations for specific complementarities while preserving their market share, subsequently resulting in clustering of FDI as discovered conditions within a particular region suit a number of participants. Such circumstances support oligopolistic structures motivated by protection of the investment and lowering of risk while, in the process, forming an agglomeration of often interdependent firms (Knickerbocker, 1973).

Other studies of the subject of agglomeration patterns also explore why economic activities agglomerate in a rather limited number of places. Fujita and Thisse (1996) answer this question in a threefold way: pointing out, first, the limitations of the workforce mobility; second, the relatively low costs of transportation; and, third, the size of the urban population, which is an important determinant in the structure of the urban agglomeration economy.

In addition to Knickerbocker's (1973) focus on risk aversion as a motive for choosing common locations, Leahy and Pavelin in their 2003 study conclude that firms sharing a common country-of-origin may follow each other, whether in a competitive or collaborative way, to set up proximate operations in a host economy to benefit from "tacit collusion equilibrium" and "execute symmetric FDI strategies." In each case, the firms may benefit from the ability to bring common suppliers, which further strengthens the reasons for choosing common host locations.

Therefore, the strong presence of foreign firms, although very important, seems to have a binary influence on the decision making process of prospective entrant firms: this presence can either attract or discourage the entry of new firms (Shaver, 1998b). Ceteris paribus, firms depending on their own strength and business strategy may see the presence of competition as a benefit – a resource of knowledge, skilled labor, tacit capabilities – or as a threat, where their own resources, knowledge, ability to innovate, and labor force will be subject to extraction by the competitors. Therefore, despite perceived value of agglomeration, clusters of global FDI distribution locating multinational leading firms within an agglomeration may not benefit all businesses equally (Shaver, 1998a; Shaver and Flyer, 2000; Alcácer and Chung, 2007; Berry, 2006). For that reason alone, some firms, especially those leading within their industry class, may choose to locate apart from clusters in order to protect their competitive advantage. Hence, some new entrants may choose to locate far from existing industrial centers.

Lin and Saggi (1999), by studying the symmetric mixed strategy equilibrium of a dynamic model of the probability choice of FDI by exporting firms, determined similarly that an increase of imitation risk usually makes FDI less likely. However, they also suggest that faster arrival of imitation, a follower, may increase the leader's advantage by delaying further FDI, although their study also proposes that faster arrival of imitation can actually increase the likelihood of FDI. In other research, Leahy and Pavelin (2008) concluded that, although firms often make decisions regarding foreign direct investment rather interdependently, when facing competition firms decide to set up operations in markets in which they would profit more by exporting to those markets instead.

These findings will offer a foundation for the hypotheses testing of the dependencies between various types of firms – leaders and followers – posed further in this research.

2.3 Location choices and clustering of foreign firms

The focus of the theoretical framework of this study will be the work of Ellison and Glaeser (1997) who, following von Thünen (1826) and others, explored the nature of agglomeration forces in researching patterns of concentration, the geographic scope of localization, and the coagglomeration of related industries – the industries with strong upstream–downstream industrial relationships in the United States. Ellison and Glaeser followed a previous concept which held that "all industries are somewhat localized," in order to empirically determine the level of geographic concentration of industries in some U.S. regions. Although Ellison and Glaeser (1997) also concentrated on knowledge spillovers, their model empirically tested the collocation of firms within specialized and traditionally industry-concentrated regions, and reaffirm a degree of agglomeration of firms within the selected industries. They found a strong empirical relationship between agglomeration size and degree of collocation of foreign firms in a particular region.

Barrios et al. (2006) find coagglomeration to be important for a number of industries in Ireland, but mainly for the purposes of employment growth only. Considering types of firms, high-tech, and rather traditionally low-technology intensive firms, Devereux and colleagues (2004) do not find any evidence to suggest that high-tech industries are more agglomerated than firms (belonging to an industrial class) which are less technology intensive. In fact these researches find the opposite effect in British firms. Further exploring the matter of agglomeration, Kolko (2010) finds that services are more urbanized yet less agglomerated than is the manufacturing industry. This present study will further explore concentration patterns of a number of industries across regions in the developing economy of Poland.

2.4 Regional industrial specialization patterns of foreign firms

The agglomeration of economic activity has been a subject intriguing economists for nearly two centuries now. The long tradition of location analysis descending from von Thünen (1826), then furthered by Marshall (1920) and Krugman (1991), does an excellent job of explaining the pattern of land use around a city or central business district. It simply assumes the existence of the central focus (Marshall, 1920; Krugman, 1991; Fujita and Krugman, 2004).

A general consensus, developed by research and practice, affirms that agglomeration of firms in a region promotes economic development of that region. Firms agglomerate within particular locales for a specific purpose (Marshall, 1920, Krugman, 1991; Ellison and Glaeser, 1997). Those purposes are, and can be motivated by, a proximity to suppliers or markets and the availability of skilled labor or cheap labor or other resources. Yet other reasons for a particular location choice may include a proximity to leading firms within the industry, or locational advantages (von Thünen, 1826; Marshall, 1920; Krugman, 1991; Ellison and Glaeser, 1997) enabling exploitation of existing endogenous advantages and tacit capabilities (knowledge and processes) of the investing firm (Dunning, 1997). The presence of the above-mentioned resources is relevant to local firms, to investors entering the agglomeration, and to regional policy.

Exploring the nature of agglomerative forces in patterns of concentration of firms, Ellison and Glaeser (1997) followed a previous conception which held that "all industries are somewhat localized." They tested this statement by empirically determining the level of geographic concentration of industries in some U.S. regions. In particular they tested the collocation of firms within specialized and traditionally industry-concentrated regions, and reaffirmed a degree of agglomeration of firms within the dominant industry in a region. Also, Cantwell and Vertova (2004) and Cantwell (2009) point out the inevitability of regional specialization of activity promoted by MNC subsidiaries collocating in a particular locale.

Additionally, these researchers found a strong empirical relationship between agglomeration size and degree of collocation of foreign firms in the particular region. The higher the number of firms in a region, the higher the level of upstream–downstream relationships within the region's firms (Venables, 1996). Also, Smith and Florida (1994) see the density of firms within a location as a factor attracting foreign investors due to the locale's ability to provide skilled labor and technology intermediate input suppliers and buyers, therefore strengthening the cluster (also Venables, 1996 and Ellison and Glaeser, 1997). Also, Feenstra and Hanson (1997) determine that growth of FDI in Mexican regions is positively related to industries' need for skilled labor.

This study will view clusters as a regionally proximate group of loosely interrelated foreign companies. The analysis of the clusters will have a dual focus – industry classification and country-of-origin classification. An industry is categorized by the Polish Classification of Activity[2] as defined by the Statistical Classification of Economic Activities in the European Community, which is similar to that of Porter (1985), in which the classification groupings of economic subjects (companies) are made based on relatedness of processes and products. Further, in this work firms will be viewed from the perspective of their types, whether they are leaders or small and medium enterprises, and which regions are hosting and attracting to form sustainable agglomerations of economic activity. Clusters are not limited to a particular industrial class but consist of a number of related, or often even non-related, industries or they have common origins.

Studying reasons behind the dynamics for industrial change in regions, Malecki (1997) concluded that R&D is necessary for competitiveness, but is not enough. He explores major reasons for economic activity in the regions, determining two major sets of influences on the innovativeness and competitiveness of agglomerations: (a) technical skills and information are key in the process of technological change and competition; and (b) urban areas contain a complex synergy of factors that smaller, more remote, places cannot attain (Malecki, 1997). These factors, among others, will be explored here in the context of economic activity in the developing economy of Poland across regions.

Brülhart (1998) explored another relevant element in industrial specialization literature regarding location of manufacturing in the European Union. The study reflects a strong concentration of Europe's economic core along with a heavy concentration of high-tech industries, while the less skill-intensive and more labor-intensive industries were dispersed around the periphery of the Union's boundaries. These aspects will also be explored in this book.

2.5 An industrial specialization and a country-of-origin trajectory development

2.5.1 A regional industrial specialization trajectory

The existence of an agglomeration economy formed of foreign-owned firms may further be a motivator for such firms to cluster together. These conditions may be favorable to exploitation of factors specifically needed by foreign firms, that is, skilled labor or specialized input providers. Obviously, due to risks and costs involved, firms must carefully consider advantages available at particular locations before establishing a subsidiary. Birkinshaw and Hood (1998) and Cantwell and Mudambi (2005) identify the elements of the group strategy based on the initiatives given to subsidiaries by their parent firms to identify characteristics of the location and type of firms that are attracted to the location (whether strong attract weak or reverse dynamics). They also emphasize the dichotomy – enhancement versus depletion of capabilities in a subsidiary – which may result in an explicit change of the subsidiary's business direction. Since not all firms have the same motivation and capability, a set of particular economic factors will have a different effect on each participant dependent on the industry and on the firm's level of capability.

Related empirical studies of FDI location choices have uncovered the importance of agglomeration effects emanating from clusters of inter-firm linkages (Wheeler and Mody, 1992; Harrison, 1994; Audretsch and Feldman, 1994; Cantwell and Piscitello, 1997). Addressing the emergence of corporate international networks, Cantwell and Piscitello (1997) considered intra-industry and inter-industry spillovers, the science base, and the influence educational institutions have on the presence of MNCs within particular regions. These authors concluded that the benefits from spillovers decline with distance; therefore, clustering of firms is a very important aspect of knowledge creation and the sustainability of firms within a region. Analysis of regional advantages – such as the existence of the industrial center's historical relationship between existing science-based divisions of the MNCs and local educational institutions – is used to explain location choices made by foreign-owned firms (Jaffe et al., 1993; Audretsch and Feldman, 1994; Audretsch and Stephan, 1996; Cantwell and Piscitello, 1997; Acs et al., 2000).

Locations offering specific university–industry linkages are of particular interest to foreign subsidiaries, which in general have a higher degree of mobility than do local firms (Porter and Stern, 2001; Alcácer and Chung, 2007). In the 1960s, scholars such as Vernon (1966, 1974) and Wells (1972), working on the determinants of FDI, gave priority of place to location variables, particularly to those determining the location of U.S. FDI seeking markets in advanced industrial countries (Bandera and White, 1968; Scaperlanda and Mauer, 1969). Very few studies address this question in context of the developing country, however, and the goal here is to offer insights as to the country in question, Poland.

In particular, the advanced stage of cluster development – knowledge creation – is highly dependent on the relationships between industry and universities as reflected in studies by Jaffe and colleagues (1993); Audretsch and Feldman (1994); Audretsch and Stephan (1996); Cantwell and Piscitello (1997); Kuemmerle (1999b); Acs et al. (2000); and Adams (2001). A trajectory of development within a national and regional economic structure is closely linked to its industrial success (Cantwell, 2000). The continuity of technological specialization and industry–university cooperation within a location – may lead to development of advantages in attracting FDI within a particular industry. The greater the value-added content of FDI-related production, the greater the impact of foreign investment on host firms. In such instances productivity spillovers associated with FDI lead to rising returns in production by domestic firms (de Mello Jr, 1997). Following this argument, Jaffe (1989) recognizes the productivity effects and, therefore, increasing returns (also, Arthur, 1989 as likely outcomes of the historical path-dependence, and of locational "lock-in" as a motive for proximate location of new investors.

Further exploring the matter of the university–industry correlation to industrial productivity and specialization in Swedish regions, Braunerhjelm (2008) found a correspondence in specialization, as well as positive productivity effects within the regions hosting universities. The study determined considerable differences in the level of specialization and productivity of the regions not related to the length of university existence in the region.

In addition, new investments may also bring badly needed skills and technologies into the host economy (Lansbury et al., 1996; Kuemmerle, 1999b). All elements – early stage of entry into a new territory, agglomeration and cluster creation, then knowledge creation and innovation – are interdependent phases. Linking many economic factors, for example, a highly developed transportation network may exert a positive influence on foreign firms looking for a new location for their production plants (Bartik, 1985; Coughlin et al., 1991; Hogenbirk and Narula, 2004), provided that it also implies good accessibility to surrounding markets (Krugman, 1991; Chung and Alcácer, 2002).

The element of specialization within an agglomeration more sharply defines that cluster (Krugman, 1998; Fujita, 2002). The linkages and complementarities that develop between the firms in a region, even when only loosely developed, improve productivity and innovation in the firms within the cluster (e.g., Cantwell, 1991a; Porter, 2000). On the other hand, considering a particular combination of diversification of location-specific assets may become a source of competitive advantage for a region (Cantwell, 2009).

Conversely, possible co-location of firms into specific regions, as per country-of-origin, could be an indicator of a particular region's international relationship or interest. The existence of agglomeration economies formed of foreign-owned firms may also be a motivator for the foreign firms to cluster among themselves. Such conditions may be favorable to allowing exploitation of specifically needed factors by the foreign firms, that is, skilled labor or specialized input providers (Dunning, 1997).

Related empirical studies of FDI location choices have uncovered the importance of agglomeration effects emanating from clusters of inter-firm linkages arising among firms locating within one region (Wheeler and Mody, 1992; Harrison, 1994; Audretsch and Feldman, 1994; Cantwell and Piscitello, 1997). Those inter-firm linkages develop through formal and, also unintentional, sharing of suppliers of intermediate inputs, and also through intentional and informal knowledge sharing. Related to the access to new inputs, output growth can be a consequence of the use of a broader range of intermediate inputs in foreign investment-related production (Feenstra and Markusen, 1994). Such geographic relationships are important and essential for further development of the region's attractiveness to FDI.

Linking collocation of firms to FDI is not, in itself, a new idea. Cantwell (1991a), for example, shows that there are significant benefits to both domestic and foreign firms from agglomeration (also, Shaver, 1998a). Location advantages at the local or regional level could be self-perpetuating where further development of a local industry makes the location even more attractive for doing business, potentially drawing in additional new investment and technological capability (Head et al., 1995; Krugman, 1991; Wheeler and Mody, 1992; De Propris et al., 2005).

2.5.2 Regional attractiveness trajectory factors

Further following the line of earlier review, the theory developed by Knickerbocker (1973) and published by Harvard University Press identified a "follow-my-leader" hypothesis which presents an explanation for clustering of multinational firms from the same country-of-origin or multinational firms within a particular industry in a specific proximity. Knickerbocker (1973) concludes that MNCs choose to follow in a collusive way in order to address the risk aversion and to benefit from complementary interdependence of FDI. A number of co-dependencies develop when they pull other firms into the region for the purpose of filling those needs based on the existing relationships or ties attributed to a country-of-origin or an industrial specialization.

The strong presence of foreign firms in a location, although very important, seems to have a binary influence on the decision making process of prospective entrant firms. Such a presence can either attract or discourage a foreign firm's entry (Shaver, 1998b). *Ceteris paribus* firms depending on their own strength and business strategy may see the presence of competition as a benefit – a resource of knowledge, of skilled labor, and tacit capabilities – or as a threat where their resources, knowledge, ability to innovate, and labor force will be a subject to extraction by competitors. Therefore, despite the perceived salience of agglomeration clusters of global FDI distribution, locating leading firms within an agglomeration may not benefit all businesses equally (Shaver, 1998b; Shaver and Flyer, 2000; Alcácer and Chung, 2007; Berry, 2006). For that reason alone, some firms, especially those leading within their industry class, may choose to locate apart from clusters in order to protect their competitive advantage. Hence, some new entrants may choose to locate far from existing industrial centers.

Lin and Saggi (2002) tested the importance of timing-of-entry and determined that the follower (a firm that entered a particular market second) had lower entry costs; however the second firm did not fare better over the period of the study, supporting that the first-mover advantage may be important despite the higher initial costs.

Alcácer and Chung (2007) also addresses the issue of location of companies leading in industrial innovation and worried about knowledge spillover when establishing subsidiaries in foreign locations. This concern emphasizes the dichotomy – enhancement versus depletion of capabilities in a subsidiary (also, Rugman and Verbeke, 2001; Birkinshaw and Hood, 1998) – which may result in an explicit change in the subsidiary's business direction. Since not all firms have the same motivation and capability, a set of particular local economic factors will have a different effect on each participant (Cantwell, 2009). The question here is whether leading foreign firms present in Poland prefer to locate near existing industrial agglomerations or independently of them.

Conversely, Cantwell and Iammarino (1998) address the role of direct investment, which may be dependent on the status of the region in the national system (also, Cantwell, 2009). They identify higher-order locations (Cantwell and Iammarino, 1998) which tend to attract the largest share of both domestic and foreign technology development and have a much broader range of technological specialization or activity that is likely interdependent. Such group strategies may develop by collusive actions of foreign investors (Cantwell and Mudambi, 2005) and may have a dominant effect on a selected region (also, Birkinshaw and Hood, 1998).

As firms often seek an advantage through generating new technological capabilities and assets (Cantwell, 1989; Dunning and Narula, 1996; Florida, 1997; Kuemmerle, 1999a, 1999b; Mowery, 1998), firms also must protect their knowledge and know-how, especially if they are in the lead. For these strategic reasons, the periphery of clusters, or areas outside of an industrial cluster, may be attractive to industry leaders. A number of studies (Cantwell and Janne, 1999; Chung and Alcácer, 2002; Berry, 2006) further determine that location choices for their subsidiaries, especially knowledge-creating subsidiaries are locating separately from the clusters to protect their internal knowledge and tacit capability. These studies also look at the firms which invest abroad as attempting to source the knowledge and access this necessary capability via FDI (Berry, 2006).

Small enterprises and upstart companies can challenge industry leaders (Acs et al., 1996) and thus are critical of public policy concerns. In their work, authors identify two key factors in the economic environment that gain importance: property rights and barriers to entry. Poland's accession to the EU in 2004 has leveled the playing field for investment originating in the EU and might have become a deterrent to potential investors from outside of the EU.

In the framework proposed by Kojima (2000) through the flying geese model,[3] he recognizes three aspects of catching-up by developing elements of: intra-industry, inter-industry, and international economies. Internal company strategies and interaction between regional advantages are also included in the framework.

In the 1930s, the phrase "flying geese pattern of development" was coined by Kaname Akamatsu.[4] The flying geese (FG) model intends to explain the catching-up process of industrialization of latecomer economies from the following three aspects:

Intra-industry aspect: product development within a particular developing country, with a single industry growing over three time-series curves, that is, import (M), production (P), and export (E).

Inter-industry aspect: sequential appearance and development of industries in a particular developing country, with industries being diversified and upgraded from consumer goods to capital goods and/or from simple to more sophisticated products.

International aspect: subsequent relocation process of industries from advanced to developing countries during the latter's catching-up process.

The regional transmission of FG industrialization, driven by the catching-up process through diversification of industries, has become famous as an engine of Asian economic growth (Kojima, 2000) and can also be used to effectively explain industrial location patterns in other developing economies.

Most often, foreign firms move their production operations in order to substitute for exports and to preserve their market share, subsequently resulting in clustering of FDI as discovered conditions within a particular region may suit and support a number of participants. Such circumstances also support an oligopolistic structure motivated by protection of the investment and lowering the risk (Knickerbocker, 1973) while, in the process, forming an agglomeration of often interdependent firms (Marshal, 1920; Kojima, 2000). A similar conclusion was reached by Krugman (1991) when discussing that economies of scale also lower the risk of investment for firms in agglomerations as agglomerations become more sustainable therefore being a more attractive place for an investment location for new firms, which also drives concentration of FDI.

Further, foreign firms may locate in a host-country based on the country's regional industrial strengths, and also in proximity to firms that have common origins in a national system of innovation and are likely to cluster near related industrial centers and in specific technological fields, in comparison with groups of firms that instead originated in other countries (Cantwell, 2000: p. 6). Cantwell and Iammarino (2000) also studied the importance of regional concentration of firms in the location hierarchy of FDI in the UK and the role of regional concentration in innovative activities. They concluded that the technological specialization of foreign-owned affiliates in different regional locations depends upon the position of the region in the hierarchy, which suggests the importance of the early economic development phase, the clustering of firms, for the successful development of subsidiaries within a chosen location over time. Later, Berry (2006), in examining the significance of the knowledge strength of the firms investing in foreign economies, concluded that a firm's prior possession of relevant knowledge and skills is crucial for the success of the investment venture in the new location.

Specific strategies are identified in the literature (Shaver, 1998b; Shaver and Flyer, 2000; Alcácer and Chung, 2007; Berry, 2006) where various industrial groups follow or attract intermediate input providers while others may choose to locate independently, especially those without a dependence on the suppliers. Their research also clearly identifies examples where smaller firms, or firms with possession of a lesser endogenous knowledge base, follow industry leaders, while the industry leaders prefer to locate separately but still require access to labor, preferably skilled, or to markets.

2.6 The effect of R&D activity, market size, availability of skilled labor, and labor costs on FDI attractiveness

2.6.1 The effect of R&D activity on FDI attractiveness

Other aspects explored in this study (relevant to the questions raised earlier) are related to additional economic factors influencing the dependent variables. One of particular significance is promotion of research and development facilities, private and public, which plays an important role in determining the location choices of investments by MNCs, especially the knowledge-seeking types, and by local stakeholders (regional governments and also academic institutions). A number of studies and policy advisors suggest establishment of the special economic zone (SEZ) as a means of promoting the attraction of foreign investment and of regional innovation via research and development activity (Porter and Ketels, 2006; Ketels and Memedovic, 2008). Ketels and Memedovic (2008) suggest that within countries, regions and cities, local competition raises the stakes and motivation for "how to improve productivity and attract firms in specific fields beyond providing low factor costs and subsidies," especially for countries rich in natural resources and with transition economies – but also for developed countries that have launched competitiveness policies and cluster initiatives involving various local stakeholders (Ketels and Memedovic, 2008).

Discussing location of innovation matters related to the host economy, Cantwell et al. (2000) state that particular countries receiving FDI must consider a proper mix of innovative activity which will be able to enhance existing capabilities in the country. Although their argument relates to technological innovation across countries, a similar theoretical conjecture can be made relating to the choice between regions of a country for the location of firms – a conjecture made for the purposes of assessing necessary resources or capabilities, and to attract investment to increase productivity within a region (also, Krugman, 1991, 1998).

Baptista and Swann (1998) asked the question: Do firms in clusters innovate more? Their findings determined that innovation within clusters of firms will be more rapid than innovation in firms locating outside of the clusters, which is due to supporting factors such as concentration of skills needed by a particular industry.

Most relevant studies conclude that FDI provides a vital source of investment for modernizing the industrial structure of these regions and for improving quality and competitiveness. In addition, new investments may also bring badly needed skills and technologies into the host economy.

Mariotti and Piscitello (1995) analyzed quality of labor force, using skill and education as its measure. Their results followed the conclusion made by Little (1978), who determined that the availability of skilled and qualified workers is a positive FDI-attraction factor. Additionally, the regions hosting research and development activity become attractive locations for foreign-owned R&D in its sectors of specialization (Cantwell, 1991a; Cantwell and Janne, 1999).

Most recent studies of FDI location and industrial clusters focus on the knowledge creation of localized foreign investment (Cantwell and Piscitello, 1997, 2002; Cantwell et al., 2000; Porter et al., 2006). The present research analyzes only early phases of the development of economies joining the free markets, including the location choices of MNCs which, in general, only later lead to technology transfers and the innovation phase of foreign investment in host regions. Nevertheless, this early stage is crucial in laying foundations but is not a guarantee of successful economic development.

2.6.2 Markets, labor, and other relevant economic factors

The transition from low value-added activity towards higher value-added activity (Dunning, 1997), proximity to large markets and region's own market size (Maleckie, 1980; Dunning, 1981) help to sustain the industrial development trajectory. The established industrial development path indicates that agglomeration of firms over time should lead to a higher concentration of firms and a sharpening of local specialization (Cantwell, 1994; Cantwell and Iammarino, 2000). The geography of international business activity is not independent of its entry mode, nor, indeed, of the competitive advantages of the investing firms.

Further, Krugman (1991) emphasized strength of the industry center versus the periphery in economic activity. The regions located along the periphery are historically less attractive to foreign investors as compared to other, proximately located regions (e.g., Cheng and Kwan, 2000; Evans, 2003; Cieślik, 2004). The periphery has generally less internal market power and is also more distant from exogenous markets, but it may offer substantial benefits to foreign firms, such as lower labor and overhead costs (Alcácer and Chung, 2007).

An opposite view was presented earlier by Porter (2000), who states that in order for companies to serve large markets, firms do not have to locate near those markets. This view offers an opportunity to remote regions, which can become production platforms, most likely due to lower costs, and can compete with more developed and highly populated regions. Linking many economic factors – for example a highly developed transportation network – may exert a positive influence on foreign firms looking for new locations for their production plants (Bartik, 1985; Coughlin et al., 1991; Hogenbirk and Narula, 2004), provided that this also implies good accessibility to surrounding markets (e.g., Chung and Alcácer, 2002; Dunning, 1997).

Researching border effects on concentration of economic activity, Cieślik (2004) concluded that existing economic factors along the western border of Poland far outweigh the advantages of such factors along the eastern border. He also suggests that Poland's accession to the European Union may even further broaden the disparities between the western and eastern regions in Poland.

In studying the effect of activities by MNCs in Poland that lead to benefits in social and economic conditions, Chidlow and colleagues

(2009), determined that four specific factors affect the formation of such relationship linkages: the foreign investor's mode of entry, the subsidiary's autonomy (including the availability of infrastructure and skills needed by foreign investors), protection of data and intellectual property rights, and government incentives. The researchers determined that the success of the developed linkages manifests in job creation and knowledge-absorptive capacity.

As foreign direct investment is often a lifeline of the economic recovery, growth, and sustainability of developing economies, those economies participating in the process of transition must consider a number of significant factors: national and regional competitiveness, existing industries, advanced technologies, available knowledge base, and policy issues. The complexity of the relationships and interests linking those factors fuel uncertainty with regard to recovery and growth, thereby multiplying the pressure on participating economies and the players within them, as well as influencing the decisions of further investment from abroad. In most cases, especially in developing economies, FDI provides a vital source of investment for modernizing the industrial structure of these economies and for improving quality and competitiveness of their products and services. In addition, new investments may bring desperately needed skills and technologies into the host economy (Borensztein et al., 1993). Lastly, the size of the local market and proximity to exogenous markets also play significant roles in determining a location for investment in the same way as do labor costs and skill availability (Buckley and Casson, 1981; Borensztein, et al., 1993; Dunning, 1993, 1995). Those relationships will be tested here to determine their influence on the location of foreign firms across regions in Poland.

Already in 1920. Marshall, in discussing new economic geography, emphasized the linkages effect: users and suppliers of intermediate inputs cluster near each other because the large market provides greater demand for goods and supply of inputs. Further, as argued by Dunning (1997) among others, a substantial local market size may help the participating firms to move toward higher value-added activities within the region.

This view supports Mariotti and Piscitello (1995), who analyzed quality of labor force, using skill and education as its measure. They reached similar results as Little (1978), who determined that the availability of qualified manpower is a positive FDI-attraction factor. The results vary between labor-intensive and skill-intensive industries as each requires different types of specialized labor input.

2.7 Specificities of transition economies

Most transition economies actively attract FDI. For the most part the existing literature describes benefits of FDI to the host economies, such as jobs creation, technological upgrades, and knowledge access, among others. This is taking place because transition economies such as Poland, a country studied here, and also other emerging economies (including the BRIC nations: Brazil, Russia, India, and China), rely on foreign investment to develop their production, technology, and knowledge base. The trend of attracting foreign investment is prevalent among developing nations despite the warnings and actions of intergovernmental agencies, such as the International Trade Organization (ITO), International Monetary Fund (IMF), and the World Bank, among others, cautioning investment-receiving economies against the risk of suppressing host-country growth by displacing local firms and obstructing their technological progress, and by exploiting the local labor force (Lipsey, 2002).

There is, however, another side to the effect of foreign investment on host economies. Aitken and Harrison (1999), in studying the effect of FDI on Venezuelan firms, determined that foreign investment negatively impacts the productivity of domestically owned plants. Further, in studying the effect of foreign investment on the economies of the Czech Republic, Hungary, Poland and Slovakia in the 1990s, Pavlínek (2004) determined that developing economies become dependent on FDI for further development and do not benefit from development of its own capacity based on spillovers from foreign subsidiaries. These studies point out the risks which host countries, recipients of FDI, must consider when attracting particular types of foreign investment.

We can assume here that for all host nations the presence of foreign subsidiaries is also expected to deliver much-needed knowledge and capability to local firms. Studying the linkages between foreign and local firms, Javorcik and Spatareanu (2003), among others, find that the evidence from Central Europe suggests that "fully owned foreign subsidiaries use newer or more sophisticated technologies than jointly owned investment projects and thus may have higher requirements vis-à-vis suppliers" (Javorcik and Spatareanu, 2003). Therefore, foreign firms also choose to source from foreign suppliers instead and leave local suppliers behind, not only by not contracting with them but, more importantly, by not sharing know-how and technological capability.

The literature on the subject also takes into consideration whether brownfield investment is of comparable value to greenfield investment. A number of studies suggest that benefits to productivity of domestic firms (Aitken and Harrison, 1999) and avoidance of competition (Cheng, 2009) by investing in existing host-country firms is a preferred entry strategy from the perspective of the investor, but is not equally beneficial to the local economy. Cheng (2009) also tests the impact on the mobility of firms with foreign investment and concludes that only those firms which have specific resource advantages in the acquired firm will be a primary choice for the investor who otherwise may want to consider a greenfield investment. This seems to be the preferred choice for the majority of foreign investors locating in Poland, as found in the study of Chidlow and colleagues (2009).

The number of foreign firms investing in Poland is taken as a whole without distinction between brownfield or greenfield investment and, as far as the data allow, it can be determined that only a small number of foreign investors in Poland were involved in greenfield investments over the period of the study. Following the opening of the Polish economy, the first privatization wave followed, making a number of potential target companies available for investment. At the same time, a number of special economic zones were established to promote the attraction of investment into the regions. By the end of the study period, every region had at least one SEZ, while most regions had numerous SEZs.[5] This allows potential investors to have a choice of greenfield versus brownfield investment types available to them. At this early stage of Poland's economic liberalization, the specific choice of location and type of investment are equal to all investors.

Another dimension often considered in studies of flows of foreign direct investment is the amount of risk present in the host-country. In the case of Poland, such risk is rather minimal, taking into account its history and the study period under consideration. Since the study period spans the time before Poland's European Union accession to a number of years following its EU membership, this aspect will be viewed only as a peripheral factor. EU membership may be seen by potential investors as reducing country risk due to meeting the requirements for admission, which presupposes an added degree of political and economic stability along with a well-developed institutional and legal environment (Bevan and Estrin, 2004).[6]

2.8 Summary and expected contribution

In practical and theoretical terms, multinational corporations provide a vital source of investment for modernizing the industrial structure of developing countries and for improving the quality and reliability of

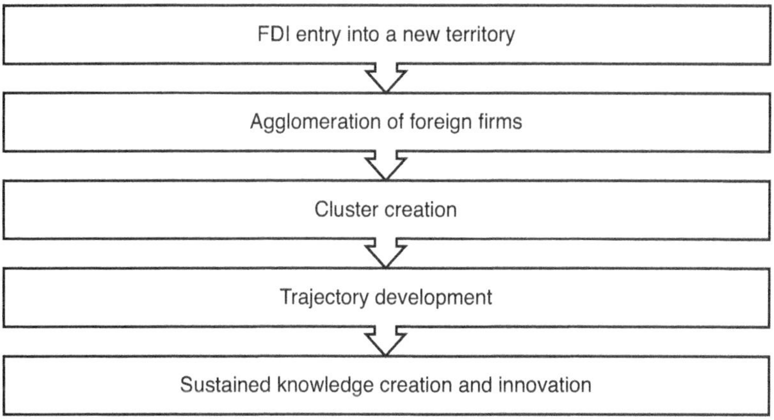

Figure 2.1 Steps of host region's adaptation of FDI

infrastructures. Most importantly, new investments may also bring badly needed skills and technologies into the host economy (Lansbury et al., 1996). All elements – early stage of entry into a new territory, agglomeration of foreign firms, cluster creation, trajectory development, then knowledge creation and innovation – are interdependent phases.

No space (a country or a region) remains homogeneous in economic, social, and political terms. Spaces are generally explicitly or implicitly divided and polarized by a number of forces that influence their development. This research identifies and reveals the existing location strengths within Poland, applying proposed index measures. It also seeks to determine specific geographic advantages and heterogeneity of regions. The methodology used here and the findings will be relevant to other developing and developed nations – and also to future investors – in determining preferred locations for establishing their businesses, a decision which depends on those factors applicable to the firm's industrial specialization and country-of-origin criteria. In this study, industrial trajectory developments are tested along with industrial dependencies on specific regional strengths as represented by regional economic factors.

The evidence of patterns in clustering of firms within particular regions has been sought out and analyzed to determine the reasons why foreign firms are attracted to those particular regions. This evidence will be discussed on the basis of what strengths the regions have that would be attractive to new foreign entrants. The strength of the existing relationships would indicate the ability of a locale to attract future foreign investment into a region, allowing both new incoming foreign investors and local policy developers to position themselves based on the advantages of the region.

This study will reveal the strengths of regions within Poland, a developing economy, to attract particular types of FDI and will offer an explanation as to what regions new investors will move into to establish their operations. The regional motivators and prevailing strengths of location choice – by industrial specialization and country-of-origin – will also be determined.

In addition, the present study determines the impact of foreign industry-leading firms on continuing foreign investment trends into the host regions. The study examines whether there are strategic interaction effects at the firm level, beyond the industry-level and country-of-origin effects in a transition economy. Observations on those interactions, reflected in regional proximity, assess future trends in the development of regional capacity for facilitating foreign direct investment in economies transitioning into a free market and driven in the same way and by the same trends as the regions of developed countries (Mariotti and Piscitello, 1995).

Finally, this study presents considerations of motivating factors for decision making by multinational corporations – the investors – and local stakeholders. This research also reveals whether concentrations have emerged where they did not previously exist or are present in areas where firms of a particular industrial class did not concentrate before.

As most research focuses on international, or inter-country, locational advantages, this research specifically focuses on intra-country aspects of location advantages to foreign investors and on strategic location choices available to leading-industry firms' subsidiaries and small and medium foreign investors (and collocation among them at a regional level).

This study forms a framework for establishing the patterns of location of foreign firms across regions in Poland, and it examines existing industrial trajectories' development and the elements supporting them. Finally, the requirements in location choice as to interaction between the leading firms and the small and medium foreign investors are examined via determination of collocation between those two classifications of firms.

3

Local Strengths and Foreign Firms' Location Choice: The Research Design, Data, and Methodology

3.1 Introduction – dependent variable

To determine the location patterns of FDI in Poland, the following data set on foreign investors in the country will be used, including their country-of-origin and industrial classification and their location within Poland – down to the level of sub-region of Polish administration. The goal of this study will be to measure the degree of geographic concentration of foreign firms across the voivodships (and, where warranted by the scale of intensity, also across *powiats*,[1] sub-regions) and attempt to determine causes of concentration of FDI according to both industrial activity class and country-of-origin of the investment, while investigating their potential for future ability to attract foreign investment into the regions. A further goal would be to examine the existence and development of industrial trajectories and the level of proximity between the leading firms and small and medium enterprises (SMEs) investing in Poland.

3.2 Methods of analysis

3.2.1 Data set description

The fundamental data set for this research consists of the lists of major foreign investors in Poland for the years 2000–2006 compiled by the Polish Information and Foreign Investment Agency – Polska Agencja Infirmacji i Investycji Zagranicznych (PAIIZ).[2] In addition, this data will be supported by statistical information obtained from the Polish Central

Statistical Office (CSO), Główny Urząd Statystyczny (GUS), describing the control measures for the economic situation of the regions. The Regional Data Bank (RDB) of the Central Statistical Office is the main organized information bank for socio-economic situations and for demographical, and environmental matters in Poland.[3]

The data used here was prepared in accordance with the Nomenclature of Territorial Statistics (NTS) and based on the European Nomenclature of Territorial Units of Statistics (NUTS). NTS divides Poland into hierarchically connected territorial units on five levels, of which three are characterized as regional levels, and two as local ones.[4] The data used for this research will be at NTS Level 2, reflective of the presence of foreign firms within voivodships. In only a few instances will additional criteria be used:

a) when regions with a high degree of activity are converging, bordering each other but distributed within two separate regions according to territorial division;
b) when a degree of presence of foreign regions is high only in some parts of a region; then data at Level 3 – sub-regions (*powiats* groups) applies.

The regional level covers:

- NUTS Level 1 – region area [on May 1, 2004, 6 regions were created; they cover several (2 to 4) voivodships];
- NUTS Level 2 – voivodships, 16 units;
- NUTS Level 3 – sub-regions (*powiats* groups).

NUTS Local level covers:

- NUTS Level 4 – *powiats*,
- NUTS Level 5 – *gminas*.

NUTS Levels 2, 4 and 5 are compliant with the territorial division of Poland. Presently, the country of Poland is divided into 16 provinces (*województwo*), which are subdivided into 308 *powiats* (districts), and the *powiats* into 2489 *gminas* (communes, primary level units). Poland's population remains very homogeneous.[5]

3.2.2 Data set and organization

The data set used here consists of a number of foreign firms investing in Poland between the years 2000 to 2006. The total number ranges from 886 firms in the year 2000 to 1,091 in 2006, with a slow decline from a high of 1,150 firms in 2005.

Figure 3.1 Regional subdivision of Poland by voivodships

Source: Central Statistical Office. Nomenclature NTS 2 Voivodships. http://www.stat.gov.pl/gus/5840_5960_ENG_HTML.htm

Table 3.1 Presence of foreign firms in Poland 2000–2006

	Total Number of Foreign Firms						
Year	**2000**	**2001**	**2002**	**2003**	**2004**	**2005**	**2006**
Number of foreign firms	886	906	978	996	1,101	1,150	1,091

Source: Based on data obtained from the Polish Information and Foreign Investment Agency (PAIIZ) and the author's own analysis.

The section that follows will introduce the data and the methodology which operationalizes this data with the purpose of deriving results and determining concentrations of foreign firms in Polish Classification of Activity (PKD) and country-of-origin of the participating foreign firms.

The outcome of the analysis will help determine the effect of country-of-origin and of industry concentration on location selection of FDI in Poland's emerging economy.

3.2.3 Data related to the investors per industrial classification of activity

The final count of the data on the presence of foreign firms used for this research shows that 36 industries are located across all 16 regions within Poland. The data includes lists of investors by company name, country-of-origin, activity class, and Polish Classification of Activity – Polska Klasyfikacja Dzialalnosci (PKD). The data also includes firms' operational locations in Poland.[6] This data was organized and grouped by region, voivodship, and by industry separately and will be used via the proposed model.

The industrial sectors are specified according to the Polish Classification of Activity without division for sub-classes of activities, thus following the main, primary, unit of industrial class specification.[7] The Central Statistical Office organization collecting PKD[8] data adopts a classification method which complies with the (changing) rules of the European Union and subsequent international organizations that have followed. One of those changes took place in 2004, which resulted in the obtained data sets for the years 2004–2006 to have a somewhat different classifications than earlier data for the period 2000–2003. That was corrected by adjusting the industrial category for data in the years that followed. Careful attention was made to maintain the distribution of firms via tests of industrial anomalies derived from the data.

After finalizing the organization of data, as could be expected, some samples with incomplete relevant information related to the PKD class and location in Poland were eliminated. The final count of the firms possessing complete relevant information that reflects the results in real terms (not RLA index) is contained in Table 3.2.

This data, reflecting aggregate countrywide distribution of foreign firms presented in real terms, follows fairly predictable patterns described in many aspects of research on FDI in Poland (Despiney-Zochowska, 2001; Cieślik, 2004; Chidlow et al., 2009). Despiney-Zochowska (2001), while comparing the Marshalian understanding of economic districts in terms of Poland's economic landscape when centrally governed and after joining "free market" economies, determined that disparities between regions exist and, with time, will become even more accentuated (Sampson, 2004). Further, Despiney-Zochowska (2001) concluded that Poland's leading

Table 3.2 Number of foreign firms by industrial activities (PKD)

	Number of Foreign firms by activities (PKD)						
Voivodship	**2000**	**2001**	**2002**	**2003**	**2004**	**2005**	**2006**
Dolnośląskie	66	70	79	78	94	92	95
Kujawsko-Pomorskie	21	18	18	20	26	19	24
Łódzkie	47	43	54	49	65	65	68
Lubelskie	15	16	13	13	16	17	16
Lubuskie	15	21	19	20	24	22	22
Małopolskie	35	35	41	38	45	41	42
Mazowieckie	277	328	382	373	411	422	427
Opolskie	16	16	17	18	20	22	22
Podkarpackie	20	25	25	25	28	27	29
Podlaskie	8	7	8	9	11	11	9
Pomorskie	38	38	45	45	51	53	52
Śląskie	60	56	59	74	81	86	89
Świętokrzyskie	13	13	12	12	15	13	13
Warmińsko-Mazurskie	11	10	10	12	13	13	13
Wielkopolskie	92	92	97	94	109	107	107
Zachodnio-pomorskie	17	19	19	23	24	33	31
Number of foreign firms	886	906	978	996	1,101	1,150	1,091
Total viable	751	807	898	903	1,033	1,043	1,059
Firms with incomplete data	–135	–99	–80	–93	–68	–107	–32

Source: Based on panel data obtained from PAIIZ and the author's own analysis.

regions centered on the following cities: Warsaw (Mazowieckie), Gdansk (Pomorskie), Szczecin (Zachodnio-pomorskie), Poznan (Wielkopolskie), Wroclaw (Dolnośląskie), and Krakow (Małopolskie). They concentrate the majority of economic activity and also support concentric circles of activity around them. That activity is supported by the strength of historical centers, availability of skilled labor, and proximity to Western European markets. Those cities lie, if not in proximity to Western Europe, on major transportation routes between Eastern and Western Europe, which gives them a considerable advantage.

The data shows concentrations of investment in the areas historically possessing substantial amounts of economic activity. As a result, these areas have been historically attracting the workforce needed to support their economic activity, reinforcing the existing industrial trajectory of the regions and becoming a stronger platform in which future investors can settle their operations. In general, most of the research conducted on Poland concludes, similarly to Despiney-Zochowska (2001) and Cieślik (2004), that three, or at most four, regions in Poland have a particular dominance. They are Mazowieckie (capital region), Wielkopolskie, Dolnośląskie, and Śląskie (Cieślik, 2004 and Chidlow et al., 2009). It is also evident from the data used here that those are the regions of focus for this research. However, as a result of the proposed analysis of the data, particular strengths are expected to be found in other (including peripheral) regions of Poland. Although, in the scale of the country's economy, those revealed strengths are not as significant, they may nevertheless be detrimental to those regions' future success.

Table 3.3 Number of foreign firms by country-of-origin designation

	RLAco in year						
Voivodship	**2000**	**2001**	**2002**	**2003**	**2004**	**2005**	**2006**
Dolnośląskie	66	72	76	79	96	92	98
Kujawsko-Pomorskie	21	18	18	21	27	19	24
Łódzkie	47	53	57	56	65	64	66
Lubelskie	15	17	13	14	16	17	16
Lubuskie	15	21	19	20	24	22	22
Małopolskie	36	39	43	40	46	40	41
Mazowieckie	317	349	403	410	432	411	407
Opolskie	16	16	17	19	20	23	22
Podkarpackie	20	25	25	25	28	27	29
Podlaskie	8	7	8	7	9	10	8
Pomorskie	44	47	51	48	54	54	53
Śląskie	64	62	66	76	86	86	89
Świętokrzyskie	15	14	12	12	15	13	13
Warmińsko-Mazurskie	11	10	10	12	13	13	13
Wielkopolskie	99	100	105	101	109	109	107
Zachodnio-pomorskie	17	18	19	22	24	33	31
Number of foreign firms	886	906	978	996	1,101	1,150	1,091
Total viable	811	868	942	962	1,064	1,033	1,039
Firms with incomplete data	75	38	36	34	37	117	52

Source: Based on panel data obtained from PAIIZ and the author's own analysis.

3.2.4 Data related to the investor's country-of-origin

Using the same set of data as above, the classification as to the investors' country-of-origin was isolated and grouped. The firms represent 43 countries of origin of investment, located across all 16 regions within Poland. In a few cases where investors represented multiple nationalities, they were reviewed and attributed as investors from the country-of-origin where the firms are headquartered. In a few cases in which the nationality was given as "international," and the country-of-origin could not be identified, the data were not included in further analysis and were removed from the data set.

Upon completion of data verification and arrangement, a number of firms were eliminated due to incomplete information related to the country-of-origin. The final count of firms containing complete relevant information reflects the results in real terms (not RLA index).

This data represents a countrywide macro perspective of the endogenous presence among individual regions in Poland in terms of the investors' location choice across the regions. The patterns of quantum investment across Poland follow in similar configurations, as in industrial classification in which concentrations of firms, as per country-of-origin, develop a similar distribution as above, without particular anomalies.

3.3 Organization methods

The analysis of data by region, used for the purpose of this research, will be able to determine preferred locations of firms within Poland according to the country-of-origin of firms and across industrial activity classes of participating firms. The level of distribution of foreign firms among regions will be examined to determine levels of concentration, in real terms, derived from panel data and relative terms measured by the proposed RLAco and RLAis index models described in the section that follows.

3.3.1 Method of analysis – the dependent variables

The data on the location of foreign firms in Poland, including firms' country-of-origin and their industrial category, will be analyzed independently of each other. The result of the statistical analysis (Appendix 1 and 2) will allow the determining of the longitudinal concentration of firms across the regions, using actual location of foreign firms present in Poland to the level of municipality, NTS level 5, a firm's type of industrial activity, and country-of-origin of foreign investment. An examination of locations of foreign companies within the 16 regions of Poland will determine to what degree co-agglomeration between them exists, and changes over time.

Given that the use of absolute numbers of data indicating the presence of foreign firms across regions – or their industrial specialization – to make comparisons between regions' strengths is not reflective of the regions' relative strengths (Cantwell, 1989, and elsewhere), the relative level of strength can be derived and explained by employing the Revealed Technological Advantage (RTA) index, a technique first applied by Soete (1987) and further developed by Cantwell (1989, 1991b).[9] This method is able to equalize the results between heterogeneous regions. Without its application, a meaningful comparison of the strengths of regions from the primary data would be quite difficult. This measure will be used here as a proxy for industrial specialization of the regions and foreign country investment concentration in the regions.

The RLAco and RLAis index measures will also allow normalizing the difference between regions with high and low numbers of participants. Soete (1987), following the research of Ergas (1986) that compared growth rates of economies of various size countries used the same method to determine the influence level on small and large countries. Therefore, also following Soete, this research should show small regions as being more specialized than larger regions.

The model adopted from the above-mentioned and presented here, will determine the level of presence of foreign firms across regions in Poland allowing measuring for industrial and country-of-origin concentration of firms among the regions. The Revealed Location Advantage for a country-of-origin (RLAco) and Regional Industrial Specialization (RLAis) will be calculated to reveal the strengths in both industrial and geographic proximity trajectories in the following ways.[10]

RLA Foreign Industry Specialization: This dependent variable will reflect the level of concentration of foreign firms across regions using the same set of data with the RLAis, PKD class, attribute for all foreign firms in the data set. For the purposes of analysis, the data will be operationalized as follows:

Equation 1: RLAis – Regional Industrial Specialization index of foreign firms in Poland

$$RLAis = \frac{Fyat / Fat}{Fyt / Ft}$$

Where:

$$RLAis = \frac{\text{Number of foreign firms in industry } y\text{, in region } a\text{, in year } t \text{ / all foreign firms in region } a \text{ in year } t}{\text{Number of foreign firms in industry } y \text{ in all regions in year } t \text{ / all foreign firms in all regions in year } t}$$

Similarly, to make the calculation for the RLA for the Foreign Industry Concentration (RLAis): The number of foreign firms in the industry *y* in region *a* in year *t*, divided by all foreign firms in region *a* in year *t*, divided by the number of foreign firms in industry *y* in all regions in year *t* divided by all foreign firms in all regions in year *t*.

And also the concentration of a country-of-origin measure is calculated in the following way:

Equation 2: RLAco – Country-of-origin index of foreign firms in Poland

$$RLAco = \frac{Fxat / Fat}{Fxt / Ft}$$

Where:

$$RLAco = \frac{\text{Number of firms from country-of-origin } x\text{, in region } a\text{, in year } t \text{ / all foreign firms present in region } a\text{, in year } t}{\text{Number of firms from country } x \text{ in all regions in year } t \text{ / all foreign firms in all regions in year } t}$$

To operationalize this model for the country-of-origin (RLAco) the following is considered: a number of firms from country-of-origin *x* in region *a* in year *t*, divided by all foreign firms present in region *a* in year *t*, divided by the number of firms from country *x* in all regions in year *t* divided by all foreign firms in all regions in year *t*.

As expected, the results obtained from the analysis of location advantages as per country-of-origin of the investment (RLAco) may show that the actual strength revealed from data as to the location of firms from a country-of-origin in a given area often does not correspond with RLAco index evaluation results. (Appendix 1).

With regard to the clustering of firms revealing a country-of-origin (RLAco), it is expected to possibly indicate a region's strength of a particular concentration of firms (from a country-of-origin of the investment and the host region) and to possibly also define a relationship for the historical presence of investors from a country in the region. This index measure will offer the evidence for the hypotheses presented earlier in this research as to the patterns of location for foreign investment in Poland.

The results obtained from operationalizing these models will paint the patterns of distribution of firms among regions and concentration of types of foreign investment within regions. This analysis should be able to establish the level of attractiveness to foreign investors of particular regions according to their regional industrial specialization and country-of-origin groups. The measures produced by the model will indicate the strength, for values above 1 (RLA >1), and the weakness of a region in a particular class, for values below 1 (RLA <1). The result of value of RLA = 1 indicates neither a strength nor a weakness – but a neutral equilibrium.

The results of the analysis of the data helps to identify trends in location choice made by foreign firms across regions in Poland based on regional industrial specialization and country-of-origin attributes. The outcome will allow making a comparison of concentration levels of RLAis and RLAco in order to reveal the levels of concentration measure of the two criteria.

Analyzing the data from these models can provide answers to the questions asked earlier in this book. More importantly, knowing the most-preferred location choices will help in understanding why incoming foreign firms may choose specific locations in Poland. In addition, such results will help determine the hierarchy of the regions patterned by Cantwell and Iammarino (2001 and 2003), by analysing regions in Poland based on their degree of attractiveness to foreign firms in participating industries. The revelation of particular existing strengths, and conversely of weaknesses, of these regions should also suggest the patterns of entry of future investors.

To accomplish the objectives, the following hypotheses are initially proposed:

H1: Regions in which foreign firms of a given industry participate at a relatively higher extent are more attractive to other foreign firms from the same industry.

H2: Regions in which foreign firms of a given home country participate to a relatively higher extent are more attractive to other foreign firms from the same home country.

These hypotheses give an indication of relative existing concentration levels of foreign firms in Poland, based on the set criteria. Review of the index results is expected to reveal the patterns of concentration of firms and allow consideration of the historical development path of agglomerative forces (Ellison and Glaeser, 1997) existing in Poland since the times of the centrally governed economy. The results of index measures also allow identification of higher order locations (Cantwell and Iammarino, 1998 and 2000) which tend to attract the largest share of foreign technology development.

The hypotheses H2 is expected to reveal whether firms from the same country-of-origin tend to settle in a common location (Knickerbocker, 1973; Leahy and Pavelin, 2003). These studies conclude that firms sharing common country-of-origin may follow each other while having both direct and indirect connections, such as common intermediate input providers, presence of specifying country, and language-related services, which make settling in the new locale much easier for the new entrants.

The review of the results of the RLAis and RLAco indexes allow the establishment of the level of strengths of the presence of foreign firms as per their industrial class and country-of-origin in all regions in Poland. Also, a concentration of those strengths, RLAis and RLAco, and formation of local specialized clusters give further opportunity for examination of whether such strengths are not just isolated events, but prolonged and sustainable activities (Kojima, 2000). Further, analysis of the index data will be examined by using the multiple regression method and also, for the purposes of control, using a dummy measure for each industry class and country-of-origin. This result will show the relationship between the index measure data for each year. The index measure results obtained in RLAis will further be used along with additional explanatory variables to offer supporting evidence to the hypotheses raised in the section that follows.

3.4 Examination of regional industrial specialization trajectories of FDI and their determinants

3.4.1 Method of analysis and introduction of the independent variables

The existing development path of the industrial class concentrations of firms (revealed from calculation results with the RLAis model) will also be tested against locational factors. The results will indicate the location trends of foreign firms in Poland for the period studied here. The data is expected to yield results that follow Akamatsu's flying geese criteria, followed later by Kojima (2000), which can be summarized with the following elements:

- intra-industry aspect reflected in the degree of collocation of firms representing the same industrial class – RLAis;
- inter-industry aspect reflected by the data on locational proximity of firms representing related industries and, especially, industries that took their origin in the basic and developed into more advanced ones;
- international aspect reflected in the data on the concentration of foreign firms as per country-of-origin and/or from a cluster of countries – reviewed in H2.

The first two aspects, intra-industry and inter-industry, will be examined here further along with another main objective of this study, which is to determine the conditions supporting the collocation of foreign firms of the same or related industries and the probability of future location choices of foreign firms in the same or related industries across regions – voivodships and *powiats*[11] – in Poland. In order to answer this question, this study explores the strength and motivation behind the existing industrial trajectories across regions in Poland by determining the relationship between dominant industries of the regions represented by the RLAis index and relevant economic factors of those regions (which empirically and theoretically have a supporting effect on industrial activity within said regions). For that purpose a multiple regression analysis between the average RLAis for all years of the study and the economic factors will be performed to measure the relationships and their strength.

The proposed further tests measure the relationship between the existing regional industrial specializations within the regions, revealed in H1, and regional economic factors to assess whether a degree of industrial specialization in total FDI activity of a region is more likely to develop in regions in which the most relevant economic factors for that industry are available.

Some regional economic factors contribute to the strengthening of agglomeration rates of FDI and regional industrial trajectory development. The goal here is to determine which factors (tested below) support industrial trajectory development of foreign investors agglomeration. The strength of a relationship between the region's foreign firms industrial agglomeration level, RLAis, and local economic factors are tested here using the statistical regression analysis method. The nature of the relationship between these variables can be positive or negative and is represented by R, ranging from 1 as a perfect relationship, to –1 denoting negative relationship, while 0 (zero) reflects no relationship between the variables. The measure of the strength of the relationship between the dependent variable and each explanatory variable will be revealed. Also a degree of goodness of fit will be represented by the measure R^2. The regional concentrations of foreign firms in Poland will be analyzed here using the revealed location advantage index measuring the strength of regional industrial specialization (RLAis) to provide a measure of preferred location choice based on industrial class (RLAis) of the investors. Then the presence and strength of the relationship between the factors relating to the location preferences of foreign investors among the country's 16 regions – voivodships (*województwo*), will be examined. The derived regression measures between the RLAis index and local factors will test what regional elements support the attraction of specific types of FDI into the regions. For that purpose, a number of sets of regressions will be used to test and answer the following supporting hypotheses.

Further analysis, to the *powiat* level (sub-regions next level administrative division) to isolate further geographic proximity of foreign firms (Alcácer and Chung, 2007), can be made. Such analysis should only be necessary for those regions with a high presence of foreign firms that are not located within a region's center of activity, in order to examine whether industrial agglomerations may form along the borders of two or more regions.

3.5 Data and method – explanatory variables

The following explanatory variables will be used to test and explain the posed hypotheses. These variables represent relevant economic factors of the regions relative to attracting foreign investors by providing access to existing indigenous and foreign firms, local and proximate markets, labor pool size and skill, amount of FDI, a region's GDP, and investment in R&D. The collected data will correspond to the time period and industries represented by foreign firms used in the dependent variable. With the exception of situations in which obtaining complete sets was not possible, the information may represent only selected industries, a shorter period, or may be cross-sectional.

At first multiple regression sets between each year for the RLAis and RLAco separately will be presented and, to offer an additional measure and robustness check for the test of panel data as a whole, further regression analysis for single or multiple sets of data will be used to determine the presence of the relationship and their level of fit within each industry and country-of-origin index measures. A statistical software tool, SPSS, is used to determine the results between the variables (Appendix 3).

3.5.1 FDI flow patterns and regional industrial class investment

The total amount of FDI into Poland for the period in question continued to increase with a dip in total investment just before the accession of Poland into the European Union in 2004. The decline in investment between 2000 and 2003, seen in Figure 3.2 below, can be explained by a number of macroeconomic reasons at global and regional levels and is probably not attributable to Poland's economic climate, which was rather conducive to foreign investment (Cieślik, 2004).

The overall flow of FDI into the individual regions contributes relatively more to growth than domestic investment (Borensztein et al., 1993); this finding supports a general practical view towards FDI. Indeed, it falls into the creation of a common view that foreign direct investment also contributes to increased productivity within the locale; however, the higher productivity of foreign firms, also tested in a study by Borensztein et al. (1993), proves to be increasing only when "the host country has a minimum threshold stock of human capital." In other words, "FDI contributes to economic growth only when a sufficient absorptive capability of the advanced technologies is available in the host economy," (Borensztein et al., 1993). This finding suggests that only regions with existing skilled human capital and advanced technological capability may benefit from the presence of foreign investors in those regions.

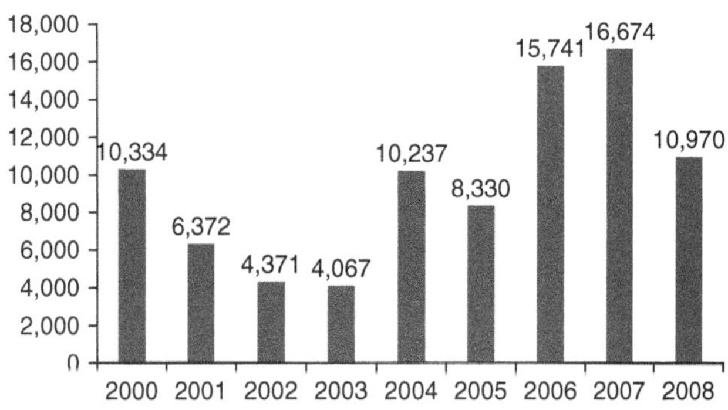

Figure 3.2 Flows of FDI into Poland in the years 2000–2008 in billions of Euros
Source: Based on data from the Central Bank of Poland and the author's own analysis.

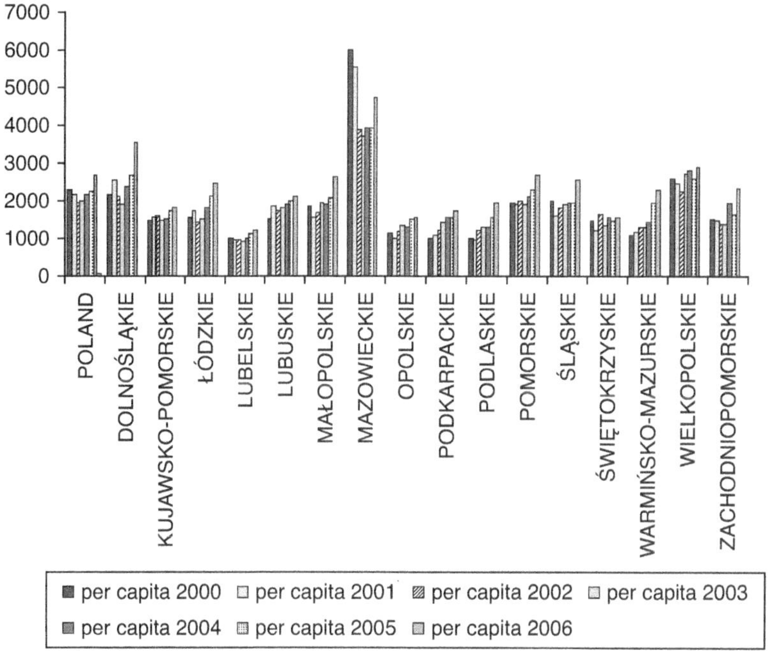

Figure 3.3 Regional investments outlays per capita by PKD (2004 sections)

Source: Based on data from the Central Statistical Office (GUS) and the author's own analysis.

To test whether the regional amount of total (foreign and domestic) investment in specific industries contributes to the attraction of foreign firms into the regions, the following hypothesis is proposed:

> H3a: A relatively high regional amount of total investment in an industry will contribute to higher attractiveness of FDI into the region.

The regression results between regions RLAis classes and the total regional investment in select industrial classes for which data is available are used for analysis. The available data allows testing the relationship between the concentration of foreign firms in the regions and regions' investment in the following areas of economic activity:

- Agriculture, hunting, and forestry
- Construction
- Electricity, gas, and water supply
- Financial intermediation

- Health and social work
- Hotels and restaurants
- Manufacturing[12]
- Mining and quarrying
- Other community, social and personal-service activities
- Real estate, rental and business activities
- Trade and repair
- Transport, storage, and communication

Additionally, the level of foreign investment per capita in the regions for the period 2000–2006 will be used in the multiple regression model for the purposes of a robustness check.

3.5.2 Value-added as a measure of attractiveness of FDI

Since foreign companies tend to bring technology and methods improving productivity, it would be expected that regions with a higher degree of regional industrial specialization of foreign firms may also have a higher value-added in those industries. This finding would follow a common view that foreign firms contribute to increased productivity within the locale, (Borensztein et al., 1993). This finding also follows Weber (1929) in describing regional forces supporting economic activity of the region as "locational factors," which provide a set of advantages creating economic conditions and giving access to processes for a particular business difficult, if not impossible, to replicate elsewhere and leading to increased value-added. Here, the following hypothesis is proposed:

> H3b: Industries with higher FDI geographic concentration in a region should also have higher value-added in aggregate for those industries in that region.

The available data allow the testing of the relationship between the concentration of foreign firms in the regions and the value-added per capita in the following areas of economic activity. For each region's concentration of FDI measured by RLAis in available industrial categories in value-added data, a regression variable will be testing the relationship between them for all years represented in this study.

3.5.3 Labor cost

To measure the influence of labor cost on the attraction of foreign firms into the regions of Poland, wage level as a percentage of the national average will be used. It is expected to help reveal the relationship between the level of presence of foreign investors in the regions and regions' labor cost. Additionally, as indicated earlier, the study by Borensztein et al. (1993) concluded that foreign investment into a locale is increasing only when "the host country has a minimum threshold stock of human capital." In other words, "FDI contributes to economic growth with a sufficient absorptive capability of the advanced technologies available in the host economy" Borensztein, et al. (1993).

At an early development stage, labor cost proxied on a wage level often has a potential dual effect on FDI attraction into a region; higher labor cost may in fact act as a deterrent to foreign investors (Culem, 1988, Mariotti and Piscitello, 1993). On the other hand, the investment attracted due to attractively low labor cost may increase with the rise of industrial specialization in a region and, in turn, becomes an obstacle to attracting further investment. Therefore, a test was carried out to determine:

> H3c: An increasing cost of labor in a region would be a deterrent to attracting FDI into that region.

The proposed measure will be an outcome of a regression between regions' RLAis of participating industries and the wage level for each region as a percentage of the national average. The result is expected to reveal the relationship between the level of presence of foreign investors in the regions and said regions' labor cost. The cost and availability of labor may be a significant factor in the location choice for investment. The data on wage levels in the regions covers the period from 2002 to 2006, so it does not cover the entire period of the study.

3.5.4 Workforce and skill availability effect on FDI attraction

The data regarding the level of presence of FDI in the regions with the availability of skilled labor (within the pool of employed) per industry is used to test the dependency between the RLAis and the proposed measures. This reasoning follows Mariotti and Piscitello (1995), who analyzed the quality of labor force using skill and education as measures. They followed the conclusion made by Little (1978), who determined that the availability of qualified manpower is a positive FDI attraction factor. This, however, varies between labor-intensive and skill intensive industries

It will also be possible here to use the outcome of H3e to compare the size of agglomeration in terms of population in a similar fashion as did Ellison and Glaeser, who also tested the effect of the agglomeration size and its correspondence to the level of collocation of firms within the regions tested (Smith and Florida, 1994; Venables, 1996; Ellison and Glaeser, 1997). Data on regional population from GUS, the main statistical body office, will be used to explain the relationship between the concentration of foreign investment and the necessary workforce, including the industry-specific skilled workforce necessary to facilitate such investment. This will be tested through regression analysis between the proposed variables to determine if:

> H3d: Availability of skilled workforce related to an industry attracts industry-related investment into those regions across Poland.

3.5.5 Market size and wages

Some foreign firms establish operations in locations suitable for a market-seeking FDI. Such a decision often is made for a firm to serve local and proximate markets (e.g., Dunning, 1993). In this case the main deciding factor is the size of a local market along with proximity to neighboring markets. Earlier, Marshall (1920), discussing new economic geography, emphasized the linkages effect: users and suppliers of intermediate inputs cluster near each other because the large market provides greater demand for goods and supply of inputs. Further, as argued by Dunning (1997), a substantial local market size may help the participating firms to move toward higher value-added activities within the region. Also, access to the neighboring markets may have a similar effect on a foreign investor's choice of location in a host economy.

Campos and Kinoshita (2003), in reviewing FDI flows in Central and Eastern Europe, concluded that a large domestic market size might be important if FDI aims to serve a domestic consumer market. But more specifically, the data sample they used determined that market size effect on overall FDI flows is rather limited. This and other studies suggest that with a decline of transportation costs (e.g., Langhorne, 2001; Glaeser and Kohlhase, 2003) a distance to proximate markets, internal or such as the EU, has limited consequence (Porter, 2000).

In Hypothesis 3e the relationship between the concentration of FDI, the size of the regions' internal markets, and the regions' average wage level as a percentage of the national level will be measured. This multiple regression analysis is expected to reveal a relationship between the level of presence of foreign investors in the regions and said regions' labor cost in attracting FDI. The test will reveal if

> H3e: Higher than average level of income per capita in a region attracts market seeking investment into the region.

3.5.6 Research and development activity in the regions and attraction of FDI into them

Foreign firms are also often sources of R&D activity and funding (Cantwell, 1991a). The success of R&D activity or spending, however, requires absorptive capacity of the locale (Lipsey and Kravis, 1985; Blomstrom, 1991). In practical and theoretical terms MNCs provide a vital source of investment for modernizing the industrial structure of developing countries and for improving the quality and reliability of infrastructure, including R&D. The linkages and complementarities that develop between the firms in a region, even when only loosely developed, improve productivity and innovation in the firms within the cluster (e.g., Cantwell, 1991a; Porter, 2000). Therefore the higher the concentration of FDI in a region the higher should be the propensity to spend on R&D. If the same is to hold true in the transition economies, then

> H3f: Regions with higher degree of R&D activities and investment will also see a higher concentration of FDI in those regions.

The relationship of regions' investment in research and development-related activity will be tested here to determine the correlation of that activity with the level of concentration of foreign firms in the regions. Also, data on the amount of investment, distinguished as private and total investment, including public and academic research facilities, combined for the years 2000–2005, will be used to test the correlation of the level of R&D spending in the regions and the regional industrial specialization of FDI RLAis. An analysis of the trends of regional industrial specialization of FDI in the regions related to R&D spending will be used to examine the presence and strength of the relationship of foreign firms' industrial specialization and R&D activity.

The regions showing such a correlation should become therefore an attractive location for foreign-owned R&D in their sectors of specialization (Cantwell, 1991a; Cantwell and Janne, 1999). The data on total R&D spending per region will be used to offer a robustness test for the strength of R&D spending in the region and attraction of FDI and regional industrial specialization of foreign firms.

3.6 Summary

In summary, the RLAis index measure, along with the proposed explanatory data analysis, should allow further determination of the specific existing strengths of the regions in Poland in attracting foreign investment, as stated in H3's. This analysis will reveal the extent of the existing relationships between economic factors across the regions, while the strengths of the relationships between the explanatory data relevant to the regions will provide further insights and help explain the raised hypotheses. This will be accomplished by measuring the availability or absence of the tested regional economic factors and their relevance to the attraction of the FDI in such a way that regional industrial development will lead to a narrowing path of an industry.

The results derived from data analysis should allow answering the proposed hypotheses in a meaningful way. Also, a determination as to the particular strengths of existing agglomerations of firms and reasons forming them should be established. With robustness tests, the explanatory data should yield the outcome signifying the influence of local factors supporting the reasons behind the decisions of foreign investors to locate within Poland. The revealed strengths between industrial agglomerations and economic factors supporting them should be also a good indication of future location patterns of foreign investment based on industrial class of activity across regions in Poland.

3.7 The effect of the presence of industry leaders investing in Poland on the location choices of small and medium-size foreign investors

3.7.1 Introduction

In addition to the consideration given to the concentration of foreign firms in Poland by industrial classification of activity and by country-of-origin, and regions' advantages in location factors, this research also takes into consideration another important aspect of the FDI strategic decision making process for companies, namely, the evaluation of types of foreign companies participating in a region and the interaction between them.

The separation of the leading foreign-owned firms and other non-leading companies investing in Poland is analyzed here to examine whether collocations exist at a firm level, beyond the industry level and country-of-origin effects. The leading firms identified as Fortune 500 companies are identified within the 16 Polish regions. An examination is made as to the effect of the presence of leading companies on the presence of other leading investors and of non-leading firms by measuring change in the types of firms in the participating regions.

For the purpose of this research, a cross-sectional result for the years 2000 and 2006 is used to reflect the relationship between different types of firms in Poland throughout the period. However, the results across the period vary insignificantly, as most of the firms remain throughout the period. It may be an indication that leading firms are also in a better position to establish their operations in developing economies first, and only then do the non-leading firms follow.

3.7.2 Do leaders lead?

To test the theory developed by Knickerbocker (1973), who identified the "follow-my-leader" hypothesis – which presents an explanation for clustering of multinational firms – the conclusion seems to predict that MNCs choose to follow a leader in "a collusive way" in order to address risk aversion and benefit from a complementary interdependence of FDI. Firms within the same, or related, industrial classes or country-of-origin may choose to follow one another and settle nearby while forming a new, or adding to the existing, cluster. Such interdependence, where established, may add a tacit element of security of dealing with a known partner from the host or home country and also of being able to exploit the shared industry-related resources at a lower entry cost. For this reason alone, some firms, especially those leading within their industry class, may choose to locate apart from clusters in order to protect their competitive advantage, while small and medium-size new entrants may choose to locate near the leading firms.

The participation of leading firms identified as Fortune 500 companies will be examined across regions, and their particular locations will be acknowledged as to their participation in the existing agglomerations. The differentiation between various strategic types of firms, leaders versus followers, will also become an additional attribute of regional industry strengths, based on the "follow-my-leader" conceptual results cited earlier. Here, the follower firm is measured by its size and understood as one that relies on expertise transfers, explicit and tacit, from other, leading firms. As per the Polish Agency on Foreign Investment, small-size enterprises are defined as firms with less than 50 employees which have an annual turnover of less than 10 million Euros; medium-size firms are those with less than 250 employees and less than 50 million Euros annual turnover. Such definitions are also the designation of the Polish government.[13]

Therefore, despite the perceived salience of agglomeration clusters of global FDI distribution, locating leading multinationals within an agglomeration may not benefit all businesses equally (Shaver, 1998b; Shaver and Flyer, 2000; Alcácer and Chung, 2007; Berry, 2006). The location patterns of leading firms that prefer locations not attractive to non-leading firms will be a confirmation of such a hypothesis in the regions tested here.

Although attracting foreign investors to developing regions seems an appealing option to increase their competitiveness, this poses its own threats: along the way of developing a certain level of attractiveness, these regions run the risk of becoming victims of their own success. The same factors that attracted the investment in the first place become threatened by it. As presented by Martin and Sunley (2003), congestion effects negatively impact a region's attractiveness due to the rising costs of labor and increasing living standards, additional costs, and other benefits – as listed by Martin and Sunley (2003), in Table 3.4.

The strategic role of this tradeoff is a key element in creating a balance of growth at a rate which would be sustainable in the long term. Such would be possible via increasing a region's capacity for continuing attractiveness due to the increase of its technological capability and a move to a higher grade of technological specialization. This last step is the most difficult to achieve and to measure in practice.

Cantwell and Iammarino (1998 and 1999) identify higher order locations as those which tend to attract the largest share of both domestic and foreign technology development and have a much broader range of technological specialization or activity that is likely interdependent. They also address the role of direct investment, which may be dependent on the status of the region in the national system (also in Cantwell, 2009). Such group strategies may develop by collusive actions of foreign investors (Cantwell and Mudambi, 2005) and may have a dominant effect on a selected region (also, Birkinshaw and Hood, 1998).

Establishing the most-preferred location choices for industry-leading firms in a region will help in increasing understanding of why incoming

Table 3.4 Cluster costs and benefits

Claimed advantages	**Potential disadvantages**
Higher innovation	Technological isomorphism
Higher growth	Labor cost inflation
Higher productivity	Inflation of land and housing costs
Increased profitability	Widening of income disparities
Increased competitiveness	Over-specialization
Higher new firm formation	Institutional and industrial lock-in
Higher job growth	Local congestion and environment pressure

Source: Based on Martin and Sunley (2003: p. 27).

foreign firms may choose specific locations in Poland. In addition, such results will determine the effect of the hierarchy of the regions (Cantwell and Iammarino, 2001, 2003) in Poland based on degree of attractiveness of leading foreign firms in participating industries. The revelation of particular existing strengths of the regions, and conversely of weaknesses, should also suggest the patterns of entry of future investors.

For that purpose an identification of Fortune 500 firms within the regions will be made and used to analyze the relationships raised between different types and sizes of firms. To determine these relationships, the cross-sectional analysis data on the presence of leading firms' concentration in regions hosting Fortune 500 firmswill be made. The analysis should show a measure of a degree of presence between the subsidiaries of Fortune 500 companies (leaders) and those firms that are of small and medium-size (the followers) as measured by their regional participation, will give an answer to the hypothesis H4's:

> H4a: A presence of an industry leading firm(s) in a region within a transitioning economy is a deterrent to attracting additional leading firms of the same industry to the same region.

A percentage change between the level of presence of leading firms for years 2000 and 2006 will be made to assess the relationship. The data set also allows for differentiation between industries and tests leading firms' participation across industries. Next, the co-location between the leading firms and small and medium-size companies present in the same regions as leaders is made as follows:

> H4b: A presence of an industry-leading firm(s) in a region within a transition economy will contribute to higher industrial agglomeration of foreign investors from the same industry in the region (all participating foreign firms in the industry).

This will require an analysis of change, measured by percentages between data on the Fortune 500 firms and RLAis, for all participating industries. The outcome of the H3 tests can also be used here to explain the existing relationships.

The strategic interdependence between location choices of the leading foreign investors and small and medium-size foreign firms will be tested by answering for the above-mentioned hypotheses. The cross-sectional analysis of the described data should offer insights as to the level of collocation and level of interaction at a firm level in the regions. Additionally, the results of the RLAis and RLAco will be used to determine the level of collocation from the data described in the earlier sections.

The pattern of distribution of leading firms will be determined, as well as whether they are the drivers of economic activity in the regions, and whether they were the first to move into the area. Particular attention is placed on the results of the test in order to determine whether leaders are drawn to the same strategic location, and followers to other locations – H4a (Knickerbocker, 1973; Alcácer and Chung, 2007) by RLAis index measure of foreign firms' participation in an industry and whether the presence of the Fortune 500 firms attracts further specialized investment, therefore establishing a location choice pattern for other firms – H4b. The proposed test should also reveal whether leaders have dominant presence in the region, that is to say, are representing the industry, or whether their presence is attracting other companies within the same or related industry into the region. The data review on location patterns should reveal the level of participation of foreign firms within the same industrial category as participating leading firms in the region and, therefore, possible interaction of the medium and small-size foreign firms, with the Fortune 500 firms present within the same region based on this relationship and its strength. Data at level NTS 5 covering the lowest administrative region and individual cities can be used, where needed, to determine the proximity of leaders to nearby clusters. Further control data may be used to explain possible existing dependencies between leaders and follower firms in the regions. Lastly, the analysis will explore whether new peripheral centers in Poland – locations hosting leading firms – emerge (Alcácer and Chung, 2007).

A review of location of foreign leading firms and the regional RLAis strength measure will enable answering whether an existing industrial strength of presence of FDI increases over time and attracts more foreign firms in that and related industries into the region due to the presence of a leading firm in the region.

In summary the results are expected to show a pattern of collocation of various types of firms across regions in Poland and to determine preferred location choice by type of firm, industrial class, and country-of-origin. The proposed tests will allow the development of meaningful results, answering the hypotheses presented.

4
Concentration of Foreign Firms in Poland based on Industrial Specialization and Country-of-Origin Criteria: The Results and Summary of the Evidence

Spaces are generally explicitly or implicitly divided and polarized by a number of intrinsic and extrinsic forces that influence their development. This research identifies and reveals the existing location strengths within Poland – applying proposed index measures RLAis-H1 and RLAco-H2 – and seeks to determine specific geographic advantages and heterogeneity of the regions. Further, analysis is made based on the existing industrial development path and local factor endowments supporting the investment in them – H3s. Also, further strategic location choices between leading industry firms and followers will be revealed from the results.

The analysis of the results of the RLAis and RLAco indexes answer for the proposed hypotheses H1 and H2, and provide supporting explanation to H3s and H4s as well. Although the aggregate data shows a slow but steady increase of investors' presence within the country, a number of regions, especially those attracting the fewest foreign firms, are increasingly showing less ability to attract foreign investors. In many cases the regions' level of participating foreign firms decreases or only slightly increases. Above all, many peripheral regions, especially along the eastern border, show narrowing industrial specializations and diminishing country-of-origin presence of the participating foreign firms investing in those regions.

The regions located along the Polish segment of the eastern border of the enlarged European Union are historically less attractive to foreign investors compared to Poland's southern and central regions (Cieślik, 2004). This eastern periphery is more distant from the higher-priced European Union markets, but may offer some substantial benefits to foreign firms such as lower labor, operational, and overhead costs.

The H3s reveal specific geographic advantages and heterogeneity of the regions by analyzing the relationships and their strengths between regional industrial specialization of foreign firms across Poland and the elements attracting FDI and influencing the decision making process of investors. Such is expected to show the preferred location choices of various industrial types of investor groups.

4.1 Regional industrial specialization patterns of foreign investment

This research is motivated by a broader question regarding where foreign investors would choose to locate within Poland, and what would be the prevailing trajectories of their location choices. Also, as a result, one would want to know what the impact would be of the location choice and presence of foreign investors on the various types of investing firms – leaders and followers. We know from the research presented here earlier – for example, von Thünen (1826), Marshall (1920), Knickerbocker (1973), Krugman, (1991), Cantwell and Piscitello (1997), and Ellison and Glaeser (1997) – that firms engaged in economic activity choose to locate in close proximity to each other, whether they engage in the same, similar, or different types of activities, to draw on the existing (in the agglomerations) mutually beneficial economic factors such as labor, markets, natural resources, and skills. It is also important to keep in mind that not all industries present in a locale benefit from FDI (Hirschman, 1958).

The attempt here is to determine the existing patterns of location choice by foreign firms in Poland based on the country-of-origin and PKD class of activity and, further, to examine the dominant strengths between those patterns and whether they are influenced by the presence of industry-leading firms.

In general, the location of foreign firms in Poland seems to follow the existing locational patterns related to historical presence of industries across regions. The investigation of the elements of the data on 16 regions within Poland reveals specific differences in strengths of those regions and is a good predictor of differences in regions' attractiveness to foreign investors using RLAco and RLAis models. The results indicate that regional strength divergences are directly related to the regions' existing industrial and technological base, size of skilled workforce, size of the endogenous market, and proximity to exogenous markets in both cases – industrial specialization and country-of-origin.

As a result of the RLAis analysis, unexpected from a look at the raw data, relative strengths emerged in peripheral regions. Those, however, are narrowly focused and present only in few select regions in Poland where industrial activities class generally depend on natural resources:

Manufacture of wood and wooden products in Podlaskie, Kujawsko-Pomorskie, and Lubuskie regions;
Mining and quarrying in Małopolskie region;
Manufacture of metals and metal products in Opolskie region;
Manufacture of fabrics and textiles in Podlaskie region;
Supply of electricity, gas, and water in Świętokrzyskie, Podlaskie, Zachodnio-Pomorskie, and Pomorskie regions;
Agriculture, hunting, and forestry in Pomorskie, and Warmińsko-Mazurskie regions;
Manufacture of furniture and consumer products in Zachodnio-Pomorskie region;
Manufacture of leather and leather products in Zachodnio-Pomorskie region (this activity may be related to the consumer products category above); (Data: Appendix 1). For the most part, the regions listed above hold other relative advantages in related industries: manufacture of metal and metal products in Małopolskie region (Data: Appendix 1.)

While some of the industries are located in only a few regions, others have a presence in a majority of them. These are:

Supply of electricity, gas, and water (11);
Manufacture of chemicals and chemical products (14);
Manufacture of electrical machinery (9);
Manufacture of fabrics and textiles (12);
Manufacture of food, drinks and tobacco (16);
Manufacture of furniture and consumer goods (10);
Manufacture of machinery and equipment (10);
Manufacture of metals and metal products (15);
Manufacture of other non-metal goods (15);
Manufacture of pulp and paper (14);
Manufacture of rubber and plastics (14);
Manufacture of transport equipment (13);
Real estate, rental, and business activities (9);

Table 4.1 PKD Correlation matrix and industry effect for years 2000–2006

	Correlations								
	2000 PKD	**2001 PKD**	**2002 PKD**	**2003 PKD**	**2004 PKD**	**2005 PKD**	**2006 PKD**		
2000 PKD	1								
2001 PKD	0.227	1							
2002 PKD	0.489	0.796	1						
2003 PKD	0.459	0.251	0.258	1					
2004 PKD	0.522	0.122	0.144	0.932	1				
2005 PKD	0.574	0.04	0.149	0.844	0.925	1			
2006 PKD	0.382	0.07	0.033	0.849	0.925	0.949	1		
	Constant							**R**	**R square**
Agriculture	0.238	0.071	0.029	0.453	0.48	0.474	0.465	.840a	0.706
Std. error	0.193	0.087	0.073	0.124	0.18	0.162	0.222		
Construction	–0.068	–0.052	–0.053	–0.05	–0.048	–0.025	–0.026	.840a	0.706
Std. error	0.195	0.085	0.072	0.124	0.18	0.16	0.221		
Electricity	0.137	0.068	–0.004	0.205	0.18	0.031	0.067	.850a	0.722
Std. error	0.187	0.083	0.07	0.121	0.179	0.157	0.215		
Finance	–0.025	–0.02	–0.013	–0.073	–0.082	–0.059	–0.071	.839a	0.705
Std. error	0.196	0.086	0.072	0.124	0.18	0.16	0.221		
Hotel	–0.048	–0.037	–0.048	–0.051	–0.058	–0.04	–0.044	.840a	0.705
Std. error	0.196	0.086	0.072	0.124	0.18	0.16	0.221		
Man. chemic	–0.071	–0.087	–0.073	–0.071	–0.071	–0.049	–0.054	.840a	0.705
Std. error	0.199	0.086	0.072	0.124	0.18	0.16	0.221		
Man. elecmac	–0.031	–0.044	–0.04	–0.073	–0.046	–0.028	–0.016	.840a	0.705
Std. error	0.195	0.086	0.072	0.125	0.18	0.16	0.222		
Man. fabrics	0.007	0.001	0.002	0.014	0.031	0.03	0.062	.840a	0.706

Std. error	0.193	0.086	0.073	0.124	0.179	0.161	0.223		
Man. food	–0.071	–0.064	–0.053	–0.043	–0.051	–0.027	–0.023	.840a	0.705
Std. error	0.199	0.086	0.072	0.124	0.18	0.16	0.221		
Man. furniture	0.003	0.058	0.031	0.053	0.06	0.013	0.025	.840a	0.705
Std. error	0.193	0.086	0.072	0.124	0.181	0.16	0.221		
Man. machinery	–0.033	–0.03	–0.019	–0.008	–0.011	–0.011	0.02	.840a	0.706
Std. error	0.194	0.086	0.073	0.124	0.179	0.161	0.223		
Man. metal	–0.06	–0.055	–0.032	–0.033	–0.035	–0.015	–0.006	.840a	0.705
Std. error	0.197	0.086	0.072	0.124	0.18	0.16	0.222		
Man. non-metal	–0.048	–0.04	–0.035	–0.014	–0.029	–0.002	–0.003	.840a	0.705
Std. error	0.198	0.086	0.072	0.124	0.18	0.16	0.221		
Man. paper	0.018	0	–0.015	0.028	0	–0.039	–0.048	.840a	0.705
Std. error	0.197	0.086	0.072	0.125	0.18	0.16	0.222		
Man. rubber	–0.049	–0.057	–0.056	–0.032	–0.046	–0.014	–0.009	.840a	0.705
Std. error	0.198	0.086	0.072	0.125	0.181	0.16	0.221		
Man. transp. eq	–0.07	–0.104	–0.097	–0.102	–0.062	–0.023	–0.019	.840a	0.705
Std. error	0.198	0.086	0.072	0.125	0.179	0.16	0.221		
Mining	0.088	0.235	0.083	0.004	0.05	0.032	0.047	.840a	0.705
Std. error	0.192	0.091	0.074	0.127	0.181	0.161	0.223		
Community serv.	0.355	0.144	0.342	0.021	0.056	0.071	–0.045	.841a	0.707
Std. error	0.192	0.085	0.073	0.126	0.183	0.16	0.224		
Real estate	–0.03	–0.059	–0.042	–0.059	–0.061	–0.051	–0.056	.839a	0.705
Std. error	0.196	0.086	0.072	0.124	0.18	0.16	0.221		
Transport	–0.04	0.757	0.715	0.161	–0.019	–0.011	–0.01	.900a	0.810
Std. error	0.165	0.071	0.061	0.107	0.161	0.128	0.182		
Wholesale	–0.043	–0.017	–0.023	–0.045	–0.039	–0.065	–0.078	.841a	0.707
Std. error	0.196	0.085	0.072	0.124	0.18	0.159	0.221		

Note: a Dependent Variable: 2000 RLAcoN=212

Source: Based on data obtained from the Polish Information and Foreign Investment Agency (PAIIZ) and the author's own analysis.

Transport, storage, and communication (10);
Wholesale and retail trade; repair of motor vehicles (13).

Despite a broad presence across regions, a number of industries maintain a relative advantage within a number of regions. Such relative strengths often follow existing historical trajectory but for the most part decline in relative strength despite increasing presence of firms in the real terms data.

The result of multiple leaner regression of the index measure for PKD classes in years 2000 to 2006 (Table 4.5 below), with year 2000 index results being a dependent variable, show weak correlation in the early years of the study and increasingly strengthening correlation for the concentration of foreign firms according to industry in the later part of the period. In the year 2003, immediately before Poland joined the European Union, the coefficient results reached a level of significance and are increasing in the following years of the study period. In addition, this measure, controlled for the effect of each industry present in the country, shows the effect of a particular industry on the remaining industries represented in this study. The regression results, using a dummy descriptor for particular industries, yielded results that are further tested in an individual regression within each industry alone.

The correlation coefficients between data sets representing all industries for each year of the study show increasing significance over the period. The results meaningfully increase in significance following the year 2004, the year in which Poland joined the European Union. The correlation coefficient for the multiple regression test with dummy variables is at 0.706, with significance level of 0.840. The individual effect of the tested industries do not present a significant effect on the remaining data.

To further analyze the results, this research looks at the correlation results of the RLAis index measures for each participating class. Investment in the supply of electricity, gas, and water represented in 11 regions shows a broad range of privatization effect on such generally centralized economic activity. Still, in the year 2000 most of this activity was centralized in the capital region of Mazowieckie; already in the following year, however, it was significantly distributed with participation of few regions previously not participating. In fact, in relative terms, by the year 2006 concentration of FDI in the supply of electricity, gas, and water for Mazowieckie falls to the lowest level in Poland.

The RLAis index shows that all other regions hosting supply of electricity, gas, and water investment (with the exception of only

Table 4.2 Investment in the supply of electricity, gas, and water across regions in Poland

	Electricity, gas, and water supply													
	Firms per PKD class							**RLAis**						
Voivodship	2000	2001	2002	2003	2004	2005	2006	2000	2001	2002	2003	2004	2005	2006
Dolnośląskie	0	0	1	2	2	2	2	0.00	0.00	0.48	8.62	5.86	0.86	0.82
Małopolskie	1	1	2	1	2	2	2	1.81	1.52	1.83	1.12	24.47	1.93	1.86
Mazowieckie	22	4	7	2	5	2	3	5.03	0.65	0.69	1.78	3.35	0.19	0.27
Podkarpackie	3	2	0	1	1	1	1	9.49	4.26	0.00	13.28	9.83	1.47	1.34
Podlaskie	0	1	1	2	1	1	1	0.00	7.61	4.70	5.15	4.00	3.61	4.33
Pomorskie	2	3	4	4	4	4	4	3.33	4.21	3.34	3.69	3.45	2.99	3.00
Śląskie	2	1	3	4	4	4	4	2.11	0.95	1.91	2.24	2.17	1.84	1.75
Świętokrzyskie	3	2	1	0	2	2	2	14.60	8.20	3.13	0.00	5.87	6.10	5.99
Warmińsko-Mazurskie	1	1	1	1	1	1	1	5.75	5.33	3.76	3.46	3.39	3.05	3.00
Wielkopolskie	3	1	3	3	3	4	4	2.06	0.58	1.18	10.60	7.58	1.48	1.46
Zachodnio-Pomorskie	1	1	2	3	2	3	3	3.72	2.80	3.96	5.41	3.67	3.61	3.77

Source: Based on data obtained from the Polish Information and Foreign Investment Agency (PAIIZ) and the author's own analysis.

Mazowieckie and Dolnośląskie), show significant level of RLAis. The regions of Małopolskie, Podlaskie, Pomorskie, Pomorskie, Świętokrzyskie, Warmińsko-Mazurskie, and Zachodnio-Pomorskie show relative strength for such an activity.The concentration of investment is distributed quite evenly across participating regions with not-necessarily obvious observation of two regions in northern Poland – Pomorskie and Zachodnio-Pomorskie – and two regions in southern Poland, Małopolskie and Świętokrzyskie, more obvious due to the availability of coal, are gaining strength despite rising sustainability and environmental issues.

Manufacture of chemicals and chemical products including pharmaceuticals (14)

The manufacturing of chemicals and chemical products shows a degree of fluidity regarding foreign investors, which means that some regions traditionally involved in the production of chemicals and chemical products – Mazowieckie, Wielkopolskie and, to a lesser extent, Zachodnio-Pomorskie – lose their attractiveness to foreign investors while other regions – Kujawsko-Pomorskie and Łódzkie – become of stronger interest.

The foreign investors' participation levels in those regions follow the country's trajectory of moving away from basic chemicals and, instead, attracting manufacturers of higher-grade chemicals. This conclusion is based on the detailed review of data related to individual participating companies and trade reports on chemical and plastic industries,[1] which show an increasing influx of foreign investment in the industry, which in total has about 50 percent of firms engaged in that economic activity. Also, the diversification of investment in various chemical products such as cosmetics and biochemicals slowly increases in dominance within this sector.[2]

Foreign investment in the manufacture of pharmaceuticals (a sub-class of chemical manufacturing activity) is contained in the data on the manufacturing of chemicals. However, data can be distinguished as to this important sub-class. As per the PAIIZ report on the related biotechnology industry,[3] Poland has been primarily involved in the production of generic drugs, owing to insufficient funds, low purchasing power and lengthy application policies. The generic drug market was greatly encouraged by the limited availability of originator medicines and the three-year exclusivity period. With domestically produced drugs being cheaper than imported drugs, there was an increase in revenue in addition to an increase in export.

Table 4.3 Manufacture of chemicals and chemical products across regions in Poland

	Manufacture of chemicals and chemical products including pharmaceuticals													
	Firms per PKD class							RLAis						
Voivodship	2000	2001	2002	2003	2004	2005	2006	2000	2001	2002	2003	2004	2005	2006
Dolnośląskie	5	6	7	7	9	7	8	1.34	1.44	1.29	1.39	1.46	1.23	1.24
Kujawsko-Pomorskie	1	0	0	1	2	1	2	0.84	0.00	0.00	0.77	1.18	0.85	1.23
Łódzkie	4	4	8	4	7	9	10	1.51	1.56	2.16	1.25	1.65	2.24	2.17
Lubelskie	0	0	1	1	2	2	2	0.00	0.00	1.12	1.18	1.91	1.91	1.84
Lubuskie	0	2	2	2	2	1	1	0.00	1.60	1.54	1.53	1.27	0.74	0.67
Małopolskie	3	3	3	4	4	3	3	1.52	1.44	1.07	1.66	1.36	1.19	1.05
Mazowieckie	20	24	29	32	29	30	27	1.28	1.23	1.11	1.31	1.08	1.15	0.93
Opolskie	2	1	1	1	1	2	2	2.22	1.05	0.86	0.85	0.76	1.47	1.34
Podkarpackie	4	4	4	4	5	3	4	3.54	2.68	2.34	2.45	2.73	1.80	2.03
Pomorskie	1	1	2	1	1	1	1	0.47	0.44	0.65	0.34	0.30	0.31	0.28
Śląskie	1	2	1	2	4	4	5	0.30	0.60	0.25	0.41	0.76	0.75	0.83
Świętokrzyskie	1	0	0	0	0	0	0	1.36	0.00	0.00	0.00	0.00	0.00	0.00
Wielkopolskie	6	6	7	5	4	5	5	1.16	1.09	1.06	0.82	0.56	0.76	0.69
Zachodnio-Pomorskie	1	1	1	1	1	4	2	1.04	0.88	0.77	0.67	0.64	1.96	0.95

Source: Based on data obtained from the Polish Information and Foreign Investment Agency (PAIIZ) and the author's own analysis.

The majority of pharmaceutical production in the country continues to be state-owned (at least as of the end of 2006). The remaining share of 22.6 percent is held mainly by four foreign companies in Poland: GlaxoSmithKline, Novartis, Servier, and Polpharma.[4]

That fact may explain the lack of steady investment in this sector. Overall, however limited, the presence of foreign firms in the pharmaceutical and related biotech industries create a hopeful sign for further developments in the fields if proper investment is available and conditions for applied research are created. Although presumably again the focus on investment in this PKD class is Mazowieckie where pharmaceutical facilities and research universities are present. According to the above-mentioned report, the Warsaw Scientific Consortium agreement, the region provides for a technology park to be set up in Warsaw to conduct research in medicine and biotechnology.[5]

By 2011 a number of additional major pharmaceutical companies, including Roche, Servier, Merck, Pfizer, and AstraZeneca, have established their presence in Poland. The major customers for Polish drugs are: Germany (16.8 percent), Russia (10.5 percent), and Italy (9.4 percent), while major drugs suppliers are Germany (17.6 percent), France (17 percent), and Great Britain (12.3 percent).[6]

Foreign firms in the class have a presence, not just in the central region, but also in Dolnośląskie, Lubelskie, and Wielkopolskie voivodships, where Lubelskie attracts a single investor, Herbapol, Inc., which specializes in the manufacture of pharmaceutical products from herbal raw materials. For over 50 years the company has been a major manufacturer of herbal preparations in Poland. That single presence along with another chemical manufacturer give this region positive RLAis. Dolnośląskie also has a positive RLAis in the class, while Wielkopolskie, despite steadily attracting five firms, has a rather negative (below 1) RLAis index, ranging around 0.7 for the last four years of the study period.

Above all, skills and expertise are necessary to develop and manufacture higher-grade chemical products, and some regions, along with support of the existing industrial base and policy activity, can be more accommodating than others in offering such prerequisite conditions for growth.

Manufacture of electrical machinery (9)

Manufacture of electrical machinery by foreign investors is concentrated in five regions, with a presence of foreign investment in nine regions. Although mostly concentrated in the regions with highest foreign investment levels and the best access to existing skilled labor, this manufacturing sector's concentration is shifting. Mazowieckie, although

Table 4.4 Manufacture of electrical machinery (combined with electrical, computers, and radio) across regions in Poland

	Manufacture of electrical machinery and apparatus													
	Firms per PKD class							RLAis						
Voivodship	**2000**	**2001**	**2002**	**2003**	**2004**	**2005**	**2006**	**2000**	**2001**	**2002**	**2003**	**2004**	**2005**	**2006**
Dolnośląskie	1	2	2	1	3	3	4	0.38	0.76	0.73	0.38	0.84	0.85	1.02
Kujawsko-Pomorskie	0	0	0	0	0	0	1	0.00	0.00	0.00	0.00	0.00	0.00	1.01
Łódzkie	1	1	1	0	0	0	0	0.54	0.62	0.53	0.00	0.00	0.00	0.00
Mazowieckie	13	12	14	13	17	16	14	1.19	0.97	1.05	1.02	1.08	0.99	0.79
Podkarpackie	1	1	1	0	1	2	2	1.27	1.07	1.15	0.00	0.94	1.94	1.67
Pomorskie	1	2	2	2	2	4	5	0.67	1.40	1.28	1.30	1.03	1.97	2.33
Śląskie	5	5	5	6	8	6	6	2.11	2.38	2.44	2.38	2.59	1.82	1.63
Wielkopolskie	4	5	4	6	7	8	8	1.10	1.45	1.20	1.87	1.68	2.77	1.81
Zachodnio-Pomorskie	5	3	3	0	3	2	3	7.45	4.21	4.54	0.00	3.28	1.58	2.35

Source: Based on data obtained from the Polish Information and Foreign Investment Agency (PAIIZ) and the author's own analysis.

still dominant in real terms of presence of foreign firms, is losing its relative advantage over other regions. Mostly the beneficiaries in this class are the Dolnośląskie, Pomorskie and Wielkopolskie voivodships, which attracted more firms and also increased their relative advantage index. Śląskie is a region where FDI in the manufacture of electrical machinery remains steady, and the region maintains its relative advantage as well.

The three regions listed above benefit the most from, and show steady progress in attracting, investors – in both actual number of investors and comparative RLAis terms. Such a steady progressive attractiveness of the regions to foreign firms can be attributed to a number of factors, the most dominant of which are: existing industrial base; proximity to investor country; and availability of skilled labor due to both the existence of the industry in the region and presence of academic institutions.

Manufacture of computers and related activities which are part of the manufacture of electrical machinery in Poland are quite dispersed and scarce, appearing only sporadically in three regions of Mazowieckie, Dolnośląskie and Zachodnio-Pomorskie, with the first having had one steady investor, Intel Europe, which withdrew in 2005 and moved to Pomorskie. The second, Zachodnio-Pomorskie, managed to attract three foreign investors in the class for only one-year and, after a two-year interlude, one foreign investor in the class.

Although Poland is perceived by a number of analysts and intergovernmental organizations as a viable location for investment in the IT sector overall,[7] due to the availability of skilled labor, facilities and markets, this opinion does not translate into interest among foreign IT firms. Politically and economically, equally stable neighboring countries are often cited as those attracting such an investment. Especially in the production of computer hardware, southern neighbors become more interesting locales (Barry and Van Egeraat, 2005). Only in a few isolated instances is Poland chosen as a home for an IT consulting hub, as in the case of Zachodnio-Pomorskie.[8] Both the Pomorskie and Zachodnio-Pomorskie regions have a strong RLA measure and a relative advantage in the PKD class of manufacture of electrical machinery. A similar level of foreign investment in the information technology industry remains until 2011, as per the latest report obtained from PAIIZ.[9]

Another sub-section of the manufacture of electrical machinery is the production of radio, television and communication equipment and apparatus that is present in three regions. This manufacturing augments the existing core activity of the class and is present in the areas with the most developed research and skill, the Mazowieckie and Wielkopolskie regions. According to the PAIIZ report on the electronic industry,[10] the

Polish electronics market is one of the sectors that have attracted the largest amounts of capital in the form of foreign direct investment over the last 15 years. Poland records a deficit in its foreign trade in electronic goods of EUR 3,997.2 million. This deficit was lower than in 2006 by over 13 percent and still creates strong market attractiveness. The main exporters in this class are:

manufacturers of TV sets: LG Electronics, Thomson (TTE) and Jabil;
TV tube manufacturer: Videocon;
LCD modules: Sharp, LG Philips LCD, Toshiba, Funai Electric, TPV Displays Polska;
electronic components and devices: Philips (energy-saving lighting bulbs and magnetic elements);
Foreign investment in the manufacturing of fabrics and textile

Foreign investment in the manufacturing of fabrics and textile is represented in 12 regions, with one, Łódzkie, showing significant dominance in that industry, in both real and RLAis terms. Mazowieckie, on the other hand, shows the highest loss of participating foreign firms in this industry on both real participation and index measures. Regions of Dolnośląskie, Lubuskie, and Wielkopolskie (this last bordering the leading region of Łódzkie) all show relative strengths in the manufacturing of fabrics and textiles. However, the participating number of firms in those regions is not high compared to Łódzkie. This finding is similar to the conclusion made by Deichmann, Kaiser, Lall, and Shalizi (2005) regarding attraction of industries to secondary locations in Indonesia, which has a limited rate of success, as firms prefer to locate in leading regions instead of secondary industrial centers outside of Java.

One region also shows an unusually high RLAis index relative to the number of firms participating (only ranging between one and two), however, the high RLAis index is a result of an overall low participation of FDI in Podlaskie, a region along the eastern border of Poland. This high measure cannot be taken as a representation of an actual strength of the industry in the region. However, this example shows that even low participation of foreign investors in a region with a low FDI level can be an indication of an area of economic activity which can potentially attract further investment.

The area of the economy not requiring a highly trained workforce can especially become competitive for foreign investors. Carstensen and Toubal (2003), among others, determined in their empirical study of Central and Eastern European countries that low labor costs and skill-specific factors can be detrimental to the success of investment in the region.

Overall, foreign direct investment participation in the industry remains quite constant, with a slight locational shift away from the capital region of Mazowieckie and a slow draw towards the Łódzkie region historically remaining the industry's center of activity.

Manufacture of food, drinks, and tobacco is present in all 16 regions across Poland. Obviously, the country's historically strong involvement in agriculture remains important to its economic performance. More than half of the regions, nine, show positive RLAis index for the industry. Again, Podlaskie, a peripheral region, hosting only three foreign investors, comes up on top of the RLAis index scale for the industry. Indeed, regions along the eastern border of Poland are considered in a number of studies as those that can benefit from organic and pesticide-free food production trends in the EU (Despiney-Zochowska, 2001).

In the meantime, one region, Świętokrzyskie, shows a decreasing presence of foreign investors for the last two years of the period studied, 2005 and 2006. Overall, the peripheral region, along the western border, and with close proximity to the EU markets, shows an increasing presence of foreign investors.

Poland's accession to the European Union on May 1, 2004 has improved the position and competitiveness of the Polish food and agricultural sector. Manufacturers now have to comply with the rules and regulations imposed by the EU, and therefore food products made in Poland have broader access and acceptance in the EU market.

According to the PAIIZ report on the food production and processing industry,[11] the European Union has removed duty-free and quota restrictions for some food and agricultural products (e.g., meat), which previously had protected the Common Market from the inflow of large quantities of cheaper food from Poland. Exports by the Polish food industry have become intra-EU sales since burdensome customs inspections of Polish goods crossing the EU border have been eliminated, allowing delivery time to be shortened. Exporters in the Polish food sector can use the same mechanisms supporting the export of goods to markets outside the European Union as do firms from other EU countries.

The full opening of the markets and the removal of customs formalities have resulted in higher demand for products of the Polish food and agricultural sector, especially meat and meat products, milk and dairy goods. Consequently, both the procurement prices of slaughter animals and milk, and the prices of processed goods have risen considerably in

Table 4.5 Manufacture of fabrics and textiles across regions in Poland

	Manufacture of fabrics and textiles													
	Firms per PKD class							RLAis						
Voivodship	**2000**	**2001**	**2002**	**2003**	**2004**	**2005**	**2006**	**2000**	**2001**	**2002**	**2003**	**2004**	**2005**	**2006**
Dolnośląskie	2	2	2	2	4	4	3	0.96	1.04	0.83	1.00	1.42	1.61	1.15
Kujawsko-Pomorskie	0	0	0	0	1	1	1	0.00	0.00	0.00	0.00	1.28	1.95	1.52
Łódzkie	8	7	9	4	11	9	9	5.39	5.90	5.43	3.13	5.65	5.14	4.81
Lubuskie	5	4	4	3	4	4	4	10.55	6.90	6.86	5.75	5.56	6.74	6.61
Małopolskie	0	0	0	0	1	1	2	0.00	0.00	0.00	0.00	0.74	0.90	1.73
Mazowieckie	6	6	7	3	3	3	3	0.69	0.66	0.60	0.31	0.24	0.26	0.26
Opolskie	1	1	1	1	1	1	1	1.98	2.27	1.92	2.13	1.67	1.69	1.65
Podlaskie	1	1	2	2	2	1	1	3.96	5.18	8.15	8.51	6.07	3.37	4.04
Śląskie	0	0	1	2	2	2	2	0.00	0.00	0.55	1.04	0.82	0.86	0.82
Świętokrzyskie	0	0	0	0	1	1	1	0.00	0.00	0.00	0.00	2.22	2.85	2.80
Warmińsko-Mazurskie	1	1	1	1	1	1	1	2.88	3.62	3.26	3.19	2.57	2.85	2.80
Wielkopolskie	3	3	3	2	2	2	2	1.03	1.18	1.02	0.82	0.61	0.69	0.68

Source: Based on data obtained from the Polish Information and Foreign Investment Agency (PAIIZ) and the author's own analysis.

Table 4.6 Manufacture of food, drinks, and tobacco across regions in Poland

	Manufacture of food, drinks, and tobacco products													
	Firms per PKD class							RLAis						
Voivodship	2000	2001	2002	2003	2004	2005	2006	2000	2001	2002	2003	2004	2005	2006
Dolnośląskie	6	4	2	3	4	5	5	0.66	0.47	0.21	0.32	0.37	0.51	0.46
Kujawsko-Pomorskie	6	5	6	7	8	6	7	2.07	2.27	2.79	2.86	2.69	2.98	2.57
Łódzkie	7	5	5	4	5	7	7	1.08	0.95	0.77	0.67	0.67	1.02	0.91
Lubelskie	3	3	3	3	3	2	2	1.45	1.53	1.93	1.88	1.64	1.11	1.10
Lubuskie	1	2	2	3	4	3	4	0.48	0.78	0.88	1.22	1.46	1.29	1.60
Małopolskie	5	4	5	5	5	3	4	1.04	0.93	1.02	1.10	0.97	0.69	0.84
Mazowieckie	32	34	34	29	28	34	31	0.84	0.85	0.74	0.63	0.60	0.76	0.64
Opolskie	2	3	5	6	5	6	6	0.91	1.53	2.46	2.72	2.18	2.57	2.40
Podkarpackie	3	4	5	5	4	4	4	1.09	1.31	1.67	1.63	1.25	1.40	1.21
Podlaskie	2	2	2	2	3	4	3	1.82	2.33	2.09	1.81	2.38	3.43	2.93
Pomorskie	10	10	10	10	10	12	11	1.91	2.15	1.86	1.81	1.71	2.13	1.86
Śląskie	3	3	3	3	2	3	4	0.36	0.44	0.43	0.33	0.22	0.33	0.40
Świętokrzyskie	1	1	1	1	1	0	0	0.56	0.63	0.70	0.68	0.58	0.00	0.00
Warmińsko-Mazurskie	3	2	2	2	2	1	1	1.98	1.63	1.67	1.36	1.34	0.73	0.68
Wielkopolskie	21	23	19	19	20	22	22	1.66	2.04	1.65	1.65	1.60	1.94	1.81
Zachodnio-Pomorskie	5	5	6	7	8	10	10	2.14	2.15	2.64	2.48	2.91	2.86	2.84

Source: Based on data obtained from the Polish Information and Foreign Investment Agency (PAIIZ) and the author's own analysis.

Poland. Also, according to the PAIIZ report, the comparative advantages of the Polish food and agricultural sector vis-a-vis the EU food and agricultural sector, in terms of prices for raw materials and labor costs, make it possible to forecast further growth of this sector of the Polish economy and of expansion of exports to the EU markets. That fact in itself makes the industry attractive to investors, including foreign ones searching for a low factor of production costs.

Finally, the report also points out that the demand for edible oils will increase further thanks to the growth of demand for bio-fuels, which is good news for Polish food producers and is highly attractive to foreign investors.[12]

Manufacture of furniture and consumer goods has a broad but very shallow presence in ten regions. Only Dolnośląskie, Pomorskie, Wielkopolskie, and Zachodnio-Pomorskie have between three and seven participating foreign investors and all have a positive RLAis index, while Mazowieckie has five participating investors and a negative RLAis index. Although Dolnośląskie had a presence of 12 foreign firms in the class pre-2004, it can be understood that the decline is not due to diminished economic activity but rather to the reclassification of industries.[13] For that reason, an overall declining trajectory as of 2003 levels is observed in both the actual number of firms and the index measure.

The remaining regions show a very low (one or two firms) level of participation. Again, the regions displaying the RLAis advantage in the industry are those aligned by or close to the western border and with ample access to raw materials. Investment in this industry comes mostly from the neighboring countries of Germany and Denmark, allowing these production platforms access to exogenous markets in Western Europe, investors' main markets, and also offer the benefit of lower labor costs.

Foreign investment in the manufacture of machinery and equipment is present in ten regions. However only four regions traditionally active and specialized in the manufacturing of machinery and equipment – Dolnośląskie, Mazowieckie, Śląskie, and Wielkopolskie – benefit from the closely related manufacture of transport equipment. Mazowieckie, however, does not reflect this industry as a strength in RLAis terms, despite having (equal to Dolnośląskie) the highest number of participating investors present.

For few regions with lower participation of FDI across industry classes, even a low number of actual participants translates into relative strength for the regions. These are: Łódzkie, Lubelskie, Opolskie, and Świętokrzyskie, with the last one, Świętokrzyskie, having the highest

Table 4.7 Manufacture of furniture and consumer goods across regions in Poland

	Manufacture of furniture and consumer goods													
	Firms per PKD class							RLAis						
Voivodship	**2000**	**2001**	**2002**	**2003**	**2004**	**2005**	**2006**	**2000**	**2001**	**2002**	**2003**	**2004**	**2005**	**2006**
Dolnośląskie	6	5	12	9	7	7	7	2.88	2.23	5.71	6.85	3.28	3.50	3.09
Kujawsko-Pomorskie	1	1	1	0	1	0	0	1.51	1.74	2.09	0.00	1.69	0.00	0.00
Łódzkie	0	0	0	3	1	0	0	0.00	0.00	0.00	7.62	0.68	0.00	0.00
Lubelskie	1	1	1	1	1	1	1	2.11	1.95	2.89	4.51	2.75	2.71	2.62
Mazowieckie	8	6	5	4	3	5	5	0.91	0.57	0.49	0.63	0.32	0.55	0.49
Pomorskie	2	2	2	3	2	3	3	1.67	1.64	1.67	3.91	1.73	2.60	2.42
Śląskie	2	1	0	1	0	1	1	1.05	0.56	0.00	0.79	0.00	0.53	0.47
Warmińsko-Mazurskie	1	2	1	1	1	1	1	2.88	6.25	3.76	4.88	3.39	3.54	3.23
Wielkopolskie	7	7	5	5	5	4	4	2.41	2.38	1.96	3.12	2.02	1.72	1.57
Zachodnio-Pomorskie	0	2	2	3	3	3	3	0.00	3.29	3.96	7.64	5.51	4.18	4.06

Source: Based on data obtained from the Polish Information and Foreign Investment Agency (PAIIZ) and the author's own analysis.

RLAis for the industry while steadily hosting two investors, with a short-term climb to three investors for the years 2003 and 2004.

The presence of this PKD class investors in the regions showing high real data and index results is closely related to the next industry covered, namely, the manufacture of metals and metal products.

Manufacture of metals and metal products is quite a traditional industry in Poland and all of the regions, with the exception of two, have steady foreign investment in this class. The most obvious hosts in the class show the highest rates of investment: Małopolskie, Mazowieckie, Śląskie, and Wielkopolskie. For two of these regions – Małopolskie and Śląskie – manufacture of metals and metal products is also indicative of strength, while for Wielkopolskie the RLAis index in the industry is just slightly above 1, indicating marginal strength. Mazowieckie, again, despite attracting the second-highest number of firms in the industry, does not reveal strength in the industry due to the highest total participation of foreign investment in the region.

The regions of Dolnośląskie and Podkarpackie show the highest increase in number of investors participating in this activity class, with only one, Podkarpackie, also showing strength for the manufacture of metals and metal products in the RLAis index measure. For Dolnośląskie, foreign investment in this industry does not become a strength despite an increase from two to five firms investing. One remaining region that deserves attention is Opolskie, which steadily attracts a small number of firms, initially three, with a dip to two and a rise to four, but steadily reflecting an RLAis strength due to an overall low attractiveness of foreign firms. Manufacture of metals and metal products maintains its historical strength.

The manufacture of other non-metal goods is represented in 15 regions, but shows statistically significant participation strengths in only four of those regions: Dolnośląskie, Łódzkie, Mazowieckie, and Śląskie. The location pattern in this class closely follows the trajectory of the manufacture of metal and metal products as well as the manufacture of transport equipment PKD classes. Interestingly enough, for the regions showing the highest strength in the beginning of the study period the participation has declined and only one region, Łódzkie, shows a steady increase of participants numbers and RLAis strength.

The remaining regions show relatively low participation of foreign investors in the PKD class ranging from two to four foreign investors. However, most still consistently reflect RLAis strength for the industry.

Foreign investors in the manufacture of pulp and paper are present in 14 regions. Despite most of the regions participating, only a handful

Table 4.8 Manufacture of machinery and equipment across regions in Poland

	Manufacture of machinery and equipment													
	Firms per PKD class							RLAis						
Voivodship	**2000**	**2001**	**2002**	**2003**	**2004**	**2005**	**2006**	**2000**	**2001**	**2002**	**2003**	**2004**	**2005**	**2006**
Dolnośląskie	6	7	6	5	10	10	10	2.98	3.36	2.65	1.75	2.66	2.98	2.73
Łódzkie	1	1	2	0	3	4	4	0.70	0.78	1.29	0.00	1.15	1.68	1.53
Lubelskie	0	0	0	1	2	2	2	0.00	0.00	0.00	2.07	3.13	3.22	3.25
Mazowieckie	8	8	6	9	9	10	10	0.95	0.82	0.55	0.65	0.55	0.65	0.61
Opolskie	1	1	2	2	1	1	2	2.05	2.10	4.11	2.99	1.25	1.24	2.36
Śląskie	1	1	1	3	6	5	5	0.55	0.60	0.59	1.09	1.85	1.59	1.46
Świętokrzyskie	2	2	2	3	3	2	2	5.05	5.16	5.82	6.73	5.00	4.21	4.00
Warmińsko-Mazurskie	0	0	0		0	0	1	0.00	0.00	0.00	0.00	0.00	0.00	2.00
Wielkopolskie	6	7	7	7	7	5	5	2.14	2.55	2.55	2.00	1.61	1.28	1.21
Zachodnio-Pomorskie	1	1	1	1	1	0	0	1.93	1.77	1.84	1.17	1.04	0.00	0.00

Source: Based on data obtained from the Polish Information and Foreign Investment Agency (PAIIZ) and the author's own analysis.

Table 4.9 Manufacture of metals and metal products across regions in Poland

	Manufacture of metals and metal products													
	Firms per PKD class							RLAis						
Voivodship	**2000**	**2001**	**2002**	**2003**	**2004**	**2005**	**2006**	**2000**	**2001**	**2002**	**2003**	**2004**	**2005**	**2006**
Dolnośląskie	2	2	2	3	5	5	5	0.60	0.56	0.51	0.79	1.01	0.99	0.90
Kujawsko-Pomorskie	2	2	3	2	2	2	2	1.88	2.19	3.33	2.03	1.46	1.92	1.42
Łódzkie	1	1	2	2	2	2	2	0.42	0.46	0.74	0.83	0.58	0.56	0.50
Lubelskie	1	1	1	0	0	1	1	1.31	1.23	1.54	0.00	0.00	1.07	1.07
Lubuskie	0	0	0	0	1	0	0	0.00	0.00	0.00	0.00	0.79	0.00	0.00
Małopolskie	6	6	6	6	8	6	7	3.38	3.38	2.92	3.30	3.37	2.67	2.84
Mazowieckie	5	6	8	9	10	10	10	0.36	0.36	0.42	0.49	0.46	0.43	0.40
Opolskie	3	3	2	2	4	4	4	3.69	3.69	2.35	2.26	3.80	3.32	3.10
Podkarpackie	1	3	4	4	5	5	5	0.98	2.36	3.19	3.25	3.39	3.38	2.94
Podlaskie	1	1	1	1	1	1	1	2.46	2.81	2.49	2.26	1.73	1.66	1.89
Pomorskie	1	1	1	2	2	3	3	0.52	0.52	0.44	0.90	0.74	1.03	0.98
Śląskie	11	9	8	9	9	13	14	3.61	3.17	2.71	2.47	2.11	2.76	2.68
Świętokrzyskie	0	0	3	2	2	2	2	0.00	0.00	4.99	3.39	2.53	2.81	2.62
Wielkopolskie	6	6	6	6	5	7	7	1.28	1.28	1.25	1.30	0.87	1.19	1.12
Zachodnio-Pomorskie	0	0	0	0	1	2	2	0.00	0.00	0.00	0.00	0.79	1.11	1.10

Source: Based on data obtained from the Polish Information and Foreign Investment Agency (PAIIZ) and the author's own analysis.

Table 4.1C Manufacture of other non-metal goods across regions in Poland

	Manufacture of other non-metal goods													
	Firms per PKD class							RLAis						
Voivodship	**2000**	**2001**	**2002**	**2003**	**2004**	**2005**	**2006**	**2000**	**2001**	**2002**	**2003**	**2004**	**2005**	**2006**
Dolnośląskie	10	12	10	9	6	6	6	2.40	2.88	2.13	1.85	1.06	1.25	1.15
Kujawsko-Pomorskie	1	1		1	0	0	0	0.75	0.83	0.00	0.79	0.00	0.00	0.00
Łódzkie	6	8	7	9	11	10	11	2.02	2.76	2.19	2.90	2.82	2.95	2.94
Lubelskie	2	2	1	2	2	2	1	2.11	1.86	1.30	2.43	2.09	2.25	1.14
Lubuskie	2	2	2	2	2	3	2	2.11	1.41	1.77	1.58	1.39	2.61	1.65
Małopolskie	5	6	5	4	4	4	4	2.26	2.55	2.06	1.71	1.48	1.87	1.73
Mazowieckie	12	12	12	14	13	9	9	0.69	0.54	0.53	0.59	0.53	0.41	0.38
Opolskie	2	1	3	4	4	4	3	1.98	0.93	2.98	3.51	3.34	3.48	2.48
Podkarpackie	1	2	1	1	1	1	1	0.79	1.19	0.67	0.63	0.60	0.71	0.63
Pomorskie	2	2	2	1	3	2	3	0.83	0.78	0.75	0.35	0.98	0.72	1.05
Śląskie	6	4	6	6	9	8	7	1.58	1.06	1.71	1.28	1.85	1.78	1.43
Świętokrzyskie	3	3	3	3	3	3	3	3.65	3.43	4.22	3.95	3.34	4.42	4.20
Warmińsko-Mazurskie	1	3	3	3	3	3	3	1.44	4.46	5.06	3.95	3.85	4.42	4.20
Wielkopolskie	2	2	4	4	4	2	3	0.34	0.32	0.70	0.67	0.61	0.36	7.65
Zachodnio-Pomorskie	0	0	0	1	1	1	1	0.00	0.00	0.00	0.69	0.70	0.58	8.80

Source: Based on data obtained from the Polish Information and Foreign Investment Agency (PAIIZ) and the author's own analysis.

exhibit this PKD class at a level of significance. Most regions have only one or two foreign investors in this class, with only two regions being a bit stronger, having four foreign investors: Kujawsko-Pomorskie and Łódzkie. Although both regions steadily attract three or four investors in this class, Kujawsko-Pomorskie maintains an increasing trajectory in actual number of firms and a relatively high 3.637 RLAis index, while Łódzkie has a flat number of investors participating, at three, with a few years' increase to four. Łódzkie, in the last year of the studied period, 2006, drops in terms of RLAis index measure to 0.963, from its highest point, matching that of Kujawsko-Pomorskie, therefore reflecting a weakening trend for the industry.

The region attracting the highest number of foreign investors in this PKD class, seven times as many as the next highest, is Mazowieckie, the biggest market. As the data on the actual terms is not a surprise, of most interest here is the fact that Mazowieckie also shows a quite high RLAis index for the class. Although this index strength is on a declining course, it remains relatively strong at 1.431. Investment in manufacture of pulp and paper shows strength when located near the market, not near the regions offering the raw materials. Those regions seem incapable of attracting investment directly.

Manufacture of rubber and plastics is one of the industries widely distributed across most of the regions – 14. As with the industries discussed above, it also concentrates in a few regions to a statistically significant level: Dolnośląskie, Łódzkie, Mazowieckie, Śląskie, and Wielkopolskie. All the regions except Mazowieckie also have a positive RLAis index for the PKD class. The highest number of participants is attracted to the region of Śląskie, 12, and this participation gives an RLAis index of 2.263 for the region. This index measure is the second-highest for the industry, higher only in Lubelskie, a region along the southeast border of Poland, hosting only three firms in the PKD class, which results in an RLAis index of 3.147 for the region.

Similarly the manufacture of transport equipment is conducted in 13 regions in Poland. This PKD class also covers auto manufacturing, which before 2004 was listed as a separate class present only in four voivodships: Dolnośląskie, Łódzkie, Lubelskie, and Małopolskie, with only Dolnośląskie having a significant presence and strength in the index measure. After 2004 all transportation manufacturing is combined and represented in 13 regions. Its strengths are in Dolnośląskie, Mazowieckie, and Śląskie, with Podkarpackie, Pomorskie, and Wielkopolskie being in a distant second tier.

Table 4.11 Manufacture of pulp and paper, publishing, and printing across regions in Poland

	Manufacture of pulp and paper, publishing, and printing													
	Firms per PKD class							RLAis						
Voivodship	**2000**	**2001**	**2002**	**2003**	**2004**	**2005**	**2006**	**2000**	**2001**	**2002**	**2003**	**2004**	**2005**	**2006**
Dolnośląskie	3	3	3	2	2	2	2	1.61	1.14	1.49	1.18	0.81	0.49	0.46
Kujawsko-Pomorskie	3	3	3	2	4	4	4	5.06	6.29	6.52	4.53	5.84	4.75	3.64
Łódzkie	3	3	4	4	3	3	3	2.26	2.63	2.90	3.70	1.75	1.04	0.96
Lubelskie	1	1	1	1	1	1	1	2.36	2.36	3.01	3.48	2.37	1.33	1.36
Lubuskie	1	2	2	2	2	2	2	2.36	3.60	4.12	4.53	3.16	2.05	1.98
Małopolskie	1	3	3	1	2	2	2	1.01	3.24	2.86	1.22	1.69	1.10	1.04
Mazowieckie	20	21	23	31	29	29	28	2.56	2.42	2.36	3.76	2.68	1.55	1.43
Podlaskie	2	0	0	0	0	0	0	8.86	0.00	0.00	0.00	0.00	0.00	0.00
Pomorskie	1	1	2	1	1	0	1	0.93	0.99	1.74	1.01	0.74	0.00	0.42
Śląskie	3	2	2	2	2	2	2	1.77	1.35	1.33	1.22	0.94	0.52	0.49
Świętokrzyskie	1	1	0	1	1	1	1	2.73	2.90	0.00	3.77	2.53	1.73	1.68
Warmińsko-Mazurskie	0	0	0	0	1	1	1	0.00	0.00	0.00	0.00	2.92	1.73	1.68
Wielkopolskie	1	0	2	2	2	3	1	0.39	0.00	0.82	0.96	0.70	0.63	10.20
Zachodnio-Pomorskie	1	2	1	1	1	1	0	2.08	3.97	2.06	1.97	1.58	0.68	0.00

Source: Based on data obtained from the Polish Information and Foreign Investment Agency (PAIIZ) and the author's own analysis.

Table 4.12 Manufacture of rubber and plastics across regions in Poland

	Manufacture of rubber and plastics													
	Firms per PKD class							RLAis						
Voivodship	2000	2001	2002	2003	2004	2005	2006	2000	2001	2002	2003	2004	2005	2006
Dolnośląskie	1	4	4	4	6	6	6	0.50	1.73	1.55	1.10	1.19	1.21	1.06
Kujawsko-Pomorskie	1	1	1	1	2	1	1	1.56	1.68	1.70	1.06	1.44	0.98	0.70
Łódzkie	3	3	4	4	6	7	7	2.09	2.11	2.26	1.73	1.72	2.00	1.73
Lubelskie	2	2	2	2	2	3	3	4.38	3.78	4.70	3.26	2.33	3.27	3.15
Lubuskie	0	0	0	1	2	2	2	0.00	0.00	0.00	1.06	1.56	1.69	1.53
Małopolskie	1	1	1	3	3	4	4	0.94	0.86	0.75	1.72	1.24	1.81	1.60
Mazowieckie	5	4	5	7	10	8	10	0.59	0.37	0.40	0.40	0.45	0.35	0.39
Podkarpackie	1	3	1	2	2	2	2	1.64	3.62	1.22	1.70	1.33	1.37	1.16
Podlaskie	0	0	0	1	1	1	1	0.00	0.00	0.00	2.35	1.70	1.69	1.86
Pomorskie	2	1	1	3	4	4	4	1.73	0.79	0.68	1.41	1.46	1.40	1.29
Śląskie	5	6	7	9	10	11	12	2.73	3.24	3.63	2.58	2.30	2.37	2.26
Warmińsko-Mazurskie	1	0	0	1	1	2	2	2.98	0.00	0.00	1.77	1.44	2.85	2.58
Wielkopolskie	5	5	6	7	10	10	10	1.78	1.64	1.91	1.58	1.71	1.73	16.99
Zachodnio-Pomorskie	0	0	0	0	0	1	1	0.00	0.00	0.00	0.00	0.00	0.56	5.87

Source: Based on data obtained from the Polish Information and Foreign Investment Agency (PAIIZ) and the author's own analysis.

Table 4.13 Manufacture of transport equipment across regions in Poland

	Manufacture of transport equipment													
	Firms per PKD class							RLAis						
Voivodship	2000	2001	2002	2003	2004	2005	2006	2000	2001	2002	2003	2004	2005	2006
Dolnośląskie	8	7	9	11	19	18	20	1.63	1.24	1.51	1.44	3.23	3.52	3.70
Kujawsko-Pomorskie	1	1	1	1	1	1	1	0.64	0.69	0.73	0.50	0.61	0.95	0.73
Łódzkie	3	1	1	1	2	1	1	0.86	0.29	0.24	0.21	0.49	0.28	0.26
Lubelskie	1	1	1	1	1	1	1	0.89	0.78	1.02	0.77	1.00	1.06	1.10
Lubuskie	2	1	1	1	1	1	1	1.79	0.59	0.70	0.50	0.66	0.82	0.80
Małopolskie	1	2	3	2	2	0	0	0.38	0.71	0.97	0.54	0.71	0.00	0.00
Mazowieckie	4	5	4	3	4	9	9	0.19	0.19	0.14	0.08	0.16	0.38	0.37
Opolskie	1	1	0	0	2	2	2	0.84	0.78	0.00	0.00	1.60	1.63	1.60
Podkarpackie	3	1	3	6	7	7	7	2.01	0.50	1.59	2.41	3.99	4.66	4.25
Pomorskie	5	4	3	2	5	5	5	1.77	1.31	0.88	0.45	1.56	1.70	1.69
Śląskie	12	11	12	14	14	11	11	2.68	2.44	2.69	1.90	2.76	2.30	2.17
Świętokrzyskie	2	2	0	0	1	1	1	2.07	1.91	0.00	0.00	1.06	1.38	1.35
Wielkopolskie	4	4	1	2	3	5	5	0.58	0.54	10.19	0.21	0.44	0.84	0.78

Source: Based on data obtained from the Polish Information and Foreign Investment Agency (PAIIZ) and the author's own analysis.

The leading region for the class is Dolnośląskie, which managed to attract a number of significant names in auto manufacturing: Volvo, Toyota, and Greenbrier Europe B.V., among others. Its existing machinery manufacturing base, access to raw materials, and proximity to the external markets allow for a good combination of necessary factors. Śląskie is second only to Dolnośląskie in attracting investors to the region, with the long-established presence of Fiat. The region also hosts a number of mostly European firms in the PKD class. For both regions the actual number of participants and the RLAis index show a significant strength for the industry class.

Mazowieckie also manages to attract a steadily increasing number of investors in the PKD class. However, its auto manufacturing base, which was leading in Poland, virtually disappeared with a number of unsuccessful investments. Remaining component manufacturers seem to operate without forming a particular cluster and are scattered across the region's large territory. The most significant names are General Motors, Delphi Automotive Systems, Toyota, and Peugeot. The origin of investment in this PKD class is also derived from three continents and does not form a particular pattern or strength. Hence, the investment RLAis index for this PKD class in Mazowieckie does not reflect strength.

The second-tier regions – Podkarpackie, Pomorskie, and Wielkopolskie – in this PKD class also show RLAis advantage for the region, with the exception of Wielkopolskie, which has the second-largest foreign investment base in Poland. Pomorskie and Wielkopolskie offer an existing industrial base for auto components manufacturing and proximity to the exogenous markets west of Poland. Podkarpackie, however, had a historical presence of truck production, and it maintains that trajectory by attracting manufacturers of heavy vehicles in addition to following its second line of expertise, which is the manufacture of aircraft and spacecraft and attracting such investors as: Goodrich Aerospace Canada LTD, Valin, Lear Corporation, and United Technologies Holding S.A. Although combined with the manufacture of transport equipment, the last class follows a particular existing location path for a cluster.

The remaining regions attract only one or two investors and, although not significant in real number strength, that low participation translates into an RLAis advantage for their economies. Another fact worth mentioning is that the Aviation Sector in Poland, a sub-section of manufacture of transport equipment and manufacture of electrical machinery (sections discussed above), forms a very distinct cluster in the south-eastern region of Poland – Podkarpackie. A number of foreign firms are

Table 4.14 Real estate, rental, and business activities across regions in Poland

	Real estate, rental, and business activities													
	Firms per PKD class							RLAis						
Voivodship	**2000**	**2001**	**2002**	**2003**	**2004**	**2005**	**2006**	**2000**	**2001**	**2002**	**2003**	**2004**	**2005**	**2006**
Dolnośląskie	2	1	1	0	1	2	2	1.49	0.72	0.59	0.00	0.47	0.42	0.41
Łódzkie	0	0	2	1	1	2	2	0.00	0.00	1.72	0.92	0.68	0.60	0.57
Małopolskie	3	1	4	3	3	3	3	4.22	1.44	4.54	3.67	73.40	1.43	1.39
Mazowieckie	7	9	10	13	16	38	38	1.24	1.38	1.22	1.58	42.86	1.76	1.73
Opolskie	0	0	0	0	1	1	1	0.00	0.00	0.00	0.00	2.20	0.89	0.89
Pomorskie	2	2	2	1	1	2	2	2.59	2.65	2.07	1.01	0.86	0.74	0.75
Śląskie	0	0	0	0	0	1	1	0.00	0.00	0.00	0.00	0.00	0.30	0.22
Wielkopolskie	1	0	1	1	3	3	3	0.54	0.00	0.49	0.48	1.21	0.55	1.33
Zachodnio-Pomorskie	1	1	0	0	0	1	1	2.90	2.65	0.00	0.00	0.00	0.59	1.53

Source: Based on data obtained from the Polish Information and Foreign Investment Agency (PAIIZ) and the author's own analysis.

located in relative proximity, following the existing path and depending on expertise and skilled labor offered by the region.

So called the Aviation Valley, an organization located in southeastern Poland, is known for its aerospace industry and pilot training centers.[14] This region has a heavy concentration of aerospace industry and scientific research centers, as well as educational and training facilities. Among the main activities are organization and development of a low-cost supply chain and further development of aerospace research, aptitude, and skill. Evident here is cooperation with universities of technology, which can promote new ideas and scientific research within the aerospace industry. According to the PAIIZ report, the Aviation Valley Association currently represents 72 companies within the region and employs over 20,000 experienced workers.[15] The association's role is the creation of favorable conditions for enhancing the development of aerospace industry enterprises in the region and for closer cooperation between R&D units and the small and medium enterprise (SME) sector.

Real estate, rental, and business activities by foreign investors are present in nine regions across Poland. Despite this wide presence, one region, Mazowieckie, dominates in both number of foreign investors in the PKD class and in the index measure. This region steadily attracts investors, with a rapid increase to 38 firms in the PKD class after Poland's accession to the EU. The RLAis index for the PKD class also shows a steady advantage, and its increase to 1.734 for 2006. It is the highest for the class and one of only two positive index measures for real estate, rental, and business activities within Poland.

One additional region showing a positive RLAis index is Małopolskie, home of the major city of Krakow. Its advantage in the industry derives from the region's overall lower attractiveness to foreign investors. The remaining regions manage to attract only one or two investors in the class, and not always consistently.

Foreign direct investment in the transport, storage, and communication PKD class is present in ten regions of Poland. This PKD class, however, is only emerging after a new PKD classification was adopted. Before the reclassification took place, the data were separated into a number of other categories and the class itself was not present. Reliable data for this PKD class are available only for the years 2004–2006. Since the record for this class has been kept, foreign investors in it seem to be attracted to the region with the largest market, Mazowieckie, where the majority of the foreign firms investing in transport, storage, and communication are present. In this case, Mazowieckie also shows a positive RLAis measure for the industry.

Table 4.15 Transport, storage, and communication across regions in Poland

	Transport, storage, and communication													
	Firms per PKD class							RLAis						
Voivodship	2000	2001	2002	2003	2004	2005	2006	2000	2001	2002	2003	2004	2005	2006
Dolnośląskie	2	1	4	1	1	2	1					0.27	0.57	0.27
Łódzkie	1	2	3	2	2	2	2	0.00	0.00	0.00	0.00	0.79	0.80	0.76
Lubuskie	0	1	1	1	1	1	1	0.00	43.14	51.47	9.96	1.07	1.19	1.18
Mazowieckie	4	11	13	20	22	23	24					1.28	1.42	1.46
Podkarpackie	1	3	3	1	1	1	1					0.91	0.97	0.90
Pomorskie	2	1	3	3	3	3	2	1.33	0.77			1.51	1.48	1.00
Śląskie	1	1	1	1	1	1	1					0.32	0.12	0.29
Warmińsko-Mazurskie	1	1	1	0	0	0	0				0.00	0.00	0.00	0.00
Wielkopolskie	4	2	4	5	6	5	5					1.41	1.22	50.98
Zachodnio-Pomorskie	1	1	1	1	0	1	1					0.00	0.79	35.19

Source: Based on data obtained from the Polish Information and Foreign Investment Agency (PAIIZ) and the author's own analysis.

Table 4.16 Wholesale and retail trade; repair of motor vehicles across regions in Poland

	Wholesale and retail trade; repair of motor vehicles, motorcycles and personal and household goods													
	Firms per PKD class							**RLAis**						
Voivodship	**2000**	**2001**	**2002**	**2003**	**2004**	**2005**	**2006**	**2000**	**2001**	**2002**	**2003**	**2004**	**2005**	**2006**
Dolnośląskie	3	7	6	7	6	5	5	1.15	90.60	2.86	2.11	1.63	0.54	0.51
Kujawsko-Pomorskie	3	2	1	2	2	2	3	3.62	3.25	1.81	2.32	1.97	1.05	1.21
Łódzkie	5	1	2	7	6	5	6	2.69	0.68	1.21	3.31	2.36	0.77	0.85
Lubelskie	1	1	1	1	1	1	1	1.69	1.83	2.51	1.78	1.60	0.59	0.60
Lubuskie	1	1	0	0	0	0	0	1.69	1.39	0.00	0.00	0.00	0.00	0.00
Małopolskie	5	5	5	5	6	9	7	3.62	4.18	3.98	3.13	3.41	2.20	1.61
Mazowieckie	37	41	44	47	60	78	80	3.38	3.65	3.75	2.92	3.74	1.85	1.81
Opolskie	1	2	2	2	1	1	1	1.58	3.65	3.84	2.57	1.28	0.45	0.44
Podlaskie	1	1	1	0	2	2	1	3.16	4.18	4.08	0.00	4.66	1.82	1.07
Śląskie	0	1	1	1	1	2	2	0.00	0.52	0.55	0.31	0.32	0.02	0.22
Świętokrzyskie	0	1	1	1	0	0	0	0.00	2.25	2.72	1.93	0.00	0.00	0.00
Wielkopolskie	9	10	15	17	21	13	13	2.48	3.18	5.09	4.19	4.93	1.21	3.16
Zachodnio-Pomorskie	0	0	0	0	1	1	1	0.00	0.00	0.00	0.00	0.00	0.30	0.84

Source: Based on data obtained from the Polish Information and Foreign Investment Agency (PAIIZ) and the author's own analysis.

A distant second, attracting only one fifth of the firms in Mazowieckie, is the region of Wielkopolskie. The region's strength include: its strategical location, situated halfway between Mazowieckie and the border with Germany; and it has the second-largest industrial base in Poland. This region shows strength in RLAis measure as well.

Wholesale trade and retail trade and the repair of motor vehicles are present in 13 regions across Poland. Again, as in the above PKD class, Mazowieckie has a distinct lead in being able to attract foreign investors. Exactly two thirds, 80 out of 120, of foreign firms in the industry locate in this region. Since it is a central, capital region with Poland's largest market and a good presence of economic activity, the region seems to be an obvious choice. This leadership in the class for the region was established very early on after the opening of the national economy and adoption of a free-market system. Again a distant second, with 13 foreign investors, is Wielkopolskie, the second most economically active region in this class. The remaining regions attract significantly less than 5 percent of foreign investors in the PKD class.

In total, five regions reflect the strength in RLAis measure: Mazowieckie, Wielkopolskie, Małopolskie, Kujawsko-Pomorskie, and Podlaskie. Although for the last one, Podlaskie, the measure can be indicative of strength due to an overall weak attraction of FDI into the region. It attracts only one foreign investor in this PKD class.

Further, the industries (by PKD class) representing investors only in a minority of regions (up to eight), but with the exception of industries present only in a single region which are discussed separately. Certain industries are equally important to Poland's economic development and even may be a sign of development of the regions they locate in; they are:

Agriculture, hunting, and forestry (4)
Capital investment (4)
Computer and related activities (2)
Construction (7)
Financial intermediation (8)
Hotels and restaurants (8)
Manufacture of leather and leather products (6)
Manufacture of radio, television and communication equipment and apparatus (3)
Manufacture of wood and wooden products (8)
Mining and quarrying (5)
Other community, social and personal service activities (8)

Table 4.17 Agriculture, hunting, and forestry across regions in Poland

	Agriculture, hunting and forestry													
	Firms per PKD class							RLAis						
Voivodship	**2000**	**2001**	**2002**	**2003**	**2004**	**2005**	**2006**	**2000**	**2001**	**2002**	**2003**	**2004**	**2005**	**2006**
Lubelskie	0	1	0	0	0	0	0	0.00	2.10	0.00	0.00	0.00	0.00	0.00
Pomorskie	2	2	2	2	2	1	1	11.66	11.92	10.87	11.07	10.79	7.23	5.25
Warmińsko-Mazurskie	1	0	0	2	2	2	2	20.14	0.00	0.00	41.50	42.35	58.97	41.96
Wielkopolskie	1	1	1	0	0	0	0	2.41	2.46	2.55		0.00	0.00	0.00

Source: Based on data obtained from the Polish Information and Foreign Investment Agency (PAIIZ) and the author's own analysis.

Table 4.13 Capital investment across regions in Poland

	Capital investment													
	Firms per PKD class							RLAis						
Voivodship	**2000**	**2001**	**2002**	**2003**	**2004**	**2005**	**2006**	**2000**	**2001**	**2002**	**2003**	**2004**	**2005**	**2006**
Dolnośląskie	0	1	1	0	1	0	0	0.00	1.29	1.24	0.00	0.53	0.00	0.00
Lubelskie	1	1	0	0	0	0	0	3.11	2.83	0.00	0.00	0.00	0.00	0.00
Małopolskie	1	1	1	0	1	0	0	3.62	2.59	2.39	0.00	1.11	0.00	0.00
Mazowieckie	5	8	22	0	14	0	0	2.28	2.21	5.63	0.00	1.70	0.00	0.00

Source: Based on data obtained from the Polish Information and Foreign Investment Agency (PAIIZ) and the author's own analysis.

Foreign investment in agriculture, hunting and forestry is present in only four regions across Poland. It is constant, at however low a level, in only two regions, Pomorskie and Warmińsko-Mazurskie. The foreign investment in this class, although closely connected to the regulation of purchase of land by foreign entities,[16] which can take place only after 12 years have passed since Poland's accession to the EU (which took place on May 1, 2004).

Regions where investment is present attract foreign investors in fishing industries is Warmińsko-Mazurskie region attracting investors in this category is located along Poland's eastern border and despite its lower level of technological development offers investment opportunities in this PKD class. According to the study by Despiney-Zochowska (2001) farmers along Poland's eastern border, generally small and medium size farms, lack expertise and access to modern technologies and farm subsidies. Action undertaken in that area by the European Union is expected to improve that situation. Its success may attract further foreign investment. This situation poses a significant opportunity of outside investors in the future.

The capital investment PKD class is represented in four (4) regions with one, Mazowieckie, clearly dominating the class. The remaining regions – Dolnośląskie, Lubelskie, and Małopolskie – attract only one investor each in the class. Mazowieckie has both theoretical and practical advantages of being the capital region with a central financial and economic government present, and also being the region attracting most of the country's economic activity. Also, the RLAis index for the PKD class reflects location advantage for this type of investment in the region. For the year 2003, there are no data for this PKD class. However, for all the regions, FDI in the class ceased after 2004. That can be a result of changing regulation and also of the global economic environment and decline of FDI levels.

FDI in the financial intermediation class is located in eight regions and reflects a slightly broader presence and a somewhat deeper distribution than the capital investment class. The majority of financial intermediation firms locate in the Mazowieckie region. The only other region with a steady increase of foreign presence in the class is Śląskie. However, Śląskie attracts less than 10 percent of firms compared to Mazowieckie, and its RLAis index for the class is rated below 1. Another region, Pomorskie, had a rise in the FDI within the PKD class in the years 2002–2005, peaking with the presence of six foreign firms in the PKD class. However, that interest has steadily declined to one foreign firm in 2006.

The remaining regions have only sporadically managed to attract foreign investors in the class. That trend seems to be mostly the result of opportunism and does not add a steady value to the local economy. In fact, it may pose a threat to indigenous financial institutions. As the study by Farnoux et al. (2004) indicates, since 1999 profitability of commercial banks under Polish control in terms of return on equity (ROE)[17] has been declining much faster than that of commercial banks under foreign control for the same period.

The financial intermediation (which includes banking and insurance) and capital investment classes have undergone a series of regulatory changes in the last two decades. The transition of these industries from a centrally governed system was quite expensive. According to a study by Tang et al. (2000), Poland's total fiscal cost of bank restructuring during the 1991–1998 period is estimated at 8 percent of 1998 GDP.

According to another study, this one by the European Central Bank (2002),[18] the development of financial and banking sector industries has a direct positive correlation in the economic development of a country. It is important for real convergence, because financial development – understood as an increase in the size, depth and efficiency of the financial sector – is closely linked to developments in the real economy.

Strong regulation of an industry allows for its stability, which may attract foreign investors. Nevertheless, in the case of Poland, after the initial strong increase, the presence of foreign investment in both financial activity classes indexes has sharply declined.

Foreign investment in the construction PKD class is present in seven regions. The majority of investment is mostly concentrated in Mazowieckie, with the remaining portion disbursed among other most-vital regions: Pomorskie, Śląskie, and Wielkopolskie. This class covers foreign investment in public and private construction as well as building activity and production of building materials. According to a PAIIZ report,[19] foreign investment in the construction market in Poland makes up 20 percent of total direct foreign investment in Poland.

Again the capital region of Mazowieckie dominates, attracting 28 foreign firms in this PKD class out of 42 present in the country. Investment in this class has steady growth, and its class RLAis index also shows increasing advantage and strength. Another two regions with quite interesting dynamics of foreign firm presence in the PKD class are Pomorskie and Śląskie, which also have steadily growing RLAis strength, although they only attract four foreign firms each in the PKD class. Where Pomorskie manages to have a strong positive RLAis index of 2, Śląskie stays only slightly above 1 only in 2003 and 2005, indicating

Table 4.19 Construction across regions in Poland

	Construction													
	Firms per PKD class							RLAis						
Voivodship	**2000**	**2001**	**2002**	**2003**	**2004**	**2005**	**2006**	**2000**	**2001**	**2002**	**2003**	**2004**	**2005**	**2006**
Łódzkie	1	2	0	0	0	0	0	0.45	1.05	0.00	0.00	0.00	0.00	0.00
Małopolskie	3	2	3	2	2	2	2	1.81	1.29	1.52	1.42	1.14	1.30	1.24
Mazowieckie	20	20	26	26	28	27	28		1.38	1.42	1.83	1.74	1.71	1.70
Pomorskie	1	2	2	1	4	4	4	0.56	1.19	0.92	0.58	2.01	2.02	2.00
Śląskie	2	1	2	3	2	4	3	0.70	0.40	0.71	1.06	0.63	1.24	0.88
Świętokrzyskie	0	1	1	1	1	1	1	0.00	1.74	1.73	2.18	1.71	2.06	2.00
Wielkopolskie	3	3	2	2	4	4	4	0.69	0.74	0.43	0.56	0.94	1.00	0.97

Source: Based on data obtained from the Polish Information and Foreign Investment Agency (PAIIZ) and the author's own analysis.

Table 4.20 Hotels and restaurants across regions in Poland

	Hotels and restaurants													
	Firms per PKD class							RLAis						
Voivodship	2000	2001	2002	2003	2004	2005	2006	2000	2001	2002	2003	2004	2005	2006
Dolnośląskie	3	1	1	1	1	1	1	1.83	0.68	0.62	0.62	0.53	0.54	0.50
Lubelskie	1	1	0	0	0	0	0	2.68	2.98	0.00	0.00	0.00	0.00	0.00
Lubuskie	0	1	1	1	1	1	1	0.00	2.27	2.57	2.37	2.09	2.27	2.16
Mazowieckie	11	11	14	15	16	15	15	1.60	1.60	1.79	1.91	1.95	1.78	1.67
Pomorskie	1	1	1	1	1	1	1	1.06	1.25	1.09	1.05	0.98	0.94	0.91
Śląskie	1	1	1	1	1	1	1	0.67	0.85	0.83	0.64	0.62	0.58	0.53
Wielkopolskie	0	0	0	0	0	1	1	0.00	0.00	0.00	0.00	0.00	0.47	0.44
Zachodnio-Pomorskie	1	1	1	1	1	1	1	2.37	2.51	2.57	2.06	2.09	1.52	1.53

Source: Based on data obtained from the Polish Information and Foreign Investment Agency (PAIIZ) and the author's own analysis.

Table 4.21 Manufacture of leather and leather products across regions in Poland

	Manufacture of leather and leather products													
	Firms per PKD class							RLAis						
Voivodship	**2000**	**2001**	**2002**	**2003**	**2004**	**2005**	**2006**	**2000**	**2001**	**2002**	**2003**	**2004**	**2005**	**2006**
Kujawsko-Pomorskie	1	1	1	1	1	0	0	7.03	8.39	10.87	8.30	7.06	0.00	0.00
Łódzkie	1	1	1	1	1	1	1	3.14	3.51	3.62	3.39	2.82	2.95	2.67
Lubuskie	1	3	2	2	2	2	2	9.84	21.57	20.59	16.60	15.29	17.42	16.53
Mazowieckie	0	0	0	1	1	1	1	0.00	0.00	0.00	0.45	0.45	0.45	0.43
Podkarpackie	1	1	1	1	1	1	1	7.38	6.04	7.82	6.64	6.55	7.10	6.27
Zachodnio-Pomorskie	0	0	0	0	0	1	1	0.00	0.00	0.00	0.00	0.00	5.81	5.87

Source: Based on data obtained from the Polish Information and Foreign Investment Agency (PAIIZ) and the author's own analysis.

relative strength while, for the remaining years, its RLAis for the class remains below 1.

Although also attracting four foreign firms in the PKD class, Wielkopolskie shows quite a steady presence of foreign investors. However, this PKD class reflects a weak RLAis index of just below 1, only reaching the index of 1 in 2005. The remaining regions host only one or two foreign firms in the class and show weakening RLAis index in the class.

The hotels and restaurants PKD class attracts foreign firms in eight regions. In this PKD class, three-quarters of foreign investment firms locate in the Mazowieckie region. This region also has a constant positive RLAis index for the PKD class in the period studied. The positive constant RLAis concentration in the class is also reflected in the western Polish regions of Lubuskie and Zachodnio-Pomorskie, although each attracts only one foreign investor in the class.

The remaining regions participating in this PKD class attract one foreign investor each year at most and not consistently, while also showing a low RLAis index. Although closely related to tourism, this industry seems not to show particular locational trends, that is, attracting foreign investors into the traditional vacation spots in the southern regions, the mountains, and the coastal regions of northern Poland. The clear center of activity in this PKD class is the capital region of Mazowieckie.

Foreign investment in Poland in the manufacture of leather and leather products can be found in six regions across the country. There is very little concentration of foreign presence in the PKD class. The region with the highest number of firms in the class is Lubuskie, attracting two foreign firms and maintaining a high RLAis index for the class, mostly due to low overall foreign firms' presence in the region.

The region of Lubuskie, however, benefits from an existing base: manufacturing of leather and leather products; access to raw materials; and proximity to external markets. With the exception of the Mazowieckie and Łódzkie regions, which attract one firm in the PKD class each, the remaining regions attracting firms in this PKD class belong to the group attracting the fewest foreign firms across all industries (below 10 percent than Mazowieckie alone) and, as a result, even the presence of one firm in the industry with a relatively low number of investors in the whole country translates into a strength for those regions.

FDI in the production of wood and manufacture of wooden products is present in eight regions across Poland. This type of foreign investment is one of the most evenly distributed across participating regions where each, with the exception of Wielkopolskie, has one foreign investor.

Table 4.22 Manufacture of wood and wooden products across regions in Poland

	Manufacture of wood and wooden products													
	Firms per PKD class							RLAis						
Voivodship	**2000**	**2001**	**2002**	**2003**	**2004**	**2005**	**2006**	**2000**	**2001**	**2002**	**2003**	**2004**	**2005**	**2006**
Dolnośląskie	1	1	1	1	1	1	1	1.92	1.62	1.55	2.59	1.46	1.56	1.44
Kujawsko-Pomorskie	1	1	1	1	1	1	1	6.03	6.29	6.79	9.96	5.29	7.57	5.68
Lubelskie	1	1	1	0	1	1	1	8.44	7.08	9.40	0.00	8.60	8.46	8.52
Lubuskie	1	1	1	1	1	1	1	8.44	5.39	6.43	9.96	5.73	6.53	6.20
Podkarpackie	0	0	1	0	0	0	1	0.00	0.00	4.89	0.00	0.00	0.00	4.70
Podlaskie	1	1	1	1	1	1	1	15.82	16.18	15.28	22.13	12.51	13.07	15.15
Wielkopolskie	1	1	1	0	2	2	2	1.38	1.23	1.27	0.00	2.53	2.69	2.55
Zachodnio-Pomorskie	0	1	1	1	1	1	0	0.00	5.96	6.43	8.66	5.73	4.36	0.00

Source: Based on data obtained from the Polish Information and Foreign Investment Agency (PAIIZ) and the author's own analysis.

Table 4.23 Mining and quarrying across regions in Poland

	Mining and quarrying													
	Firms per PKD class							RLAis						
Voivodship	**2000**	**2001**	**2002**	**2003**	**2004**	**2005**	**2006**	**2000**	**2001**	**2002**	**2003**	**2004**	**2005**	**2006**
Dolnośląskie	2	2	3	3	3	2	2	6.71	8.63	9.28	9.70	7.03	5.00	4.59
Małopolskie	0	0	0	0	1	1	1	0.00	0.00	0.00	0.00	4.89	5.61	5.20
Mazowieckie	1	1	1	1	1	1	1	0.80	0.92	0.64	0.67	0.54	0.55	0.51
Opolskie	1	1	1	0	0	0	0	13.84	18.88	14.38	0.00	0.00	0.00	0.00
Śląskie	0	2	0	0	1	1	1	0.00	10.79	0.00	0.00	2.72	2.67	2.45

Source: Based on data obtained from the Polish Information and Foreign Investment Agency (PAIIZ) and the author's own analysis.

Although the single foreign firm present is not statistically significant in this industry; it gives the participating regions a positive RLAis index. Also, it is worth noting that the majority of regions attracting foreign investment in this PKD class attract the lowest total number of foreign firms.

The majority of foreign firms participating in this sector invest in production of raw materials with little value-added: milling and planing of wood; pressure-treated wood; manufacture of veneer sheets; and manufacture of plywood, laminate board, and particle board.[20] They are providers of raw materials to furniture manufacturers and are located in their proximity. A vast portion of wood materials also become exports as construction materials.

Mining and quarrying attracts foreign investment to five regions, mostly those having a long-term tradition of mining for coal or other raw materials, for various forms of minerals and metals, and also for silicon. Although foreign investors are attracted to five regions, two of them, Dolnośląskie and Śląskie, have the most stable foreign investments. Dolnośląskie is of most interest, since the region attracts investment in the mining of minerals, metals, and silicon. This investment is represented only by two or three firms in the region and manages to have a positive and strong RLAis index for the PKD class. Śląskie, on the other hand, attracts one foreign investor to the region that specializes in extraction of hard coal. The same level of foreign participation in the PKD class can be seen in the neighboring region of Małopolskie, which has attracted one foreign investor since 2004, for the quarrying of stone. For all three regions, the investment in this PKD class represents a strong advantage in the RLAis index measure.

The exception here is Mazowieckie, which also attracts one foreign investor in the PKD class investing in a single year, classified in the subsections ranging from extraction of crude petroleum and natural gas to mining of non-ferrous metal ores (except uranium and thorium ores). The firms are involved in the country's range of industry specializations that are generally located outside of the Mazowieckie region.

Foreign investment in a broadly described class as "other community, social and personal service activities" is reflected in eight regions. This class covers a range of activity, from sewage and refuse disposal, sanitation and similar activities, to sporting activities and arena management, radio and television activities, and distribution of motion pictures and videos. Exactly half of the foreign firms, as of 2006, locate in the Mazowieckie region, and the other half are distributed across seven other regions. Three of those regions attract more than one firm:

Table 4.24 Other community, social, and personal service activities across regions in Poland

	Other community, social and personal service activities													
	Firms per PKD class							RLAis						
Voivodship	2000	2001	2002	2003	2004	2005	2006	2000	2001	2002	2003	2004	2005	2006
Dolnośląskie	1	1	1	3	2	2	3	3.36	4.31	4.13	2.43	1.80	1.09	1.50
Łódzkie	0	1	1	2	2	2	2	0.00	7.02	6.04	2.54	2.61	1.54	1.40
Małopolskie	0	0	0	1	1	1	1	0.00	0.00	0.00	1.68	1.88	1.22	1.13
Mazowieckie	2	4	3	5	19	11	10	3.20	2.76	1.10	0.83	3.92	1.30	1.11
Pomorskie	1	1	2	2	2	1	1	11.66	7.95	14.49	2.77	3.32	2.71	0.91
Śląskie	1	2	1	3	1	2	2	7.38	10.79	5.53	2.52	1.05	0.45	1.07
Warmińsko-Mazurskie	1	0	1	1	1	1	0	40.27	0.00	32.60	5.19	6.51	3.85	0.00
Wielkopolskie	1	2	2	1	1	1	1	4.82	6.57	2.91	0.66	3.37	0.47	2.04

Source: Based on data obtained from the Polish Information and Foreign Investment Agency (PAIIZ) and the author's own analysis.

Dolnośląskie (3), Łódzkie (2), Śląskie (2). For each of those regions, the RLAis index reflects a positive measure.

The remaining regions, attracting only a single investor in the PKD class, show mixed results ranging from a slightly positive to marginally negative RLAis. The exceptions are Wielkopolskie, which has an RLAis index of 2.04, and Warmińsko-Mazurskie, which had significant strength over the years only to lose it when its lone investor withdrew.

As a diverse sub-class, participation indicates (with the exception of Mazowieckie) the remaining regions hosting foreign investors in this PKD class in sewage and refuse disposal, sanitation and similar activities. The remaining activities (i.e., sporting activities and arena management, radio and television activities, motion picture and video distribution) are located in Mazowieckie. The concentration there of these activities is logical, as the capital region is the most preferred locale for production, management, and distribution of such products and services.

The following industries attract foreign investors in their class only in a single region:

Distribution of petroleum products, retail trade
Manufacture of glass
Media and entertainment
Postal services
Supply of electricity, gas, and water

The majority of these PKD classes are closely connected to the industries and PKD classes discussed earlier. However, the present PKD indexing system lists them separately. In general, the industries present only in one region do not-necessarily indicate a relative strength but, in fact, often produce a high quite RLAis index measure that seems distorted.[21] However, after a closer look at the data and the RLAis measure, some of the index measurement begins making sense in practical terms as, for example, in the case of the manufacture of glass in the Podkarpackie region, which has a low presence of foreign investors, meaning that even the presence of one foreign firm becomes important for the region. In fact, a single investor in an industry that is vital for a region may be that region's ticket out of an economic lag.

Also, especially in the case of an industry represented in a single, or even a few regions, the need for progression to higher grade technologies production may be indicated. Such would be a highly desirable outcome for any region, without regard to its size, population, skilled labor, and economic strength.

Table 4.25 Foreign investors by class present only in a single region in Poland

	Distribution of petroleum products, retail trade													
	Firms per PKD Class							**RLAis**						
Voivodship	**2000**	**2001**	**2002**	**2003**	**2004**	**2005**	**2006**	**2000**	**2001**	**2002**	**2003**	**2004**	**2005**	**2006**
Mazowieckie	2	4	4	2	0.00	0.00	0.00	0.80	1.38	1.71	2.67	0.00	0.00	0.00
	Manufacture of glass													
	Firms per PKD Class							**RLAis**						
Voivodship	**2000**	**2001**	**2002**	**2003**	**2004**	**2005**	**2006**	**2000**	**2001**	**2002**	**2003**	**2004**	**2005**	**2006**
Podkarpackie	1	1	1	0	0	0	0	8.8.	9.06	9.78	0	0	0	0
	Media and entertainment													
	Firms per PKD Class							**RLAis**						
Voivodship	**2000**	**2001**	**2002**	**2003**	**2004**	**2005**	**2006**	**2000**	**2001**	**2002**	**2003**	**2004**	**2005**	**2006**
Mazowieckie	3	21	7	4	0	0	0	1.07	6.45	1.63	2.67	0	0	0
	Postal services													
	Firms per PKD Class							**RLAis**						
Voivodship	**2000**	**2001**	**2002**	**2003**	**2004**	**2005**	**2006**	**2000**	**2001**	**2002**	**2003**	**2004**	**2005**	**2006**
Mazowieckie	3	1	5	2	0	0	0	9.60	2.76	2.13	2.67	0	0	0
	Power, gas and water supply													
	Firms per PKD Class							**RLAis**						
Voivodship	**2000**	**2001**	**2002**	**2003**	**2004**	**2005**	**2006**	**2000**	**2001**	**2002**	**2003**	**2004**	**2005**	**2006**
Mazowieckie	1	1	1	5	0	0	0	0.23	0.16	0.10	0.56	0	0	0

Source: Based on data obtained from the Polish Information and Foreign Investment Agency (PAIIZ) and the author's own analysis.

Distribution of petroleum products, retail trade; supply of electricity, gas, and water

Distribution of petroleum products, retail trade; is one class combined with supply of electricity, gas, and water are closely related but are displayed as separate industries under the PKD classification. They concentrate only in Mazowieckie, the capital region, with access to industry regulators and a financing base. This location choice and the relationship between classes relates to the earlier, centrally governed system of petroleum and power management and processing that are dependent on supplies of raw materials sourced from the former Eastern Bloc, the present Russia. This region has historic ties, established by the pre-democratic government of Poland, in the industry that continues its strategic presence even now.

The manufacture of glass attracted foreign investment to a single firm in the region of Podkarpackie until the year 2002. Since then, the firm has been operating without additional influx of foreign finance.[22] It maintains a long tradition of glass working in the region and depends on skilled local craftsmen. Along with foreign financing, the firm benefited from access to foreign markets offered by the investor.

Foreign investment in media and entertainment is located, for obvious reasons, only in Mazowieckie. This industry is dependent on local access to a skilled workforce, artists, and media regulators. Main news outlets and media production companies locate there while having satellite offices across Poland for local news-gathering production, and local distribution.

The postal service class was a separate class until adoption of a new PKD classification when, after 2004, it was reclassified as part of the transport, storage and communication PKD activity. Investment in the postal service is only located in Mazowieckie for the obvious reason that it is a region with most of the activity, and is a communications hub that is centrally located in the country. Although it has varied over the years, the PKD class activity attracted between one and five foreign investors.

4.2 Summary

This chapter presents an examination of the location strengths as per PKD classification in hosting foreign investors in Poland. The outcome of the review presents a degree of complexity, although many foreign investors seem to form concentrations of activity at or near the regions where relevant industrial activity has already existed. Such established centers probably offer a degree of attractiveness to the regions possessing them and, in turn, also impact the decisions of foreign firms. The existence and formation of new centers of economic activity increase the probability of interaction between participating firms and local policy makers. The awareness of needs and opportunities may be one of the factors that may impact locational decision making by foreign firms and enable local governments to focus activities necessary to create productive environments for business leveraged by the existing presence of firms in key industries.

The outcome of the multiple linear regression of the index measure for PKD classes in the years 2000 to 2006 shows a weak correlation in the early years of the study and an increasingly strengthening correlation for the concentration of foreign firms according to industry in the later part of the period. Starting in the year 2003, immediately before Poland joined the European Union, the coefficient results reached a level of significance and they are strengthening in the following years of the study period.

Although, for the majority of the regions, industrial trajectories remain stable, in some regions a transition is observed, showing sharpening of concentrations in actual presence of investors, as in: financial intermediation in Mazowieckie; the manufacture of rubber and plastics in Śląskie; and the real estate rental, and business activity class in Mazowieckie. Also, in RLAis measures, as in: the manufacture of chemicals and chemical products in Łódzkie; manufacture of food, drinks and tobacco products in Podlaskie and Zachodnio-Pomorskie; manufacture of metal and metal products in Podkarpackie; manufacture of rubber and plastics in Małopolskie; manufacture of transport equipment in Dolnośląskie and Podkarpackie; and wholesale and retail trade in Wielkopolskie.

Some industries weaken or disappear from the regions where previously they had an economic advantage, as in the case of: the manufacture of chemicals in Wielkopolskie; manufacture of fabrics and textile in Mazowieckie; manufacture of food, drinks and tobacco products in Warmińsko-Mazurskie; and manufacture of transport equipment in Małopolskie.

These results support the findings of Piscitello (1998), whose study reviewed Italian firms in mining and manufacturing industries in the period 1986–1993 and determined that a result of regional industrial specialization is often narrowing and cannot always be created effectively by indigenous firms but requires knowledge and processes drawn from the outside via the attraction of foreign investors who supply them. Further trajectory development of foreign firms in a location is an indicator of strength of a particular location for a specific type of investment (Cantwell, 2000). That trajectory is generally developed over time and is difficult, and most often nearly impossible, to establish (Cantwell, 2000) through national or local economic policy influence, including offering preferential entry conditions for the investing firms.

Further development of the technological specializations within a national and regional economic structure is closely linked to the industrial success (Cantwell, 2000) of regions. A continuity of technological specialization within a location may lead to advantages in attracting FDI within a particular industry. Cantwell (1991a) and Shaver (1998) among others, show that agglomerations of specialized economic activity offer significant benefits to both domestic and foreign firms. Therefore, firms generally follow an industrial development trajectory (Cantwell and Piscitello, 1997). As a result, further location advantages at a local or regional level could be self-perpetuating, where additional development of the local industry makes the location even more attractive to do business in (Head et al., 1995; Krugman, 1991; Wheeler and Mody, 1992; De Propris, Driffield, Menghinello, 2005), subsequently drawing in additional investors.

Across all industrial activity classes, Mazowieckie attracts the highest number of investors in most of the participating PKD classes, but with low RLAis measures. On the other side of the spectrum is Podkarpackie, with one of the lowest total levels of participating investors, maintaining the highest degree of location advantage for the industry.

The analysis of data on location patterns in real terms shows a southwestern trajectory of concentration (Śląskie, Dolnośląskie, and Wielkopolskie) related proximately to the exogenous Western European markets. The geographical exception is Mazowieckie, capital region in the east-central portion of the country, which has the advantage of better infrastructure and regulatory and financial institutions. That finding is supported by Campos and Kinoshita's (2006)[23] framework, where workforce size and skill, and population size of the region's internal market are the drivers behind the motivation to locate there.

The results of regional industrial specialization of foreign firms in Poland reveal a hierarchy of location order between the regions where higher-order regions, as measured by the level of RLAis, have narrower specializations and, in some cases, began the process of transitioning from lower-grade to higher-grade technologies production, indicating a possibility of growing competitiveness. The findings also suggest that for the majority of the regions across all levels of the hierarchy of attractiveness to foreign firms, regional industrial specializations tend to narrow.

Furthermore, the pattern of trajectory of industrial specialization is clearly evident in the peripheral regions, especially along the eastern border. Those, however, are of lower significance in an immediate countrywide perspective, but remain vital for their local economies, as they are less developed and not capable of attracting foreign investors at the same pace as more developed regions, mainly due to weaker infrastructure and distance to external markets.

The level of statistical significance of the results derived from data in the regions with low levels of total firms participating may need to be discounted. Although the importance of a single or few investors for a region with a very low participation of foreign investors across industries or countries of origin may be meaningful, and it will need to be placed into a proper regional context.

4.3 Country-of-origin – RLAco – concentration patterns of foreign investment

Often, foreign firms move their production operations in order to substitute for exports and to preserve their market share, subsequently resulting in clustering of FDI as discovered conditions within a particular region may suit and support a number of participants. Such circumstances support an oligopolistic structure motivated by protection of the investment and lowering the risk (Knickerbocker, 1973), while in the process forming an agglomeration of often interdependent firms (Marshall, 1920 and Kojima, 2000) but sharing the same origins, therefore enabling transfer and building on existing relationships and national customs for more effective collaboration.

Discussed above, Kojima's (2000) flying geese (FG) model recognizes three aspects of catching-up by developing elements of intra-industry, inter-industry, and international economies but driven by country-of-origin relationship of the investment. The regional transmission of FG industrialization, motivated by the catching-up process through diversification/rationalization of industries, has become famous as an engine of Asian economic growth (Kojima, 2000) and can also be used to effectively explain industrial location advantages by following location patterns of firms sharing the same country-of-origin.

4.4 The results of the RLAco data analysis

The same set of data as in the previous section, with the classification as to the investors' country-of-origin RLAco grouping, was used here.

Table 4.26 Country-of-origin correlation matrix of foreign investors for years 2000–2006

	Correlations								
	2000 RLAco	2001 RLAco	2002 RLAco	2003 RLAco	2004 RLAco	2005 RLAco	2006 RLAco		
2000 RLAco	1								
2001 RLAco	0.224	1							
2002 RLAco	0.082	0.258	1						
2003 RLAco	0.004	0.101	0.181	1					
2004 RLAco	0.043	0.152	0.393	0.489	1				
2005 RLAco	–0.007	0.111	0.306	0.657	0.743	1			
2006 RLAco	–0.015	0.089	0.244	0.643	0.723	0.982	1		
	Constant							**R**	**R square**
Austria	0.031	0.036	0.046	0.045	0.055	0.041	0.014	0.234	0.055
Std. error	0.845	0.013	0.033	0.021	0.049	0.151	0.129		
Belgium	–0.055	0.017	0.005	0.022	0.018	0.011	0.008	0.241	0.058
Std. error	0.842	0.013	0.033	0.021	0.049	0.149	0.127		
Canada	–0.008	–0.07	–0.081	–0.035	0.037	0.018	0.018	0.233	0.054
Std. error	1.088	0.013	0.033	0.021	0.049	0.15	0.128		
Denmark	0.038	0.008	–0.024	0	–0.024	0.01	0.012	0.237	0.056
Std. error	0.882	0.013	0.033	0.021	0.049	0.15	0.128		
Finland	–0.031	0.032	0.032	0.035	0.042	0.028	0.026	0.236	0.056
Std. error	0.958	0.013	0.033	0.021	0.049	0.15	0.128		
France	0.1	0.028	–0.158	0.038	0.016	0.006	0.005	0.253	0.064
Std. error	0.802	0.013	0.033	0.021	0.049	0.149	0.127		
Germany	0.068	0.008	0.019	0.028	0.024	0.004	0.004	0.242	0.058
Std. error	0.76	0.013	0.033	0.021	0.049	0.149	0.127		
Italy	0.05	0.04	0.051	0.042	0.057	0.042	0.038	0.237	0.056
Std. error	0.81	0.013	0.033	0.021	0.049	0.15	0.128		
Japan	–0.196	0.028	–0.006	0.013	0.012	0.011	0.017	0.308	0.095
Std. error	0.992	0.012	0.032	0.02	0.048	0.146	0.125		
Luxemburg	–0.166	0.011	0.025	0.023	0.031	0.022	0.021	0.228	0.083
Std. error	1.334	0.013	0.032	0.02	0.048	0.147	0.126		
Netherlands	0.062	0.019	0.034	0.039	0.041	0.029	0.03	0.24	0.058
Std. error	0.759	0.013	0.033	0.021	0.049	0.149	0.127		
Norway	–0.019	0.023	0.009	0.026	0.03	0.013	0.025	0.234	0.055
Std. error	0.963	0.013	0.033	0.021	0.049	0.15	0.128		
So. Korea	–0.07	0.012	–0.011	0.008	–0.033	–0.021	–0.003	0.244	0.059
Std. error	1.155	0.013	0.033	0.021	0.049	0.15	0.128		
Spain	–0.13	–0.005	–0.016	0.002	–0.012	0.019	0.018	0.265	0.07
Std. error	1.507	0.013	0.032	0.02	0.048	0.148	0.127		
Sweden	0.069	0.023	0.029	0.028	0.017	0.014	0.012	0.242	0.058
Std. error	0.875	0.013	0.033	0.021	0.049	0.149	0.127		
Switzerland	0.008	0.028	0.027	0.033	0.043	0.03	0.029	0.233	0.054
Std. error	0.842	0.013	0.033	0.021	0.049	0.15	0.128		
Turkey	–0.112	–0.394	0.005	0.013	–0.004	0.019	0.019	0.235	0.055
Std. error	1.496	0.014	0.033	0.021	0.049	0.15	0.128		
UK	0.054	0.023	0.008	–0.341	–0.141	–0.237	–0.237	0.237	0.056
Std. error	0.85	0.013	0.033	0.021	0.049	0.15	0.128		
USA	0.064	–0.014	–0.002	0.013	–0.185	–0.018	–0.012	0.347	0.061
Std. error	0.824	0.013	0.033	0.021	0.05	0.149	0.127		

Note: a Dependent Variable: 2000 RLAco

N=212.

Source: Based on data obtained from the Polish Information and Foreign Investment Agency (PAIIZ) and the author's own analysis.

The firms represent 43 countries of origin of investment located across all 16 regions within Poland. In a few cases an investor represented multiple nationalities; those were reviewed and attributed as investors from the country-of-origin where the firms are headquartered. In some cases in which the nationality was given as international and the country-of-origin could not be identified, the data were not included.

Further, upon completion of data verification and arrangement, a number of firms were eliminated due to incomplete information related to the country-of-origin. The final count of the firms containing the complete data set reflects the results further discussed here.

Countries with statistically significant levels (above 10 firms) of FDI participation in Poland are: Austria, Belgium, Denmark, Finland, France, Germany, Italy, Japan, Luxemburg, Norway, South Korea, Sweden, Switzerland, the Netherlands, the United Kingdom, and the United States. The remaining countries – those with participation of a single investor in a region and those with less than 10 investors across the country – again, as in the RLAis index, fall into a unique, though not statistically significant, measurement. The results for these countries will not be individually analyzed here but looked at as a group.

Further, the result of the multiple linear regression of the RLA country-of-origin index measure in the years 2000 to 2006 (Table 4.29), with the average of the RLAis index results being a dependent variable, shows a weak positive correlation in the early years of the study and, in the later part of the period, an increasing correlation for the concentration of foreign firms according to industry.

In the year 2003, immediately before Poland joined the European Union, the coefficient results reached a level of significance and are increasing in the following years of the study period. In addition, this measure also controlled for the effect of each industry present in the country by using dummy variables represented by 0 for each industry in separate tests. These results reflect a correlation coefficient for the data set at 0.234 and a degree of fit at 0.057 not having high significance level. The dummy tests also reflect weak correlation effects for firms from each tested country-of-origin. The trend observed for each country-of-origin data set, however, shows declining correlations as the years of study progress.

A substantial number of firms from Austria, 20 out of 31 foreign firms in 2006, are located in Mazowieckie. The country-of-origin also manages to gain a positive RLAco index measure in this region. These investing Austrian firms specialize mostly in financial intermediation and related fields, with real estate investment as another sector. Łódzkie is another

Table 4.27 Regional concentration of Austrian firms in Poland

	Austria													
	Firms per country-of-origin							RLAco						
Voivodship	2000	2001	2002	2003	2004	2005	2006	2000	2001	2002	2003	2004	2005	2006
Dolnośląskie	1	1	1	1	1	1	1	0.35	0.33	0.33	0.32	0.27	0.30	0.27
Kujawsko-Pomorskie	5	3	2	2	3	2	2	5.55	3.97	2.79	2.43	2.84	2.88	2.16
Łódzkie	2	2	2	2	6	5	4	0.99	0.90	0.88	0.91	2.36	2.14	1.57
Małopolskie	3	4	4	0	3	3	2	1.94	2.45	2.33	0.00	1.67	2.05	1.27
Mazowieckie	17	16	18	20	19	16	20	1.25	1.09	1.12	1.25	1.13	1.07	1.28
Opolskie	2	1	2	2	2	2	2	2.91	1.49	2.95	2.69	2.56	2.38	2.36
Podkarpackie	0	0	0	0	0	0	1	0.00	0.00	0.00	0.00	0.00	0.00	12.99
Pomorskie	2	2	1	2	1	2	3	1.06	1.01	0.49	1.06	0.47	1.01	1.47
Śląskie	2	2	2	2	2	2	2	0.73	0.77	0.76	0.67	0.60	0.64	0.58
Świętokrzyskie	1	1	1	1	1	1	1	1.55	1.70	2.09	2.13	1.71	2.11	2.00
Warmińsko-Mazurskie	0	1	0	0	0	0	0	0.00	2.38	0.00	0.00	0.00	0.00	0.00
Wielkopolskie	1	1	2	2	2	2	2	0.39	0.24	0.48	0.51	0.47	0.50	0.49
Zachodnio-Pomorskie	1	1	1	1	1	2	1	1.37	1.32	1.32	1.16	1.07	1.66	0.84

Source: Based on data obtained from the Polish Information and Foreign Investment Agency (PAIIZ) and the author's own analysis.

Table 4.28 Regional concentration of Belgian firms in Poland

	Belgium													
	Firms per country-of-origin							RLAco						
Voivodship	2000	2001	2002	2003	2004	2005	2006	2000	2001	2002	2003	2004	2005	2006
Dolnośląskie	2	1	2	2	3	3	3	1.17	0.57	1.12	1.10	1.27	1.44	1.28
Kujawsko-Pomorskie	1	1	0	1	2	0	1	1.83	2.29	0.00	2.06	3.02	0.00	1.75
Łódzkie	0	0	1	1	1	1	1	0.00	0.00	0.75	0.77	0.63	0.69	0.64
Lubelskie	1	2	1	1	0	2	2	2.57	4.84	3.27	3.09	0.00	5.20	5.25
Lubuskie	1	0	0	0	1	0	0	2.57	0.00	0.00	0.00	1.70	0.00	0.00
Mazowieckie	5	5	7	6	6	5	5	0.61	0.59	0.74	0.63	0.57	0.54	0.52
Opolskie	3	3	3	3	3	3	3	7.22	7.72	7.50	6.84	6.12	5.77	5.72
Pomorskie	0	0	0	0	1	1	1	0.00	0.00	0.00	0.00	0.76	0.82	0.79
Śląskie	2	3	2	3	2	2	1	1.20	1.99	1.29	1.71	0.95	1.03	0.47
Świętokrzyskie	4	4	3	2	3	2	2	10.27	11.77	10.63	7.22	8.16	6.80	6.46
Warmińsko-Mazurskie	1	1	1	1	1	1	1	3.50	4.12	4.25	3.61	3.14	3.40	3.23
Wielkopolskie	1	1	3	3	3	5	5	0.47	0.41	1.21	1.29	1.12	2.03	1.96
Zachodnio-Pomorskie	0	0	0	0	0	1	1	0.00	0.00	0.00	0.00	0.00	1.34	1.35

Source: Based on data obtained from the Polish Information and Foreign Investment Agency (PAIIZ) and the author's own analysis.

region where Austrian firms gather in higher numbers, second-highest for country-of-origin: four firms in 2006. This region also manages a positive RLAco measure for Austrian firms and has an index above 1 for the last three years of this study period. The index general trajectory for the region is positive. Another region, Pomorskie, manages to maintain, on and off, a positive index, finally peaking at three firms in 2006.

Another interesting region where Austrian firms agglomerate is Kujawsko-Pomorskie. This region manages to attract five firms in 2000, but the presence of Austrian firms in the region declines to two in 2006 while also maintaining a positive RLAco index throughout the entire period. The remaining regions manage to attract, at most, only two or even one Austrian firm.

The Belgian firms investing in Poland also can be found in 13 regions. However, they are much more evenly distributed than the Austrian firms. The highest concentration of Belgian firms is in the Mazowieckie and Wielkopolskie regions, at five firms each. Mazowieckie has a quite steady presence, although declining in recent years, with a negative RLAco index. The participating Belgian firms in the region are classified under financial intermediation, manufacture of chemicals, and non-metal goods. Wielkopolskie steadily attracts more firms and, starting in 2002, maintains a strengthening positive RLAco index for the country-of-origin. Belgian firms attracted to this region are in the food manufacturing and retail trade industries.

The Opolskie region attracts a constant presence of three firms with a positive although declining RLAco measure. The Belgian firms in Opolskie are in the manufacturing of metals and metal products and manufacturing of non-metal products classes. Dolnośląskie also manages to attract three firms from 2004–2006, which gives this region an increasing trajectory of presence and also a positive RLAco index for Belgian investors. The firms here specialize in the manufacture of non-metal products and retail PKD classes.

The remaining regions attract only one or two firms. Worth mentioning is Świętokrzyskie, which at the beginning of the study period attracted four firms annually but faced continuing decline to two firms for the last two years of the study. Even with that decline the region maintains a positive RLAco with the representation of manufacturers of non-metal goods and energy distributors.

Denmark has a strong presence of investors in Poland with a quite significant growth, from 32 investors in 2000 to 52 in 2006. The largest group is located in the Mazowieckie region, with a major share of investors participating in financial intermediation, real estate management, manufacturing of electrical equipment, and food processing.

Table 4.29 Regional concentration of Danish firms in Poland

	Denmark													
	Firms per country-of-origin							RLAco						
Voivodship	2000	2001	2002	2003	2004	2005	2006	2000	2001	2002	2003	2004	2005	2006
Dolnośląskie	1	1	1	1	1	2	2	0.39	0.33	0.30	0.29	0.24	0.49	0.41
Kujawsko-Pomorskie	1	1	1	1	1	1	1	1.24	1.32	1.26	1.08	0.85	1.19	0.84
Łódzkie	2	2	3	3	3	4	5	1.11	0.90	1.20	1.21	1.06	1.41	1.53
Lubuskie	1	1	1	1	1	1	1	1.74	1.14	1.20	1.13	0.96	1.02	0.92
Małopolskie	1	1	1	2	2	2	2	0.72	0.61	0.53	1.13	1.00	1.13	0.99
Mazowieckie	14	17	18	15	19	19	21	1.15	1.16	1.02	0.83	1.01	1.04	1.04
Podkarpackie	0	1	2	2	2	1	1	0.00	23.84	22.74	22.64	22.94	11.27	10.10
Pomorskie	3	2	2	2	2	2	2	1.78	1.01	0.89	0.94	0.85	0.84	0.76
Śląskie	2	2	2	2	2	2	2	0.81	0.77	0.69	0.60	0.53	0.52	0.45
Warmińsko-Mazurskie	1	1	1	1	1	1	1	2.37	2.38	2.27	1.89	1.76	1.73	1.55
Wielkopolskie	4	5	5	6	5	5	5	1.05	1.19	1.08	1.34	1.05	1.03	0.94
Zachodnio-Pomorskie	2	3	5	7	7	8	9	3.07	3.97	5.99	7.20	6.69	5.47	5.87

Source: Based on data obtained from the Polish Information and Foreign Investment Agency (PAIIZ) and the author's own analysis.

Table 4.30 Regional concentration of Finnish firms in Poland

	Finland													
	Firms per country-of-origin							RLAco						
Voivodship	2000	2001	2002	2003	2004	2005	2006	2000	2001	2002	2003	2004	2005	2006
Dolnośląskie	1	1	2	1	1	0	0	0.67	0.70	1.61	0.66	0.55	0.00	0.00
Łódzkie	0	0	0	1	1	2	2	0.00	0.00	0.00	0.94	0.81	1.89	1.74
Małopolskie	0	0	0	0	1	1	1	0.00	0.00	0.00	0.00	1.14	1.51	1.40
Mazowieckie	8	10	8	11	12	9	9	1.12	1.44	1.21	1.41	1.46	1.33	1.27
Opolskie	1	1	1	1	1	1	1	2.91	3.15	3.60	2.76	2.62	2.63	2.61
Podlaskie	1	0	0	0	0	0	0	5.54	0.00	0.00	0.00	0.00	0.00	0.00
Pomorskie	1	0	0	1	1	1	1	1.01	0.00	0.00	1.09	0.97	1.12	1.08
Śląskie	3	2	1	1	2	3	3	2.08	1.62	0.93	0.69	1.22	2.11	1.94
Warmińsko-Mazurskie	2	1	1	1	1	1	1	8.05	5.03	6.11	4.37	4.03	4.66	4.42
Wielkopolskie	1	2	2	1	1	1	1	0.45	1.01	1.16	0.52	0.48	0.56	0.54

Source: Based on data obtained from the Polish Information and Foreign Investment Agency (PAIIZ) and the author's own analysis.

The region with the highest growth in number of Danish investors is Zachodnio-Pomorskie. Participation here grew steadily, from two Danish firms in 2000 to nine in 2006. Also, the RLAco index for the region maintains a high positive measure of 5.87 for Danish firms. The main concentration of investment is represented in the production of food and furniture, and the production and distribution of electricity. Another area of investment is the manufacture of medical and surgical equipment and orthopedic appliances, where there is one firm.

Łódzkie and Wielkopolskie attract five firms each, while Łódzkie maintains a slow increase. Wielkopolskie has a quite steady presence of four to six investors from Denmark over the years. The Łódzkie region also maintains an increasing RLAco index for the period, while the index measure for Wielkopolskie remains only slightly above 1 for most of the years, with a decline to 0.94 for the year 2006, indicating decreasing strength of the Danish investment presence.

Both regions attract quite similar types of investment in the manufacture of fabrics, other non-metal goods, food processing, and retail. Although these are neighboring regions, both form their own centers of activity. The remaining participating regions attract either one or two investors only.

The concentration of Finnish firms in Poland is clearly in the Mazowieckie region, which attracts nine firms at the end of the study period, with an overall presence in ten regions across the country. The only other region having more than two Finnish firms is Śląskie, which attracts three. The Finnish firms locating in Mazowieckie participate in financial intermediation and production of non-metal materials, plastics, and the manufacture of pulp and paper, as well as publishing and printing. Meanwhile, firms in Śląskie participate in the manufacture of metals and metal products, rubber, and plastics, and in production of electricity.

Finnish firms in the remaining regions have a relatively even distribution of investment across participating industries with no pronounced concentrations. The only industries that attract slightly more Finnish investors than any other is the manufacture of pulp and paper, and publishing and printing. In both regions, investors from Finland maintain a positive RLAco index.

French firms locate in 15 regions across Poland. The predominant concentration of presence of French firms is found in Mazowieckie, with 44 firms. Other regions attract less than ten firms each: Wielkopolskie with eight, Śląskie with seven, Łódzkie and Pomorskie with five each, Podkarpackie with four, and Małopolskie with three. This thin spread of

Table 4.31 Regional concentration of French firms in Poland

	France													
	Firms per country-of-origin							RLAco						
Voivodship	**2000**	**2001**	**2002**	**2003**	**2004**	**2005**	**2006**	**2000**	**2001**	**2002**	**2003**	**2004**	**2005**	**2006**
Dolnośląskie	4	5	2	2	2	2	2	0.77	0.72	0.28	0.28	0.22	0.26	0.22
Kujawsko-Pomorskie	0	0	1	1	1	1	1	0.00	0.00	0.58	0.53	0.40	0.62	0.45
Łódzkie	6	6	5	5	6	4	5	1.62	1.18	0.92	0.99	1.00	0.73	0.83
Lubelskie	1	1	1	1	1	2	2	0.84	0.61	0.81	0.79	0.67	1.38	1.36
Lubuskie	0	1	1	1	1	1	1	0.00	0.50	0.55	0.55	0.45	0.53	0.50
Małopolskie	4	4	5	4	3	2	3	1.41	1.07	1.22	1.11	0.70	0.59	0.80
Mazowieckie	32	44	49	47	53	49	44	1.28	1.31	1.28	1.27	1.32	1.40	1.18
Opolskie	0	0	0	1	1	1	1	0.00	0.00	0.00	0.58	0.54	0.51	0.50
Podkarpackie	1	2	3	2	4	4	4	0.63	20.83	91.69	11.07	21.59	23.47	21.82
Podlaskie	0	1	1	1	2	1	2	0.00	1.49	1.31	1.58	2.40	1.17	2.73
Pomorskie	2	3	3	4	4	4	5	0.58	0.66	0.62	0.92	0.80	0.87	1.03
Śląskie	4	4	5	5	6	8	7	0.79	0.67	0.80	0.73	0.75	1.09	0.86
Świętokrzyskie	0	1	1	1	2	2	2	0.00	0.74	0.88	0.92	1.44	1.81	1.68
Warmińsko-Mazurskie	1	0	0	1	0	1	2	1.15	0.00	0.00	0.92	0.00	0.90	1.68
Wielkopolskie	6	11	10	8	9	8	8	0.77	1.15	1.00	0.88	0.89	0.86	0.82

Source: Based on data obtained from the Polish Information and Foreign Investment Agency (PAIIZ) and the author's own analysis.

firms manages to maintain a strong positive RLAco in Podkarpackie, with specialization in the manufacturing of transport equipment, including two firms manufacturing aircraft equipment.

The industrial specializations for the remaining regions fall along the following lines: Wielkopolskie attracts firms in the manufacture of electrical machinery and apparatus; the manufacture of food and drink; and wholesale and retail trade classes. The region does not manage to show a positive RLAco for French firms at the end of the study period; Śląskie also has a degree of specialization among French firms, with three out of seven in the manufacture of rubber and plastic. The remaining firms are classified under financial intermediation, food production, and the manufacture of other non-metal goods and pulp. Łódzkie attracts an eclectic variety of firms, with some following the region's strength in the manufacture of fabrics, textiles, and leather products. Pomorskie and Małopolskie also have no distinct strength of French firms, although Pomorskie manages a positive RLAco for French firms in the last year of the study period, and Małopolskie shows a declining RLAco index throughout the period and ends the last few years with an RLAco below 1. The remaining regions reviewed also have a weak RLAco index measurement for French firms.

Germany is represented in all 16 regions of Poland, with a total of 236 firms in 2006. That number has grown steadily throughout the period studied, beginning with 190 firms in 2000. The highest concentration of German firms is found in the Mazowieckie region, with 65 in 2006. However that presence does not translate into a positive RLAco index for Germany; the index is at 0.71 in 2006, which is observed as constant for the entire study period.

The industries represented in the Mazowieckie region primarily are financial intermediation, the manufacture of chemicals, manufacture of pulp and paper, publishing and printing, and wholesale and retail trade. Besides Mazowieckie, a group of regions attract a significant number of firms each: Dolnośląskie, Łódzkie, Pomorskie, Śląskie, and Wielkopolskie. That group attracts at least 15 German investors each. Most of the regions in this group manage a positive RLAco for German firms, the exception here being Śląskie which, starting in 2003, maintains a declining RLAco index, with about 0.9 for the year 2006. The highest out-of-scale index measure is derived for Podkarpackie, in which ten out of its 29 foreign firms are German. The remaining regions maintain a stable index ranging from about 1.2 to 1.7.

The industrial specializations of German firms in the regions are as follows: Dolnośląskie attracts manufacturers of chemicals and chemical

Table 4.32 Regional concentration of German firms in Poland

	Germany													
	Firms per country-of-origin							RLAco						
Voivodship	2000	2001	2002	2003	2004	2005	2006	2000	2001	2002	2003	2004	2005	2006
Dolnośląskie	24	25	30	32	34	33	31	1.54	1.52	1.67	1.81	1.54	1.66	1.41
Kujawsko-Pomorskie	9	8	8	8	9	8	8	1.82	1.95	1.88	1.70	1.44	1.95	1.48
Łódzkie	13	14	16	14	19	18	19	1.17	1.16	1.19	1.12	1.27	1.30	1.28
Lubelskie	4	4	3	3	5	4	4	1.13	1.03	0.98	0.96	1.35	1.09	1.11
Lubuskie	2	6	5	6	8	8	8	0.57	1.25	1.11	1.34	1.44	1.69	1.62
Małopolskie	8	6	8	8	9	6	7	0.94	0.67	0.79	0.89	0.85	0.70	0.76
Mazowieckie	46	50	67	63	69	68	65	0.62	0.63	0.70	0.69	0.69	0.77	0.71
Opolskie	5	5	5	6	7	8	8	1.32	1.37	1.25	1.41	1.52	1.61	1.62
Podkarpackie	5	8	7	7	7	9	10	1.06	35.01	14.82	15.63	15.17	20.87	22.27
Podlaskie	0	3	3	2	2	2	1	0.00	1.88	1.59	1.28	0.96	0.93	0.56
Pomorskie	11	13	16	15	17	17	15	1.06	1.21	1.33	1.40	1.36	1.46	1.26
Śląskie	17	15	17	16	19	17	18	1.13	1.06	1.09	0.94	0.96	0.92	0.90
Świętokrzyskie	2	2	1	1	1	1	1	0.57	0.63	0.35	0.37	0.29	0.36	0.34
Warmińsko-Mazurskie	3	3	3	3	5	5	5	1.16	1.31	1.27	1.12	1.67	1.78	1.71
Wielkopolskie	37	34	33	29	32	33	31	1.58	1.49	1.33	1.28	1.27	1.40	1.29
Zachodnio-Pomorskie	4	3	4	3	4	5	5	1.00	0.73	0.89	0.61	0.72	0.70	0.72

Source: Based on data obtained from the Polish Information and Foreign Investment Agency (PAIIZ) and the author's own analysis.

products, of rubber and plastics and transport equipment, which are traditional industrial strengths for the region; Łódzkie attracts the manufacture of chemicals and chemical products, fabrics and textiles, and the wholesale and retail trade; Pomorskie, the manufacture of food, drinks and tobacco products, furniture and other consumer products, and food, drinks and tobacco products; Śląskie, the manufacture of other non-metal goods, transport equipment, machinery, and equipment; and Wielkopolskie the manufacture of food products, transport equipment, rubber and plastics, metals and metal products, and wholesale and retail trade.

Another group of regions attracting between three and nine German firms are Kujawsko-Pomorskie, Lubelskie, Lubuskie, Małopolskie, Opolskie, Warmińsko-Mazurskie, and Zachodnio-Pomorskie. This group locates predominantly along both the eastern and western borders. The industrial specialization for these regions seems to be as follows: Kujawsko-Pomorskie, with food processing and the manufacture of pulp and paper, and publishing and printing; Lubelskie, with diverse investment in only four firms; Lubuskie, with the manufacture of fabrics and textiles, rubber, and plastics; Małopolskie, with the manufacture of metals and metal products; Opolskie, with the manufacture of food, drinks and tobacco products, metal and non-metal goods; Warmińsko-Mazurskie, with the manufacture of furniture, consumer goods, and related products; and Zachodnio-Pomorskie, with the manufacture of furniture, consumer goods, and non-metal goods.

All the regions attracting between three and nine German firms, with the exception of Małopolskie and Zachodnio-Pomorskie, have a positive RLAco index for these firms.

Italian firms investing in Poland locate in 14 regions throughout the country and maintain the most stable level of investment across the study period, with 60 firms in 2000 and 63 by 2006. The decided concentrations of Italian investment in Poland are in the Mazowieckie and Śląskie regions. Mazowieckie does not have a positive RLAco for Italian firms, while Śląskie maintains a relatively high RLAco of 3.06.

Mazowieckie attracts firms in the manufacture of food, drinks and tobacco products, metals and metal products, and related product classes, as well as other community, social- and personal service activities in the radio and television activity sub-class. Śląskie maintains a long-term relationship with Fiat, which began during the time of the centrally governed system in control of economic activity in Poland until 1989. Fiat survived successfully in the free-market economy. The Italian investment in this region is specifically concentrated on supporting the

Table 4.33 Regional concentration of Italian firms in Poland

	Italy													
	Firms per country-of-origin							RLAco						
Voivodship	2000	2001	2002	2003	2004	2005	2006	2000	2001	2002	2003	2004	2005	2006
Dolnośląskie	2	2	2	1	3	3	3	0.41	0.41	0.42	0.20	0.49	0.59	0.52
Kujawsko-Pomorskie	2	2	1	1	1	0	0	1.30	1.65	0.88	0.74	0.58	0.00	0.00
Łódzkie	6	8	9	9	9	8	8	1.74	2.24	2.49	2.50	2.18	2.25	2.07
Lubelskie	1	2	0	1	1	1	1	0.91	1.75	0.00	1.11	0.98	1.06	1.07
Lubuskie	3	4	4	4	4	4	4	2.73	2.83	3.32	3.11	2.62	3.27	3.10
Małopolskie	4	4	3	3	2	2	2	1.51	1.52	1.10	1.17	0.68	0.90	0.83
Mazowieckie	23	22	24	24	23	23	21	0.99	0.94	0.94	0.91	0.84	1.01	0.88
Opolskie	0	0	0	0	0	1	1	0.00	0.00	0.00	0.00	0.00	0.78	0.77
Pomorskie	1	2	2	2	3	2	2	0.31	0.63	0.62	0.65	0.87	0.67	0.64
Śląskie	12	12	12	14	19	15	16	2.56	2.87	2.87	2.87	3.47	3.13	3.06
Świętokrzyskie	2	2	2	2	2	2	2	1.82	2.12	2.63	2.59	2.10	2.76	2.62
Warmińsko-Mazurskie	1	0	0	1	1	1	1	1.24	0.00	0.00	1.30	1.21	1.38	1.31
Wielkopolskie	2	1	1	1	1	1	1	0.28	0.15	0.15	0.15	0.14	0.16	0.16
Zachodnio-Pomorskie	1	0	0	0	0	1	1	0.80	0.00	0.00	0.00	0.00	0.54	0.55

Source: Based on data obtained from the Polish Information and Foreign Investment Agency (PAIIZ) and the author's own analysis.

activity of the main investor, Fiat, and also focuses on: financial intermediation, the manufacture of transport equipment, and manufacture of metal products classes of PKD activity. The early existing relationship between the region and Italian investors has been a basis for continuing, steady, and further Italian investment in the region.

Dolnośląskie, Łódzkie, and Lubuskie attract between three to eight firms each, with the remaining regions attracting only one or two investors. While Dolnośląskie has an RLAco index below 1 for Italian firms, indicating a lack of strength for the firms in the region, the Łódzkie and Lubuskie regions maintain a steady, positive RLAco index for this group throughout the period. The regions and their participating industries are: Dolnośląskie, with the manufacture of chemicals and chemical products and metal products; Łódzkie with the manufacture of fabrics and textiles (the region's historical expertise), of chemicals and chemical products, and of food; and Lubuskie with the manufacture of fabrics and textiles and leather.

Japanese investors are present in nine regions in Poland, with two significant concentrations in the Mazowieckie and Dolnośląskie regions. Mazowieckie attracts ten firms in 2006, steadily growing its Japanese presence from four firms in 2000. The Japanese presence in the region manages only to maintain an occasional above 1 RLAco, while in most of the years the index indicator remains well below 1 for Japanese firms. Dolnośląskie, on the other hand, the study period began with no Japanese participants, then had one representative investor but, since 2004, Japanese investment in the region increased to seven firms and remains constant. Dolnośląskie also maintained a low RLAis in the beginning of the study period; however, that has changed since 2004, and the Japanese investors RLAco index ranges from 2.69 to 3.5, maintaining a high relative strength of Japanese presence in the region.

Mazowieckie decidedly attracts the largest share of Japanese investment, including wholesale and retail trades (which involves repair and sale of motor vehicles, motorcycles and personal and household goods), with the manufacture of rubber and plastics and financial intermediation classes following the lead. Dolnośląskie Japanese firms focus on the manufacture of transport equipment, machinery, and on equipment PKD classes, concerned with resource and intermediate component production. Thus far, this investment is the most concentrated.

Two other regions, Śląskie and Wielkopolskie, attract three Japanese firms each. The data paint stories that look quite different from each other. Śląskie manages slowly to attract additional firms to the region, starting from one in 2000, while Wielkopolskie has three Japanese firms

Table 4.34 Regional concentration of Japanese firms in Poland

	Japan													
	Firms per country-of-origin							RLAco						
Voivodship	2000	2001	2002	2003	2004	2005	2006	2000	2001	2002	2003	2004	2005	2006
Dolnośląskie	0	1	0	1	7	7	7	0.00	0.33	0.00	0.57	2.97	3.50	2.69
Kujawsko-Pomorskie	0	0	0	0	0	1	1	0.00	0.00	0.00	0.00	0.00	2.42	1.57
Lubelskie	0		0	1	1	0	0	0.00	0.00	0.00	3.23	2.55	0.00	0.00
Małopolskie	1	1	1	2	2	2	2	1.17	1.94	1.42	2.26	1.77	2.30	1.84
Mazowieckie	4	3	4	10	9	9	10	1.02	0.65	0.88	1.10	0.85	1.01	0.92
Podlaskie	3	0	1	1	1	1	1	30.20	0.00	11.11	6.47	4.53	4.60	4.70
Śląskie	1	2	1	2	2	2	3	1.26	2.44	1.35	1.19	0.95	1.07	1.27
Świętokrzyskie	1	1	1	2	2	1	1	5.37	5.39	7.41	7.55	5.44	3.54	2.89
Wielkopolskie	3	4	3	3	3	3	3	2.44	3.02	2.54	1.34	1.12	1.27	1.05

Source: Based on data obtained from the Polish Information and Foreign Investment Agency (PAIIZ) and the author's own analysis.

investing there in 2000 and maintains that level consistently. Both regions maintain a positive RLAco for Japanese firms, with Wielkopolskie's index slowly declining, while Śląskie maintains steady RLAco index measure with a one-year drop below 1.

Śląskie attracts investment in the manufacture of rubber and plastics and other non-metal goods; in Wielkopolskie, two out of three Japanese firms focus on the manufacture of electrical machinery and apparatus.

Luxembourg firms are present in five Polish regions throughout the study period. Their concentration is significant in the Mazowieckie and Śląskie regions only. These regions exhibit a slow increase in investment participation that translates into RLAco strength for both regions, at the levels of 1.51 and 3.06 respectively. In Mazowieckie, Luxembourger investment concentrates predominantly on the wholesale and retail trade, and construction PKD classes, and in Śląskie on the manufacture of electrical machinery and apparatus and related products.

Investment from the Netherlands in Poland is present across all 16 regions of the country. The most intense concentration of Dutch investor presence is in Mazowieckie, with 39 in 2006, and in Wielkopolskie, with 16 Dutch investors in the same year. Both regions manage also a positive RLAco index measure of Dutch investors, although Mazowieckie only entered positive index measure territory starting in 2004, making the region more vital to Dutch investors. Until that year its RLAco for Dutch firms was below 1. Wielkopolskie continues a steady RLAco measure for Dutch firms throughout the period.

Dutch investment is concentrated mainly in four sectors: financial intermediation; real estate, rental, and business activities; wholesale and retail trade; and manufacturing of consumer products, paper, food, and chemicals. Dutch firms in the region are also almost exclusively, partly as a nature of their business demands, in Warsaw, or in very close proximity to the city.

Wielkopolskie attracts Dutch firms participating in the manufacture of food, drinks, and tobacco products; transport, storage and communication (telecommunication sub-class of activity); and wholesale and retail trade. The Dutch investors in the region are not as concentrated as are those in Mazowieckie.

Other regions with at least three Dutch firms do not show strength in terms of RLAco for Dutch firms, with the exception of Małopolskie with five firms and Zachodnio-Pomorskie with three firms in 2006. Both regions have a continuing positive RLAco index throughout the study period. Małopolskie hosts two out of five firms engaged in the manufacture of non-metal goods, with the remaining firms participating in

Table 4.35 Regional concentration of Luxembourger firms in Poland

	Luxebourg													
	Firms per country-of-origin							RLAco						
Voivodship	2000	2001	2002	2003	2004	2005	2006	2000	2001	2002	2003	2004	2005	2006
Dolnośląskie	1	1	1	2	2	2	2	4.47	2.10	3.22	1.80	1.43	1.56	1.39
Lubelskie	1	1	0	0	0	0	0	19.69	8.88	0.00	0.00	0.00	0.00	0.00
Mazowieckie	1	4	8	8	10	9	9	0.93	1.73	1.94	1.39	1.59	1.57	1.51
Śląskie	0	0	1	4	4	4	4	0.00	0.00	1.48	3.74	3.20	3.34	3.06
Wielkopolskie	0	0	0	0	0	1	1	0.00	0.00	0.00	0.00	0.00	0.66	0.64

Source: Based on data obtained from the Polish Information and Foreign Investment Agency (PAIIZ) and the author's own analysis.

Table 4.36 Regional concentration of Dutch firms in Poland

	The Netherlands													
	Firms per country-of-origin							RLAco						
Voivodship	2000	2001	2002	2003	2004	2005	2006	2000	2001	2002	2003	2004	2005	2006
Dolnośląskie	5	5	7	8	7	5	5	1.02	0.85	0.99	1.03	0.76	0.63	0.56
Kujawsko-Pomorskie	1	1	2	2	2	3	3	0.64	0.68	1.19	0.97	0.78	1.83	1.38
Łódzkie	3	4	5	7	4	5	5	0.86	0.92	0.94	1.27	0.65	0.91	0.83
Lubelskie	1	1	2	1	2	0	0	3.11	3.55	1.65	0.73	1.31	0.00	0.00
Lubuskie	1	1	1	1	2	2	2	0.89	0.58	0.57	0.51	0.87	1.06	1.00
Małopolskie	3	4	5	6	6	5	5	1.12	1.26	1.25	1.52	1.37	1.45	1.34
Mazowieckie	20	26	33	39	45	39	39	0.85	0.91	0.88	0.97	1.09	1.10	1.06
Opolskie	1	1	1	1	1	1	1	0.84	0.77	0.63	0.53	0.52	0.51	0.50
Podkarpackie	1	2	2	2	2	2	2	0.67	24.49	10.75	10.16	10.49	11.62	11.02
Podlaskie	0	0	0	0	1	1	1	0.00	0.00	0.00	0.00	1.17	1.16	1.38
Pomorskie	3	3	4	4	4	3	4	0.92	0.78	0.84	0.85	0.78	0.65	0.83
Śląskie	4	4	6	5	5	7	8	0.84	0.79	0.98	0.67	0.61	0.95	0.99
Świętokrzyskie	2	2	1	2	2	2	2	1.79	1.75	0.90	1.69	1.40	1.79	1.70
Warmińsko-Mazurskie	0	0	1	1	2	2	1	0.00	0.00	1.07	0.85	1.61	1.79	0.85
Wielkopolskie	12	12	13	13	15	17	16	1.63	1.47	1.33	1.31	1.44	1.81	1.65
Zachodnio-Pomorskie	3	5	4	3	3	3	3	2.37	3.40	2.26	1.39	1.31	1.06	1.07

Source: Based on data obtained from the Polish Information and Foreign Investment Agency (PAIIZ) and the author's own analysis.

Table 4.37 Regional concentration of Norwegian firms in Poland

	Norway													
	Firms per country-of-origin							RLAco						
Voivodship	**2000**	**2001**	**2002**	**2003**	**2004**	**2005**	**2006**	**2000**	**2001**	**2002**	**2003**	**2004**	**2005**	**2006**
Dolnośląskie	1	0	0	0	0	0	0	2.68	0.00	0.00	0.00	0.00	0.00	0.00
Kujawsko-Pomorskie	0	0	1	1	1	0	0	0.00	0.00	4.18	3.39	2.72	0.00	0.00
Lubuskie	0	1	1	1	1	1	1	0.00	2.88	3.96	3.56	3.06	3.73	3.10
Małopolskie	0	0	0	0	1	1	1	0.00	0.00	0.00	0.00	1.60	2.05	1.66
Mazowieckie	5	5	4	5	5	4	6	1.00	0.87	0.75	0.87	0.85	0.80	1.01
Opolskie	1	1	1	1	1	1	0	3.96	3.78	4.43	3.74	3.67	3.57	0.00
Pomorskie	2	3	2	1	2	2	2	2.88	3.86	2.95	1.48	2.72	3.04	2.57
Śląskie	1	1	1	1	1	1	1	0.99	0.97	1.14	0.94	0.85	0.96	0.77
Wielkopolskie	2	1	1	1	2	1	2	1.28	0.60	0.72	0.70	1.35	0.75	1.27
Zachodnio-Pomorskie	2	2	1	1	0	2	2	7.45	6.71	3.96	3.23	0.00	4.98	4.40

Source: Based on data obtained from the Polish Information and Foreign Investment Agency (PAIIZ) and the author's own analysis.

construction, production of food, drinks and tobacco products (Philip Morris Holland BV), while Zachodnio-Pomorskie attracts the production of food, drinks and tobacco products.

Firms from Norway can be found in ten regions across Poland. Their concentration, however, is very low, mostly one or two firms per region, in some years none. The most significant concentration of Norwegian firms is in the Mazowieckie region which hosted six firms in 2006. In the previous years of the study only four or five firms were present there. This slight increase also gives Norwegian firms an RLAco index of 1.01 for 2006, while in previous years that index strength was below 1.

Norwegian firms in Mazowieckie form an eclectic group, ranging from the manufacture of pulp and paper, publishing and printing, manufacturing of non-metal goods, and wholesale and retail sales with a subclass activity of retail sales of automotive fuel. Norwegian investment in other regions is also quite diverse, but mostly focused on manufacturing of consumer products and retail.

South Korean firms invest sporadically in seven regions in Poland between 2000 and 2006. The only consistent South Korean investment is in the Mazowieckie region, while all remaining regions have investors in a single year only. Investment in Mazowieckie ranges from two to four firms per year and, until 2005, the region maintains a positive RLAco for South Korean firms. That RLAco advantage is lost in 2006 due to a sudden investment by five South Korean firms in the Dolnośląskie region. As such, RLAco for Mazowieckie in 2006 declines to 0.89 from 1.39 in 2005.

The predominant industries present in the Mazowieckie region are wholesale and retail trade, financial intermediation, and manufacture of radio, television and communication equipment and apparatus, with the last two classes attracting only one firm each. The Dolnośląskie region's sudden influx of five investors from South Korea brings investors in one PKD class – manufacture of radio, television and communication equipment and apparatus – with some differentiation in sub-classes ranging from the manufacture of electronic valves and tubes and other electronic components to one investor in retail sales of electrical household appliances and radio and television goods. South Korean firms in this region are most concentrated and manage a high positive RLAco for the region at 4.64.

Investors from Sweden participate in economic activities within 12 regions in Poland. The regions attracting most of the Swedish firms are Mazowieckie, with 18, and Wielkopolskie, with 10. In Mazowieckie, the presence of Swedish investors seems to be on a declining trajectory in

Table 4.38 Regional concentration of South Korean firms in Poland

	South Korea													
	Firms per country-of-origin							**RLAco**						
Voivodship	**2000**	**2001**	**2002**	**2003**	**2004**	**2005**	**2006**	**2000**	**2001**	**2002**	**2003**	**2004**	**2005**	**2006**
Dolnośląskie	0	0	0	0	0	0	5	0.00	0.00	0.00	0.00	0.00	0.00	4.64
Kujawsko-Pomorskie	0	0	0	0	2	0	2	0.00	0.00	0.00	0.00	13.59	0.00	7.58
Łódzkie	2	1	0	0	0	0	0	7.54	4.27	0.00	0.00	0.00	0.00	0.00
Lubelskie	0	1	1	1	1	1	1	0.00	13.32	18.81	17.79	11.47	11.27	5.68
Lubuskie	1	0	0	0	0	0	0	11.81	0.00	0.00	0.00	0.00	0.00	0.00
Mazowieckie	2	2	3	3	3	3	4	1.12	1.30	1.82	1.82	1.27	1.40	0.89
Zachodnio-Pomorskie	0	0	0	0	0	2	0	0.00	0.00	0.00	0.00	0.00	11.62	0.00

Source: Based on data obtained from the Polish Information and Foreign Investment Agency (PAIIZ) and the author's own analysis.

Table 4.39 Regional concentration of Swedish firms in Poland

Voivodship	Sweden													
	Firms per country-of-origin							RLAco						
	2000	2001	2002	2003	2004	2005	2006	2000	2001	2002	2003	2004	2005	2006
Dolnośląskie	1	1	3	3	4	4	4	0.25	0.22	0.68	0.68	0.75	0.85	0.78
Kujawsko-Pomorskie	0	1	1	1	1	1	1	0.00	0.88	0.95	0.85	0.67	1.03	0.80
Łódzkie	0	1	0	0	0	0	0	0.00	0.30	0.00	0.00	0.00	0.00	0.00
Lubelskie	1	1	1	0	0	0	0	1.11	0.93	1.32	0.00	0.00	0.00	0.00
Lubuskie	2	1	2	3	3	3	3	2.23	0.76	1.81	2.67	2.26	2.66	2.61
Mazowieckie	27	29	28	25	25	21	18	1.42	1.32	1.19	1.08	1.04	1.00	0.85
Podkarpackie	1	1	1	1	1	1	1	0.84	15.89	8.58	8.89	9.02	9.75	9.57
Podlaskie	0	0	0	0	1	1	1	0.00	0.00	0.00	0.00	2.01	1.95	2.39
Pomorskie	2	3	3	3	4	3	3	0.76	1.01	1.01	1.11	1.34	1.08	1.08
Śląskie	4	4	3	3	3	3	4	1.04	1.03	0.78	0.70	0.63	0.68	0.86
Wielkopolskie	7	9	10	12	12	11	10	1.18	1.43	1.63	2.11	1.99	1.97	1.79
Zachodnio-Pomorskie	2	2	2	4	7	7	7	1.97	1.77	1.81	3.23	5.26	4.13	4.32

Source: Based on data obtained from the Polish Information and Foreign Investment Agency (PAIIZ) and the author's own analysis.

both real and index terms. The region has 27 Swedish firms in 2000 and only 18 in 2006. That course also translates into a declining RLAco index for Swedish firms in Mazowieckie from 1.42 in the year 2000 to 0.85 in 2006, indicating weakening importance of the strength offered for Swedish firms in the Mazowieckie region. Wielkopolskie, on the other hand, manages positive growth throughout the period, with peak presence and index levels in 2003 and 2004.

Mazowieckie attracts Swedish investment predominantly in the manufacture of electrical machinery and apparatus, with a focus on manufacture of office machinery and computers, and manufacture of pulp and paper, publishing and printing, with a focus on production of paper products and printing. Wielkopolskie attracts a less-focused group of investors from Sweden, with few firms in manufacture of metals and metal products and the related class in manufacture of machinery, with a sub-class of the production and use of mechanical power.

The next tier of regions – Dolnośląskie, Lubuskie, Pomorskie, Śląskie, and Zachodnio-Pomorskie – attract between three to seven Swedish investors each and, with the exception of Dolnośląskie and Śląskie, all manage to maintain positive, in some cases even strong, RLAco for Swedish firms. Swedish investment in Dolnośląskie specializes in the manufacture of transport equipment with a focus on manufacture of parts and accessories for motor vehicles and their engines; Lubuskie has an eclectic group, with a focus on the manufacture of pulp and paper and on publishing and printing; Pomorskie attracts a diverse group; Śląskie hosts investors in manufacture of metals and metal products and of plastics; and Zachodnio-Pomorskie, the region with the highest number of Swedish participants gained in the study period, hosts investors in the manufacture of food, drinks and tobacco products.

Switzerland's investors are present in 13 regions in Poland, with a focus on Mazowieckie, which hosts nine Swiss investors in 2006. This level of investors' presence does not contribute to a strong RLAco index measure, as it remains below 1 at 0.86 in 2006. Swiss investment in the region is not specifically focused, instead ranging from financial intermediation to the manufacture of food, drinks and tobacco products and of non-metal products.

The only two other areas of investment focus worth mentioning are Dolnośląskie and Wielkopolskie, with three firms each. What is noteworthy is the fact that Dolnośląskie increases the presence of Swiss firms from 1 to 3 during the period, while Wielkopolskie experiences a drop from five to three firms. Dolnośląskie and Wielkopolskie both attract

Table 4.4C Regional concentration of Swiss firms in Poland

	Switzerland													
	Firms per country-of-origin							RLAco						
Voivodship	2000	2001	2002	2003	2004	2005	2006	2000	2001	2002	2003	2004	2005	2006
Dolnośląskie	1	3	3	3	3	3	3	0.71	1.72	1.61	1.58	1.27	1.29	1.19
Kujawsko-Pomorskie	0	0	0	0	0	1	1	0.00	0.00	0.00	0.00	0.00	2.09	1.62
Łódzkie	0	1	1	1	1	2	2	0.00	0.78	0.71	0.74	0.63	1.24	1.18
Lubelskie	1	1	1	1	1	1	1	2.81	2.42	3.13	2.96	2.55	2.33	2.44
Lubuskie	1	2	1	1	1	1	1	3.11	3.92	2.14	2.08	1.70	1.80	1.77
Małopolskie	0	2	2	2	2	2	2	0.00	2.11	1.90	2.08	1.77	1.98	1.90
Mazowieckie	6	7	9	10	10	10	9	0.88	0.83	0.91	1.01	0.94	0.96	0.86
Opolskie	0	1	1	1	1	1	1	0.00	2.57	2.40	2.18	2.04	1.72	1.77
Podlaskie	1	1	1	1	1	1	1	5.83	5.88	5.09	5.93	4.53	3.97	4.87
Pomorskie	3	1	1	0	0	2	2	3.18	0.88	0.80	0.00	0.00	1.47	1.47
Śląskie	0	0	0	0	1	1	1	0.00	0.00	0.00	0.00	0.47	0.46	0.44
Wielkopolskie	5	4	4	4	5	3	3	2.36	1.65	1.55	1.64	1.87	1.09	1.09
Zachodnio-Pomorskie	1	1	1	1	1	1	0	2.74	2.29	2.14	1.89	1.70	1.20	0.00

Source: Based on data obtained from the Polish Information and Foreign Investment Agency (PAIIZ) and the author's own analysis.

Table 4.41 Regional concentration of United Kingdom firms in Poland

	United Kingdom													
	Firms per country-of-origin							RLAco						
Voivodship	**2000**	**2001**	**2002**	**2003**	**2004**	**2005**	**2006**	**2000**	**2001**	**2002**	**2003**	**2004**	**2005**	**2006**
Dolnośląskie	6	6	4	4	7	7	8	2.30	1.89	1.14	1.07	1.51	1.68	1.75
Kujawsko-Pomorskie	0	0	0	0	1	1	1	0.00	0.00	0.00	0.00	0.77	1.16	0.89
Łódzkie	2	3	4	2	1	2	2	1.08	1.28	1.53	0.76	0.32	0.69	0.65
Lubelskie	1	1	0	2	2	2	0	1.69	1.33	0.00	142.29	2.60	2.60	0.00
Lubuskie	0	1	1	1	1	1	0	0.00	1.08	1.14	1.06	0.87	1.01	0.00
Małopolskie	2	3	3	3	3	3	3	1.41	1.74	1.52	1.59	1.35	1.66	1.57
Mazowieckie	11	16	21	18	18	19	19	0.88	1.04	1.13	0.93	0.87	1.02	1.00
Opolskie	1	1	1	1	1	1	1	1.58	1.42	1.28	1.12	1.04	0.96	0.97
Podkarpackie	1	1	2	2	2	2	2	1.27	22.65	21.73	21.19	20.77	22.12	21.39
Pomorskie	0	1	1	1	2	2	2	0.00	0.48	0.43	0.44	0.77	0.82	0.81
Śląskie	2	1	1	5	6	4	4	0.79	0.37	0.33	1.39	1.45	1.03	0.96
Świętokrzyskie	2	1	2	1	1	1	1	3.38	1.62	3.62	1.77	1.38	1.70	1.65
Warmińsko-Mazurskie	1	0	0	0	0	0	0	2.30	0.00	0.00	0.00	0.00	0.00	0.00
Wielkopolskie	3	2	3	3	3	4	4	0.77	0.45	0.62	0.63	0.57	0.81	0.80

Source: Based on data obtained from the Polish Information and Foreign Investment Agency (PAIIZ) and the author's own analysis.

an eclectic investment from Switzerland, which falls along the lines of regional strengths.

Firms from the United Kingdom invest in 14 regions in Poland throughout the period. The most substantial concentrations of investors are in Mazowieckie, with 19 firms, and Dolnośląskie, with eight firms in 2006. The RLAco for the UK firms in Dolnośląskie remains constantly above 1, in fact often close to 2. Mazowieckie, on the other hand maintains an index measure just slightly above or below 1 for most of the years with the exception of 2006 when it is exactly at 1 for the UK firms.

In Mazowieckie, UK firms form concentrations in real estate, rental, and business activities, transport, storage, and communication (with specialization in telecommunication), and wholesale and retail trade. In Dolnośląskie, pronounced concentrations of the manufacture of chemicals and chemical products and of transport equipment are revealed.

The remaining regions worth noting are: Małopolskie, Śląskie, and Wielkopolskie, each attracting three or four UK investors. Only Małopolskie has a positive RLAco index for UK firms. Małopolskie attracts investment in the manufacture of metals and metal products and of non-metal products (ceramics), and wholesale and retail trade (oil and gas distributor, BP). Śląskie attracts an eclectic group, and Wielkopolskie has two out of four firms in the manufacture of food, drinks and tobacco products, one in the manufacture of chemicals and chemical products, and one in the manufacture of other non-metal goods (glass). The remaining regions attract only a low number of UK investors, some even only intermittently.

U.S. investors are located across 15 regions in Poland. This country's investment grows slowly from 116 firms in 2000 to 130 in 2006. The highest concentration is apparent in Mazowieckie, with almost half the firms, 64, locating there. Over the study period, investment from the United States in Mazowieckie increases from 58 to 64 firms and maintains a steady positive RLAco index strength above 1.2. The region attracts investment in construction, financial intermediation, real estate and hotels, wholesale and retail trade, and the manufacture of various consumer products.

The next groups attracting investment from the United States are Dolnośląskie with 13 firms, Łódzkie with eight firms, Małopolskie with eight firms, Podkarpackie with eight firms, Pomorskie with seven firms, Śląskie with six firms, and Wielkopolskie with seven firms. The regions of Dolnośląskie, Małopolskie, Podkarpackie, and Pomorskie maintain a positive RLAco index for investment from the United States, while the

Table 4.42 Regional concentration of U.S. firms in Poland

	USA													
	Firms per country-of-origin							RLAco						
Voivodship	**2000**	**2001**	**2002**	**2003**	**2004**	**2005**	**2006**	**2000**	**2001**	**2002**	**2003**	**2004**	**2005**	**2006**
Dolnośląskie	8	11	12	11	13	12	13	0.83	1.11	1.21	1.03	1.10	1.14	1.08
Kujawsko-Pomorskie	1	1	1	1	1	0	1	0.32	0.40	0.42	0.35	0.30	0.00	0.34
Łódzkie	5	5	5	6	7	8	8	0.73	0.68	0.67	0.80	0.88	1.09	0.99
Lubelskie	1	1	1	1	1	2	2	0.45	0.43	0.59	0.53	0.51	1.02	1.02
Małopolskie	7	8	10	9	9	8	8	1.33	1.49	1.78	1.67	1.60	1.74	1.59
Mazowieckie	58	60	60	69	67	64	64	1.25	1.25	1.14	1.25	1.26	1.36	1.28
Opolskie	2	2	2	2	2	2	2	2.91	0.91	0.90	0.78	0.82	0.76	0.74
Podkarpackie	10	8	7	8	10	8	8	3.41	57.98	26.74	29.73	40.78	34.85	32.57
Podlaskie	2	2	2	1	0	1	1	1.70	2.07	1.91	1.06	0.00	0.87	1.02
Pomorskie	8	8	10	7	7	8	7	1.24	1.23	1.50	1.08	1.06	1.29	1.08
Śląskie	6	5	6	10	8	5	6	0.64	0.58	0.69	0.98	0.76	0.51	0.55
Świętokrzyskie	1	0	0	0	1	1	1	0.45	0.00	0.00	0.00	0.54	0.67	0.63
Warmińsko-Mazurskie	0	1	1	1	0	0	0	0.00	0.72	0.76	0.62	0.00	0.00	0.00
Wielkopolskie	7	6	7	7	8	7	7	0.48	0.43	0.51	0.52	0.60	0.56	0.53
Zachodnio Pomorskie	0	0	0	0	0	1	2	0.00	0.00	0.00	0.00	0.00	0.26	0.53

Source: Based on data obtained from the Polish Information and Foreign Investment Agency (PAIIZ) and the author's own analysis.

regions of Łódzkie, Śląskie, and Wielkopolskie maintain a steady RLAco index measure below 1.

In terms of investment concentration in those regions, Dolnośląskie attracts the manufacture of machinery and equipment and of transport equipment; Łódzkie attracts an eclectic variety of manufacturers, from electrical machinery and apparatus, to fabrics and textiles, to food, drinks and tobacco products; Małopolskie attracts real estate, rental, and business activities and manufacture of metal and metal products; Podkarpackie attracts the manufacture of transport equipment with a specific concentration of manufacture of aircraft and spacecraft sub-class; Pomorskie attracts the manufacture of metals and metal products, and real estate, rental, and business activities; Śląskie attracts a diverse group; and Wielkopolskie attracts the manufacture of food, drinks and tobacco products and of electrical machinery and apparatus.

Foreign firms showing a minority presence representing the following countries of origin are: Australia, Canada, China, Croatia, Cyprus, Czech Republic, Greece: 3; Hungary: 5; India: 2; Ireland: 6; Israel: 1; Liechtenstein: 4; Malta: 1; Mexico: 1; Monaco: 1; Philippines: 1; Portugal: 6; Russia: 2; Slovenia: 2; South Africa: 4; Spain: 4; Taiwan: 1; Turkey: 1; Ukraine: 1. Individually, they do not yield statistically significant results during the period of this study; as such they are not analyzed here.

4.5 Summary

This analysis reveals the patterns of location of foreign investors in Poland. The emerging concentrations of investment suggest a correlation of economic factors that support and attract a particular economic activity and are conducive to investors from particular countries of origin of the investment. The result of multiple linear regression of the RLAco index measure in years 2000 to 2006, before Poland joined the European Union and immediately after accession, shows weak correlation in the early years of the study and increasing correlation for the concentration of foreign firms according to industry in the later part of the period. In the year 2003, immediately before Poland joined the EU, the coefficient results reach a level of significance and are increasing in the following years of the study period, after entry into the EU.

The results reveal, as expected, that the central capital region of Mazowieckie attracts the largest investment share from most participating countries in real terms. This, however, does not always mean that the region attracts the most investors in RLAco terms. The Mazowieckie region manages only a slightly positive RLAco for a number of countries, with at least ten or more investors in the region despite a relatively high concentration of firms there. These countries include: Austria, with RLAco of 1.28, Finland, with RLAco of 1.27, France, with RLAco of 1.18, the Netherlands, with RLAco of 1.06, and the United States, with RLAco of 1.28. A number of countries with a much lower concentration of investing participants in the region manage to secure a higher RLAco due to a lower participation of investors in the country as a whole. As a consequence, other regions may offer them a more significant advantage.

For the most part, these are border regions, which seem to attract investors from neighboring and nearby countries. An example is Zachodnio-Pomorskie, which has a strong and steadily increasing RLAco index of 5.87 in 2006 for Danish firms, 4.32 for Swedish investors, and 4.4 for Norwegian investors.

There are specific concentrations of German investors in Poland's western regions (Dolnośląskie and Lubuskie) and southern and central regions (Łódzkie, Pomorskie, Śląskie, and Wielkopolskie). All of the above-named regions maintain a positive RLAco index measure and attract at least around 10 percent of total firms investing in Poland.

The region with the highest concentration measures of RLAco for a number of countries is Podkarpackie in the southeast region. Although the overall number of participating investors in the region is one of the lowest, at 29 in 2006, over the years this region has hosted investors from only ten countries. This fact gives an opportunity to maintain a high location advantage measure for participating countries.

Italian firms investing in Poland locate in 14 regions across the country and maintain the most constant level of investment, with almost no growth, across the study period, from 60 firms in 2000 to 63 in 2006. German firms are most concentrated in Mazowieckie, Dolnośląskie, Wielkopolskie, Łódzkie, and Śląskie in real terms. Of these, Mazowieckie and Śląskie do not manage to have a positive RLAco index measure.

Swedish firms outside of the Mazowieckie region concentrate in the Zachodnio-Pomorskie and Wielkopolskie regions, which are located in geographical proximity to the source of investment and leverage host regions' strengths. Worth noting is the Podkarpackie region, which has the highest concentration of firms from very few countries of origin: France, Germany, and the United States. Also, these firms operate in the related industries of transport and manufacturing of machinery, which makes the region the most specialized of the small regions in the country. The region of Podkarpackie is narrowly specialized in both

RLAco and RLAis index measures, and that fact helps it achieve high index measures for participating countries.

4.6 The influence of local economic factors on the location choices of foreign investors in Poland

Questions regarding the effect of availability of regional economic factors (H3s) on trajectory development patterns will be answered by the results of the raised hypotheses (H3a-f) that follow. The results obtained in each of the following regressions will offer an insight to the correlation of the considered factors in the decision making of foreign investors entering Poland. Each of those factors potentially has a significant economic influence on the location decisions of foreign firms. These factors are good indicators of the motives behind particular location selections and are good predictors of future decisions by foreign investors.

At first, the results of a multiple regression between dependent variable, an average of the RLAis for all the years of the study, and the proposed economic factors offer weak negative results across the subjects (Appendix 3). Further the outcome reveals that unemployment in both secondary and tertiary education levels has an increasingly strong correlation with investment in R&D across regions, while private investment in R&D has the strongest relationship, slightly higher than total investment in R&D, with wage measure and this relationship increasing during the study period (Appendix 3). The interaction between wage and unemployment rates do correlate at a lower level than the remaining variables, which can be an indicator that higher availability of skilled labor force may not have an attraction effect for foreign investment in the early years of the study. With the progression of time, this measure shows a stronger relationship, which may in turn mean that availability of skilled labor may be an attractive element for foreign corporations to locate investment in Poland.

4.6.1 Regional investment per industry along with total amount of investment in a region and RLAis regression results

The results of the regression analysis of RLAis and total regional investment along with the total amount of investment in a region in selected industries (H3a) reveals that the investment level in an industry has the following relationships with the level of presence of foreign firms in the regions:

Foreign investment in agriculture, hunting and forestry in the region Warmińsko-Mazurskie maintains the highest relationship.

Foreign investment in the manufacture of transport equipment maintains the highest relationship in Podkarpackie, which is mainly focused on the production of aviation components, a sub-class of the manufacturing of transport equipment category. Further, the Kujawsko-Pomorskie and Pomorskie regions maintain a high relationship between the level of investment in the above-mentioned industry and the concentration of foreign firms in them. Even though the region of Dolnośląskie, a long-term center of automotive manufacturing, also maintains a high relationship in the class with two other regions, Mazowieckie and Śląskie, historically hosting foreign auto manufacturers in Poland, it does not show relationship strength between the variables.

Foreign investment in construction maintains the highest relationship in the Wielkopolskie, Mazowieckie, and Łódzkie regions, with the highest of all presence of foreign investors, economic activity, and population.

Foreign investment in the supply of electricity, gas, and water has the strongest relationship in Pomorskie, at 0.621, and in Warmińsko-Mazurskie and Małopolskie, closely following at 0.584 and 0.557, respectively.

Foreign investment in financial intermediation has decisively the strongest degree of fit in Wielkopolskie, at 0.879, with Lubuskie earning a distinct second at 0.685, while Mazowieckie hosts the highest number of foreign firms in the class, exhibiting one of the weakest relationships.

Foreign investment in hotels and restaurants in Zachodnio-Pomorskie, Śląskie, and Pomorskie maintains a strong relationship. The regions with the highest degree of economic activity, Mazowieckie and Wielkopolskie, which also attract a relatively high level of investment in the class, maintain virtually no relationship.

Foreign investment in the manufacture of chemicals and chemical products, although present in all regions except for Podlaskie and Warmińsko-Mazurskie, shows the strongest goodness-of-fit measure in Podkarpackie, at 0.692, and in Dolnośląskie and Wielkopolskie, at around 0.430 each.

The manufacture of consumer products shows the strongest relationship in Dolnośląskie, at 0.741, with a degree of fit of 0.550, while the second region, Mazowieckie, shows a relationship strength of 0.642 and R square of 0.413.

Foreign investment in the manufacture of electrical machinery and apparatus shows a strong relationship compared to overall investment (in a region) in the regions of Dolnośląskie and Śląskie, while the remaining participating regions show only a weak relationship between these two variables.

The manufacture of fabrics and textiles, although present in the majority of the regions, shows the strongest relationship compared to the total amount of foreign investment in a region (with a value of around 0.860 and goodness-of-fit of 0.750) in Małopolskie, Mazowieckie, Opolskie, and Wielkopolskie. The historically dominant region in the industry, Łódzkie, shows the weakest relationship of all participating regions, therefore indicating that other economic factors contribute to attracting foreign investors in the class.

Foreign investors in the manufacture of food, drinks, and tobacco products are present in all regions across Poland, with the strongest measures of fit being in the regions of Warmińsko-Mazurskie, Podlaskie, Świętokrzyskie and Mazowieckie. However, the majority of regions perform relatively weakly in both measures.

The manufacture of furniture and of consumer goods exhibit a strong relationship among participating regions only in Warmińsko-Mazurskie, in the same way as does the manufacture of glass in Podkarpackie. The latter region, however, maintains sole representation of said industry.

The manufacture of leather and leather products has a distinctly strong relationship in Mazowieckie, with Łódzkie following closely with an R square of 0.786; third is Kujawsko-Pomorskie, with an R square of 0.559.

The manufacture of machinery and equipment maintains a leading relationship in the class in Wielkopolskie, at 0.876 and R square at 0.767, with the remaining regions of Świętokrzyskie and Warmińsko-Mazurskie closely following. The regions of Łódzkie and Zachodnio-Pomorskie also maintain a relatively strong relationship and degree of fit measures.

The Dolnośląskie, Mazowieckie, and Wielkopolskie regions, while maintaining a traditional industrial relationship with the manufacture of metals and metal products, also show relatively uniform measures of goodness-of-fit. Opposite, the regions of Podlaskie and Zachodnio-Pomorskie maintain the strongest goodness-of-fit measures in the class of 0.603 and 0.615 respectively.

Foreign investment in the manufacture of other non-metal goods is present in almost all regions, with the exception of Podlaskie, showing the highest dependency between the variables in Dolnośląskie and Zachodnio-Pomorskie.

Foreign investment in the manufacture of pharmaceuticals maintains a relatively neutral relationship to industry investment in the participating regions of Mazowieckie and Wielkopolskie. Lubelskie, the region with the strongest RLAis pharmaceutical industry measure, shows almost no relationship.

Foreign investment in the manufacture of pulp and paper and in publishing and printing, although present in 14 out of 16 regions, shows a distinctly leading relationship in the class in Łódzkie and Dolnośląskie.

Foreign investment in the manufacture of radio, television and communication equipment and telecommunications apparatus has a leading goodness-of-fit measure of 0.779 in Mazowieckie, with Wielkopolskie following closely, while the remaining participating region, Kujawsko-Pomorskie (presently the home of Dell computers), shows a very weak relationship.

Foreign investment in the manufacture of rubber and plastics has a leading goodness-of-fit measure in Pomorskie at 0.523, with Podlaskie following at 0.463.

Foreign investment in the manufacture of wood and wooden products does not overall show strength in the relationship nor goodness-of-fit to the industry investment level in the participating regions.

Foreign investment in mining and quarrying has an obvious relationship in Dolnośląskie with an R square of 0.94, followed by Małopolskie and Mazowieckie, which simply show a marginally strong relationship between the variables.

Foreign investment in other community, social and personal service activities shows almost no relationship between the variables in participating regions. Exceptions are the adjacent regions of Małopolskie and Śląskie, which have respectable relationship and degree of fit measures.

Foreign investment in real estate, rental, and business activities distinctly maintains the highest relationship between the variables in Pomorskie, with an R of 0.839; while Mazowieckie, Dolnośląskie, and Wielkopolskie virtually maintain a second equal relationship at around 0.6.

Foreign investment in transport, storage and communication, although measuring only three years of activity, has the strongest relationship and goodness-of-fit in the region of Pomorskie, with an R square of 0.925, far outpacing the remaining participating regions. The remaining regions with a strong measure with the class are Śląskie and Mazowieckie.

Foreign investment in wholesale and retail trade and repair of motor vehicles, motorcycles and personal and household goods has, as expected, the strongest relationship compared to investment in the industry in Mazowieckie, the largest and most affluent market. Also, the regions of Małopolskie and Świętokrzyskie hold a somewhat distant but respectable position at 0.827 and 0.770, respectively.

This variable shows relatively strong dependency in the above-mentioned select industries in particular regions, while in remaining regions it does not show a strong correlation. Distinct examples are Łódzkie in the manufacture of fabrics and textiles, Lubelskie in pharmaceuticals, and Mazowieckie in financial intermediation – regions which are able to offer historical strength, market size, and resources as leverage to attracting foreign investors. Łódzkie shows the weakest relationship in the industry of all participating regions, indicating that other economic factors contribute to attracting foreign investors in the class.

From the data we can determine that for the remaining regions other factors, distinct from the level of investment in the industry in the region, may play a more important role in the decision making process of foreign investors. Such can be explained by the analysis that follows.

4.6.2 Value-added and regional industrial specialization regression results

The results of the ratio analysis of the value-added regional data in selected industries (H3b) reveal that the value-added has a strong relationship with regard to the level of presence of foreign firms in the manufacturing sectors across most regions. Few regions are an exception here; for these regions the value-added above the region's mean seems to correlate with higher presence of foreign firms in service industries. There are also a number of regions with strong value-added measures for a number of industries in which foreign firms do not participate.

The review of the results by region is as follows:

> The supply of electricity, gas, and water has a strong value-added ratio in Dolnośląskie; however its RLAis is below 1 at 0.82. The real estate and rental PKD classes show a similar situation.

In the region of Kujawsko-Pomorskie, no foreign investment is present in a number of PKD classes with high value-added measures, such as fishing, real estate rental, and business activity. Wholesale and retail trade is the only class with the above mean range in which foreign firms participate.

Łódzkie has a strong value-added measure and RLAis for the region's manufacturing sector only. The region's service-related industries, financial intermediation and real estate, also reflect higher than the value of the region's mean. However, they do not manage to have a sufficient foreign presence to have a positive, above 1, RLAis for those sectors.

No foreign firms are present in the Lubelskie region's economic sectors, showing positive, above mean, value-added measure – the mining and quarrying and supply of electricity, gas, and water classes. Strong value-added is also recorded in the manufacturing sector, which reflects a strong participation of foreign firms. Foreign firms seem to be drawn to manufacturing industries with a high value-added ratio. Mining and quarrying have a high value-added ratio in the region; however they have no foreign participants in the region.

The value-added strength is reflected in only a few manufacturing industries with the participation of foreign investors in the Lubuskie region. The remaining industrial classes which have above-average value-added measure are those that have no foreign investors' presence in the region.

Foreign firms in the Małopolskie region seem to invest in industries which present a high value-added measure above the regions' mean. A strong number of foreign investors in service sectors of the economy generating high value-added are also present. Małopolskie seems to be attracting FDI into industries with a high value-added indicator. PKD classes – such as the supply of electricity, gas and water, manufacturing of fabrics and textiles, metals and metal products, and manufacturing of non-metal goods – also show an above 1 RLAis measure for foreign firms participating in the region's economy.

The vast majority of industrial classes that have a value-added measure above the mean also have high RLAis for foreign firms in those classes (always within the Mazowieckie region). These industries belong to the service sector, such as financial intermediation, real estate, rental, and business activity, transport, storage and communication, and wholesale and retail trade. The only PKD class with a high value-added and low presence of foreign firms in the region is the supply of electricity, gas, and water.

The manufacturing sector shows a value-added ratio measure above the region's mean in Opolskie, and foreign firms show a positive RLAis measure for all manufacturing classes in the region. The remaining PKD classes with high value-added in the Opolskie region have no foreign participation.

Most manufacturing sectors have a high RLAis measure in the Podkarpackie region. Manufacturing as a whole also has a higher than average value-added measure in the region.

Only the industries of the supply of electricity, gas, and water, and wholesale and retail trade have both above the mean value-added and above 1 RLAis measures in the region of Podlaskie. The remaining industries with a high value-added indicator have no foreign participation in the region.

In the Pomorskie region, manufacturing displays above-average value-added measure and also has a relatively strong RLAis in a number of manufacturing PKD classes: electrical machinery; food, drink, and tobacco; furniture and consumer products; rubber and plastics, and transport equipment. Service-oriented sectors displaying a value-added measure above the region's mean show RLAis below 1 for the participating industries.

In the Śląskie region, the manufacturing sector has a strong value-added ratio between the tested periods, and it also attracts foreign investors. On the other hand, the service-related industry maintains a relatively attractive value-added measure, but it does not show a strong RLAis for foreign firms in the region.

In the Świętokrzyskie region, PKD classes in both service and manufacturing reflect a value-added higher than the mean. However, only the manufacturing sector manages to show a positive RLAis for foreign firms in the manufacturing of fabrics and textiles, machinery and equipment, metal and metal products, and other non-metal goods, among other sectors.

The manufacturing sector reflects above mean value-added ratio in the Warmińsko-Mazurskie region and has a relatively strong RLAis measure with regard to the production of non-metal goods and furniture classes. Agriculture has the highest RLAis index measure in the class in the whole country. Agriculture also has a positive but below mean level of ratio.

The Wielkopolskie region maintains positive measures in both value-added ratio and RLAis index for what concerns the manufacturing sectors, while its service-oriented classes show positive value-added and have an RLAis index at 0.54 and below.

In the region of Zachodnio-Pomorskie value-added ratio correlates with high RLAis only in the services for supply of electricity, gas, and water, and the hotel and restaurants sectors. Manufacturing sectors that show strong RLAis for foreign firms in the region have a value-added measure below the region's mean. Overall high value-added in the region's economic sector does not seem to be a factor that attracts FDI.

The above review reflects where the strongest correlation between value-added and the presence of foreign firms in the particular industries exists. This summary offers an insight into the importance of value-added as an indicator of location selection for said industries. The data also show that in some key regions value-added bears no relationship to the attraction of foreign firms into those regions. This may be an indication that firms attracted to those regions are in pursuit of specific regional resources. Noteworthy are observations reflecting no correlation between RLAis and value-added for some regions and industries: Mazowieckie, in construction and financial intermediation, industries with high levels of foreign participation; and Łódzkie in the manufacturing of textiles and consumer products, a historically strong representative of these regions.

Manufacturing of fabrics and textiles has a strong positive relationship to value-added in the regions of Małopolskie, Świętokrzyskie, Wielkopolskie, Mazowieckie, and Kujawsko-Pomorskie, while it shows no relationship between the two measures in Łódzkie, a traditionally leading region in that industry. Besides the mentioned regions, a relatively strong correlation is evident from the data indicating the positive influence of FDI on the regions' productivity.

4.6.3 Labor cost influence on foreign investment in regions of Poland

The results of the regression between regions' RLAis index of participating industries and wage level for each region (H3c) is expected to reveal the relationship between the level of presence of foreign investors in said regions and the regions' labor cost. In fact, the cost of labor may be a significant factor in the location choice for investment. The data covers the period from 2002 to 2006 and yields the following results.

Foreign investment in agriculture, hunting and forestry shows the strongest correlation with labor cost in the regions of Pomorskie and Warmińsko-Mazurskie.

Foreign investment in construction has the strongest correlation in Pomorskie and a very weak, almost nil relationship, correlation in the Mazowieckie and Śląskie regions, which have the strongest presence of foreign investors in the class. These last two regions show high RLAis in the class despite their higher cost of labor.

Foreign investment in the supply of electricity, gas, and water has the strongest relationship in the regions of Pomorskie, Śląskie, Małopolskie, Wielkopolskie, and Podkarpackie, with the weakest relationship being in Mazowieckie.

Financial intermediation has the strongest relationship in Pomorskie, while Mazowieckie has one of the weakest relationships, indicating that other factors might be attracting investors.

Hotels and restaurants form the class that, on average, shows the highest correlation between the level of participation of foreign investors and wages, again with the weakest relationship observed in Mazowieckie.

Foreign investment in the manufacture of chemicals and chemical products has the strongest relationship in Śląskie, Lubuskie, and Opolskie.

Foreign investment in the manufacture of consumer products has the strongest relationship in Dolnośląskie, at 0.956 and an R square of 0.915, and Mazowieckie at 0.781, with an R square of 0.610.

Foreign investment in the manufacture of electrical machinery and apparatus has the strongest relationship in Podkarpackie, Pomorskie, and Dolnośląskie.

Foreign investment in the manufacture of fabrics and textiles has the strongest relationship between its RLAis and wages in the regions of Małopolskie, Kujawsko-Pomorskie, and Warmińsko-Mazurskie. Łódzkie, which attracts the highest number of investors in the class and is a historic center for the manufacture of fabrics and textiles, has a weak positive relationship of 0.312 for the class. The region's high concentration in the industry indicates that there are other factors behind the attractiveness of foreign forms in the PKD class.

Foreign investment in the manufacture of food, drinks, and tobacco products class has the strongest relationship between its RLAis and wages in the regions of Warmińsko-Mazurskie, Dolnośląskie, Świętokrzyskie, and Wielkopolskie.

Foreign investment in the manufacture of furniture and consumer goods class has the strongest relationship between its RLAis and wages in the Wielkopolskie, Kujawsko-Pomorskie, and Warmińsko-Mazurskie regions.

Foreign investment in the manufacture of glass (represented only in the region of Podkarpackie) shows a very weak positive relationship to the cost of labor at 0.2 with a low degree of fit.

Foreign investment in the manufacture of leather and leather products class has the strongest relationship between its RLAis and wages in the neighboring regions of Kujawsko-Pomorskie and Zachodnio-Pomorskie.

Foreign investment in the manufacture of machinery and equipment class has the strongest relationship between its RLAis and wages in the regions of Śląskie, Zachodnio-Pomorskie, Świętokrzyskie, and Wielkopolskie.

Foreign investment in the manufacture of metals and metal products class has the strongest relationship between its RLAis and wages in Pomorskie, Kujawsko-Pomorskie, and Zachodnio-Pomorskie. These are regions that have attracted foreign investors of this class in recent years.

Foreign investment in the manufacture of the non-metal goods class has the strongest relationship between its RLAis and wages in the regions of Wielkopolskie, Dolnośląskie, and Mazowieckie, of which the last two attract the highest number of foreign investors in the class.

Foreign investment in the manufacture of pharmaceuticals shows a relatively weak relationship between its RLAis and wages in all participating regions, with the strongest region being Lubelskie at 0.524 and an R square of 0.275.

Foreign investment in the manufacture of pulp and paper and publishing and printing class has the strongest relationship between its RLAis and wages in Dolnośląskie, Pomorskie, and Śląskie. Mazowieckie also reflects a strong relationship in the class.

Foreign investment in the manufacture of radio, television and communication equipment and apparatus has a relatively weak relationship between its RLAis and wages.

Foreign investment in the manufacture of rubber and plastics class has the strongest relationship between its RLAis and wages in the regions of Kujawsko-Pomorskie, Warmińsko-Mazurskie, Lubuskie, and Śląskie. Śląskie attracts the highest number of investors in the class.

Foreign investment in the manufacture of transport equipment has the strongest relationship between its RLAis and wages in the Dolnośląskie, Wielkopolskie, Pomorskie, and Mazowieckie regions, which attract a good number of firms in that industry. Śląskie, the host of Fiat, does not have a strong coefficient measure.

Foreign investment in the production of wood and manufacture of wooden products class has the strongest relationship between its RLAis and wages in Lubuskie, Zachodnio-Pomorskie, Wielkopolskie, and Podlaskie.

Foreign investment in the other community, social and personal service activities class has the strongest relationship between its RLAis and wages in the Śląskie and Dolnośląskie regions. Mazowieckie, attracting the highest number of investors in the class, shows a weak relationship.

Foreign investment in the real estate, rental, and business activities class has the strongest relationship between its RLAis and wages in Pomorskie and Zachodnio-Pomorskie. Mazowieckie attracts the highest number of investors in the class and shows a weak positive relationship and an R square of 0.291.

Foreign investment in the trade and repair class has the strongest relationship between its RLAis and wages in the regions of Śląskie, Mazowieckie, Opolskie, and Podlaskie.

The results of the regression between RLAis of participating industries and wage level (H3c) for each region reveal that, for the most part, labor cost does not have an impact on economic activity in Mazowieckie, the region with the highest degree of FDI. A similar pattern is followed by regions showing a distinct industrial specialization: they tend to attract foreign investors despite higher labor costs. Outside of the specialized regions (Łódzkie, Wielkopolskie, and Śląskie), the relationship between the level of presence of foreign investors in the regions and regions' labor cost is high in labor-intensive rather than skill-intensive industries. In highly populated regions and regions attracting the highest number of foreign investors, other economic factors besides labor costs give advantage to such an investment by attracting especially service-oriented investment. This result may also reflect an effect of the variables across the participating industries or groups of industries, such as service, manufacturing, and raw materials processing, and shows similar negative or positive results for the class.

4.6.4 Workforce and skill availability effect on FDI attraction into Polish regions

The data measuring the availability of workforce (by using data related to the number of people unemployed per region, including the skilled workforce variable of people educated in the technical and secondary level of academic institutions (H3d), and the RLAis index yields the following results for the selected industries.

Foreign investment in agriculture, hunting and forestry has the strongest relationship to the combined variables of workforce and skills in Warmińsko-Mazurskie.

Foreign investment in construction shows the strongest relationship in Mazowieckie and Świętokrzyskie. Foreign investment in financial intermediation is strongest in Kujawsko-Pomorskie, Śląskie and Pomorskie, and Mazowieckie, with Mazowieckie having the highest RLAis in the class, showing one of the weakest relationships between the class and workforce and skills availability. This indicates that other factors attract investment. Foreign investment in hotels and restaurants shows the strongest relationship in Wielkopolskie.

Foreign investment in the manufacture of chemicals and chemical products has a positive relationship in Opolskie and a marginally positive relationship in Dolnośląskie.

Foreign investment in the manufacture of fabrics and textiles has the strongest relationship in Wielkopolskie, while the neighboring region of Łódzkie, attracting the most investors in the class, shows one of the weakest relationships between investment concentration and workforce and skills variables.

Foreign investment in the manufacture of food, drinks, and tobacco products exhibits the highest relationship in the regions of Kujawsko-Pomorskie, Lubelskie, Opolskie, and Podkarpackie.

Foreign investment in the manufacture of glass, represented only in Podkarpackie, shows almost no relationship between concentration of foreign investors and workforce and skills availability.

Foreign investment in the manufacture of leather and leather products has a strong relationship in the Mazowieckie region.

Foreign investment in the manufacture of machinery and equipment has the strongest relationship in the following regions: Wielkopolskie, Mazowieckie, and Warmińsko-Mazurskie.

Foreign investment in the manufacture of pulp and paper and in publishing and printing presents the strongest relationship in the regions of Podlaskie and Lubelskie, while the region of Mazowieckie, attracting the highest number of foreign investors, shows one of the weakest relationships.

Foreign investment in the manufacture of transport equipment has the strongest relationship in the Dolnośląskie and Lubuskie regions, with the regions of Świętokrzyskie, Łódzkie, and Wielkopolskie a close second as a group.

Foreign investment in the production of wood and manufacture of wooden products has the strongest relationship in Zachodnio-Pomorskie and Wielkopolskie.

The data gathered to measure the availability of a skilled workforce, including the skilled workforce variable of people educated in technical and secondary institutions, shows that the regions with historically present industrial specializations seem to reveal a strong relationship between the above-mentioned variables (skilled workforce and RLAis index). Again, regions with higher levels of an available skilled workforce seem to have a stronger relationship between the variables in the service-oriented industries. This would be an indication that availability of skilled labor has an impact on attracting specialized class investors and service-oriented investors.

Two additional regressions were adopted to test the robustness of this coefficient. Skilled labor with secondary and tertiary levels of education shows a very low relationship with the level of concentration of FDI in the regions and in the selected industries. Only in some instances (i.e., the service and higher-grade chemicals and electronics) does the coefficient measure become significant. This indicates that the proposed measure reflects robust results.

4.6.5 The effect of market size and wages on FDI attraction into the regions

The result of multiple regression correlating market size (represented by population and level of wages[24] in the region (H3e) and the level of industrial specialization of foreign firms in the regions are expected to test the effect of market strength on FDI. The RLAis, population and wage level variables, taken for a total sample period of five years (2002–2006), yielded the following results:

Foreign investment in agriculture, hunting and forestry has a strong correlation in all represented regions.

Foreign investment in construction has a strong relationship in the majority of participating regions, with the exception of Mazowieckie, where foreign investment exhibits the lowest relationship and goodness-of-fit measures.

Foreign investment in the supply of electricity, gas, and water shows the highest relationship in the regions of Podkarpackie at 0.994, Pomorskie at 0.959, and Dolnośląskie 0.914, with the remaining participating regions following behind.

Foreign investment in financial intermediation has the strongest relationship in Pomorskie and Lubuskie, with 0.975 and 0.889 respectively. These regions become progressively attractive to this type of investment with a growth in wages.

Foreign investment in hotels and restaurants has a relatively strong relationship in the majority of participating regions, with the lowest measure in Mazowieckie at 0.628.

Foreign investment in the manufacture of chemicals and chemical products has an overall strong relationship in the majority of participating regions, with the exceptions being Łódzkie and Lubuskie, which have negative goodness-of-fit measures and weak relationship measures.

Foreign investment in the manufacture of consumer products shows the strongest relationship in the regions of Dolnośląskie and Mazowieckie, with 0.974 and 0.956 respectively. The remaining participating regions lag behind.

Foreign investment in the manufacture of electrical machinery and apparatus has an overall strong relationship in most of the participating regions, with the distinct exception being the region Zachodnio-Pomorskie, which shows a weak relationship measure of 0.346.

Foreign investment in the manufacture of fabrics and textiles has the strongest relationship in Małopolskie, Świętokrzyskie, and Podlaskie, with the last two being the regions with a lower population density. Łódzkie, traditionally strong in the PKD class, maintains one of the lowest relationships.

Foreign investment in the manufacture of food, drinks, and tobacco products has, as expected, an overall strong relationship between the variables for H3e; the weakest relationship is recorded in the region of Mazowieckie, at 0.147.

Foreign investment in the manufacture of furniture and consumer goods has an overall strong relationship between the variables.

Foreign investment in the manufacture of glass has a strong relationship between the variables in the single participating region of Podkarpackie.

Foreign investment in the manufacture of leather and leather products has an overall strong relationship between the variables in the class in all participating regions.

Foreign investment in the manufacture of machinery and equipment has an overall strong relationship between the variables in the majority of participating regions, with the lowest being Łódzkie at 0.530.

Foreign investment in the manufacture of metals and metal products has a strong relationship in the majority of participating regions, with Małopolskie and Wielkopolskie being notable exceptions.

Foreign investment in the manufacture of other non-metal goods shows a strong relationship only in some of the participating regions, notably in Wielkopolskie, Mazowieckie, and Dolnośląskie, with the remaining regions following at a distance or indicating a weak relationship between the variables.

Foreign investment in the manufacture of pharmaceuticals has a relatively strong relationship between the variables in all participating regions.

Foreign investment in the manufacture of pulp and paper and in publishing and printing has a relatively strong relationship between the variables in most participating regions, with the exception of the region of Świętokrzyskie, which exhibits weak relationship and goodness-of-fit measures.

Foreign investment in the manufacture of radio, television and communication equipment and telecommunications apparatus has a strong relationship in two participating regions, Kujawsko-Pomorskie and Wielkopolskie, at 0.955 and 0.842, while Mazowieckie has a weak relationship.

Foreign investment in the manufacture of rubber and plastics has a strong relationship in the majority of the participating regions, with the notable exception of Łódzkie, Lubelskie, and Mazowieckie (these show weak relationship and goodness-of-fit measures).

Foreign investment in the manufacture of transport equipment has a strong relationship between the variables in the regions traditionally involved in the class activity. These regions are Dolnośląskie, Łódzkie, Świętokrzyskie, and Wielkopolskie (which leads with a relationship measure above 0.9). Several other regions follow in the score: Lubelskie, Mazowieckie, Opolskie, Podkarpackie, and Pomorskie. The remaining regions show a weaker relationship.

Foreign investment in the production of wood and manufacture of wooden products in the majority of the participating regions shows significant strength for what concerns the relationship of the variables, with the exception of Kujawsko-Pomorskie and Lubuskie, which have weak relationship measures.

Foreign investment in mining and quarrying has a strong relationship between variables in all participating regions.

Foreign investment in other community, social and personal service activities has a strong relationship between variables in all participating regions, with the exception of Warmińsko-Mazurskie, which shows a weak relationship.

Foreign investment in real estate, rental, and business activities has a strong relationship between variables in all participating regions, with the exception of Wielkopolskie, which shows a weak relationship.

Foreign investment in wholesale and retail trade and repair of motor vehicles, motorcycles and personal and household goods has an unexpectedly strong relationship (above 0.9) in the regions of Lubelskie, Opolskie, and Świętokrzyskie. Foreign investment shows the weakest relationship of 0.430 in Łódzkie.

The results of the regression analysis show a relatively high relationship between the variables. The industries dependent on local markets focus near them; however, industries requiring specialized skills tend to have a lower correlation coefficient in the majority of regions, indicating their focus on skill and production rather than on market access.

4.6.6 A higher level of FDI presence in the region should also manifest in higher private R&D investment in the region

The regions attracting a higher concentration of foreign investors are also expected to have a higher level of private investment in R&D within (H3f). Following the concept that foreign investors tend to innovate more, the current test shows the results of the correlation between these two data sets – concentration of foreign investment and private investment in R&D – and investigates whether there is a dependency. At the same time, conversely, the local investment can be made in the region to attract foreign investors. For the purpose of control, another variable is adopted in order to measure the level of presence of foreign investors in regions by considering the data on the total amount of investment in R&D in the regions.

The following are the results of the regression between the levels of foreign investors and the total amount of investment in R&D in said regions (H3f):

Foreign investment in agriculture, hunting and forestry has a strong relationship between the variables only in Pomorskie.

Foreign investment in construction has a strong relationship result for the variables in the regions of Wielkopolskie and Łódzkie, with the remaining regions lagging behind.

Foreign investment in the supply of electricity, gas and water has a relatively weak or negative relationship in the majority of the participating regions, with only Świętokrzyskie and Pomorskie having a relationship strength slightly above 0.7.

Foreign investment in financial intermediation has overall weak or negative relationship and goodness-of-fit measures across all participating regions, with the highest being Łódzkie (with an R of 0.655).

Foreign investment in hotels and restaurants has, as expected, an overall negative or weak relationship to private spending on research and development. The only exception here is Zachodnio-Pomorskie, with a strength of 0.888 and a goodness-of-fit measure of 0.789.

Foreign investment in the manufacture of chemicals and chemical products has a relatively strong relationship in only two participating regions (Zachodnio-Pomorskie, at 0.782, and Lubuskie, at 0.699). The remaining regions show a relatively weak or negative relationship.

Foreign investment in the manufacture of consumer products has a strong relationship in only one region: Dolnośląskie.

Foreign investment in the manufacture of electrical machinery and apparatus also has a negative relationship in the majority of participating regions. A strong positive relationship is evident from the analysis only in the region of Pomorskie.

Foreign investment in the manufacture of fabrics and textiles has a strong relationship between the variables in Małopolskie and Śląskie, at 0.824 and 0.705, respectively. The remaining participating regions show very weak or negative relationships.

Foreign investment in the manufacture of food, drinks, and tobacco products has a strong relationship in about half of the regions, with the remaining half maintaining only a weak or negative relationship.

Foreign investment in the manufacture of furniture and consumer goods shows strength in Lubelskie at 0.816 and Śląskie at 0.758, with the remaining participating regions maintaining only a weak or negative relationship.

Foreign investment in the manufacture of glass shows a negative relationship in the single participating region of Podkarpackie.

Foreign investment in the manufacture of leather and leather products results in a negative relationship in the majority of the participating regions, with the exception of Zachodnio-Pomorskie, in which it has a strong positive relationship.

Foreign investment in the manufacture of machinery and equipment data presents a strong positive relationship in Zachodnio-Pomorskie and Świętokrzyskie at above 0.900, with a few regions following close, while five regions exhibit a negative relationship.

Foreign investment in the manufacture of metals and metal products has a strong relationship in Zachodnio-Pomorskie, Łódzkie, and Podlaskie. The regions of Śląskie and Małopolskie follow closely, while the remaining participating regions show a negative relationship.

Foreign investment in the manufacture of other non-metal goods have overall weak and negative results, with only Kujawsko-Pomorskie and Opolskie showing relatively strong positive results.

Foreign investment in the manufacture of pharmaceuticals has a relatively strong positive relationship in all participating regions.

Foreign investment in the manufacture of pulp and paper and publishing and printing has a relatively weak or negative relationship in the majority of participating regions, with only Lubelskie and Lubuskie recording a positive relationship.

Foreign investment in the manufacture of radio, television and communication equipment and telecommunications apparatus has a positive relationship only in Wielkopolskie.

Foreign investment in the manufacture of rubber and plastics maintains a strong positive relationship between the variables in three regions (Zachodnio-Pomorskie, Małopolskie and Podlaskie), with the remaining regions having weak or negative relationships.

Foreign investment in the manufacture of transport equipment has, overall, weak or negative relationships in the majority of regions, with Wielkopolskie and Świętokrzyskie having positive relationships of 0.809 and 0.748, respectively.

Foreign investment in the production of wood and manufacture of wooden products has an overall weak relationship, with only a single region, Lubelskie, having a positive relationship at 0.8.

Foreign investment in mining and quarrying has the strongest relationship in Małopolskie, with the remaining regions staying a distance. Mazowieckie, which attracts the highest number of foreign investors in the class, has a negative relationship.

Foreign investment in other community, social, and personal service activities has overall weak or negative relationship and goodness-of-fit measures across all participating regions, with the highest rates being Wielkopolskie with R = 0.874, Małopolskie at R = 0.693 and Mazowieckie at R = 0.691 (also the most densely populated regions).

Foreign investment in real estate, rental, and business activities has, overall, weak or negative relationship and goodness-of-fit measures across all participating regions, with the highest being Łódzkie with R = 0.957.

Finally, foreign investment in wholesale and retail trade and repair of motor vehicles, motorcycles and personal and household goods has the strongest relationship in Małopolskie, at 0.951, with the regions of Kujawsko-Pomorskie and Zachodnio-Pomorskie closely following with an R measure of above 0.9. The remaining participating regions have a much lower, or negative, relationship between the two variables; notably, Mazowieckie (the largest market) maintains a relationship of only 0.664 with a goodness-of-fit measure of 0.301.

In order to measure the validity of the results, another regression analysis was performed, taking into consideration the total regional spending on R&D investment and the data on the level of presence of foreign investors in the class. From that analysis we see that the level of correlation between the variables is much weaker across most of the industries. The only strong relationship is evident in the regions which seem to have strong historical and strategic ties to particular industries, such as, for example, mining and quarrying in Małopolskie, manufacturing of consumer products in Dolnośląskie, manufacturing of electrical machinery in Wielkopolskie, and manufacturing of transport equipment in Świętokrzyskie.

These industries seem to be strategically important for the regions, many of which show signs of advancement or transformation from other, lower-end, industries into more advanced industrial sectors. Such a specifically directed investment may be a sign of a regional policy to isolate particular industries and make them competitive. An example might also be the focusing of foreign investment in the manufacture of chemicals and chemical products, which exhibits a relatively strong relationship in two of the participating regions, Zachodnio-Pomorskie, at 0.782, and Lubuskie, at 0.699. Related industries such as the manufacture of food, drinks and tobacco products, show a strong relationship in about half of the regions while the remaining half maintains only a weak or negative relationship. Further, foreign investment in the manufacture of pharmaceuticals has a relatively strong positive relationship in all participating regions.

Foreign investment in wholesale and retail trade, repair of motor vehicles, motorcycles and personal and household goods, presents the strongest relationship in Małopolskie at 0.951, together with Kujawsko-Pomorskie and Zachodnio-Pomorskie, and with an R measure of above 0.9; this class, however, might be driven by the close proximity to internal and external markets, which may also introduce to the regions the necessary improvement in process management going from the home base of the investing companies to their subsidiaries.

By examining the results of both sets of coefficients, a conclusion can be drawn that the relationship between the level of FDI and private investment in R&D in the regions showing strong relationship measures can be a good predictor of the attraction of such or similar types of investment into those regions. This result can also be an indicator that foreign firms may be the source of knowledge and know-how for those regions in addition to providing the initial investment benefit.

4.7 Summary of the results

Examining the H3 variables for the tested industries, the effect of the above-mentioned economic factors on the degree of industrial specialization is revealed. As a result, the following selected factors and conclusions related to the effect of the concentration of foreign investment per industry in the regions can be noted. Taking a look at the analysis in aggregate unemployment in both secondary and tertiary education levels of labor, wage level, and spending on R&D historically have the strongest correlation to concentration of foreign firms in Poland. This countrywide indicator of strength is a sign that these three elements (unemployment, wage level, and spending on R&D historically) and availability of skilled labor, at both lower and higher levels of skill, may be drivers for establishing subsidiaries of foreign firms in Poland. Further investment in research and development, both private and total (including public), show an indication of a relatively strong correlation and, in fact, this correlation shows a high level of growth. These three elements alone, one may argue, can be significant attraction factors to foreign investors to locate in Poland. A strong correlation to the wage variable is also an important element to support attractive conditions to foreign investors. This last variable seems to have the highest correlation over the years of the study, although its success in increasing wage levels with the increase in the number of investors may create a deterrent effect to further investment in the future.

Further evaluating the variable results between the total regional investment in particular industries at the regional level and the level of RLAis index (H3a), it is clear that this variable shows relatively strong dependency in the tested industries. This follows the findings of Porter (2000), Cantwell and Mudambi (2005), and Delgado, Porter, and Stern (2012), among others, who state that higher level of investment in an industry in a region attracts further investment (which, subsequently, often leads to more innovation). The distinct examples are Łódzkie in the manufacture of fabrics and textiles, Lubelskie in pharmaceuticals, and Mazowieckie in financial intermediation – being able to offer historical strength, market size, and resources as leverage for attracting foreign investors. Łódzkie shows the weakest relationship in the industry among all participating regions, indicating that other economic factors contribute to attracting foreign investors in the class. From the results of this regression we can determine that, for the remaining regions, other factors, distinct from the level of investment in the industry in the region, may play a more important role in the decision making process.

The summary of the results for value-added ratio (H3b) shows that in some key regions (Mazowieckie and Łódzkie), value-added bears no relationship to concentration of foreign firms there. This may be an indication that firms are attracted to those regions in pursuit of other resources or for exploitation of advantages. Noteworthy are the observations reflecting no correlation between RLAis and value-added, namely in Mazowieckie, in the construction and financial intermediation industries with high levels of foreign participation; and in Łódzkie with regard to the manufacturing of textiles and consumer products, historically strong industrial representatives of these regions. This result may be an indication of the fact that the regions are moving toward high value-added activities from within (Maleckie, 1980; Dunning, 1997). This transition would help sustain an industrial development trajectory and a move from lower-end to higher-end technologies. On the other hand, the manufacturing of fabrics and textiles has a strong positive relationship to value-added in Małopolskie, Świętokrzyskie, Wielkopolskie, Mazowieckie, and Kujawsko-Pomorskie. The results show no relationship between the two measures in Łódzkie, traditionally a leading region in the manufacturing of fabrics and textiles industry. Besides the above-mentioned regions, a relatively strong value-added ratio is evident from the data, which indicates the influence of FDI on the regions' productivity.

The results of the regression analysis between regions' RLAis of participating industries and wage level (H3c) for each region reveals that, for most industries, labor cost does not have an impact on economic activity in Mazowieckie, the region with the highest degree of FDI. A similar pattern is followed by regions showing distinct industrial specialization; these tend to attract foreign investors despite higher labor costs. At an early developmental stage, such as the time period adopted for this study on Poland, wage level often has a potential dual effect on FDI attraction into a region: higher labor costs may act as a deterrent to foreign investors (Culem, 1988, Mariotti and Piscitello, 1993). Outside of the specialized regions, for example in Łódzkie, Wielkopolskie, and Śląskie, the relationship between the level of presence of foreign investors in the regions is high in the labor-intensive rather than skill-intensive industries. This result reflects the relationship of the variables across the participating industries and groups of industries – such as services, manufacturing, and raw materials processing – and shows similar positive results. In highly specialized regions and those attracting the highest number of foreign investors, other economic factors besides labor costs offer an advantage to such an investment by attracting service-oriented investment.

Overall, for both types, where the cost of labor plays a role, either positive or negative, in relation to attracting FDI into a region, the results may have an ambiguous effect on attracting foreign investors. It may also be difficult to predict a positive or negative effect on the future success of a region similar to that observed in the cases of Ireland or Spain, where an initial fast economic growth, rise of personal incomes and standard of living, caused a deterrence to foreign investment into those countries.

The data measuring the degree of correlation between the availability of labor force and RLAis for the participating industries (H3d) – including the skilled workforce variable of educated in technical and secondary institutions presented as a control variable – show that regions with historically strong industrial specializations seem to have strong relationships between the tested variables. The regions with a larger available skilled workforce seem to have a stronger relationship between the control variables in service-oriented industries. This would be an indication that the availability of skilled labor has a positive impact on attracting a specialized class of investors, including service-oriented investors.

The data on the level of presence of FDI in regions with an availability of skilled labor per industry is used to test the dependency between the variables. The results follow Mariotti and Piscitello (1995), who analyzed the quality of the labor force using skill and education as its measure.

Their conclusion was similar to that made by Little (1978), who determined that the availability of qualified manpower is a positive FDI attraction factor. In the present analysis, some labor-intensive industries seem to have a strong correlation to the RLAis of the specific industry, as in the regions of Dolnośląskie and Wielkopolskie, where manufacturing of transport equipment and non-metal goods is dominant, or in the region of Małopolskie, with the manufacturing of fabrics class. Łódzkie, being the historical center of manufacturing of fabrics (called Manchester of Poland), shows a very weak correlation.

The availability of labor and skilled labor has a relatively strong correlation to the concentration of foreign firms in labor-intensive economic sectors. The exceptions are the regions with historically strong industrial specializations; those regions are: Łódzkie in textiles, Podkarpackie in glass production, and Dolnośląskie in the manufacturing of chemicals. These regions exhibit a weak correlation to labor availability, indicating that other factors are more important in attracting foreign investors.

In addition to the data on the total available skilled workers per region, another two regressions tested the robustness of this coefficient. Skilled labor with secondary and tertiary levels of education shows a very low relationship to the level of concentration of FDI in the regions and the selected industries. Only in some instances, such as the service-related industries and the manufacturing of higher-grade chemicals and electronics, does the coefficient measure become significant. This finding supports the result of the primary variable set in answering the H3d hypothesis.

For the measure of market-seeking motivation of investment, and for the robustness check of the cost of labor, as measured by wage level, and a population of regions was used in a multiple regression yielded supporting results to the single regression between the RLAis for PKD classes and wage level, indicating the relationship to the cost of labor. These results, however, increased in significance, indicating the expected increase in the level of the market attractiveness of foreign investment (H3e), and also showing that the market size of most regions is a relevant factor in the decision making process for a location choice (e.g., Dunning, 1993).

These results follow Dunning's (1997) claim that substantial local market size may support the participating firms and even help them move toward higher value-added activities within the region. The results also follow Campos's and Kinoshita's (2003) examination of FDI flows in Central and Eastern Europe, which concluded that a large domestic market size might be important if FDI aims to serve a domestic consumer market.

Even though the majority of the regions reveal a strong relationship, some others, especially those having historical strengths in their industries (Mazowieckie, Łódzkie, Wielkopolskie, and Dolnośląskie), seem not to have a correlation. This may be a sign of regional industrial transition into higher-grade industries. Also, more concentrated industries and more efficient firms may contribute, with above-average results. This consideration follows Blomstrom, Lipsey, and Zejan (1992), who find that for most of the developing economies, the correlation between level of GDP per capita and income does not reflect a converging trend.

The coefficient of the amount of regional, private R&D spending and concentration of foreign investment in Poland (H3f) shows a strong correlation in some industries in selected regions, such as: foreign investment in the manufacture of chemicals and chemical products in only two participating regions (Zachodnio-Pomorskie, at 0.782, and Lubuskie, at 0.699); and foreign investment in the manufacture of food, drinks and tobacco products in about half of the regions, with the remaining half maintaining only a weak or negative relationship. Also, foreign investment in the manufacture of pharmaceuticals has a relatively strong, positive relationship in all participating regions.

Finally, foreign investment in wholesale and retail trade and repair of motor vehicles, motorcycles and personal and household goods shows the strongest relationship in Małopolskie, at 0.951, with Kujawsko-Pomorskie and Zachodnio-Pomorskie following closely with an R measure of above 0.9. Although these are not highly R&D-intensive industries, the investment in R&D and RLAis correlation may be a sign of process improvement orientation of the investment in the region. The remaining participating regions have a much lower, or negative, relationship between the two variables, notably in Mazowieckie, the largest market, which maintains a relationship of only 0.664, with a goodness-of-fit measure of 0.301.

The findings of a positive effect of R&D spending on attraction of FDI follows similar conclusions reached by a number of studies on the effect of R&D on foreign investment activity (Porter and Ketels, 2006; Ketels and Memedovic, 2008). The results obtained here show that regions which have a higher effect of R&D on concentration of FDI are those where industries have a strong presence. These results also follow findings by Baptista and Swann (1998), which determined that innovation within clusters of firms is due to the presence of supporting factors such as concentration of skills needed by a particular industry. Also, Mariotti and Piscitello (1995), in their study of Italian regions, concluded that the availability of skilled and qualified manpower is a positive FDI attraction factor. Additionally, the regions hosting research and development activity become attractive locations for foreign-owned R&D in their sectors of specialization (Cantwell, 1991, a; Cantwell and Janne, 1999).

Manufacturing classes tested in this study generally have a weak correlation coefficient between the regional private amount of R&D spending and concentration of foreign investment. Also foreign investment in the supply of electricity, gas, and water shows a relatively weak or negative relationship in the majority of the participating regions, with the only exception of Świętokrzyskie and Pomorskie, which have a relationship strength slightly above 0.7. Foreign investment in the manufacture of electrical machinery and apparatus also has a negative relationship in the majority of participating regions.

Foreign investment in financial intermediation has overall weak or negative relationship and goodness-of-fit measures across all participating regions, with the highest being Łódzkie with an R of 0.655. Foreign investment in hotels and restaurants has an overall negative, or a weak, relationship to private spending on research and development. The only exception here is the region of Zachodnio-Pomorskie, with a strength of 0.888 and a goodness-of-fit measure of 0.789.

The location choice of new FDI due to existing cluster initiatives involving various local stakeholders (Ketels and Memedovic, 2008) can affect further development of a region's industrial development path. Therefore, as in many cases, the data suggests foreign firms' industrial specialization in the regions due to the presence of supporting factors is relevant to the further development and competitiveness of the regions.

4.8 Can the Polish economy do it alone from now on? Analysis of the results

The results of the preceding can offer an element of the foundation for national and regional policy considerations, based on the understanding of the drivers of regional agglomeration growth. Following the literature on the subject, starting from Weber (1929), who depicted industry location as "more-or-less foreordained by invariant geographical and technological considerations" (Arthur, 1989; David and Rosenbloom, 1990), it can be said that a continuity of technological specialization within a location may lead to advantages in attracting FDI within particular industries. These technological trajectories of development formed within national and regional economic structures are closely linked to the industrial success (Cantwell, 2000) of regions. Cantwell (1991a) also shows that there are significant benefits to both domestic and foreign firms from agglomeration (later also Shaver, 1998). Therefore, generally, firms follow industrial development trajectory (Cantwell and Piscitello, 1997).

The readily made observations from the results obtained from the analysis of the data on location of foreign firms in Poland quite fittingly follow the theoretical supposition of early economic writers von Thünen (1826) and Marshall (1920), who state that firms choose to locate near the centers of economic activity and near markets. What is more interesting is that a number of investors in PKD classes with less representation across the country become relatively small, but significant, participants in the local economies of regions attracting fewer foreign firms.

From the results obtained in all H3 hypotheses testing whether the degree of industrial specialization in total FDI activity in a region is more likely to develop in the regions in which the most relevant economic factors for a specific industry are available. The presence or absence of relevant economic factors can have specific, clear answers for some of the regions, particularly those that maintain a clear policy focus in their industrial development path. The regions with narrowing industrial paths are: Mazowieckie, in real estate management and financial intermediation (having a strong growth of concentration due to the size and strength of the market); Podkarpackie, in manufacturing of transportation, mainly aviation and equipment (due to the presence of skilled labor and the existing industrial base); and Wielkopolskie and Śląskie in labor-intensive industries, manufacture of radio, television and communication equipment and telecommunications apparatus, and manufacture of transport equipment (due to the availability of labor and skilled labor, as well as to the size of the local market).

The presence of particular location advantages, at a local or regional level, could be a self-perpetuating, a local development path where additional growth of the local industry makes the location even more attractive for doing business (Head et al., 1995; Krugman, 1991; Wheeler and Mody, 1992; De Propris, Driffield, Menghinello, 2005) and draws additional investors into the region. For industries and regions where this research has found no significant industrial specialization strengths supported by the proposed variables, the recommendations can only be less specific. Nevertheless, in some of those regions the lack of a clear direction should be interpreted as a signal for a need of a coherent policy in promoting existing regional strengths. Such regions are Kujawsko-Pomorskie, Podlaskie, and Lubuskie. They should focus on creating supportive conditions for industries that show promise of becoming strong and important to the region's development.

The Mazowieckie region is somewhat of an anomaly, producing results counter to expectations: it has a weak relationship in the PKD classes it clearly dominates (construction industry, and financial intermediation, mostly concentrated in Mazowieckie). The reasons for investment to locate there, besides the region being a policy center, are the presence of international schools and overall highest living conditions across Poland, such as access to international transportation and logistics hubs, higher average wages and the largest agglomeration in terms of population.

From the analysis it can also be determined that the pre-EU accession period of increasing openness of the economy and cautious response of foreign investors has set the foundation for the attraction of FDI into Poland. During that period, however, foreign investors clearly followed the existing path of industrial centers similar to those described by Ellison and Glaeser (1997). These centers have begun to form in Poland ever since the era of a centrally governed economy. Following the post-EU accession period, Poland's economic environment has created deeper certainty of political and economic stability, which is reflected in a relatively sharp increase in concentrations of RLAis and RLAco, with the effect of narrowing of industrial specialization in a number of regions. Such results can be interpreted as an increase in competitiveness of those regions and creation of stronger, more sustainable agglomerations (Cantwell, 1994; Cantwell and Iammarino, 2000).

The concentration of foreign investment activity across the regions in Poland is beginning to diverge along the service and manufacturing areas. Foreign investment in service industries seems to be concentrating in areas with higher wages and access to larger markets, which support them, while manufacturing and production industries seem to concentrate along the existing paths of development, where labor is readily available and where there is a strong presence of foreign firms in the same or related industry. In some regions, where the industrial specialization is beginning to transition into the more advanced industries (manufacturing of advanced chemicals, pharmaceuticals, and telecommunication equipment), the presence of skilled labor and the amount of R&D spending are supporting factors for those activities. Those regions seem to be most strongly equipped to succeed in the industrial transition and technological development in the future. This conclusion falls along the macro-level analysis of correlation between the average of RLAis and tested economic factors.

5

The Results of the Effects of Location Choices by Industry Leading Firms Investing in Poland on the Location Choices of Small and Medium-Size Foreign Investors

5.1 Do leading firms actually lead?

This chapter examines the effect of the presence in Poland of leading companies (i.e., Fortune 500 firms) on the presence of other leading investors and of non-leading firms, by measuring the change in the level of presence of both types of firms in the participating regions (H4s). For the purpose of testing these hypotheses, H4a and H4b, a cross-sectional result for the years 2000 and 2006 is used in order to reflect the relationship between different types of firms in Poland during this period.

The participation of Fortune 500 companies was examined across regions, and their particular industries and countries of origin are identified. In addition, the key differentiation between various types of firms, leaders and followers, gives an additional attribute of regional industry strengths based on the "follow-my-leader" concept proposed by Knickerbocker (1973). In spite of the perceived salience of agglomeration clusters of global FDI distribution, locating leading multinationals within an agglomeration may not benefit all businesses equally (Shaver, 1998a; Shaver and Flyer, 2000; Alcácer and Chung, 2006; Berry, 2006). The following test is offered to determine whether the presence of a leading firm in a region of a transition economy tends to deter other leading firms of the same industry from entering that same region (H4a).

Further, this study compares the level of leading FDI, large firms identified from the PAIIZ annual industry reports for the year 2008 (Appendix 4a: pp. 277–282), to determine the effect of the presence of leading firms in the regions on other leading firms in the later stage of regional economic development.

Additionally, this study reveals the determinants behind location choice strategy for investment in selected industries based on established collocation patterns between different types of firms: leaders (Fortune 500 firms) and followers (small and medium-size firms). The test offered here will determine whether the presence of industry-leading firms in a region contributes to higher agglomeration of foreign investors from the same industry in a region – H4b. Conversely, the location patterns of leading firms that prefer locations not attractive to non-leading firms will be further confirmation of this hypothesis in the regions tested (Knickerbocker, 1973).

The tests will also address the role of direct investment, which may be dependent on the status of the regions in the national hierarchy system (Cantwell and Iammarino, 1998, 2000; Cantwell, 2009), by determining whether higher-order locations, which tend to attract the largest share of both domestic and foreign investors, also attract leading firms. Establishing the most preferred location choices for industry-leading firms across regions – in relation to other leading firms – and determining the regions with industrial specialization will help to understand why incoming foreign firms choose specific locations in Poland. Such results determine the effect of the hierarchy of the regions (Cantwell and Iammarino, 2001 and 2003) in Poland, based on their degree of attractiveness to leading foreign firms. Revealing particular existing strengths and particular weaknesses in the regions should also suggest the patterns of entry for future investors, given that such group strategies may develop by collusive actions of foreign investors (Cantwell and Mudambi, 2005) and may have a dominant effect on a region (also, Birkinshaw and Hood, 1998).

Analysis of the data offers insights as to the presence and the level of interaction at a firm level in the regions. The results of the RLAis and further RLAco may be used to determine the level of collocation, taking into account the data described in earlier sections.

The pattern of distribution of the leading firms is established along with determining whether they are the drivers of economic activity in the regions, and whether participating Fortune 500 firms were the first to mover into an area. Particular attention is placed on measuring whether leaders are drawn to the same strategic locations and followers to other locations (Knickerbocker, 1973 and Alcácer and Chung, 2007). That is, whether the presence of Fortune 500 firms attracts further specialized investment, therefore establishing a location choice pattern for other firms – H4b. The test also reveals whether leaders have a dominant presence in the regions, and therefore represent the industry, or whether their presence is attracting into the region other companies within the same or related industry. The data review on location patterns reveals the level of participation of foreign firms within the same industrial class as the participating leading firms in the region, and shows possible interactions of the small and medium-size foreign firms with Fortune 500 firms within the same region (based on this relationship and its strength).

Although, for developing regions, attracting foreign investors seems an appealing way to increase a region's competitiveness, there can be threats along the way – for example, upon developing a certain level of attractiveness, these regions run the risk of congestion and subsequently of becoming a "victim of their own success." The same factors that attracted the investment in the first place now become threatened by it. As presented by Martin and Sunley (2003), congestion effects negatively impact a region's attractiveness and slows growth, due to rising costs of labor and increasing living standards. The strategic role of this trade-off is a key element in creating a balance of growth at a rate that could prove sustainable in the long term. Such would be possible via increasing the region's capacity for continuing attractiveness due to the increase of its technological capability and a move to a higher grade of technological specialization. The last step is the most difficult to achieve, but it is the most desirable transition for any locale.

The analysis presented further shows a measure of the degree of participation between the subsidiaries of Fortune 500 companies (leaders) and the participation of small and medium-size companies (the followers), as measured by their regional participation, and will give the answer to the hypotheses raised.

5.2 Review of the findings

5.2.1 Mazowieckie region

The vast majority of the Fortune 500 firms investing in Poland are located in the Mazowieckie region. Although many firms have operations in other locations across the country, they are headquartered in Mazowieckie and predominantly in or near Warsaw, the capital city. The investment participation by Fortune 500 companies represents a number of industrial classes of activity. The most represented areas are the following: financial intermediation – five firms: Ballinger Holdings Ltd., Cigna Global Holdings, Inc., Nationwide Global Holdings, Inc., Citigroup, General Electric Corporation (GE); manufacture of chemicals and chemical products – four firms: Colgate-Palmolive America, Inc., Praxir, Inc., Procter & Gamble Mexico Holding, 3M Nederland B.V.; wholesale and retail trade, repair of motor vehicles, motorcycles and personal and household goods – three firms: Eli Lilly Nederland, Xerox Ltd., and Unisys Corporation.

Since both hypotheses H4a and H4b are closely related, they will be discussed together in this section. As already mentioned, Fortune 500 firms show the strongest presence in the Mazowieckie region; they are concentrated in three areas of economic activity: financial intermediation, manufacture of chemicals, and wholesale and retail. These are also areas of economic activity in which Mazowieckie has a decisive advantage over other regions. This advantage is shown in the RLAis index of the financial intermediation, and wholesale and retail PKD classes (Appendix 4b), while the manufacture of chemicals RLAis index remained positive throughout the period until 2006, when it dropped to below 1 at 0.96.

The dominant portion of 22 Fortune 500 firms located in the Mazowieckie region – out of 29 (75 percent) – participating during the study period are from the United States. The U.S. investors maintain a positive RLAco index in the region. Other countries have only one or, at most, two, Fortune 500 firms participating. The remaining investment in Mazowieckie falls into the PKD classes that have a dominant countrywide presence reflected in Mazowieckie. This confirms that small and medium-size firms in those industries follow leading firms. From an historical perspective, these foreign investments, including investments from leading companies, are established in the PKD classes with already-existing regional strength.

5.2.2 The cases of attraction effect in Mazowieckie region

As to the concentration of industrial participation among leading firms in the Mazowieckie region, this rate is increasing in the majority of the participating industries (Appendix 4b). The financial intermediation class concentrates all of the Fortune 500 firms in the above-mentioned region and maintains an increasingly positive presence of leading firms – from three to five during the period. This class is only one of a few industries in the region to maintain a high concentration index measure of RLAis at 2.10 in the year 2006; however this index shows a decline from 4.38 in the year 2000. This result indicates that the presence of leading firms in the region also attracts other small and medium firms into the region. Besides having the highest concentration of any agglomerations in Poland and a high presence of business activity, this region also aligns with national policy, which is an additional attraction to locating foreign business there.

The manufacture of chemicals and chemical products class maintains a stable presence of four leading firms in the region; however, the RLAis index measure for the class as a whole is declining steadily, reaching a level below 1, at an RLAis of 0.93 in 2006. In this class, the decline of participation of foreign firms is observed as well. This result follows the finding of Shaver (1998b), Shaver and Flyer (2000), Alcácer and Chung (2007), and Berry (2006), who determined that the presence of leading industry firms in an agglomeration may not benefit all businesses equally. Due to a relatively high presence of leaders, smaller firms might be prone to move out of those regions. A similar effect is observed in the manufacture of machinery and equipment, and in wholesale and retail trade and repair classes, where leading firms maintain a steady presence while small and medium foreign firms move away from the region. These depend on the cost of labor and skilled labor, which is most expensive in the region and can be a significant deterrent to small and medium-size foreign investors, which also have a higher ease of movement across regions (Lin and Saggi, 1999).

In the case of the manufacture of electrical machinery and apparatus it is clear that the diminishing presence of leading firms also has a negative effect on the RLAis index of foreign firms in the industry in the region. However, looking at the actual number of participants it appears that they are moving away, or following the leading firm. Lucent Technologies Network Systems Netherlands BV has moved to the neighboring region of Kujawsko-Pomorskie; however, it did not cause small and medium-size firms to follow suit, so that the receiving region has the presence of Lucent alone. The conclusion can be drawn that small and medium firms in the industry moved out of Mazowieckie due to competition pressure and were not following the leader.

The manufacture of transport equipment maintains a steady but rotating presence with regard to leading foreign firms in Mazowieckie, with the increasing presence of small and medium-size foreign firms in the same class. The leading firms in the industry maintain the same level of presence – one moved out and one moved in – which seems to be a historical result in the region as if only one leading firm in the industry could be supported by the region. While the rotation of leading firms is taking place, the total number of foreign firms in the class is increasing in RLAis measure, which is well below 1 for the region – ranging from RLAis 0.19 in year 2000 to 0.37 in year 2006. The actual number of foreign firms in the region has increased from four to nine, with a temporary dip to three firms during the leading firms' transition period. This result for the leading firms in the industry could project a congestion effect, while for the small and medium-size firms it could be interpreted as an opportunity that they can exploit.

The real estate, rental and business activities class presents only one Fortune 500 firm in the Mazowieckie region. Its participation remains stable throughout the period. Small and medium firms, however, increased their presence in the region from seven in the year 2000 to 38 firms in the year 2006, while also increasing the RLAis index from 1.24 to 1.73 for the same period. The influx and concentration of foreign firms in the industry in Mazowieckie are driven primarily by the highest concentration of population, highest wages among the regions, and business activity level present due to the economic and political centrality of the region. This service-driven activity type shows strong growth during the period, and specifically after the accession of Poland into the European Union.

The transport, storage and communication class also has gained one Fortune 500 firm in the class during the study period, in 2004. Reclassification of PKD activity has also put this industry in the rank. Although there is only one leading firm, it has a strong presence of foreign companies in the class in the region as well. The presence of the leader seems to create an attraction effect, although this remains to be monitored further as there are only short-term results in this class for the final three years of the study.

The above-mentioned industries seem to establish themselves following the leader firm, creating an attraction effect due to sizable markets. This outcome follows the findings of Martin and Sunley (2003) and Pitelis (2010), especially with regard to the service-oriented industries – transport; storage and communication; real estate; rental and business activities; and financial intermediation. Opposite this, the production-oriented industries – the manufacture of chemicals and chemical products, and manufacture of electrical machinery and apparatus – seem to depend on the market size of the region and on the historically established base for those industries.

The region manages to capitalize on its leading position in FDI attraction and its central role for a number of industries. That position allows it to attract a substantial number of leading foreign firms in the post-study period of years 2007 and 2008 (Appendix 4a: pp. 277–282). Within those years, 15 leading firms from a number of industries establish themselves in the region, which is a 52 percent increase over the previous period of 2000 to 2006. Most noteworthy entrants are from the United States,

Germany, and South Korea. All new firms follow the existing industrial strength pattern of the region.

Of the five new entrants from the United States, three are in the business service industry, with the two others being in manufacturing of pharmaceuticals and of chemical products. The new entrants are following other leading firms located in the region and are registered as having research and development facilities.

New leading German firms in Mazowieckie are in the manufacturing of pharmaceutical products and of chemical products, with a specific activity class of biotech and pharmaceuticals, while South Korean firms' activity also possesses R&D facilities in the manufacturing of electrical machinery and apparatus and telecommunications. Additionally, single firms from France, Hungary, Sweden, and the United Kingdom in chemical and closely related pharmaceutical industries have entered the region. These new entrants seem to further indicate an upgrade of technological capability and development of industrial specialization in Mazowieckie.

5.2.3 The cases of congestion effect in Mazowieckie region

The manufacture of fabrics and textiles in the Mazowieckie region has one Fortune 500 firm moving in during the period researched, causing RLAis for the industry to decline. The manufacture of food, drinks and tobacco products similarly follows suit, having a steady presence of leading firms in the region with a slowly declining presence of other foreign firms in the class. In the mining and quarrying class, instead, one leading firm entering the region pushed out a smaller firm. These instances represent the congestion effect, especially in labor-intensive manufacturing sectors. This result follows the finding of Martin and Sunley (2003), who determined the effect of increasing cost of labor and living standards in a region on small and medium-size firms, which are generally less resilient and unable to compete effectively with the changing circumstances. In contrast, leading firms having potentially vaster resources, are able to protect their positions.

Not represented in the final year of the study were leading firms in the following classes: hotels, restaurants, and property management; manufacture of consumer products; and manufacture of other non-metal goods. The hotels, restaurants, and property management class consisting of all foreign firms managed, however, to have positive RLAis without the presence of a leading firm. While the manufacture of consumer products and manufacture of other non-metal goods classes collectively achieved very low RLAis or recorded no presence at all. This finding can be an indication of higher labor cost in the region, affecting the decision-making process of MNCs regarding locating in the region.

Capital investment was not represented in the final two years of the study due to reclassification of the PKD classes. However, the two leading firms in the class were not present at the end of the study period. During the time of leading firms' presence, the participation and presence of other foreign firms in the class also increased in real terms and declined only slightly, remaining at well above 1 for the RLAis index.

5.3 Podkarpackie and Wielkopolskie regions

Podkarpackie and Wielkopolskie each attract four Fortune 500 investors. The Podkarpackie region is host to: Owens-Illinois, Inc.; Goodrich Aerospace Canada, Ltd.; Lear Corporation; and United Technologies Holding S.A. Wielkopolskie hosts: Aesculap AG; H.J. Heinz Company; Wm. Wrigley Jr. Company; and ArvinMeritor. The Fortune 500 firms in Wielkopolskie invest in manufacture of food, drinks and tobacco products – two firms refer to the class of manufacture of electrical machinery and apparatus (with a sub-class of manufacture of medical and surgical equipment and orthopedic appliances – one firm) and of manufacture of transport equipment (with a sub-class of manufacture of parts and accessories for motor vehicles and their engines – one firm).

The presence of Fortune 500 firms in the Wielkopolskie region maintains a positive trajectory: at the beginning of the study period it hosted only two firms and ended with four fortune 500 firms in 2006. All industries with leading firms' participation maintain rising RLAis indexes, with the manufacture of electrical machinery and apparatus, and manufacture of food, drinks and tobacco products having an RLAis index above 1, at 1.81 and 1.80 respectively. At the same time, the manufacture of transport equipment maintains an RLAis index of 0.77 in the region in 2006. Although this last measure of RLAis is below 1 it has shown relative growth of concentration from an RLAis index of 0.58 in the year 2000.

Overall, industries with participation of Fortune 500 firms in the Wielkopolskie region do not seem to be affected by the congestion effect and appear to be able to attract and accommodate foreign firms regardless of the firm's size. In the immediate post-2006 period the region attracts three new leading firms. Two of those firms are in the manufacture of pharmaceuticals and medicinal chemicals PKD class and are from France and Switzerland. The third new leading foreign investor is in the manufacture of electrical machinery and apparatus PKD class and comes from the Netherlands. Their presence follows the industrial specialization pattern set in the region in the early 2000–2006 period.

Table 5.1 Fortune 500 firms in Wielkopolskie

Investor name	Fortune 500 – 2000	Fortune 500 – 2006	Fortune 500 – 2000 and 2006	% change of the 2000 RLAis	change of the 2000 RLAis	change in the presence of F500 firms	Location	Województwo	Country-of-origin	Activities (PKD)
Aesculap AG	1	1	1	1.65	+	=	Nowy Tomyśl	Wielkopolskie	Germany	Manufacture of electrical machinery and apparatus;
Wm. Wrigley Jr. Company	0	1	0	1.09	+	+	Poznań	Wielkopolskie	USA	Manufacture of food, drinks and tobacco products;
H.J. Heinz Company	0	1	0			+	Pudliszki	Wielkopolskie	USA	Manufacture of food, drinks and tobacco products;
ArvinMeritor	0	1	0	1.32	+	+	Swarzędz	Wielkopolskie	USA	Manufacture of transport equipment;
Dana Corporation	1	0	0			–	Gostyn	Wielkopolskie	USA	Manufacture of transport equipment;
Total	2	4	1							
Increase since year 2000		100%								
Present in both year 2000 and 2006			25%							

Source: Based on data obtained from the Polish Information and Foreign Investment Agency (PAIIZ) and the author's own analysis.

In the Podkarpackie region, the majority of participating Fortune 500 firms represent the manufacture of transport equipment industrial class, which reflects a positive RLAis index at 4.24. A strong RLAco index measure is registered for the American Fortune 500 firms, all four firms until 2006 and, in the post-2006 period, five out of six firms. The manufacture of non-metal goods class does not have a positive RLAis index in the region, however.

All leading firms in Podkarpackie are U.S. corporations and it is the same in Wielkopolskie, which hosts three U.S. and one German firm. The Podkarpackie region has a quite specific orientation of investment, with three firms focusing on the manufacture of transport equipment (two in the manufacture of aircraft and spacecraft, and one Fortune 500 firm investing in the manufacture of parts and accessories for motor vehicles and their engines) and one leading firm in the manufacture of other non-metal goods, sub-class of the manufacture of glass and glass products. In the manufacture of transport equipment class, one leading firm is attracted during the period of this study and the RLAis measure is nearly doubled during that period from 2.01 to 3.99 for foreign firms in the class. The manufacture of electrical machinery and apparatus with the presence of one leading firm also increases the RLAis measure for the class.

Since 2006 the region attracted one additional leading firm from the United States in the manufacture of transport equipment industrial class, and one from France in the manufacture of chemicals and chemical products PKD class. This further sharpens the industrial specialization of the region and gives it a rather rare country-of-origin locus of U.S. firms.

Un the Podkarpackie region, the manufacture of other non-metal goods is represented by one leading firm for the whole class throughout the period of this study, maintaining a monopolistic position while representing the glass manufacturing sub-class. There are no small and medium-size firms in this class in the region or in the entire country. The supply of electricity, gas, and water sector also paints another story. It is represented by one leading firm, Enron (in the beginning of the period), and due to the demise of Enron has no leading firm at the end of the period. The region's RLAis index for the class also declines, as in real terms the region is host to three foreign firms in the class in the year 2000, while it hosts only one firm in the year 2006. In this case, the presence of the leading firm is clearly an attraction to other firms to establish their operations in the region.

Table 5.2 Fortune 500 firms in Podkarpackie

Investor name	Fortune 500 – 2000	Fortune 500 – 2006	Fortune 500 – 2000 and 2006	% change of the 2000 RLAis	change of the 2000 RLAis	change in the presence of F500 firms	Location	Województwo	Country-of-origin	Activities (PKD)
United Technologies Automotive	1	1	1	1.32	+	=	Rzeszów/ Mielec	Podkarpackie	USA	Manufacture of electrical machinery and apparatus
Owens-Illinois Inc.	1	1	1	0.79	–	=	Jarosław	Podkarpackie	USA	Manufacture of other non-metal goods;
Goodrich Aerospace Canada LTD	0	1	0	1.98	+	+	Krosno	Podkarpackie	USA	Manufacture of transport equipment;
Lear Corporation	1	1	1	1.98	+	=	Mielec	Podkarpackie	USA	Manufacture of transport equipment;
Enron International	1	0	0	0.14	–	–	Nowa Sarzyna	Podkarpackie	USA	Electricity, gas and water supply
Total	4	4	3							
Increase since year 2000		0%								
Present in both year 2000 and 2006			75%							

Source: Based on data obtained from the Polish Information and Foreign Investment Agency (PAIIZ) and the author's own analysis

5.4 Pomorskie and Śląskie regions

The Pomorskie and Śląskie regions attract investment of only two and three Fortune 500 firms, respectively. All leading investors that remain in these two regions originate in the United States. The Pomorskie region has a marginally positive, and slowly declining, RLAco for U.S. investors, finishing at 1.08 in 2006. In Śląskie, on the other hand, U.S. investors have an RLAco index below 1 throughout the period, ending at 0.55.

The investment classes represented by the leading firms in the regions are: the manufacture of transport equipment, and real estate, rental and business activities in Pomorskie, and the manufacture of machinery and equipment and of transport equipment in Śląskie.

In Pomorskie, the manufacture of transport equipment presents a positive overall RLAis index, finishing at 1.692 in year 2006, while the real estate, rental and business activities have a negative index measure for the region. In the Śląskie region, the manufacture of machinery and equipment and of transport equipment both maintain positive RLAis index for the industries.

The presence of Fortune 500 firms in the Śląskie region remains at a steady level with a bit of turnover: some firms move out and others come into the region. The manufacture of transport equipment maintains a steady presence of two foreign investors, which in 2006 are: General Motors Corporation and Tenneco Global Holding, Inc. All participating foreign investors in the manufacture of transport equipment industry maintain an RLAis index of 2.17; however, this measure is slowly decreasing in the region.

The manufacture of machinery and equipment in Śląskie has added one Fortune 500 firm during the period and also maintains an increasing RLAis index at 1.46 for the PKD class. The remaining industry with a Fortune 500 firm present during the period is the manufacture of metal products. Its investor does not participate in the year 2006; however, the total industry's RLAis remains positive at 2.68 and is slowly declining.

The Pomorskie region maintains a steady presence of two Fortune 500 firms in two separate industries: the manufacture of transport equipment and the real estate, rental and business activities. Both firms entered the region during the period of research and have maintained their presence since. The RLAis measures for both industries represented by Fortune 500 firms have, however, a declining trajectory, with the measure for real estate, rental and business activities moving below 1 (ranging to 0.75 in 2006 from 2.6 in the year 2000), suggesting a dominant position

Table 5.3 Fortune 500 firms in Pomorskie

Investor name	Fortune 500 – 2000	Fortune 500 – 2006	Fortune 500 – 2000 and 2006	% change of the 2000 RLAis	change of the 2000 RLAis	change in the presence of F500 firms	Location	Województwo	Country-of-origin	Activities (PKD)
Eaton	0	1	0	0.90	–	+	Tczew	Pomorskie	USA	Manufacture of transport equipment;
Intel Europe Inc.	0	1	0	0.29	–	+	Gdańsk	Pomorskie	USA	Real estate, rental and business activities;
Total	0	2	0							
Increase since year 2000		100%								
Present in both year 2000 and 2006			0%							

Source: Based on data obtained from the Polish Information and Foreign Investment Agency (PAIIZ) and the author's own analysis.

Table 5.4 Fortune 500 firms in Śląskie

Investor name	Fortune 500 – 2000	Fortune 500 – 2006	Fortune 500 – 2000 and 2006	% change of the 2000 RLAis	change of the 2000 RLAis	change in the presence of F500 firms	Location	Województwo	Country-of-origin	Activities (PKD)
Timken Company	0	1	0	2.67	+	+	Sosnowiec	Śląskie	USA	Manufacture of machinery and equipment;
Foster Wheeler Energy	1	0	0	0.74	–	–	Sosnowiec	Śląskie	Finland	Manufacture of metal products
General Motors Corporation	1	1	1	0.81	–	+	Gliwice	Śląskie	USA	Manufacture of transport equipment;
Tenneco Global Holding Inc	0	1	0		–	+	Rybnik	Śląskie	USA	Manufacture of transport equipment;
TRW	1	0	0		–	–	Czechowice-Dziedzice	Śląskie	USA	Manufacture of transport equipment;
Total	3	3	1							
Increase since year 2000		0%								
Present in both year 2000 and 2006			33%							

Source: Based on data obtained from the Polish Information and Foreign Investment Agency (PAIIZ) and the author's own analysis.

of the leading firms and crowding out the industry's small and medium-size firms from the region.

Beyond the core period of this study, in the years 2007 and 2008, five new large investors enter the region. Three of them are from the United States, with one each from France and India. Their PKD classifications follow regional industrial specialization patterns, with three firms being engaged in the business activity class and with one in each of the supply of electricity, gas, and water, and the manufacture of electrical machinery and apparatus classes. During the same period, the Śląskie region also manages to attract four new foreign investors: two from the United States, and one each from Canada and the Netherlands. Two of the new foreign firms locating in the Śląskie region fit the existing industrial specialization pattern of the manufacture of transport equipment, and two are in the business services class, adding to one small firm present in this region in the class.

5.5 Kujawsko-Pomorskie and Łódzkie regions

The regions of Kujawsko-pomorskie and Łódzkie end the period with one Fortune 500 firm each; however, one other firm per region participates during the period. The remaining Fortune 500 investor in Kujawsko-pomorskie, Lucent Technologies Network Systems, originates from the United States and represents the manufacture of electrical machinery and apparatus class. The region does not have a strong RLAco for the U.S. investment and only a short history of investment, as Lucent entered the region only in 2006. The designated PKD class of the investor shows an RLAis index at 1.01 in that year, showing a neutral measure and no strength.

The leading firm which moved out of Kujawsko-pomorskie during the period, General Mills, participated in the manufacture of food PKD class, which continually maintains a positive RLAis at 2.57 in the year 2006, rising from 2.07 in the year 2000 for the industry in the region. Therefore, in the case of the food processing class, attraction of foreign firms is observed along with the presence of the leading firm and after it terminated its presence in the region. The fact that the industry's leading firm has left the region, where the presence of small and medium-size foreign firms is strong, apparently indicates the leader's preference to maintain a monopolistic position. The region does not attract any leading firms in the two years following the core study period.

The Łódzkie region hosts a single Fortune 500 firm, PepsiCo., which represents the United States and the manufacture of food, drinks, and

Table 5.5 Fortune 500 firms in Kujawsko-pomorskie

Investor name	Fortune 500 – 2000	Fortune 500 – 2006	Fortune 500 – 2000 and 2006	% change of the 2000 RLAis	change of the 2000 RLAis	change in the presence of F500 firms	Location	Województwo	Country-of-origin	Activities (PKD)
Lucent Technologies Network Systems Netherlands BV	0	1	0	1	+	+	Bydgoszcz	Kujawsko-Pomorskie	USA	Manufacture of electrical machinery and apparatus;
General Mills	1	0	0	1.24	+	_	Torun	Kujawsko-Pomorskie	USA	Manufacture of food processing
Total	1	1	0							
Increase since year 2000		0%								
Present in both year 2000 and 2006			0%							

Source: Based on data obtained from the Polish Information and Foreign Investment Agency (PAIIZ) and the author's own analysis.

Table 5.6 Fortune 500 firms in Łódzkie

Investor name	Fortune 500 – 2000	Fortune 500 – 2006	Fortune 500 – 2000 and 2006	% change of the 2000 RLAis	change of the 2000 RLAis	change in the presence of F500 firms	Location	Województwo	Country-of-origin	Activities (PKD)
Harris	1	0	0	0.73	–	–	Lodz	Łódzkie	Austria	wholesale and retail trade
PepsiCo	1	1	1	0.84	–	=	Łódź	Łódzkie	USA	Manufacture of food, drinks and tobacco products;
Total	2	1	1							
Increase since year 2000		–50%								
Present in both year 2000 and 2006			–50%							

Source: Based on data obtained from the Polish Information and Foreign Investment Agency (PAIIZ) and the author's own analysis.

tobacco products PKD class. Both RLAco and RLAis indexes reflect weak measures (RLA below 1) for the United States and the PKD class in the region, with seven firms participating in the industrial class activity in the year 2006. The RLAis measure however maintains a steady level of growth for the region and attracts five to seven foreign firms in the industry throughout the period. The presence in this region of the leading firm, PepsiCo., seems to offer opportunities for investment in the PKD class in the region.

The region of Łódzkie receives two leading firms in the year 2008. The new firms are in the manufacture of transport equipment and business services PKD classes, which have no significant strength in the RLAis index in the region.

5.6 The regions with a single leading firm

The regions of Dolnośląskie, Lubelskie, Lubuskie, and Opolskie each attract a single Fortune 500 investor. The mix of the firms represented in Table 5.4 below reveals little of a common thread, except that most of the leading investors in the PKD class enter the respective region during the study period (with the exception of Caterpillar, Inc., in Lubelskie, which represents an industry maintaining a strong RLAis index measure for the participating PKD class in the region).

The Fortune 500 investor in Dolnośląskie, Autoliv AB, is from Sweden and represents the manufacture of transport equipment class. For this region, Swedish investment shows weak signs of concentration, at 0; however, the manufacture of transport equipment class shows significant strength in Dolnośląskie, with an RLAis index of 3.70, while that region hosts 20 investors in the class. Therefore, both the presence of leading firms in the industrial class represented and the total regional industrial specialization of the same class have an increasing measure in the region. This result shows that the leading firm is not a threat to other types of firms in the industry entering the region.

The Lubelskie region hosts an American firm, Caterpillar, Inc., representing the manufacture of transport equipment class, with a sub-class of manufacture of parts and accessories for motor vehicles and their engines. Both RLAco and RLAis indexes in the region show a relative measure that is very close to 1, with no specific strength. Especially interesting is the fact that Caterpillar is one of two U.S. investors and the only representative of the manufacture of transport equipment class in the Lubelskie region. The presence of Caterpillar is very important for this region, which is situated along the eastern border and shows one of

Table 5.7 Regions with a single Fortune 500 firm

Investor name	Fortune 500 – 2000	Fortune 500 – 2006	Fortune 500 – 2000 and 2006	% change of the 2000 RLAis	change of the 2000 RLAis	change in the presence of F500 firms	Location	Województwo	Country-of-origin	Activities (PKD)
Autoliv AB	0	1	0	1.93	+	+	Oława	Dolnośląskie	Sweden	Manufacture of transport equipment;
Increase since year 2000		100%								
Present in both year 2000 and 2006			0%							
Caterpillar Inc.	1	1	1	1	=	=	Janów Lubelski	Lubelskie	USA	Manufacture of transport equipment;
Increase since year 2000		0%								
Present in both year 2000 and 2006			100%							
Sara Lee D/E N.V.	0	1	0	1.68	+	+	Gorzów Wielkopolski	Lubuskie	The Netherlands	Manufacture of leather and leather products;
Increase since year 2000		100%								
Present in both year 2000 and 2006			0%							
Visteon Automotive Systems	0	1	0	1.79	+	+	Praszka	Opolskie	USA	Manufacture of transport equipment;
Increase since year 2000		100%								
Present in both year 2000 and 2006			0%							

the lowest levels of foreign investment activity, but gaining singlehandedly a positive RLAis in the PKD class for the region. This example may be the case of a congestion effect, although the region's eastern location may have more to do with the actual level of attractiveness of foreign firms to it.

The Lubuskie region hosts Sara Lee D/E N.V. of the Netherlands, registered in the manufacture of leather and leather products class. The region also lists RLAco at precisely 1, which is a reflection of neither strength nor weakness for the Dutch firms in the region, and a strongly positive RLAis, registering at 16.5, mostly due to the low presence of FDI in the manufacture of leather and leather products PKD class across the country. The presence of the leading firm in the region may also be a reason for maintaining a steady presence of foreign firms in the PKD class without an increase or a decline from the time of the leader's entry. The entry of the leading firm by itself in year 2002, however, might have caused one of the investors in the class to leave the region and reduce the presence of foreign firms in the class from three to two. In this region the presence of two firms indicates a very high level of strength, which should be read in that context.

The Opolskie region hosts Visteon Automotive Systems, from the United States, participating in the manufacture of transport equipment PKD class. The region has a weak measure of RLAco index for U.S. firms, while its RLAis for the manufacture of transport equipment PKD class is relatively strong at 1.60, with only two firms in this PKD class having operations in this region. After the brief absence of firms in the PKD class in the region, and after the entry of the leading firm, another foreign investor in the class is also registered in the region.

Overall, Fortune 500 investors with a single leading firm present in a region seem to be attracted into the industry, which already exhibits strong concentration of foreign firms in the above-mentioned region. Such may be the case where the leading firm is looking for the resources-available, manufacturing-based and labor-intensive activity. In the instances discussed above, the effect of the presence of a leading firm does seem to have a positive effect on the attraction of other firms in the same industry into the region.

Out of the regions attracting only one leading investor each in the years 2000 to 2006 one, Dolnośląskie, has significantly increased the number of leading investors into the region by nine, following only the Mazowieckie region. The majority of the new foreign firms, six, are in the business services PKD class and related to the consulting or IT fields. The two following firms are in telecommunications and the manufacture of electrical machinery and apparatus classes. The remaining company is in the PKD class represented in the early period of the study, the manufacture of transport equipment. The majority of the new entrants are from the United States, which had an RLAco index of 1.08 for the U.S. firms in the region.

5.7 The reasons and method of coexistence between large firms and SMEs in Poland

The review of the location of Fortune 500 firms across Poland and a closer analysis of the specific regions indicate that the majority of Fortune 500 firms are located in regions with a strong presence of foreign firms in their PKD classes. Conversely, it can also mean that foreign small and medium enterprises (SMEs) follow the industry-leading firms and locate near them. These following firms may, indeed, be in search of both the factors of production and expertise necessary to further their activities. Since the Fortune 500 firms, in most cases, were present in the locale before the majority of the SMEs, it can be inferred that the Fortune 500 firms led the way for foreign firms to settle in the particular locations.

These results are consistent with the literature that indicates the trajectory of locational choice by firms within the same industry by following their leading peers in developed economies (Kaname Akamatsu in the 1930s; Knickerbocker, 1973; Kojima, 2000; Cantwell et al., 2000). This theoretical and empirical view is supported by the data in this study, since the majority of Fortune 500 firms in Poland, a developing economy, maintain an early presence, while the small and medium investors enter and exit the country more frequently (which is also supported by the data).

The location of the Fortune 500 firms does, however, seem to indicate that the presence of the leading firms does not attract their country-of-origin peers into the same location. In other words, firms from the same country-of-origin locating in Poland do not seem to follow in a collusive way as was suggested by the studies of Kaname Akamatsu in the 1930s, Kojima (2000) and Knickerbocker (1973), but choose locations for their operations near industry peers rather than near firms sharing a common country-of-origin. The exceptions here are the U.S. firms in Mazowieckie.

The colocation patterns between various types of foreign firms show that Fortune 500 firms have the strongest presence in the Mazowieckie region: they are concentrated in three areas of economic activity, namely financial intermediation, the manufacture of chemicals, and wholesale and retail. These are also areas of economic activities in which

Mazowieckie has a decisive advantage over other regions. This advantage is shown in the RLAis index in financial intermediation, and in wholesale and retail PKD classes. Contrarily, the manufacture of chemicals RLAis index remains positive throughout the period until 2006, when it drops to below 1 at 0.96.

Particular attention is placed on the results of the test in order to determine whether leaders are drawn to the same strategic location, and followers to other locations – H4a – (Knickerbocker, 1973; Alcácer and Chung, 2007) by evaluating the RLAis index measure of foreign firms' participation in an industry. The same focus is adopted to determine whether the presence of Fortune 500 firms attracts further specialized investment, therefore establishing a location choice pattern for other firms – H4b. The test should also reveal whether leaders have a dominant presence in the region, therefore representing the industry, or whether their presence is attracting other companies within the same or related industry into the region.

The presence of the U.S. Fortune 500 firms in Mazowieckie – the capital region, which attracts the most investors – seems to have an impact on the location of small and medium investors from the United States into the region. The RLAco index for the U.S. firms in Mazowieckie is at 1.28, which gives a relative advantage to the region, also indicating an attraction for firms originating from the United States. Some industries in the Mazowieckie region, especially those of established labor-intensive classes such as the manufacturing of transport equipment and manufacture of chemicals, tend to follow the leading firms. The majority of the region's leading foreign firms operate in service-oriented industries.

The presence of leading firms in Mazowieckie does not seem to have a deterring effect on new incoming leading firms. However, existing concentrations of leading firms in the region focus on the areas of PKD classes that depend on the expected close interaction with nationwide industrial and policy governance.

The presence of Fortune 500 investors from Cyprus in the region of Mazowieckie bears mentioning: said investors hold a positive RLAco at 2.68 for Cyprus firms in the Mazowieckie region. The result is based however on the participation of all three Cyprus firms investing in Poland and located in that region alone.

The Fortune 500 firms in the Wielkopolskie region do not seem to be affected by the congestion effect and seem to be able to attract and accommodate foreign firms regardless of the firms' size. The region receives additional foreign firms that continue to settle in the region following the leaders in the industry.

There are some distinct exceptions, however. The only eastern region maintaining a steady strong presence of Fortune 500 firms is Podkarpackie. This region maintains a high positive RLAco index for U.S. firms investing in the dominant manufacture of the transport equipment industry class, with concentrated specialization in the manufacture of aircraft and spacecraft. This concentration is significant for the region and gives Podkarpackie its clear advantage.

The regions attracting a single Fortune 500 investor – Dolnośląskie, Lubelskie, Lubuskie, and Opolskie – maintain a low RLAco index measure for the country of origin of the participating Fortune 500 investors. The most notable exception here is Lubelskie, with only a marginally positive RLAco at 1.02, but attracting only two U.S. firms. The pattern of proximate location of single leading investors in the regions show that the presence of a single leading firm in the industry may deter other leading firms in the same industry to locate within that region, therefore supporting hypothesis H4a. The same can be concluded for the majority of regions with the presence of multiple Fortune 500 firms in various industries.

The presence of leading firms in regions with the lowest presence of FDI seems, however, to be rather a deterrent for new firms in the same industry to enter the region as the leading firm, therefore having a negative effect on those regions. This result is an indication of a congestion effect, showing that not all firms are able to benefit equally from entering the same locale (also Shaver, 1998b; Shaver and Flyer, 2000; Alcácer and Chung, 2007; Berry, 2006).

The regions with three or more leading firms (with the exception of Mazowieckie) seem able to attract more foreign firms in the same industry as leading firms. The small and medium-size foreign firms in production-focused industries seem to be deterred from entering the Mazowieckie region, with its presence of leading firms. The exception here are service-oriented industries, which seem to attract foreign SMEs into the region in increasing numbers.

The period immediately following the time span of this study gives additional perspective as to the future ability of the regions to attract major investors. Overall, foreign firms that entered Poland in the years 2007 and 2009 followed the initial industrial specialization developing in particular regions. In addition, larger agglomerations – those centered in Warsaw, Mazowieckie; Poznan, Wielkopolskie, Krakow, Małopolskie; Wroclaw, Dolnośląskie; and Gdansk Pomorskie – are increasingly able to attract investment in knowledge-intensive industries, as those agglomerations and regions also offer an ample pool of skilled labor due to hosting a number of universities and technical schools. These regions are also homes to the largest markets for products and services in Poland.

In summary, the results show a pattern of colocation of various types of firms, leaders and followers, across regions in Poland, and they determine preferred location choice by type of firm, industrial class, and country-of-origin in relation to the level of existing economic activity in the regions: thereby providing answers to the hypotheses. These findings are quite important to local policy makers and foreign enterprises considering setting up operations there and, by doing so, entering one of the largest new markets of the EU.

6
Final Analysis of FDI Patterns Across Regions in Poland and Policy Recommendations

This research identifies and reveals the existing preferred location choices for FDI within Poland and determines specific geographic advantages and heterogeneity of its regions. The results may be found relevant to future investors in determining preferred locations for establishing their subsidiaries in Poland. This research also provides a framework for the analysis of location decisions by multinational firms in the regions within developing economies by addressing the questions raised.

The explored topics play an important role as components of research in the areas of global flows of foreign direct investment, location of multinational firms' subsidiaries, and the development of regions in new free-market economies. These topics recognize that FDI alone is an important economic factor substantially affecting global choices of production location based on industrial specialization of the investor and the strengths of the regions within the host country. The importance of the contribution of developing local clusters, their competitiveness and sustainability, become more significant in the increasingly globalized economic structure of production and new markets than ever before. The latest technological advancements and economic globalization manifested in lower transportation and communication costs, in access to cheaper labor and resources, and in increasing complexity of the global economy motivate multinational corporations to search for those advantages. In the process, MNCs become distributors of foreign direct investment while themselves searching to acquire needed resources and skills. On the receiving side are national and local governments attempting to attract such investment from abroad in hopes of providing a financial lifeline to their transitioning economies.

As the outcome of this research, hypotheses H1 and H2 reveal, relative agglomeration strengths of foreign investors' presence by the degree of regional industrial specialization and by country-of-origin, as measured by RLAis and RLAco indexes, the results of which show in the case of some regions, the industrial specialization and country-of-origin concentration where these advantages are not possible to distinguish from the primary data. The RLAis and RLAco index results represent the industrial specialization of foreign firms and country-of-origin concentrations by presenting a reliable measure of those strengths.

The analysis of the data on location patterns in real terms shows a southwestern trajectory of concentration of foreign firms related proximately to the exogenous – Western European – markets. The geographical exception is Mazowieckie, capital region in the east-central part of the country, which has the advantage of infrastructure and regulatory and financial institutions – as supported by Campos and Kinoshita's (2006)[1] framework, which indicates that workforce size and skill, population, and size of the internal market of a region are the drivers behind the motivation to locate there.

Additionally, many peripheral regions, especially along the eastern border (such as Lubelskie, Podkarpackie, Podlaskie, Świętokrzyskie, and Warmińsko-Mazurskie), show narrowing industrial specializations and diminishing country-of-origin presence of the participating foreign firms investing in those regions. This finding broadly follows Krugman (1991), who emphasized the strength of the industry center versus the periphery in economic activity. The regions located along the periphery are historically less attractive to foreign investors as compared to centrally located regions (e.g., Cheng and Kwan, 2000; Evans, 2003; Cieślik, 2004). These results relate to many factors but, most importantly here, the periphery generally has lower internal market power and, especially in the case of the regions along the eastern border of Poland, is also more distant from exogenous free-trade markets, although they may offer some substantial benefits to foreign firms, such as lower labor and overhead cost (Alcácer and Chung, 2007). The eastern regions should not be dismissed, as they may become vital industrial, market, and transit points when the European Union's eastern enlargement, or even openness, will continue in the future, however distant. That possibility should remain a significant motivating factor to regional and national policymakers in Poland.

The regions along the western border of Poland (Dolnośląskie, Lubuskie, and Zachodnio-Pomorskie) also have a much lower degree of foreign investment activity; however, they seem to show a degree of specialization and slightly increasing attractiveness for foreign investors in some selected industries. This finding further reveals the dichotomy between the regions located along the western and eastern borders of Poland, as they diverge in their attractiveness to foreign firms mainly due to distance, lack of a good road network, and an historical lag in infrastructure and industrial development.

The results of this research support the findings of Lundvall (1986), Arthur (1986), and Soete (1987), that small regions (countries) are more specialized. The results presented here reflect that smaller regions, even those along the peripheries, have narrowing industrial activity in them; however, some selected existing industrial activities by foreign firms tend to increase their concentration index as compared to the concentration of those industries in other regions.

The regional industrial specialization of foreign firms in Poland reveals a hierarchy of location order among the regions, where higher-order regions, as measured by the level of RLAis, have narrower specializations and, in some cases, began the process of transitioning from lower-grade to higher-grade technologies production, indicating a possibility of growing competitiveness. Regions with the highest degree of presence of foreign firms show steps of transition from lower-grade to higher-grade technologies. The regions with a mid-range of participation of foreign firms tend to narrow their industrial specializations to fewer industries, while the regions at the lowest level of participation of foreign firms tend to narrow their specializations down to only one or two industries.

The overall findings suggest that, for the majority of the regions in Poland, their industrial specializations, across all levels of the hierarchy of attractiveness to foreign firms, tend to narrow. Such results can be explained in part by the entry of foreign firms based on the existing presence of industry. In the late 1980s and early 1990s, Polish national policy allowed and promoted privatization of government-owned enterprises. The inflow of foreign investment, which this study covers, was mainly driven by the first wave of privatization during which greenfield investment was quite rare. Due to such types of activity, industrial specialization mostly follows the existing industrial patterns in Poland. With the opening of the economy and increasing entry of foreign investors, economic activity has begun to concentrate and narrow its industrial specialization across regions. Specifically, the results discussed in this book show that such narrowing of the industrial development path begins taking place after the entry of Poland into the European Union in 2004. This act offers additional protection to foreign investors with regard to their intellectual property and promotes, as the data shows, a transition towards higher-grade industrial investment. A number of new firms in electronics, pharmaceuticals, biotech, and aviation equipment have set up operations in Poland since 2006. Also, with the entry of Poland into the EU and the slow increase of living standards, Poland's own market becomes more attractive to investors offering more advanced products and services.

Further examination of economic factors to determine which support and attract particular types of FDI into the regions and which have no attraction effect provides us with the following conclusions: Although average RLAis of the study period shows weak negative correlation with tested factors, the correlation between the factors themselves shows a strong level of significance. Here, the analysis offers insights to the relationship between availability of skilled labor with a tertiary level of education and the amount of private investment in R&D across regions, which is strong and slightly increases throughout the period. This can be interpreted as foreign investors attempting to tap into the availability of the skilled workforce available across regions. Wage levels also correlate strongly with R&D, both private and total investment in R&D, which can be a sign of success – however, that dependence can also pose a risk should skilled labor cost become too expensive, leading foreign investors to move elsewhere, as happened in Spain and Ireland a few decades after they joined the EU.

Industries which are production-driven show strong relationships between the variables indicating markets, local and proximate to them, labor pool size and skill, and regional FDI levels. Some regressions clearly indicate, as in the case of investment in R&D, that private investment in this activity has a strong relationship to foreign investment presence in participating regions, while the total amount of investment in the region – including private institutions of higher learning and government spending on R&D – has a much lower correlation coefficient to the level of presence of foreign firms.

Moreover, in the final set of hypotheses raised here, determining the aspects of the relationship between leading foreign firms and the remainder of foreign investors locating in Poland, they confirm that the presence of leading firms in regions with the lowest concentration of FDI seem to be a deterrent to new firms in the same industry. The regions with multiple leading investors (three or more), other than the Mazowieckie region (generally stronger or specialized regions) seem able to attract more foreign firms in the same industry as leading firms. In other words, the stronger regions have a higher capacity to accommodate investment and seem able to attract additional firms while, as might be expected, the weaker regions do not.

6.1 Policy and further research considerations

The results of this empirical investigation determine the contributing components and the existing reasons driving location choices of MNCs' subsidiaries within Poland and help predict future location choices of foreign subsidiaries, as the strong presence of foreign firms within a particular geographic area generally creates dependencies between suppliers, manufacturers, and markets, leading to their sustainability and growth and followed in some cases by participating firms' autonomous innovation. Although separate processes, they are closely related. Many studies connect industrial clustering with technological innovation, while this research takes innovation as the ultimate important step leading to sustainability of economic development of a region or a country. This last step can be a topic of future research.

Governmental policy implications can have a detrimental impact for multinational corporations considering entry into Poland so, in order to create inviting conditions, national and local governments should adjust their own specific policies to allow for the expansion of productive local industries to position themselves in the national and international economic scene. In the process, national and local governments should offer foreign investors access to not only low-cost and skilled labor resources and markets, but also a strong tacit and explicit economic base. As a result, creation of sustainable industrial clusters in Poland may lead to increased interdependence of firms, and to increased competitiveness and innovation in the participating industries. Although knowledge spillovers are not taken into consideration here, future studies may concentrate on these issues.

Further, this research also offers local and national policy makers recommendations as to endogenous actions in furthering the economic positioning and success of their regions. These recommendations are arrived at by means of testing the existing strengths of the particular locales – mainly labor, skilled labor, and markets – and emphasizing them to present and future investors. The policies in the regions that foresee incoming foreign investment supporting the transition of the existing economic base into a higher-grade technological expertise – policies that take into consideration the peripheral regions, especially those along the eastern border – will have clear guidelines as to the specific focal industries which may be the vehicles to those regions' future growth. For both economic and policy reasons, it is important to determine and accentuate the strengths of the nation's regions and their ability to contribute to the attracting and sustaining of FDI flows. This finding follows the results of the study by de Mello Jr. (1997), suggesting that a better environment for domestic investment is necessary to increase the country's or region's ability to host foreign investment. Where competitive conditions for domestic investment are not present, the success of policies designed to attract FDI may result in adverse outcomes for local firms.

Overall, it is determined here that the economic environment of Poland offers a platform for retention and development of important strategic production capabilities, which often are moved out from the developed countries of Europe, mainly to China. Also, sustaining the presence of manufacturing capabilities can well serve Europe's economic competitiveness and security.

This book provides an original contribution to the analysis of the location decisions by multinational firms in regions within Poland, by addressing the questions raised. It also offers a framework that will allow future investors, policymakers, and researchers to determine a location selection for investment within developing economies based on the optimal benefit for their type of investment and the firm size, based on the evidence of the regions in Poland.

7
Afterword

7.1 Present situation related to FDI in Poland

Since the end of the period of the study covered in this book, Poland keeps moving steadily towards being an attractive destination for FDI in Central Europe. In fact, according to the latest available information, mainly from media reports,[1] Poland has established itself as a leader in FDI-related job creation over the last few years, and not only in Central Europe but in Europe as a whole. According to the same report, only the UK and Russia were better. Poland came in third (having been seventh last year), with a 67.3 percent increase in foreign investment related jobs.

Also for the year 2012, according to an Ernst & Young survey,[2] Poland attracted 22.3 percent more FDI projects. Most of the foreign investment projects originated with the United States and Germany, with a major industrial inclination towards automotive and logistics sectors. Not surprisingly, such is the case as these sectors seem to be industrial strengths revealed in this book as well.

A review of the latest available industry reports presented by PAIIZ further show that, in most industries, the presence of leading foreign firms is increasing. This trend tends to support further the findings of this research for the period tested and indicates that the accession of Poland into the European Union has, at least temporarily, achieved initial goals in terms of economic growth. In my view, if managed properly this foundation can serve well the country's future industrial and economic development.

Further, based on the above-mentioned reports, it is rather clear that the industrial specialization of regions in Poland continues to narrow. Such specialization is also effecting an increase of focus of FDI entering Poland on service providing industries and manufacture of higher-grade goods – mainly pharmaceuticals and electronics.

The data on GDP composition by sector for 2012 (Index Mundi 2013 profile) shows the following split between industrial sectors: agriculture 3.5 percent, industry 34.2 percent, and services 62.3 percent; this indicates that Poland's economy increasingly moves towards service industries.

According to much previous research and my own conclusions, this trend is a desirable outcome of hosting foreign multinationals, hopefully with a lasting effect on domestic industry.

7.2 Moving forward

Considering the current state of attractiveness of Poland to foreign investors in the present-day global economic situation, one can see a positive, although measured, economic outlook. Over the last two decades Poland has developed itself as a competitive platform within the EU for investment in a range of industries. Such readiness is steadily gravitating towards production of higher-grade goods and services, which is a desired outcome of attracting foreign investment.

Poland also offers a highly skilled labor force, and still at a reasonable cost, which is certainly a draw for many firms. An increasing capability to conduct research and development also offers an attractive dimension to many sectors and firms. Increased investment in pharmaceuticals, aviation, and service industries has been observed in recent years.

In the process, besides being a manufacturing base, Poland is also an attractive market for many multinational firms. Having the largest market with increasing purchasing power in Central Europe is certainly an advantage. Besides, Poland is well positioned geographically to serve as an access platform to East European neighbors of former Soviet Union, which are also an attractive market to many MNCs. To that point, for younger Polish generations that focused mainly on the West of Europe, knowledge of the Russian language is an advantage in developing future business networks.

For now, at least, industrial specialization of regions in Poland seems to have taken root. However, it is still too early to make an ultimate judgment as to such specialization's effect on Poland's long-term economic growth. Lessons drawn from the example of Poland as a developing economy can serve many other developing countries in focusing their strategies and policies towards attracting specific types of needed FDI and cultivating this investment to achieve the objectives desired by both host and investor.

Appendices

Appendix 1 Concentration of foreign firms according to industrial specialization – RLAis

	Number of Firms							RLAis Index						
All Firms Total	**886**	**906**	**978**	**996**	**1101**	**1150**	**1091**							
Activities (PKD)	**2000**	**2001**	**2002**	**2003**	**2004**	**2005**	**2006**	**2000**	**2001**	**2002**	**2003**	**2004**	**2005**	**2006**
Dolnośląskie														
Automotive; Count	7	7	8	7	12	0	0	1.42	1.24	1.34	0.90	2.04	0.00	0.00
Business activities; Count	0	1	1	1	1	0	0	0.00	1.29	1.24	0.71	0.53	0.00	0.00
Computer technology; Count	2	1	1	1	1	0	0	13.42	4.31	12.38	12.77	11.71	0.00	0.00
Electricity, gas and water supply; Count	0	0	1	2	2	2	2	0.00	0.00	0.48	8.51	5.86	0.86	0.82
Financial intermediation; Count	0	0	0	2	0	2	2	0.00	0.00	0.00	0.27	0.00	0.30	0.27
Hotels and restaurants; Count	3	1	1	1	1	1	1	1.83	0.68	0.62	0.61	0.53	0.54	0.50
Manufacture of chemicals and chemical products; Count	5	6	7	7	9	7	8	1.34	1.44	1.49	1.38	1.46	1.23	1.24
Manufacture of consumer products; Count	4	3	8	5	3	0	0	4.88	3.53	11.00	7.98	3.90	0.00	0.00
Manufacture of electrical machinery and apparatus; Count	1	2	2	1	3	3	4	0.38	0.76	0.73	0.38	0.84	0.85	1.02
Manufacture of fabrics and textiles; Count	2	2	2	2	4	4	3	0.96	1.04	0.83	0.98	1.42	1.61	1.15
Manufacture of food, drinks and tobacco products; Count	6	4	2	3	4	5	5	0.66	0.47	0.21	0.31	0.37	0.51	0.46
Manufacture of furniture and consumer goods; Count	2	2	4	4	4	7	7	1.58	1.44	2.91	3.00	2.93	3.50	3.09
Manufacture of machinery and equipment; Count	6	7	6	5	10	10	10	2.98	3.36	2.65	1.73	2.66	2.98	2.73
Manufacture of metals and metal products; Count	2	2	2	3	5	5	5	0.60	0.56	0.51	0.78	1.01	0.99	0.90

Manufacture of motor vehicles, trailers and semi-trailers; Count	1	0	0	0	0	0	2	4.47	0.00	0.00	0.00	0.00	0.00	5.74
Manufacture of other non-metal goods; Count	10	12	10	9	6	6	6	2.40	2.88	2.13	1.82	1.06	1.25	1.15
Manufacture of pulp and paper, publishing and printing; Count	3	3	3	2	2	2	2	1.61	1.14	1.49	1.16	0.81	0.49	0.46
Manufacture of rubber and plastics; Count	1	4	4	4	6	6	6	0.50	1.73	1.55	1.09	1.19	1.21	1.06
Manufacture of transport equipment; Count	0	0	1	4	7	18	18	0.00	0.00	0.17	0.52	1.19	3.52	3.33
Manufacture of wood and wooden products; Count	1	1	1	1	1	1	1	1.92	1.62	1.55	2.55	1.46	1.56	1.44
Mining and quarrying; Count	2	2	3	3	3	2	2	6.71	8.63	9.28	9.58	7.03	5.00	4.59
Other community, social and personal service activities; Count	1	1	1	3	2	2	3	3.36	4.31	4.13	2.39	1.80	1.09	1.50
Real estate, rental and business activities; construction; Count	2	1	1	0	1	2	2	1.49	0.72	0.59	0.00	0.47	0.42	0.41
Retail trade, exept of motor vehicles and motorcycles; repair of personal and household goods; Count	2	7	6	5	5	0	0	0.89	3.24	2.65	1.45	1.95	0.00	0.00
Transport, storage and communication; Count					1	2	1					0.27	0.57	0.27
Wholesale and retail trade; repair of motor vehicles, motorcycles and personal and household goods; Count	1	0	0	2	1	5	5	0.38	0.00	0.00	0.59	0.27	0.54	0.51
Total:	**64**	**69**	**75**	**77**	**94**	**92**	**95**							
					Kujawsko-Pomorskie									
Financial intermediation; Count	0	0	0	1	1	0	0	0.00	0.00	0.00	0.54	0.59	0.00	0.00
Manufacture of chemicals and chemical products; Count	1	0	0	1	2	1	2	0.84	0.00	0.00	0.77	1.18	0.85	1.23
Manufacture of electrical machinery and apparatus; Count	0	0	0	0	0	0	1	0.00	0.00	0.00	0.00	0.00	0.00	1.01
Manufacture of fabrics and textiles; Count	0	0	0	0	1	1	1	0.00	0.00	0.00	0.00	1.28	1.95	1.52
Manufacture of food, drinks and tobacco products; Count	6	5	6	7	8	6	7	2.07	2.27	2.79	2.86	2.69	2.98	2.57

Continued

Appendix 1 Continued

	Number of Firms							RLAis Index						
All Firms Total	**886**	**906**	**978**	**996**	**1101**	**1150**	**1091**							
Activities (PKD)	**2000**	**2001**	**2002**	**2003**	**2004**	**2005**	**2006**	**2000**	**2001**	**2002**	**2003**	**2004**	**2005**	**2006**
manufacture of furniture and consumer goods Count	1	1	1	0	1	0	0	2.48	2.80	3.20	0.00	2.65	0.00	0.00
Manufacture of leather and leather products; Count	1	1	1	1	1	0	0	7.03	8.39	10.87	8.30	7.06	0.00	0.00
Manufacture of metals and metal products; Count	2	2	3	2	2	2	2	1.88	2.19	3.33	2.03	1.46	1.92	1.42
Manufacture other non-metal goods and plastics Count	1	1		1	0	0	0	0.75	0.83	0.00	0.79	0.00	0.00	0.00
Manufacture of pulp and paper, publishing and printing; Count	3	3	3	2	4	4	4	5.06	6.29	6.52	4.53	5.84	4.75	3.64
Manufacture of radio, television and communication equipment and apparatus; Count	0	0		0	0	0	1	0.00	0.00	0.00	0.00	0.00	0.00	7.58
Manufacture of rubber and plastics; Count	1	1	1	1	2	1	1	1.56	1.68	1.70	1.06	1.44	0.98	0.70
Manufacture of transport equipment; Count	1	1	1	1	1	1	1	0.64	0.69	0.73	0.50	0.61	0.95	0.73
Manufacture of wood and wooden products; Count	1	1	1	1	1	1	1	6.03	6.29	6.79	9.96	5.29	7.57	5.68
Wholesale and retail trade; repair of motor vehicles, motorcycles and personal and household goods; Count	3	2	1	2	2	2	3	3.62	3.25	1.81	2.32	1.97	1.05	1.21
Total:	**21**	**18**	**18**	**20**	**26**	**19**	**24**							
				Łódzkie										
Automotive Count	1	1	1	1	1	0	0	0.29	0.29	0.24	0.21	0.25	0.00	0.00
Financial intermediation; Count	2	2	2	1	2	1	1	1.98	2.11	1.25	0.22	0.37	0.22	0.19
Construction; Count	1	2	0	0	0	0	0	0.45	1.05	0.00	0.00	0.00	0.00	0.00
Manufacture of chemicals and chemical products; Count	4	4	8	4	7	9	10	1.51	1.56	2.50	1.25	1.65	2.24	2.17
Manufacture of consumer products Count	0	0	0	3	1	0	0	0.00	0.00	0.00	7.62	1.88	0.00	0.00

Manufacture of electrical machinery and apparatus Count	1	1	1	0	0	0	0	0.54	0.62	0.53	0.00	0.00	0.00	0.00
Manufacture of fabrics and textiles; Count	8	7	9	4	11	9	9	5.39	5.90	5.43	3.13	5.65	5.14	4.81
Manufacture of food, drinks and tobacco products; Count	7	5	5	4	5	7	7	1.08	0.95	0.77	0.67	0.67	1.02	0.91
Manufacture of leather and leather products; Count	1	1	1	1	1	1	1	3.14	3.51	3.62	3.39	2.82	2.95	2.67
Manufacture of machinery and equipment; Count	1	1	2	0	3	4	4	0.70	0.78	1.29	0.00	1.15	1.68	1.53
Manufacture of metals and metal products; Count	1	1	2	2	2	2	2	0.42	0.46	0.74	0.83	0.58	0.56	0.50
Manufacture of other non-metal goods; Count	6	8	7	9	11	10	11	2.02	2.76	2.19	2.90	2.82	2.95	2.94
Manufacture of pulp and paper, publishing and printing; Count	3	3	4	4	3	3	3	2.26	2.63	2.90	3.87	1.75	1.04	0.96
Manufacture of rubber and plastics; Count	3	3	4	4	6	7	7	2.09	2.11	2.26	1.73	1.72	2.00	1.73
Manufacture of transport equipment; Count	2	0	0	0	1	1	1	0.57	0.00	0.00	0.00	0.25	0.28	0.26
Other community, social and personal service activities; Count	0	1	1	2	2	2	2	0.00	7.02	6.04	2.54	2.61	1.54	1.40
Real estate, rental and business activities; Count	0	0	2	1	1	2	2	0.00	0.00	1.72	0.92	0.68	0.60	0.57
Retail trade, except of motor vehicles and motorcycles; repair of personal and household goods; supporting and auxiliary transport activities; Count	3	0	1	5	4	0	0	1.89	0.00	0.65	2.31	2.26	0.00	0.00
Transport, storage and communication; Count					2	2	2					0.79	0.80	0.76
Wholesale and retail trade; repair of motor vehicles, motorcycles and personal and household goods; Count	2	1	1	2	2	5	6	1.08	0.68	0.60	0.95	0.79	0.77	0.85
Total:	**46**	**41**	**51**	**47**	**65**	**65**	**68**							
							Lubelskie							
Agriculture; Count	0	1	0	0	0	0	0	0.00	2.10	0.00	0.00	0.00	0.00	0.00
Automotive /Manufacture of transport equipment; Count	1	1	1	0	0	0	0	0.89	0.78	1.02	0.00	0.00	0.00	0.00
Capital investment; Count	1	1	0	0	0	0	0	3.11	2.83	0.00	0.00	0.00	0.00	0.00

Continued

Appendix 1 Continued

	Number of Firms							RLAis Index						
All Firms Total	**886**	**906**	**978**	**996**	**1101**	**1150**	**1091**							
Activities (PKD)	**2000**	**2001**	**2002**	**2003**	**2004**	**2005**	**2006**	**2000**	**2001**	**2002**	**2003**	**2004**	**2005**	**2006**
Hotels and restaurants; Count	1	1	0	0	0	0	0	2.68	2.98	0.00	0.00	0.00	0.00	0.00
Health and social work; manufacture of food, drinks and tobacco products; Count	0	0	0	1	0	1	1	0.00	0.00	0.00	0.72	0.00	67.65	68.19
Manufacture of chemicals and chemical products; Count	0	0	0	1	2	1	1	0.00	0.00	0.00	1.09	1.91	0.95	0.92
Manufacture of food, drinks and tobacco products; Count	3	3	3	3	3	2	2	1.45	1.53	1.93	1.75	1.64	1.11	1.10
Manufacture of furniture and consumer goods; Count	1	1	1	1	1	1	1	3.47	3.15	4.43	4.18	4.30	2.71	2.62
Manufacture of machinery and equipment; Count	0	0	0	1	2	2	2	0.00	0.00	0.00	1.92	3.13	3.22	3.25
Manufacture of metals and metal products; Count	1	1	1	0	0	1	1	1.31	1.23	1.54	0.00	0.00	1.07	1.07
Manufacture of other non-metal goods; Count	2	2	1	2	2	2	1	2.11	1.86	1.30	2.26	2.09	2.25	1.14
Manufacture of parts and accessories for motor vehicles and their engines; Count	0	0	0	1	0	0	0	0.00	0.00	0.00	71.14	0.00	0.00	0.00
Manufacture of pharmaceuticals; Count	0	0	1	0	0	0	0	0.00	0.00	8.36	0.00	0.00	0.00	0.00
Manufacture of pulp and paper, publishing and printing; Count	1	1	1	1	1	1	1	2.36	2.36	3.01	3.39	2.37	1.33	1.36
Manufacture of rubber and plastics; Count	2	2	2	2	2	3	3	4.38	3.78	4.70	3.03	2.33	3.27	3.15
Manufacture of transport equipment; Count	0	0	0	0	1	1	1	0.00	0.00	0.00	0.00	1.00	1.06	1.10
Manufacture of wood and wooden products; Count	1	1	1	0	1	1	1	8.44	7.08	9.40	0.00	8.60	8.46	8.52
Wholesale and retail trade; repair of motor vehicles, motorcycles and personal and household goods; Count	1	1	1	1	1	1	1	1.69	1.83	2.51	1.65	1.60	0.59	0.60
Total:	**15**	**16**	**13**	**14**	**16**	**17**	**16**							

Lubuskie														
Financial intermediation; Count	1	1	1	1	1	1	1	3.11	2.16	1.77	0.54	0.50	0.64	0.58
Hotels and restaurants; Count	0	1	1	1	1	1	1	0.00	2.27	2.57	2.37	2.09	2.27	2.16
Manufacture of chemicals and chemical products; Count	0	2	2	2	2	1	1	0.00	1.60	1.77	1.53	1.27	0.74	0.67
Manufacture of fabrics and textiles; Count	5	4	4	3	4	4	4	10.55	6.90	6.86	5.75	5.56	6.74	6.61
Manufacture of food, drinks and tobacco products; Count	1	2	2	3	4	3	4	0.48	0.78	0.88	1.22	1.46	1.29	1.60
Manufacture of leather and leather products; Count	1	3	2	2	2	2	2	9.84	21.57	20.59	16.60	15.29	17.42	16.53
Manufacture of metals and metal products; Count	0	0	0	0	1	0	0	0.00	0.00	0.00	0.00	0.79	0.00	0.00
Manufacture of other non-metal goods; Count	2	2	2	2	2	3	2	2.11	1.41	1.77	1.58	1.39	2.61	1.65
Manufacture of pulp and paper, publishing and printing; Count	1	2	2	2	2	2	2	2.36	3.60	4.12	4.74	3.16	2.05	1.98
Manufacture of rubber and plastics; Count	0	0	0	1	2	2	2	0.00	0.00	0.00	1.06	1.56	1.69	1.53
Manufacture of transport equipment; Count	2	1	1	1	1	1	1	1.79	0.59	0.70	0.50	0.66	0.82	0.80
Manufacture of wood and wooden products; Count	1	1	1	1	1	1	1	8.44	5.39	6.43	9.96	5.73	6.53	6.20
Transport, storage and communication; Count	0	1	1	1	1	1	1	0.00	43.14	51.47	9.96	1.07	1.19	1.18
Wholesale trade, automotive; Count	1	1	0	0	0	0	0	1.69	1.39	0.00	0.00	0.00	0.00	0.00
Total:	**15**	**21**	**19**	**20**	**24**	**22**	**22**							
Małopolskie														
Automotive; Count	1	2	3	1	1	0	0	0.38	0.71	0.97	0.26	0.35	0.00	0.00
Business activities; Count	1	1	1	1	1	0	0	3.62	2.59	2.39	1.46	1.11	0.00	0.00
Construction; Count	3	2	3	2	2	2	2	1.77	1.29	1.52	1.38	1.14	1.30	1.24
Electricity, gas and water supply; Count	1	1	2	1	2	2	2	1.81	1.52	1.83	1.09	1.96	1.93	1.86
Manufacture of chemicals and chemical products; Count	3	3	3	4	4	3	3	1.52	1.44	1.23	1.61	1.36	1.19	1.05
Manufacture of fabrics and textiles; Count	0	0	0	0	1	1	2	0.00	0.00	0.00	0.00	0.74	0.90	1.73
Manufacture of food, drinks and tobacco products; Count	5	4	5	5	5	3	4	1.04	0.93	1.02	1.07	0.97	0.69	0.84

Continued

Appendix 1 Continued

	Number of Firms							RLAis Index						
All Firms Total	**886**	**906**	**978**	**996**	**1101**	**1150**	**1091**							
Activities (PKD)	**2000**	**2001**	**2002**	**2003**	**2004**	**2005**	**2006**	**2000**	**2001**	**2002**	**2003**	**2004**	**2005**	**2006**
Manufacture of metals and metal products; Count	6	6	6	6	8	6	7	3.38	3.38	2.92	3.21	3.37	2.67	2.84
Manufacture of other non-metal goods; Count	5	6	5	4	4	4	4	2.26	2.55	2.06	1.66	1.48	1.87	1.73
Manufacture of pulp and paper, publishing and printing; Count	1	3	3	1	2	2	2	1.01	3.24	2.86	1.25	1.69	1.10	1.04
Manufacture of rubber and plastics; Count	1	1	1	3	3	4	4	0.94	0.86	0.75	1.67	1.24	1.81	1.60
Manufacture of transport equipment; Count	0	0	0	1	1	0	0	0.00	0.00	0.00	0.26	0.35	0.00	0.00
Mining and quarrying; Count	0	0	0	0	1	1	1	0.00	0.00	0.00	0.00	4.89	5.61	5.20
Other community, social and personal service activities; Count	0	0	0	1	1	1	1	0.00	0.00	0.00	1.64	1.53	1.22	1.13
Real estate, rental, and business activities; Count	3	1	4	3	3	3	3	4.22	1.44	4.54	3.57	2.94	1.43	1.39
Wholesale and retail trade; repair of motor vehicles, motorcycles and personal and household goods; Count	5	5	5	5	6	9	7	3.62	4.18	3.98	3.05	3.41	2.20	1.61
Total:	**35**	**35**	**41**	**38**	**45**	**41**	**42**							
					Mazowieckie									
Business activities Count	5	8	22	0	14	0	0	2.28	2.21	5.63	0.00	1.70	0.00	0.00
Construction; Count	20	20	26	26	28	27	28		1.38	1.42	1.83	1.74	1.71	1.70
Distribution of petroleum products, retail trade; Count	2	4	4	2				0.80	1.38	1.71	2.67	0.00	0.00	0.00
Electricity, gas and water supply; Count	22	4	7	2	5	2	3	5.03	0.65	0.69	1.78	3.35	0.19	0.27
Financial intermediation; Count	26	45	68	76	74	63	70	4.38	6.21	8.70	2.18	2.18	2.09	2.10
Hotels and restaurants; Count	11	11	14	15	16	15	15	1.60	1.60	1.79	1.91	1.95	1.78	1.67
Manufacture of chemicals and chemical products; Count	20	24	23	32	29	30	27	1.28	1.23	1.02	1.31	1.08	1.15	0.93
Manufacture of consumer products; Count	5	5	4	3	2			1.45	1.26	1.14	1.00	0.60	0.00	0.00

Manufacture of electrical machinery and apparatus; Count	13	12	14	13	17	16	14	1.19	0.97	1.05	1.02	1.08	0.99	0.79
Manufacture of fabrics and textiles; Count	6	6	7	3	3	3	3	0.69	0.66	0.60	0.31	0.24	0.26	0.26
Manufacture of food, drinks and tobacco products; Count	32	34	34	29	28	34	31	0.84	0.85	0.74	0.63	0.60	0.76	0.64
Manufacture of furniture and consumer goods; Count	3	1	1	1	1	5	5	0.56	0.15	0.15	0.16	0.17	0.55	0.49
Manufacture of leather and leather products; Count	0	0	0	1	1	1	1	0.00	0.00	0.00	0.45	0.45	0.45	0.43
Manufacture of machinery and equipment; Count	8	8	6	9	9	10	10	0.95	0.82	0.55	0.65	0.55	0.65	0.61
Manufacture of metals and metal products; Count	5	6	8	9	10	10	10	0.36	0.36	0.42	0.49	0.46	0.43	0.40
Manufacture of other non-metal goods; Count	12	12	12	14	13	9	9	0.69	0.54	0.53	0.59	0.53	0.41	0.38
Manufacture of pharmaceuticals Count	0	0	6					0.00	0.00	1.71	0.00	0.00	0.00	0.00
Manufacture of pulp and paper, publishing and printing; Count	20	21	23	31	29	29	28	2.56	2.42	2.36	3.94	2.68	1.55	1.43
Manufacture of radio, television and communication equipment and apparatus; Count telecommunications	0	9	10				1	0.00	1.91	1.71	0.00	0.00	0.00	0.43
Manufacture of rubber and plastic products; Count	5	4	5	7	10	8	10	0.59	0.37	0.40	0.40	0.45	0.35	0.39
Manufacture of transport equipment; Count	4	5	4	3	4	9	9	0.19	0.19	0.14	0.08	0.16	0.38	0.37
Media and entertainment Count	3	21	7	4				1.07	6.45	1.63	2.67	0.00	0.00	0.00
Mining and quarrying; Count	1	1	1	1	1	1	1	0.80	0.92	0.64	0.67	0.54	0.55	0.51
Other community, social and personal service activities; Count	2	4	3	5	19	11	10	3.20	2.76	1.10	0.83	3.18	1.30	1.11
Postal services; Count	3	1	5	2				9.60	2.76	2.13	2.67	0.00	0.00	0.00
Electricity, gas and water supply; Count	1	1	1	5				0.23	0.16	0.10	0.56	0.00	0.00	0.00
Real estate, rental and business activities; Count	7	9	10	13	16	38	38	1.24	1.38	1.22	1.58	1.71	1.76	1.73
Retail trade; Count	21	25	31	33	43	23	24	2.24	2.47	2.83	2.00	3.84		
Transport, storage and communication; Count					22	23	24					1.39	1.42	1.46
Wholesale and retail trade; repair of motor vehicles, motorcycles and personal and household goods; Count	16	16	13	14	17	55	56	1.46	1.43	1.11	0.87	1.06	1.30	1.27
Total:	**273**	**317**	**369**	**353**	**411**	**422**	**427**							

Continued

Appendix 1 Continued

	Number of Firms							RLAis Index						
All Firms Total	**886**	**906**	**978**	**996**	**1101**	**1150**	**1091**							
Activities (PKD)	**2000**	**2001**	**2002**	**2003**	**2004**	**2005**	**2006**	**2000**	**2001**	**2002**	**2003**	**2004**	**2005**	**2006**
Opolskie														
Manufacture of chemicals and chemical products; Count	2	1	1	1	1	2	2	2.22	1.05	0.99	0.85	0.76	1.47	1.34
Manufacture of fabrics and textiles; Count	1	1	1	1	1	1	1	1.98	2.27	1.92	2.13	1.67	1.69	1.65
Manufacture of food, drinks and tobacco products; Count	2	3	5	6	5	6	6	0.91	1.53	2.46	2.72	2.18	2.57	2.40
Manufacture of machinery and equipment; Count	1	1	2	2	1	1	2	2.05	2.10	4.11	2.99	1.25	1.24	2.36
Manufacture of metals and metal products; Count	3	3	2	2	4	4	4	3.69	3.69	2.35	2.26	3.80	3.32	3.10
Manufacture of other non-metal goods; Count	2	1	3	4	4	4	3	1.98	0.93	2.98	3.51	3.34	3.48	2.48
Manufacture of transport equipment; Count	1	1	0	0	2	2	2	0.84	0.78	0.00	0.00	1.60	1.63	1.50
Mining and quarrying; Count	1	1	1	0	0	0	0	13.84	18.88	14.38	0.00	0.00	0.00	0.00
Real estate, rental and business activities; Count	2	2	0	0	1	1	1			0.00	0.00	2.20	0.89	0.89
Wholesale and retail trade; repair of motor vehicles, motorcycles and personal and household goods; Count	1	2	2	2	1	1	1	1.58	3.65	3.84	2.57	1.28	0.45	0.44
Total:	**16**	**16**	**17**	**18**	**20**	**22**	**22**							
Podkarpackie														
Electricity, gas and water supply; Count	3	2	0	1	1	1	1	9.49	4.26	0.00	13.28	9.83	1.47	1.34
Manufacture of chemicals and chemical products; Count	4	4	4	4	5	3	4	3.54	2.68	2.70	2.45	2.73	1.80	2.03
Manufacture of electrical machinery and apparatus; Count	1	1	1	0	1	2	2	1.27	1.07	1.15	0.00	0.94	1.94	1.67
Manufacture of food, drinks and tobacco products; Count	3	4	5	5	4	4	4	1.09	1.31	1.67	1.63	1.25	1.40	1.21
Manufacture of glass; Count	1	1	1	0	0	0	0	8.86	9.06	9.78	0.00	0.00	0.00	0.00

Manufacture of leather and leather products; Count	1	1	1	1	1	1	1	7.38	6.04	7.82	6.64	6.55	7.10	6.27
Manufacture of metals and metal products; Count	1	3	4	4	5	5	5	0.98	2.36	3.19	3.25	3.39	3.38	2.94
Manufacture of other non-metal goods; Count	1	2	1	1	1	1	1	0.79	1.19	0.67	0.63	0.60	0.71	0.63
Manufacture of rubber and plastics, automotive; Count	1	3	1	2	2	2	2	1.64	3.62	1.22	1.70	1.33	1.37	1.16
Manufacture of transport equipment; Count	3	1	3	6	7	7	7	2.01	0.50	1.59	2.41	3.99	4.66	3.99
Manufacture of wood and wooden products; Count	0	0	1	0	0	0	1	0.00	0.00	4.89	0.00	0.00	0.00	4.70
Transport, storage and communication; Count					1	1	1					0.91	0.97	0.90
Total:	**19**	**22**	**22**	**24**	**28**	**27**	**29**							
Podlaskie														
Electricity, gas and water supply; Count	0	1	1	2	1	1	1	0.00	7.61	4.70	5.15	4.00	3.61	4.33
Manufacture of fabrics and textiles; Count	1	1	2	2	2	1	1	3.96	5.18	8.15	8.51	6.07	3.37	4.04
Manufacture of food, drinks and tobacco products; Count	2	2	2	2	3	4	3	1.82	2.33	2.09	1.81	2.38	3.43	2.93
Manufacture of metals and metal products; Count	1	1	1	1	1	1	1	2.46	2.81	2.49	2.26	1.73	1.66	1.89
Manufacture of pulp and paper; Count	2	0	0	0	0	0	0	8.86	0.00	0.00	0.00	0.00	0.00	0.00
Manufacture of rubber and plastics; Count	0	0	0	1	1	1	1	0.00	0.00	0.00	2.35	1.70	1.69	1.86
Manufacture of wood and wooden products; Count	1	1	1	1	1	1	1	15.82	16.18	15.28	22.13	12.51	13.07	15.15
Wholesale and retail trade; repair of motor vehicles, motorcycles and personal and household goods; Count	1	1	1	0	2	2	1	3.16	4.18	4.08	0.00	4.66	1.82	1.07
Total:	**8**	**7**	**8**	**9**	**11**	**11**	**9**							
Pomorskie														
Agriculture, hunting and forestry; Count	2	2	2	2	2	1	1	11.66	11.92	10.87	11.07	10.79	7.23	5.25
Construction; Count	1	2	2	1	4	4	4	0.56	1.19	0.92	0.58	2.01	2.02	2.00
Electricity, gas and water supply; Count	2	3	4	4	4	4	4	3.33	4.21	3.34	3.69	3.45	2.99	3.00
Financial intermediation; Count	2	2	4	6	4	3	1	2.45	2.38	3.00	1.43	0.95	0.79	0.25

Continued

Appendix 1 Continued

	Number of Firms							RLAis Index						
All Firms Total	886	906	978	996	1101	1150	1091							
Activities (PKD)	2000	2001	2002	2003	2004	2005	2006	2000	2001	2002	2003	2004	2005	2006
Hotels and restaurants; Count	1	1	1	1	1	1	1	1.06	1.25	1.09	1.05	0.98	0.94	0.91
Manufacture of chemicals and chemical products; Count	1	1	2	1	1	1	1	0.47	0.44	0.75	0.34	0.30	0.31	0.28
Manufacture of electrical machinery and apparatus; Count	1	2	2	2	2	4	5	0.67	1.40	1.28	1.30	1.03	1.97	2.33
Manufacture of food, drinks and tobacco products; Count	10	10	10	10	10	12	11	1.91	2.15	1.86	1.81	1.71	2.13	1.86
Manufacture of furniture and consumer goods; Count	2	2	2	3	2	3	3	2.74	2.65	2.56	3.91	2.70	2.60	2.42
Manufacture of metals and metal products; Count	1	1	1	2	2	3	3	0.52	0.52	0.44	0.90	0.74	1.03	0.98
Manufacture of other non-metal goods; Count	2	2	2	1	3	2	3	0.83	0.78	0.75	0.35	0.98	0.72	1.05
Manufacture of pulp and paper, publishing and printing; Count	1	1	2	1	1	0	1	0.93	0.99	1.74	1.05	0.74	0.00	0.42
Manufacture of rubber and plastics; Count	2	1	1	3	4	4	4	1.73	0.79	0.68	1.41	1.46	1.40	1.29
Manufacture of transport equipment; Count	5	4	3	2	5	5	5	1.77	1.31	0.88	0.45	1.56	1.70	1.59
Other community, social and personal service activities; Count	1	1	2	2	2	1	1	11.66	7.95	14.49	2.77	3.32	2.71	0.91
Real estate, rental and business activities; Count	2	2	2	1	1	2	2	2.59	2.65	2.07	1.01	0.86	0.74	0.75
Transport, storage and communication; Count					3	3	2					1.51	1.48	1.00
Total:	36	37	42	42	51	53	52							
Śląskie														
Construction; Count	2	1	2	3	2	4	3	0.70	0.40	0.71	1.06	0.63	1.24	0.88
Electricity, gas and water supply; Count	2	1	3	4	4	4	4	2.11	0.95	1.91	1.99	1.87	1.84	1.75
Financial intermediation; Count	1	1	2	3	3	4	5	0.78	0.81	1.14	0.43	0.45	0.65	0.72
Hotels and restaurants; Count	1	1	1	1	1	1	1	0.67	0.85	0.83	0.64	0.62	0.58	0.53
Manufacture of chemicals and chemical products; Count	1	2	1	2	4	4	5	0.30	0.60	0.29	0.41	0.76	0.75	0.83

Manufacture of electrical machinery and apparatus; Count	5	5	5	6	8	6	6	2.11	2.38	2.44	2.38	2.59	1.82	1.63
Manufacture of fabricated metal products, except machinery and equipment; Count	1	0	1	0	0	0	1		0.00		0.00	0.00	0.00	0.00
Manufacture of fabrics and textiles; Count	0	0	1	2	2	2	2	0.00	0.00	0.55	1.04	0.82	0.86	0.82
Manufacture of food, drinks and tobacco products; Count	3	3	3	3	2	3	4	0.36	0.44	0.43	0.33	0.22	0.33	0.40
Manufacture of furniture and consumer goods; Count	2	1	0	1	0	1	1	1.74	0.90	0.00	0.79	0.00	0.53	0.47
Manufacture of machinery and equipment; Count	1	1	1	3	6	5	5	0.55	0.60	0.59	1.09	1.85	1.59	1.46
Manufacture of metals and metal products; Count	10	9	7	9	9	13	13	3.28	3.17	2.37	2.47	2.11	2.76	2.49
Manufacture of other non-metal goods; Count	6	4	6	6	9	8	7	1.58	1.06	1.71	1.28	1.85	1.78	1.43
Manufacture of pulp and paper, publishing and printing; Count	3	2	2	2	2	2	2	1.77	1.35	1.33	1.28	0.94	0.52	0.49
Manufacture of rubber and plastics; Count	5	6	7	9	10	11	12	2.73	3.24	3.63	2.58	2.30	2.37	2.26
Manufacture of transport equipment; Count	12	11	12	14	14	11	11	2.68	2.44	2.69	1.90	2.76	2.30	2.17
Mining and quarrying; Count	0	2	0	0	1	1	1	0.00	10.79	0.00	0.00	2.72	2.67	2.45
Municipal services Count	3	2	2	1	1			11.08	8.09	4.74	2.69	2.72	0.00	0.00
Other community, social and personal service activities; Count	1	2	1	3	1	2	2	7.38	10.79	5.53	2.52	1.05	1.49	1.07
Real estate, rental and business activities; Count	0	0	0	0	0	1	1	0.00	0.00	0.00	0.00	0.00	0.23	0.22
Transport, storage and communication; Count					1	1	1					0.32	0.30	0.29
Wholesale and retail trade; repair of motor vehicles, motorcycles and personal and household goods Count	0	1	1	1	1	2	2	0.00	0.52	0.55	0.31	0.32	0.23	0.22
Total:	**59**	**55**	**58**	**73**	**81**	**86**	**89**							

Continued

Appendix 1 Continued

	Number of Firms							RLAis Index						
All Firms Total	**886**	**906**	**978**	**996**	**1101**	**1150**	**1091**							
Activities (PKD)	**2000**	**2001**	**2002**	**2003**	**2004**	**2005**	**2006**	**2000**	**2001**	**2002**	**2003**	**2004**	**2005**	**2006**
				Świętokrzyskie										
Chemicals and chemical products Count	1	0	0	0	0	0	0	1.36	0.00	0.00	0.00	0.00	0.00	0.00
Construction; Count	0	1	1	1	1	1	1	0.00	1.74	1.73	2.18	1.71	2.06	2.00
Electricity, gas and water supply; Count	3	2	1	0	2	2	2	14.60	8.20	3.13	0.00	5.06	6.10	5.99
Manufacture of fabrics and textiles; Count	0	0	0	0	1	1	1	0.00	0.00	0.00	0.00	2.22	2.85	2.80
Manufacture of food, drinks and tobacco products Count	1	1	1	1	1	0	0	0.56	0.63	0.70	0.68	0.58	0.00	0.00
Manufacture of machinery and equipment; Count	2	2	2	3	3	2	2	5.05	5.16	5.82	6.73	5.00	4.21	4.00
Manufacture of metals and metal products; Count	0	0	3	2	2	2	2	0.00	0.00	4.99	3.39	2.53	2.81	2.62
Manufacture of other non-metal goods; Count	3	3	3	3	3	3	3	3.65	3.43	4.22	3.95	3.34	4.42	4.20
Manufacture of pulp and paper, publishing and printing; Count	1	1	0	1	1	1	1	2.73	2.90	0.00	3.95	2.53	1.73	1.68
Manufacture of transport equipment; Count	2	2	0	0	1	1	1	2.07	1.91	0.00	0.00	1.06	1.38	1.35
Wholesale and retail trade, transport equipment Count	0	1	1	1	0	0	0	0.00	2.25	2.72	1.93	0.00	0.00	0.00
Total:	**13**	**13**	**12**	**12**	**15**	**13**	**13**							
				Warmińsko-Mazurskie										
Agriculture, hunting and forestry; Count	1	0	0	2	2	2	2	20.14	0.00	0.00	41.50	42.35	58.97	41.96
Electricity, gas and water supply; Count	1	1	1	1	1	1	1	5.75	5.33	3.76	3.07	2.92	3.05	3.00
Manufacture of fabrics and textiles; Count	1	1	1	1	1	1	1	2.88	3.62	3.26	3.19	2.57	2.85	2.80
Manufacture of food, drinks and tobacco products; Count	3	2	2	2	2	1	1	1.98	1.63	1.67	1.36	1.34	0.73	0.68
Manufacture of furniture and consumer goods; Count	1	2	1	1	1	1	1	4.74	10.07	5.75	4.88	5.29	3.54	3.23

Manufacture of machinery and equipment; manufacture of transport equipment; manufacture of rubber and plastics; manufacture of metals and metal products; manufacture of metals and metal products; manufacture of metals and metal products; Count	0	0	0		0	0	1	0.00	0.00	0.00	0.00	0.00	0.00	2.00
Manufacture of other non-metal goods; Count	1	3	3	3	3	3	3	1.44	4.46	5.06	3.95	3.85	4.42	4.20
Manufacture of pulp and paper, publishing and printing; Count	0	0	0	0	1	1	1	0.00	0.00	0.00	0.00	2.92	1.73	1.68
Manufacture of rubber and plastics; Count	1	0	0	1	1	2	2	2.98	0.00	0.00	1.77	1.44	2.85	2.58
Other community, social and personal service activities; Count	1	0	1	1	1	1	0	40.27	0.00	32.60	5.19	6.51	17.69	0.00
Total:	10	9	9	12	13	13	13							
Wielkopolskie														
Agriculture Count	1	1	1	0	0	0	0	2.41	2.46	2.52	0.00	0.00	0.00	0.00
Construction; Count	3	3	2	2	4	4	4	0.69	0.74	0.43	0.56	0.94	1.00	0.97
Electricity, gas and water supply; Count	3	1	3	3	3	4	4	2.06	0.58	1.16	10.60	7.58	1.48	1.46
Financial intermediation; Count	2	2	1	0	0	1	2	1.01	0.98	0.35	0.00	0.00	0.13	0.24
Hotels and restaurants; Count	0	0	0	0	0	1	1	0.00	0.00	0.00	0.00	0.00	0.47	0.44
Manufacture of chemicals and chemical products; Count	6	5	5	5	4	5	5	1.16	0.91	0.87	0.82	0.56	0.76	0.69
Manufacture of consumer products Count	2	2	1	0	1	0	0	1.75	1.79	1.12	0.00	1.12	0.00	0.00
Manufacture of electrical machinery and apparatus; Count	4	5	4	6	7	8	8	1.10	1.45	1.19	1.87	1.68	2.77	1.81
Manufacture of fabrics and textiles; Count	3	3	3	2	2	2	2	1.03	1.18	1.01	0.82	0.61	0.69	0.68
Manufacture of food, drinks and tobacco products; Count	21	23	19	19	20	22	22	1.66	2.04	1.64	1.65	1.60	1.94	1.81
Manufacture of furniture and consumer goods; Count	5	5	4	5	4	4	4	2.83	2.74	2.37	3.12	2.53	1.72	1.57
Manufacture of machinery and equipment; Count	6	7	7	7	7	5	5	2.14	2.55	2.52	2.00	1.61	1.28	1.21
Manufacture of metals and metal products; Count	6	6	6	6	5	7	7	1.28	1.28	1.23	1.30	0.87	1.19	1.12

Continued

Appendix 1 Continued

	Number of Firms							RLAis Index						
All Firms Total	**886**	**906**	**978**	**996**	**1101**	**1150**	**1091**							
Activities (PKD)	**2000**	**2001**	**2002**	**2003**	**2004**	**2005**	**2006**	**2000**	**2001**	**2002**	**2003**	**2004**	**2005**	**2006**
Manufacture of other non-metal goods; Count	2	2	4	4	4	2	3	0.34	0.32	0.70	0.67	0.61	0.36	0.51
Manufacture of pharmaceuticals Count	0	1	2	0	0	0	0	0.00	?	2.24	0.00	0.00	0.00	0.00
Manufacture of pulp and paper, publishing and printing; Count	1	0	2	2	2	3	1	0.39	0.00	0.81	1.01	0.70	0.63	0.20
Manufacture of rubber and plastics; Count	5	5	6	7	10	10	10	1.78	1.64	1.89	1.58	1.71	1.73	1.57
Manufacture of transport equipment; Count	4	4	1	2	3	5	5	0.58	0.54	10.08	0.21	0.44	0.84	0.77
Manufacture of wood and wooden products; Count	1	1	1	0	2	2	2	1.38	1.23	1.26	0.00	2.53	2.69	2.55
Other community, social and personal service activities; Count	1	2	2	1	1	1	1	4.82	6.57	20.16	0.66	3.37	0.47	0.44
Real estate, rental and business activities; Count	1	0	1	1	3	3	3	0.54	0.00	0.48	0.48	1.21	0.55	0.55
Telecommunications Count	2	2	2	0	0	0	0	1.28	1.52	1.34	0.00	0.00	0.00	0.00
Trade and repairs Count	2	3	5	4	4	0	0	0.88	0.84	1.17	0.96	0.88	0.00	0.00
Transport, storage and communication; real estate, rental and business activities; Count					6	5	5					1.27	1.22	1.21
Wholesale and retail trade; repair of motor vehicles, motorcycles and personal and household goods; Count	7	7	11	13	17	13	13	1.93	2.22	3.70	3.20	3.99	1.21	1.19
Total:	**88**	**90**	**93**	**89**	**109**	**107**	**107**							
					Zachodnio-Pomorskie									
Computer and related activities Count	0	0	0	3	0	0	1	0.00	0.00	0.00	129.91	0.00	0.00	35.19
Electricity, gas and water supply; Count	1	1	2	3	2	3	3	3.72	2.80	3.96	5.41	3.67	3.61	3.77
Hotels and restaurants; Count	1	1	1	1	1	1	1	2.37	2.51	2.57	2.06	2.09	1.52	1.53
Manufacture of chemicals and chemical products; Count	1	1	1	1	1	4	2	1.04	0.88	0.89	0.67	0.64	1.96	0.95
Manufacture of consumer products Count	0	0	0	1	1	0	0	0.00	0.00	0.00			0.00	0.00

Manufacture of electrical machinery and apparatus; Count	5	3	3	0	3	2	3	7.45	4.21	4.54	0.00	3.28	1.58	2.35
Manufacture of food, drinks and tobacco products; Count	5	5	6	7	8	10	10	2.14	2.15	2.64	2.48	2.91	2.86	2.84
Manufacture of furniture and consumer goods; Count	0	2	2	2	2	3	3	0.00	5.30	6.06	5.09	5.73	4.18	4.06
Manufacture of leather and leather products; Count	0	0	0	0	0	1	1	0.00	0.00	0.00	0.00	0.00	5.81	5.87
Manufacture of machinery and equipment Count	1	1	1	1	1	0	0	1.93	1.77	1.84	1.17	1.04	0.00	0.00
Manufacture of metals and metal products; Count	0	0	0	0	1	2	2	0.00	0.00	0.00	0.00	0.79	1.11	1.10
Manufacture of other non-metal goods; Count	0	0	0	1	1	1	1	0.00	0.00	0.00	0.69	0.70	0.58	0.59
Manufacture of pulp and paper, publishing and printing; Count	1	2	1	1	1	1	0	2.08	3.97	2.06	2.06	1.58	0.68	0.00
Manufacture of rubber and plastics; Count	0	0	0	0	0	1	1	0.00	0.00	0.00	0.00	0.00	0.56	0.54
Manufacture of wood and wooden products; Manufacture of wood and wooden products; Count	0	1	1	1	1	1	0	0.00	5.96	6.43	8.66	5.73	4.36	0.00
Real estate, rental and business activities; Count	1	1	0	0	0	1	1	2.90	2.65	0.00	0.00	0.00	0.59	0.63
Transport, storage and communication; Count					0	1	1					0.00	0.79	0.84
Wholesale and retail trade; repair of motor vehicles, motorcycles and personal and household goods; Count	0	0	0	0	1	1	1	0.00	0.00	0.00	0.00		0.30	0.32
Total:	**16**	**18**	**18**	**22**	**24**	**33**	**31**							

Source: Based on data obtained from the Polish Information and Foreign Investment Agency (PAIIZ) and the author's own analysis.

Appendix 2 Concentration of foreign firms according to country-of-origin – RLAco

Country-of-origin	2000	2001	2002	2003	2004	2005	2006	2000	2001	2002	2003	2004	2005	2006
All firms total:	**886**	**906**	**978**	**996**	**1101**	**1150**	**1091**	RLA CO						
Dolnośląskie														
Austria	1	1	1	1	1	1	1	0.35	0.33	0.33	0.32	0.27	0.30	0.27
Belgium	2	1	2	2	3	3	3	1.17	0.57	1.12	1.10	1.27	1.44	1.28
Canada	2	3	2	2	2	2	2	1.41	2.90	1.84	1.80	1.76	1.92	1.86
Czech Republic	1	1	0	0	0	0	0	3.36	3.15	0.00	0.00	0.00	0.00	0.00
Denmark	1	1	1	1	1	2	2	0.39	0.33	0.30	0.29	0.24	0.49	0.41
Finland	1	1	2	1	1	0	0	0.67	0.70	1.61	0.66	0.55	0.00	0.00
France	4	5	2	2	2	2	2	0.77	0.72	0.28	0.28	0.22	0.26	0.22
Germany	24	25	30	32	34	33	31	1.54	1.52	1.67	1.82	1.54	1.67	1.41
Ireland	0	0	0	1	1	1	1	0.00	0.00	0.00	4.20	2.29	2.08	1.59
International	1	0	0	0	0	0	0	0.64	0.00	0.00	0.00	0.00	0.00	0.00
Italy	2	2	2	1	3	3	3	0.41	0.41	0.42	0.20	0.50	0.60	0.53
Japan	0	1	0	1	7	7	7	0.00	0.33	0.00	0.57	2.97	3.50	2.69
Luxembourg	1	1	1	2	2	2	2	4.47	2.10	3.22	1.80	1.43	1.56	1.39
Monaco	0	0	0	0	1	1	1	0.00	0.00	0.00	0.00	11.47	12.50	11.13
Norway	1	0	0	0	0	0	0	2.68	0.00	0.00	0.00	0.00	0.00	0.00
Portugal	0	0	0	0	1	1	1	0.00	0.00	0.00	0.00	2.87	2.50	2.23
Russia	1	1	1	1	1	1	1	6.71	6.29	6.43	6.30	3.82	4.17	3.71
South Korea	0	0	0	0	0	0	5	0.00	0.00	0.00	0.00	0.00	0.00	4.64
Spain	2	2	1	1	1	1	2	3.84	2.80	0.99	1.15	1.04	1.25	1.86
Sweden	1	1	3	3	4	4	4	0.25	0.22	0.68	0.69	0.78	0.86	0.80
Switzerland	1	3	3	3	3	3	3	0.71	1.72	1.61	1.58	1.27	1.29	1.19
The Netherlands	5	5	7	8	7	5	5	1.02	0.85	0.99	1.03	0.76	0.63	0.56
Turkey	1	1	2	2	1	1	1	3.36	3.15	6.43	6.30	2.87	1.25	1.11
United Kingdom	6	6	4	4	7	7	8	2.30	1.89	1.14	1.07	1.51	1.68	1.75

USA	8	11	12	11	13	12	13	0.83	1.11	1.21	1.04	1.12	1.15	1.09
Wojewodztwo total:	**66**	**72**	**76**	**79**	**96**	**92**	**98**							
Kujawsko-Pomorskie														
Austria	5	3	2	2	3	2	2	5.55	3.97	2.79	2.43	2.91	2.95	2.22
Belgium	1	1	0	1	2	0	1	1.83	2.29	0.00	2.06	3.02	0.00	1.75
Denmark	1	1	1	1	1	1	1	1.24	1.32	1.26	1.08	0.85	1.19	0.84
France	0	0	1	1	1	1	1	0.00	0.00	0.58	0.53	0.40	0.62	0.45
Germany	9	8	8	8	9	8	8	1.82	1.95	1.88	1.71	1.45	1.96	1.49
Hungary	0	0	0	1	1	0	1	0.00	0.00	0.00	11.86	10.19	0.00	7.58
International	1	0	0	1	1	0	0	2.01	0.00	0.00	3.95	3.71	0.00	0.00
Italy	2	2	1	1	1	0	0	1.30	1.65	0.88	0.75	0.59	0.00	0.00
Japan	0	0	0	0	0	1	1	0.00	0.00	0.00	0.00	0.00	2.42	1.57
Norway	0	0	1	1	1	0	0	0.00	0.00	4.18	3.39	2.72	0.00	0.00
South Korea	0	0	0	0	2	0	2	0.00	0.00	0.00	0.00	13.59	0.00	7.58
Sweden	0	1	1	1	1	1	1	0.00	0.88	0.95	0.86	0.69	1.04	0.81
Switzerland	0	0	0	0	0	1	1	0.00	0.00	0.00	0.00	0.00	2.09	1.62
The Netherlands	1	1	2	2	2	3	3	0.64	0.68	1.19	0.97	0.78	1.83	1.38
United Kingdom	0	0	0	0	1	1	1	0.00	0.00	0.00	0.00	0.77	1.16	0.89
USA	1	1	1	1	1	0	1	0.32	0.40	0.42	0.36	0.31	0.00	0.34
Wojewodztwo total:	**21**	**18**	**18**	**21**	**27**	**19**	**24**							
Łódzkie														
Australia	1	1	0	0	0	0	0	6.28	8.55	0.00	0.00	0.00	0.00	0.00
Austria	2	2	2	2	5	4	1	0.99	0.90	0.88	0.91	2.02	1.75	0.40
Austria/Belgium	0	0	0	0	1	1	3	0.00	0.00	0.00	0.00	16.94	17.97	49.59
Belgium	0	0	1	1	1	1	1	0.00	0.00	0.75	0.77	0.63	0.69	0.64
Canada	0	0	1	1	1	1	1	0.00	0.00	1.23	1.27	1.30	1.38	1.38
Cyprus	1	0	0	0	0	0	0	9.43	0.00	0.00	0.00	0.00	0.00	0.00

Continued

Appendix 2 Continued

Country-of-origin	2000	2001	2002	2003	2004	2005	2006	2000	2001	2002	2003	2004	2005	2006
All firms total:	**886**	**906**	**978**	**996**	**1101**	**1150**	**1091**				**RLA CO**			
Czech Republic	1	1	1	1	2	0	0	4.71	4.27	4.29	4.45	6.78	0.00	0.00
Denmark	2	2	3	3	3	4	5	1.11	0.90	1.20	1.21	1.06	1.41	1.53
Finland	0	0	0	1	1	2	2	0.00	0.00	0.00	0.94	0.81	1.89	1.74
France	6	6	5	5	6	4	5	1.62	1.18	0.92	0.99	1.00	0.73	0.83
Germany	13	14	16	14	19	18	19	1.17	1.16	1.19	1.12	1.27	1.31	1.29
Greece	0	0	0	0	1	1	1	0.00	0.00	0.00	0.00	5.65	5.99	5.51
Italy	6	8	9	9	9	8	8	1.74	2.24	2.49	2.54	2.21	2.28	2.10
Lichtenstein	0	1	1	1	1	1	1	0.00	4.27	4.29	4.45	3.39	3.59	2.76
Portugal	1	1	1	1	1	1	1	3.77	4.27	4.29	5.93	4.23	3.59	3.31
South Korea	2	1	0	0	0	0	0	7.54	4.27	0.00	0.00	0.00	0.00	0.00
Sweden	0	1	0	0	0	0	0	0.00	0.30	0.00	0.00	0.00	0.00	0.00
Switzerland	0	1	1	1	1	2	2	0.00	0.78	0.71	0.74	0.63	1.24	1.18
Taiwan	1	1	1	0	0	0	0	18.85	17.09	17.16	0.00	0.00	0.00	0.00
The Netherlands	3	4	5	7	4	5	5	0.86	0.92	0.94	1.27	0.65	0.91	0.83
Turkey	1	1	1	1	1	1	1	4.71	4.27	4.29	4.45	4.23	1.80	1.65
United Kingdom	2	3	4	2	1	2	2	1.08	1.28	1.53	0.76	0.32	0.69	0.65
USA	5	5	5	6	7	8	8	0.73	0.68	0.67	0.80	0.89	1.10	0.99
Wojewodztwo total:	**47**	**53**	**57**	**56**	**65**	**64**	**66**							
							Lubelskie							
Belgium	1	2	1	1	0	2	2	2.57	4.84	3.27	3.09	0.00	5.20	5.25
Canada	1	0	0	0	0	1	1	3.11	0.00	0.00	0.00	0.00	5.20	5.68
Cyprus	1	1	1	0	0	0	0	29.53	26.65	25.08	0.00	0.00	0.00	0.00
France	1	1	1	1	1	2	2	0.84	0.61	0.81	0.79	0.67	1.38	1.36
Germany	4	4	3	3	5	4	4	1.13	1.03	0.98	0.96	1.36	1.10	1.12
International	0	0	1	1	1	1	1	0.00	0.00	4.43	5.93	6.26	7.52	7.58

Italy	1	2	0	1	1	1	1	0.91	1.75	0.00	1.13	1.00	1.07	1.08
Japan	0		0	1	1	0	0	0.00	0.00	0.00	3.23	2.55	0.00	0.00
Luxemburg	1	1	0	0	0	0	0	19.69	8.88	0.00	0.00	0.00	0.00	0.00
Mexico	0	0	0	0	0	0	1	0.00	0.00	0.00	0.00	0.00	0.00	68.19
South Korea	0	1	1	1	1	1	1	0.00	13.32	18.81	17.79	11.47	11.27	5.68
Sweden	1	1	1	0	0	0	0	1.11	0.93	1.32	0.00	0.00	0.00	0.00
Switzerland	1	1	1	1	1	1	1	2.81	2.42	3.13	2.96	2.55	2.33	2.44
The Netherlands	1	1	2	1	2	0	0	3.11	3.55	1.65	0.73	1.31	0.00	0.00
United Kingdom	1	1	0	2	2	2	0	1.69	1.33	0.00	142.29	2.60	2.60	0.00
USA	1	1	1	1	1	2	2	0.45	0.43	0.59	0.53	0.52	1.03	1.03
Wojewodztwo total:	**15**	**17**	**13**	**14**	**16**	**17**	**16**							
Lubuskie														
Belgium	1	0	0	0	1	0	0	2.57	0.00	0.00	0.00	1.70	0.00	0.00
Croatia	1	1	1	1	1	0	1	29.53	21.57	25.74	24.90	22.94	0.00	24.80
Denmark	1	1	1	1	1	1	1	1.74	1.14	1.20	1.13	0.96	1.02	0.92
France	0	1	1	1	1	1	1	0.00	0.50	0.55	0.55	0.45	0.53	0.50
Germany	2	6	5	6	8	8	8	0.57	1.25	1.11	1.35	1.45	1.69	1.63
Greece	1	1	1	0	0	0	0	29.53	21.57	12.87	0.00	0.00	0.00	0.00
International	1	1	0	0	0	0	0	2.81	2.40	0.00	0.00	0.00	0.00	0.00
Italy	3	4	4	4	4	4	4	2.73	2.83	3.32	3.16	2.66	3.32	3.15
Norway	0	1	1	1	1	1	1	0.00	2.88	3.96	3.56	3.06	4.02	3.31
South Korea	1	0	0	0	0	0	0	11.81	0.00	0.00	0.00	0.00	0.00	0.00
Sweden	2	1	2	3	3	3	3	2.23	0.76	1.81	2.72	2.33	2.70	2.66
Switzerland	1	2	1	1	1	1	1	3.11	3.92	2.14	2.08	1.70	1.80	1.77
The Netherlands	1	1	1	1	2	2	2	0.89	0.58	0.57	0.51	0.87	1.06	1.00
United Kingdom	0	1	1	1	1	1	0	0.00	1.08	1.14	1.06	0.87	1.01	0.00
Wojewodztwo total:	**15**	**21**	**19**	**20**	**24**	**22**	**22**							

Continued

Appendix 2 Continued

Country-of-origin	2000	2001	2002	2003	2004	2005	2006	2000	2001	2002	2003	2004	2005	2006
All firms total:	**886**	**906**	**978**	**996**	**1101**	**1150**	**1091**				**RLA CO**			
							Małopolskie							
Australia	0	0	0	1	1	1	1	0.00	0.00	0.00	12.45	7.98	14.38	8.87
Austria	3	4	4	0	3	3	2	1.94	2.45	2.33	0.00	1.71	2.10	1.30
Croatia	1	1	1	1	1	1	1	12.31	11.62	11.37	12.45	11.97	14.38	13.30
Denmark	1	1	1	2	2	2	2	0.72	0.61	0.53	1.13	1.00	1.13	0.99
Finland	0	0	0	0	1	1	1	0.00	0.00	0.00	0.00	1.14	1.51	1.40
France	4	4	5	4	3	2	3	1.41	1.07	1.22	1.11	0.70	0.59	0.80
Germany	8	6	8	8	9	6	7	0.94	0.67	0.79	0.90	0.85	0.70	0.76
International	1	1	0	0	0	0	0	1.17	1.29	0.00	0.00	0.00	0.00	0.00
Italy	4	4	3	3	2	2	2	1.51	1.52	1.10	1.19	0.69	0.91	0.84
Japan	1	1	1	2	2	2	2	1.17	1.94	1.42	2.26	1.77	2.30	1.84
Lichtenstein	0	0	0	0	1	1	1	0.00	0.00	0.00	0.00	4.79	5.75	4.43
Norway	0	0	0	0	1	1	1	0.00	0.00	0.00	0.00	1.60	2.21	1.77
Portugal	1	0	0	0	0	0	0	4.92	0.00	0.00	0.00	0.00	0.00	0.00
Switzerland	0	2	2	2	2	2	2	0.00	2.11	1.90	2.08	1.77	1.98	1.90
The Netherlands	3	4	5	6	6	5	5	1.12	1.26	1.25	1.52	1.37	1.45	1.34
Turkey	0	0	0	0	1	1	1	0.00	0.00	0.00	0.00	5.98	2.88	2.66
United Kingdom	2	3	3	3	3	3	3	1.41	1.74	1.52	1.59	1.35	1.66	1.57
USA	7	8	10	9	9	8	8	1.33	1.49	1.78	1.68	1.62	1.76	1.60
Wojewodztwo total:	**36**	**39**	**43**	**40**	**46**	**40**	**41**							
							Mazowieckie							
Australia	2	1	2	2	2	1	1	1.86	1.30	2.43	2.43	1.70	1.40	0.89
Austria	17	16	18	20	19	16	20	1.25	1.09	1.12	1.25	1.15	1.09	1.31

Belgium	5	5	7	6	6	5	5	0.61	0.59	0.74	0.63	0.57	0.54	0.52
Canada	8	3	3	3	3	3	3	1.18	0.60	0.52	0.52	0.59	0.65	0.67
China	1	1	1	1	1	1	1	1.40	1.30	1.21	1.21	1.27	1.40	1.34
Croatia	0	0	0	0	0	1	0	0.00	0.00	0.00	0.00	0.00	1.40	0.00
Cyprus	0	0	1	1	2	2	3	0.00	0.00	0.81	1.21	1.70	1.87	2.68
Czech Republic	1	2	3	3	3	2	2	0.70	1.30	1.82	1.82	1.53	1.40	1.34
Denmark	14	17	18	15	19	19	21	1.15	1.16	1.02	0.83	1.01	1.04	1.04
Finland	8	10	8	11	12	9	9	1.12	1.44	1.21	1.41	1.46	1.33	1.27
France	32	44	49	47	53	49	44	1.28	1.31	1.28	1.27	1.32	1.40	1.18
Germany	46	50	67	62	68	67	64	0.62	0.63	0.70	0.68	0.69	0.76	0.70
Germany/Finland	0	0	0	1	1	1	1	0.00	0.00	0.00	2.43	2.55	2.80	2.68
Greece	1	1	3	2	1	1	1	1.40	1.30	1.82	2.43	0.85	0.93	0.89
Hungary	0	0	2	2	2	2	3	0.00	0.00	1.62	1.21	1.27	0.93	1.34
India	0	0	0	0	0	1	1	0.00	0.00	0.00	0.00	0.00	1.40	1.34
International	11	10	8	6	6	6	6	1.46	1.44	1.14	1.21	1.39	1.87	1.79
Ireland	1	1	0	0	2	2	2	0.93	0.87	0.00	0.00	1.02	0.93	0.77
Israel	4	3	3	3	3	3	0	2.24	1.95	1.82	1.82	1.91	2.10	0.00
Italy	23	22	24	24	23	23	21	0.99	0.94	0.94	0.93	0.85	1.02	0.89
Japan	4	3	4	10	9	9	10	1.02	0.65	0.88	1.10	0.85	1.01	0.92
Lichtenstein	1	1	1	1	1	1	2	0.70	0.65	0.61	0.61	0.51	0.56	0.89
Luxembourg	1	4	8	8	10	9	9	0.93	1.73	1.94	1.39	1.59	1.57	1.51
Norway	5	5	4	5	5	3	5	1.00	0.87	0.75	0.87	0.85	0.65	0.89
Norway, Germany	0	0	0	0	0	1	1	0.00	0.00	0.00	0.00	0.00	2.80	2.68
Portugal	1	2	2	1	1	1	1	0.56	1.30	1.21	0.81	0.64	0.56	0.54
South Africa	1	0	0	0	0	0	0	1.40	0.00	0.00	0.00	0.00	0.00	0.00
Russia	1	1	2	2	2	2	2	1.40	1.30	4.85	1.62	1.70	1.87	1.79
Slovenia	1	2	2	2	2	1	2	2.79	2.60	2.43	2.43	2.55	1.40	2.68
South Korea	2	2	3	3	3	3	4	1.12	1.30	1.82	1.82	1.27	1.40	0.89
Spain	3	4	8	7	7	7	7	1.20	1.15	1.49	1.55	1.62	1.96	1.56
Sweden	27	29	28	24	24	20	18	1.42	1.32	1.19	1.06	1.04	0.96	0.86

Continued

Appendix 2 Continued

Country-of-origin	2000	2001	2002	2003	2004	2005	2006	2000	2001	2002	2003	2004	2005	2006
All firms total:	**886**	**906**	**978**	**996**	**1101**	**1150**	**1091**				RLA CO			
Sweden/Switzerland	0	0	0	1	1	1	0	0.00	0.00	0.00	2.43	2.55	2.80	0.00
Switzerland	6	7	9	10	10	10	9	0.88	0.83	0.91	1.01	0.94	0.96	0.86
The Netherlands	20	26	33	39	45	39	39	0.85	0.91	0.88	0.97	1.09	1.10	1.06
Turkey	1	1	1	1	1	7	7	0.70	0.65	0.61	0.61	0.64	1.96	1.88
United Kingdom	11	16	21	18	18	19	19	0.88	1.04	1.13	0.93	0.87	1.02	1.00
USA	58	60	60	68	66	63	63	1.25	1.25	1.14	1.24	1.26	1.35	1.27
USA/United Kingdom	0	0	0	1	1	1	1	0.00	0.00	0.00	2.43	1.27	2.80	2.68
Wojewodztwo total:	**317**	**349**	**403**	**410**	**432**	**411**	**407**							
							Opolskie							
Austria	2	1	2	2	2	2	2	2.91	1.49	2.95	2.69	2.62	2.44	2.42
Belgium	3	3	3	3	3	3	3	7.22	7.72	7.50	6.84	6.12	5.77	5.72
Finland	1	1	1	1	1	1	1	2.91	3.15	3.60	2.76	2.62	2.63	2.61
France	0	0	0	1	1	1	1	0.00	0.00	0.00	0.58	0.54	0.51	0.50
Germany	5	5	5	6	7	8	8	1.32	1.37	1.25	1.42	1.52	1.62	1.63
Hungary	0	0	0	0	0	1	1	0.00	0.00	0.00	0.00	0.00	8.33	8.27
Italy	0	0	0	0	0	1	1	0.00	0.00	0.00	0.00	0.00	0.79	0.79
Norway	1	1	1	1	1	1	0	3.96	3.78	4.43	3.74	3.67	3.85	0.00
Switzerland	0	1	1	1	1	1	1	0.00	2.57	2.40	2.18	2.04	1.72	1.77
The Netherlands	1	1	1	1	1	1	1	0.84	0.77	0.63	0.53	0.52	0.51	0.50
United Kingdom	1	1	1	1	1	1	1	1.58	1.42	1.28	1.12	1.04	0.96	0.97
USA	2	2	2	2	2	2	2	2.91	0.91	0.90	0.79	55.05	0.76	0.75
Wojewodztwo total:	**16**	**16**	**17**	**19**	**20**	**23**	**22**							

Podkarpackie														
Austria	0	0	0	0	0	0	1	0.00	0.00	0.00	0.00	0.00	0.00	13.30
Canada	0	1	1	1	0	0	0	0.00	69.69	34.93	35.57	0.00	0.00	0.00
Denmark	0	1	2	2	2	1	1	0.00	23.84	22.74	22.64	22.94	11.27	10.10
France	1	2	3	2	4	4	4	0.63	20.83	91.69	11.07	21.59	23.47	21.82
Germany	5	8	7	7	7	9	10	1.06	35.01	14.82	15.70	15.23	20.95	22.36
Sweden	1	1	1	1	1	1	1	0.84	15.89	8.58	9.05	9.33	9.91	9.74
The Netherlands	1	2	2	2	2	2	2	0.67	24.49	10.75	10.16	10.49	11.62	11.02
Turkey	1	1	0	0	0	0	0	11.08	226.50	0.00	0.00	0.00	0.00	0.00
United Kingdom	1	1	2	2	2	2	2	1.27	22.65	21.73	21.19	20.77	22.12	21.39
USA	10	8	7	8	10	8	8	3.41	57.98	26.74	29.95	41.39	35.11	32.81
Wojewodztwo total:	**20**	**25**	**25**	**25**	**28**	**27**	**29**							
Podlaskie														
Canada	1	0	0	0	0	0	0	5.83	0.00	0.00	0.00	0.00	0.00	0.00
Finland	1	0	0	0	0	0	0	5.54	0.00	0.00	0.00	0.00	0.00	0.00
France	0	1	1	1	2	1	2	0.00	1.49	1.31	1.38	2.16	1.07	2.42
Germany	0	3	3	2	2	2	1	0.00	1.88	1.59	1.12	0.87	0.85	0.50
Japan	3	0	1	1	1	1	1	30.20	0.00	11.11	5.66	4.08	4.18	4.18
Slovenia	0	0	0	0	0	1	0	0.00	0.00	0.00	0.00	0.00	52.27	0.00
South Africa	0	0	0	1	1	1	0	0.00	0.00	0.00	124.50	110.10	104.55	0.00
Sweden	0	0	0	0	1	1	1	0.00	0.00	0.00	0.00	1.87	1.80	2.16
Switzerland	1	1	1	1	1	1	1	5.83	5.88	5.09	5.19	4.08	3.61	4.33
The Netherlands	0	0	0	0	1	1	1	0.00	0.00	0.00	0.00	1.05	1.06	1.22
United Kingdom/USA	0	0	0	1	1	1	1	0.00	0.00	0.00	124.50	55.05	104.55	121.22
USA	2	2	2	1	0	1	1	1.70	2.07	1.91	0.94	0.00	0.80	0.91
Wojewodztwo total:	**8**	**7**	**8**	**8**	**10**	**11**	**9**							

Continued

Appendix 2 Continued

Country-of-origin	2000	2001	2002	2003	2004	2005	2006	2000	2001	2002	2003	2004	2005	2006
All firms total:	**886**	**906**	**978**	**996**	**1101**	**1150**	**1091**				RLA CO			
							Pomorskie							
Austria	2	2	1	2	1	2	3	1.06	1.01	0.49	1.06	0.49	1.04	1.51
Belgium	0	0	0	0	1	1	1	0.00	0.00	0.00	0.00	0.76	0.82	0.79
Canada	2	2	3	3	3	2	1	2.12	2.97	4.11	4.45	4.71	3.28	1.72
China	1	1	1	1	1	1	1	10.07	9.64	9.59	10.38	10.19	10.65	10.29
Denmark	3	2	2	2	2	2	2	1.78	1.01	0.89	0.94	0.85	0.84	0.76
Finland	1	0	0	1	1	1	1	1.01	0.00	0.00	1.09	0.97	1.12	1.08
France	2	3	3	4	4	4	5	0.58	0.66	0.62	0.92	0.80	0.87	1.03
Germany	11	13	16	15	17	17	15	1.06	1.21	1.33	1.40	1.37	1.47	1.27
International	2	3	2	1	1	1	1	1.92	3.21	2.26	1.73	1.85	2.37	2.29
Ireland	1	0	0	0	0	0	0	6.71	0.00	0.00	0.00	0.00	0.00	0.00
Italy	1	2	2	2	3	2	2	0.31	0.63	0.62	0.66	0.89	0.68	0.65
Norway	2	3	2	1	2	2	2	2.88	3.86	2.95	1.48	2.72	3.28	2.74
Philippines	0	0	0	1	1	1	1	0.00	0.00	0.00	20.75	20.39	21.30	20.58
Sweden	2	3	3	3	4	3	3	0.76	1.01	1.01	1.13	1.38	1.10	1.10
Switzerland	3	1	1	0	0	2	2	3.18	0.88	0.80	0.00	0.00	1.47	1.47
The Netherlands	3	3	4	4	4	3	4	0.92	0.78	0.84	0.85	0.78	0.65	0.83
United Kingdom	0	1	1	1	2	2	2	0.00	0.48	0.43	0.44	0.77	0.82	0.81
USA	8	8	10	7	7	8	7	1.24	1.23	1.50	1.09	1.07	1.30	1.08
Wojewodztwo total:	**44**	**47**	**51**	**48**	**54**	**54**	**53**							
							Śląskie							
Austria	2	2	2	2	2	2	2	0.73	0.77	0.76	0.67	0.61	0.65	0.60
Belgium	2	3	2	3	2	2	1	1.20	1.99	1.29	1.71	0.95	1.03	0.47
Czech Republic	0	0	0	0	0	2	2	0.00	0.00	0.00	0.00	0.00	6.69	6.13

Denmark	2	2	2	2	2	2	2	0.81	0.77	0.69	0.60	0.53	0.52	0.45
Finland	3	2	1	1	2	3	3	2.08	1.62	0.93	0.69	1.22	2.11	1.94
France	4	4	5	5	6	8	7	0.79	0.67	0.80	0.73	0.75	1.09	0.86
Germany	17	15	17	16	19	17	18	1.13	1.06	1.09	0.94	0.96	0.92	0.90
Hungary	0	0	0	0	0	1	0	0.00	0.00	0.00	0.00	0.00	2.23	0.00
India	0	0	0	0	1	1	1	0.00	0.00	0.00	0.00	12.80	6.69	6.13
International	2	2	2	1	1	1	1	1.32	1.62	1.74	1.09	1.16	1.49	1.36
Ireland	0	0	0	0	0	1	1	0.00	0.00	0.00	0.00	0.00	2.23	1.75
Italy	12	12	12	13	18	14	15	2.56	2.87	2.87	2.70	3.34	2.97	2.92
Italy/USA	0	0	0	1	1	1	1	0.00	0.00	0.00	13.11	12.80	13.37	12.26
Japan	1	2	1	2	2	2	3	1.26	2.44	1.35	1.19	0.95	1.07	1.27
Luxembourg	0	0	1	4	4	4	4	0.00	0.00	1.48	3.74	3.20	3.34	3.06
Norway	1	1	1	1	1	1	1	0.99	0.97	1.14	0.94	0.85	1.03	0.82
Portugal	0	0	0	0	0	1	1	0.00	0.00	0.00	0.00	0.00	2.67	4.09
South Africa	1	1	1	0	0	0	0	6.92	7.31	14.82	0.00	0.00	0.00	0.00
Spain	1	2	3	2	2	2	2	1.98	3.25	3.42	2.38	2.33	2.67	2.04
Sweden	4	4	3	3	3	3	4	1.04	1.03	0.78	0.71	0.65	0.69	0.88
Switzerland	0	0	0	0	1	1	1	0.00	0.00	0.00	0.00	0.47	0.46	0.44
The Netherlands	4	4	6	5	5	7	8	0.84	0.79	0.98	0.67	0.61	0.95	0.99
Ukraine	0	0	0	0	0	1	1	0.00	0.00	0.00	0.00	0.00	13.37	12.26
United Kingdom	2	1	1	5	6	4	4	0.79	0.37	0.33	1.39	1.45	1.03	0.96
USA	6	5	6	10	8	5	6	0.64	0.58	0.69	0.99	0.77	0.51	0.55
Wojewodztwo total:	**64**	**62**	**66**	**76**	**86**	**86**	**89**							
Świętokrzyskie														
Austria	1	1	1	1	1	1	1	1.55	1.70	2.09	2.13	1.75	2.16	2.05
Belgium	4	4	3	2	3	2	2	10.27	11.77	10.63	7.22	8.16	6.80	6.46
France	0	1	1	1	2	2	2	0.00	0.74	0.88	0.92	1.44	1.81	1.68
Germany	2	2	1	1	1	1	1	0.57	0.63	0.35	0.37	0.29	0.36	0.34
Italy	2	2	2	2	2	2	2	1.82	2.12	2.63	2.63	2.13	2.81	2.66
Japan	1	1	1	2	2	1	1	5.37	5.39	7.41	7.55	5.44	3.54	2.89

Continued

Appendix 2 Continued

Country-of-origin	2000	2001	2002	2003	2004	2005	2006	2000	2001	2002	2003	2004	2005	2006
All firms total:	**886**	**906**	**978**	**996**	**1101**	**1150**	**1091**				RLA CO			
The Netherlands	2	2	1	2	2	2	2	1.79	1.75	0.90	1.69	1.40	1.79	1.70
United Kingdom	2	1	2	1	1	1	1	3.38	1.62	3.62	1.77	1.38	1.70	1.65
USA	1	0	0	0	1	1	1	0.45	0.00	0.00	0.00	0.55	0.68	0.63
Wojewodztwo total	**15**	**14**	**12**	**12**	**15**	**13**	**13**							
Warmińsko-Mazurskie														
Austria	0	1	0	0	0	0	0	0.00	2.38	0.00	0.00	0.00	0.00	0.00
Belgium	1	1	1	1	1	1	1	3.50	4.12	4.25	3.61	3.14	3.40	3.23
Denmark	1	1	1	1	1	1	1	2.37	2.38	2.27	1.89	1.76	1.73	1.55
Finland	2	1	1	1	1	1	1	8.05	5.03	6.11	4.37	4.03	4.66	4.42
France	1	0	0	1	0	1	2	1.15	0.00	0.00	0.92	0.00	0.90	1.68
Germany	3	3	3	3	5	5	5	1.16	1.31	1.27	1.12	1.67	1.79	1.72
Ireland	0	1	1	1	1	1	1	0.00	30.20	48.90	27.67	16.94	14.74	11.99
Italy	1	0	0	1	1	1	1	1.24	0.00	0.00	1.32	1.23	1.40	1.33
Spain	1	1	1	1	1	0	0	11.51	10.07	7.52	7.55	7.70	0.00	0.00
The Netherlands	0	0	1	1	2	2	1	0.00	0.00	1.07	0.85	1.61	1.79	0.85
United Kingdom	1	0	0	0	0	0	0	2.30	0.00	0.00	0.00	0.00	0.00	0.00
USA	0	1	1	1	0	0	0	0.00	0.72	0.76	0.62	0.00	0.00	0.00
Wojewodztwo total:	**11**	**10**	**10**	**12**	**13**	**13**	**13**							
Wielkopolskie														
Austria	1	1	2	2	2	2	2	0.39	0.24	0.48	0.51	0.48	0.51	0.50
Belgium	1	1	3	3	3	5	5	0.47	0.41	1.21	1.29	1.12	2.03	1.96
Canada	3	3	3	3	3	3	3	1.41	2.09	2.00	2.11	2.33	2.43	2.55

Denmark	4	5	5	6	5	5	5	1.05	1.19	1.08	1.34	1.05	1.03	0.94
Finland	1	2	2	1	1	1	1	0.45	1.01	1.16	0.52	0.48	0.56	0.54
France	6	11	10	8	9	8	8	0.77	1.15	1.00	0.88	0.89	0.86	0.82
Germany	37	34	33	29	32	33	31	1.58	1.49	1.33	1.29	1.28	1.41	1.30
Hungary	0	0	1	1	1	1	1	0.00	0.00	3.10	2.47	2.53	1.76	1.70
Ireland	1	1	1	1	1	1	1	2.98	3.02	4.66	3.29	2.02	1.76	1.46
Italy	2	1	1	1	1	1	1	0.28	0.15	0.15	0.16	0.15	0.17	0.16
Japan	3	4	3	3	3	3	3	2.44	3.02	2.54	1.34	1.12	1.27	1.05
Lichtenstein	2	2	2	2	2	2	2	4.47	4.53	4.66	4.93	4.04	4.22	3.40
Luxembourg	0	0	0	0	0	1	1	0.00	0.00	0.00	0.00	0.00	0.66	0.64
Malta	1	0	0	0	0	0	0	8.95	0.00	0.00	0.00	0.00	0.00	0.00
Norway	2	1	1	1	2	1	2	1.28	0.60	0.72	0.70	1.35	0.81	1.36
Portugal	1	1	1	1	1	0	0	1.79	2.27	2.33	3.29	2.53	0.00	0.00
South Africa	0	0	0	0	0	0	1	0.00	0.00	0.00	0.00	0.00	0.00	10.20
Sweden	7	9	10	12	12	11	10	1.18	1.43	1.63	2.15	2.05	2.00	1.82
Switzerland	5	4	4	4	5	3	3	2.36	1.65	1.55	1.64	1.87	1.09	1.09
The Netherlands	12	12	13	13	15	17	16	1.63	1.47	1.33	1.31	1.44	1.81	1.65
United Kingdom	3	2	3	3	3	4	4	0.77	0.45	0.62	0.63	0.57	0.81	0.80
USA	7	6	7	7	8	7	7	0.48	0.43	0.51	0.52	0.61	0.56	0.54
Wojewodztwo total:	**99**	**100**	**105**	**101**	**109**	**109**	**107**							
Zachodnio-Pomorskie														
Austria	1	1	1	1	1	2	1	1.37	1.32	1.32	1.16	1.09	1.70	0.86
Belgium	0	0	0	0	0	1	1	0.00	0.00	0.00	0.00	0.00	1.34	1.35
Cyprus	0	1	1	1	1	0	0	0.00	25.17	17.16	22.64	15.29	0.00	0.00
Denmark	2	3	5	7	7	8	9	3.07	3.97	5.99	7.20	6.69	5.47	5.87
Germany	4	3	4	3	4	5	5	1.00	0.73	0.89	0.61	0.73	0.71	0.72
International	1	0	0	1	0	0	0	2.48	0.00	0.00	3.77	0.00	0.00	0.00

Continued

Appendix 2 Continued

Country-of-origin	2000	2001	2002	2003	2004	2005	2006	2000	2001	2002	2003	2004	2005	2006
All firms total:	**886**	**906**	**978**	**996**	**1101**	**1150**	**1091**	RLA CO						
Italy	1	0	0	0	0	1	1	0.80	0.00	0.00	0.00	0.00	0.55	0.56
Norway	2	2	1	1	0	2	2	7.45	6.71	3.96	3.23	0.00	5.36	4.69
South Korea	0	0	0	0	0	2	0	0.00	0.00	0.00	0.00	0.00	11.62	0.00
Sweden	2	2	2	4	7	7	7	1.97	1.77	1.81	3.29	5.44	4.21	4.40
Switzerland	1	1	1	1	1	1	0	2.74	2.29	2.14	1.89	1.70	1.20	0.00
The Netherlands	3	5	4	3	3	3	3	2.37	3.40	2.26	1.39	1.31	1.06	1.07
USA	0	0	0	0	0	1	2	0.00	0.00	0.00	0.00	0.00	0.27	0.53
Wojewodztwo total:	**17**	**18**	**19**	**22**	**24**	**33**	**31**							

Source: Based on data obtained from the Polish Information and Foreign Investment Agency (PAIIZ) and the author's own analysis.

Appendix 3 Multiple regression coefficients for years 2000–2006

		Correlations													
		1	2	3	4	5	6	7	8	9	10	11	12	13	14
1	PKD Average	1													
2	2000 R&D – Private	–0.14	1												
3	2000 R&D – Total	–0.13	0.99	1											
4	2000 Unemployment-secondary	–0.17	0.74	0.7	1										
5	2000 Unemployment-tertiary	–0.18	0.074	0.71	0.94	1									
6	2000 Population	–0.19	0.79	0.75	0.93	0.88	1								
7	2001 R&D – Private	–0.14	1	0.98	0.76	0.76	0.81	1							
8	2001 R&D – Total	–0.14	0.99	1	0.71	0.71	0.76	0.98	1						
9	2001 Unemployment-secondary	–0.17	0.76	0.72	1	0.93	0.96	0.78	0.73	1					
10	2001 Unemployment-tertiary	–0.18	0.78	0.75	0.95	1	0.9	0.8	0.75	0.95	1				
11	2001 Population	–0.19	0.79	0.75	0.93	0.88	1	0.81	0.76	0.96	0.9	1			
12	2002 R&D private	–0.15	0.87	0.87	0.77	0.76	0.82	0.87	0.87	0.79	0.78	0.82	1		
13	2002 R&D-Total	–0.13	0.98	1	0.7	0.71	0.75	0.97	1	0.72	0.74	0.75	0.88	1	
14	2002 Unemployment-secondary	–0.18	0.79	0.75	0.99	0.92	0.96	0.81	0.76	1	0.94	0.96	0.8	0.74	1
15	2002 Unemployment-tertiary	–0.19	0.81	0.78	0.95	0.98	0.91	0.83	0.78	0.95	1	0.91	0.79	0.77	0.95
16	2002 Population	–0.19	0.79	0.75	0.93	0.88	1	0.81	0.76	0.96	0.9	1	0.82	0.75	0.96
17	2002 Wage	–0.13	0.96	0.94	0.69	0.69	0.78	0.96	0.94	0.72	0.74	0.78	0.83	0.93	0.76
18	2003 R&D – Private	–0.15	0.98	0.98	0.76	0.75	0.82	0.97	0.98	0.78	0.78	0.82	0.94	0.98	0.8
19	2003 R&D – Total	–0.14	0.99	1	0.71	0.71	0.76	0.98	1	0.73	0.75	0.77	0.88	1	0.75
20	2003 Unemployment-secondary	–0.18	0.79	0.75	0.99	0.91	0.96	0.81	0.76	1	0.94	0.96	0.8	0.74	1
21	2003 Unemployment-tertiary	–0.19	0.82	0.78	0.96	0.98	0.93	0.84	0.79	0.96	0.99	0.93	0.8	0.78	0.96
22	2003 Population	–0.19	0.79	0.76	0.93	0.87	1	0.81	0.76	0.95	0.9	1	0.82	0.76	0.96
23	2003 Wage	–0.13	0.96	0.94	0.69	0.68	0.79	0.96	0.94	0.72	0.74	0.79	0.83	0.93	0.76
24	2004 R&D – Private	–0.15	0.99	0.99	0.73	0.72	0.787	0.98	0.99	0.75	0.76	0.78	0.91	0.99	0.77

Continued

Appendix 3 Continued

		Correlations													
		1	2	3	4	5	6	7	8	9	10	11	12	13	14
25	2004 R&D – Total	–0.13	0.98	1	0.7	0.71	0.76	0.97	1	0.72	0.74	0.76	0.89	1	0.75
26	2004 Unemployment-secondary	–0.18	0.79	0.76	0.99	0.92	0.97	0.81	0.76	0.99	0.94	0.97	0.8	0.75	1
27	2004 Unemployment-tertiary	–0.19	0.81	0.77	0.95	0.98	0.93	0.83	0.78	0.95	0.99	0.92	0.78	0.77	0.96
28	2004 Population	–0.19	0.79	0.76	0.93	0.87	1	0.81	0.77	0.95	0.9	1	0.83	0.76	0.96
29	2004 Wage	–0.14	0.95	0.93	0.7	0.7	0.79	0.96	0.93	0.73	0.75	0.79	0.84	0.92	0.77
30	2005 R&D – Private	–0.15	0.98	0.98	0.74	0.73	0.79	0.97	0.98	0.76	0.76	0.79	0.94	0.98	0.78
31	2005 R&D – Total	–0.14	0.98	0.99	0.71	0.71	0.77	0.97	1	0.73	0.75	0.77	0.9	1	0.75
32	2005 Unemployment-secondary	–0.18	0.81	0.78	0.98	0.92	0.96	0.83	0.79	0.99	0.95	0.96	0.82	0.78	1
33	2005 Unemployment-tertiary	–0.19	0.79	0.76	0.93	0.87	1	0.81	0.77	0.95	0.99	0.91	0.8	0.8	0.95
34	2005 Population	–0.19	0.79	0.76	0.93	0.87	1	0.81	0.77	0.95	0.9	1	0.83	0.76	0.96
35	2005 Wage	–0.15	0.94	0.91	0.69	0.69	0.78	0.94	0.91	0.72	0.74	0.78	0.84	0.91	0.76
36	2006 Unemployment-secondary	–0.17	0.84	0.81	0.98	0.93	0.95	0.85	0.81	0.98	0.95	0.95	0.84	0.8	0.99
37	2006 Unemployment-tertiary	–0.18	0.84	0.8	0.94	0.98	0.91	0.85	0.81	0.94	0.99	0.9	0.8	0.8	0.94
38	2006 Population	–0.19	0.8	0.76	0.93	0.87	1	0.81	0.77	0.95	0.9	1	0.83	0.76	0.96
39	2006 Wage	–0.14	0.93	0.91	0.7	0.69	0.79	0.94	0.91	0.73	0.74	0.79	0.84	0.9	0.77

N=213

For all the results correlation is significant at the $P<.05$ level

		Correlations												
		15	16	17	18	19	20	21	22	23	24	25	26	27
1	PKD Average													
2	2000 R&D – Private													
3	2000 R&D – Total													
4	2000 Unemployment-secondary													
5	2000 Unemployment-tertiary													
6	2000 Population													
7	2001 R&D – Private													
8	2001 R&D – Total													
9	2001 Unemployment-secondary													
10	2001 Unemployment-tertiary													
11	2001 Population													
12	2002 R&D – Private													
13	2002 R&D – Total													
14	2002 Unemployment-secondary													
15	2002 Unemployment-tertiary	1												
16	2002 Population	0.91	1											
17	2002 Wage	0.78	0.78	1										
18	2003 R&D – Private	0.8	0.82	0.92	1									
19	2003 R&D – Total	0.78	0.77	0.93	0.98	1								
20	2003 Unemployment-secondary	0.95	0.96	0.76	0.8	0.75	1							
21	2003 Unemployment-tertiary	1	0.93	0.79	0.81	0.78	0.96	1						
22	2003 Population	0.91	1	0.79	0.82	0.77	0.96	0.92	1					
23	2003 Wage	0.78	0.79	1	0.92	0.93	0.76	0.79	0.79	1				
24	2004 R&D – Private	0.78	0.78	0.93	0.99	0.99	0.77	0.79	0.78	0.93	1			

Continued

Appendix 3 Continued

		Correlations												
		15	16	17	18	19	20	21	22	23	24	25	26	27
25	2004 R&D – Total	0.77	0.76	0.93	0.98	1	0.93	0.78	0.76	0.93	0.99	1		
26	2004 Unemployment-secondary	0.95	0.97	0.77	0.8	0.76	0.99	0.96	0.97	0.77	0.78	0.75	1	
27	2004 Unemployment-tertiary	1	0.92	0.78	0.8	0.77	0.95	1	0.92	0.78	0.78	0.77	0.96	1
28	2004 Population	0.91	1	0.79	0.82	0.77	0.96	0.92	1	0.79	0.79	0.77	0.97	0.92
29	2004 Wage	0.79	0.8	1	0.91	0.92	0.77	0.8	0.8	1	0.92	0.92	0.78	0.79
30	2005 R&D – Private	0.79	0.8	0.94	0.99	0.99	0.78	0.8	0.8	0.93	0.99	0.99	0.79	0.78
31	2005 R&D – Total	0.77	0.77	0.93	0.98	1	0.76	0.78	0.77	0.92	0.99	1	0.76	0.77
32	2005 Unemployment-secondary	0.99	0.91	0.78	0.83	0.79	1	0.96	0.96	0.78	0.81	0.78	1	0.96
33	2005 Unemployment-tertiary	0.91	1	0.79	0.83	0.77	0.96	0.92	1	0.79	0.79	0.77	0.97	0.92
34	2005 Population	0.78	0.78	0.99	0.9	0.9	0.77	0.79	0.79	0.99	0.91	0.9	0.77	0.78
35	2005 Wage	0.96	0.95	0.8	0.85	0.81	0.99	0.97	0.95	0.8	0.83	0.81	0.99	0.96
36	2006 Unemployment-secondary	0.99	0.9	0.78	0.83	0.8	0.93	0.99	0.9	0.78	0.81	0.8	0.94	0.99
37	2006 Unemployment-tertiary	0.91	1	0.79	0.83	0.78	0.96	0.92	1	0.79	0.79	0.77	0.97	0.92
38	2006 Population	0.91	1	0.79	0.83	0.78	0.96	0.92	1	0.79	0.79	0.77	0.97	0.92
39	2006 Wage	0.78	0.79	0.99	0.9	0.9	0.77	0.8	0.8	0.99	0.91	0.9	0.78	0.78

N=213

For all the results correlation is significant at the P<.05 level

		Correlations													
		28	29	30	31	32	33	34	35	36	37	38	39	40	41
1	PKD Average														
2	2000 R&D – Private														
3	2000 R&D – Total														
4	2000 Unemployment-secondary														
5	2000 Unemployment-tertiary														
6	2000 Population														
7	2001 R&D – Private														
8	2001 R&D – Total														
9	2001 Unemployment-secondary														
10	2001 Unemployment-tertiary														
11	2001 Population														
12	2002 R&D – Private														
13	2002 R&D – Total														
14	2002 Unemployment-secondary														
15	2002 Unemployment-tertiary														
16	2002 Population														
17	2002 Wage														
18	2003 R&D – Private														
19	2003 R&D – Total														
20	2003 Unemployment-secondary														
21	2003 Unemployment-tertiary														
22	2003 Population														
23	2003 Wage														
24	2004 R&D – Private														

Continued

Appendix 3 Continued

		Correlations													
		28	29	30	31	32	33	34	35	36	37	38	39	40	41
25	2004 R&D – Total														
26	2004 Unemployment-secondary														
27	2004 Unemployment-tertiary														
28	2004 Population	1													
29	2004 Wage	0.8	1												
30	2005 R&D – Private	0.8	0.93	1											
31	2005 R&D – Total	0.78	0.92	0.99	1										
32	2005 Unemployment-secondary	0.96	0.79	0.81	0.79	1									
33	2005 Unemployment-tertiary	0.91	0.79	0.81	0.8	0.96	1								
34	2005 Population	1	0.8	0.8	0.78	0.96	0.91	1							
35	2005 Wage	0.79	1	0.92	0.9	0.78	0.78	0.79	1						
36	2006 Unemployment-secondary	0.95	0.8	0.83	0.81	1	0.97	0.95	0.79	1					
37	2006 Unemployment-tertiary	0.9	0.78	0.81	0.8	0.95	1	0.9	0.77	0.96	1				
38	2006 Population	1	0.8	0.81	0.78	0.96	0.91	1	0.79	0.96	0.9	1			
39	2006 Wage	0.8	1	0.92	0.9	0.79	0.78	0.8	1	0.79	0.77	0.8	1		
	N=213														
	For all the results correlation is significant at the P<.05 level														

Source: Based on data obtained from the Polish Information and Foreign Investment Agency (PAIIZ) and the author's own analysis.

Appendix 3a Results of regression – RLAis and amount of total regional investment in select industries (H3a) control

Investment per Industry & Total Investment (2000–2006)	DOLNOŚLĄSKIE	KUJAWSKO-POMORSKIE	ŁÓDZKIE	LUBELSKIE	LUBUSKIE	MAŁOPOLSKIE	MAZOWIECKIE	OPOLSKIE	PODKARPACKIE	PODLASKIE	POMORSKIE	ŚLĄSKIE	ŚWIĘTOKRZYSKIE	WARMIŃSKO-MAZURSKIE	WIELKOPOLSKIE	ZACHODNIOPOMORSKIE
Agriculture, hunting and forestry																
Multiple R				0.360							0.963			0.856	0.848	
R Square				0.129							0.928			0.733	0.719	
Adjusted R Square				–0.306							0.892			0.599	0.578	
Mining and quarrying																
Multiple R	0.986					0.734	0.787	0.910				0.571				
R Square	0.973					0.539	0.620	0.828				0.326				
Adjusted R Square	0.959					0.308	0.429	0.742				–0.012				
Manufacturing: Chemicals & Chemical Products																
Multiple R	0.654	0.334	0.419	0.351	0.677	0.604	0.277	0.077	0.835		0.506	0.452	0.444		0.853	0.117
R Square	0.428	0.112	0.176	0.123	0.459	0.364	0.077	0.006	0.697		0.257	0.204	0.197		0.728	0.014
Adjusted R Square	0.142	–0.332	–0.236	–0.315	0.188	0.046	–0.385	–0.491	0.545		–0.115	–0.194	–0.204		0.592	–0.479
Manufacturing: Consumer Products																
Multiple R	0.790		0.366				0.668								0.636	1.000
R Square	0.625		0.134				0.446								0.405	1.000
Adjusted R Square	0.437		–0.300				0.169								0.107	1.000

Continued

Investment per Industry & Total Investment (2000–2006)	DOLNOŚLĄSKIE	KUJAWSKO–POMORSKIE	ŁÓDZKIE	LUBELSKIE	LUBUSKIE	MAŁOPOLSKIE	MAZOWIECKIE	OPOLSKIE	PODKARPACKIE	PODLASKIE	POMORSKIE	ŚLĄSKIE	ŚWIĘTOKRZYSKIE	WARMIŃSKO–MAZURSKIE	WIELKOPOLSKIE	ZACHODNIOPOMORSKIE
Manufacturing: Electrical Machinery and Apparatus																
Multiple R	0.828	0.862	0.593				0.200		0.556		0.886	0.740			0.496	0.278
R Square	0.686	0.743	0.352				0.040		0.309		0.784	0.547			0.246	0.077
Adjusted R Square	0.529	0.615	0.027				–0.440		–0.037		0.676	0.321			–0.131	–0.384
Manufacturing: Fabrics & Textiles																
Multiple R	0.642	0.693	0.295		0.921	0.909	0.948	0.858		0.800		0.531	0.541	0.625	0.900	
R Square	0.413	0.481	0.087		0.847	0.827	0.900	0.736		0.640		0.282	0.292	0.390	0.811	
Adjusted R Square	0.119	0.221	–0.370		0.771	0.740	0.849	0.604		0.460		–0.077	–0.061	0.085	0.716	
Manufacturing: Food, Drinks & Tobacco Products																
Multiple R	0.483	0.405	0.435	0.892	0.937	0.477	0.868	0.710	0.348	0.867	0.124	0.616	0.774	0.949	0.117	0.657
R Square	0.233	0.164	0.189	0.796	0.877	0.228	0.753	0.505	0.121	0.751	0.015	0.379	0.599	0.900	0.014	0.431
Adjusted R Square	–0.150	–0.254	–0.217	0.694	0.816	–0.159	0.630	0.257	–0.319	0.626	–0.477	0.068	0.398	0.850	–0.480	0.147
Manufacturing: Furniture & Consumer Goods																
Multiple R	0.943	0.686		0.760			0.620				0.535	0.468		0.862	0.815	0.186
R Square	0.890	0.470		0.577			0.384				0.287	0.219		0.743	0.664	0.035
Adjusted R Square	0.834	0.206		0.366			0.076				–0.070	–0.171		0.614	0.496	–0.448
Manufacturing: Glass																
Multiple R									0.919							
R Square									0.845							
Adjusted R Square									0.768							

Manufacturing: Leather & Leather Products																
Multiple R		0.781	0.887		0.473		0.958		0.333							0.646
R Square		0.611	0.787		0.224		0.918		0.111							0.417
Adjusted R Square		0.416	0.680		–0.164		0.877		–0.334							0.125
Manufacturing: Machinery & Equipment																
Multiple R	0.747		0.662	0.630			0.887	0.715				0.508	0.782	0.781	0.898	0.695
R Square	0.559		0.439	0.397			0.787	0.512				0.258	0.612	0.610	0.806	0.484
Adjusted R Square	0.338		0.158	0.096			0.680	0.268				–0.113	0.418	0.415	0.709	0.226
Manufacturing: Metals & Metal Products																
Multiple R	0.868	0.151	0.557	0.473	0.623	0.785	0.948	0.725	0.758	0.785	0.655	0.302	0.780		0.747	0.804
R Square	0.754	0.023	0.310	0.224	0.388	0.616	0.898	0.525	0.575	0.616	0.428	0.091	0.609		0.558	0.647
Adjusted R Square	0.631	–0.466	–0.035	–0.164	0.081	0.424	0.847	0.288	0.362	0.425	0.143	–0.363	0.413		0.337	0.470
Manufacturing: Other Non-Metal Goods																
Multiple R	0.981	0.627	0.634	0.844	0.544	0.547	0.425	0.684	0.685		0.658	0.422	0.588	0.832	0.363	0.789
R Square	0.963	0.394	0.402	0.712	0.295	0.299	0.180	0.468	0.469		0.432	0.178	0.345	0.693	0.132	0.622
Adjusted R Square	0.944	0.091	0.104	0.568	–0.057	–0.052	–0.229	0.202	0.203		0.149	–0.233	0.018	0.539	–0.302	0.433
Manufacturing: Pharmaceuticals																
Multiple R				0.862			0.847								0.875	
R Square				0.744			0.717								0.765	
Adjusted R Square				0.615			0.576								0.648	
Manufacturing: Pulp & Paper / Publishing & Printing																
Multiple R	0.905	0.692	0.918	0.902	0.686	0.736	0.194			0.385	0.722	0.646	0.769	0.588	0.124	0.756
R Square	0.818	0.479	0.843	0.815	0.471	0.542	0.038			0.148	0.521	0.417	0.592	0.345	0.015	0.572
Adjusted R Square	0.728	0.219	0.765	0.722	0.207	0.314	–0.443			–0.278	0.282	0.125	0.388	0.018	–0.477	0.358
Manufacturing: Radio, Television, Communication Equipment & Apparatus																
Multiple R		0.862					0.910								0.857	
R Square		0.743					0.829								0.734	
Adjusted R Square		0.615					0.743								0.600	

Continued

Appendix 3a Continued

Investment per Industry & Total Investment (2000–2006)	DOLNOŚLĄSKIE	KUJAWSKO-POMORSKIE	ŁÓDZKIE	LUBELSKIE	LUBUSKIE	MAŁOPOLSKIE	MAZOWIECKIE	OPOLSKIE	PODKARPACKIE	PODLASKIE	POMORSKIE	ŚLĄSKIE	ŚWIĘTOKRZYSKIE	WARMIŃSKO-MAZURSKIE	WIELKOPOLSKIE	ZACHODNIOPOMORSKIE
Manufacturing: Rubber & Plastics																
Multiple R	0.174	0.801	0.485	0.368	0.772	0.739	0.622		0.566	0.681	0.745	0.776		0.968	0.753	0.628
R Square	0.030	0.642	0.235	0.135	0.595	0.546	0.387		0.320	0.464	0.556	0.603		0.937	0.568	0.394
Adjusted R Square	–0.455	0.462	–0.148	–0.297	0.393	0.320	0.080		–0.020	0.195	0.333	0.404		0.906	0.352	0.092
Manufacturing: Transport Equipment																
Multiple R	0.810	0.947	0.684	0.616	0.808	0.234	0.351	0.840	0.913		0.815	0.574	0.785		0.481	
R Square	0.656	0.897	0.467	0.380	0.653	0.055	0.123	0.705	0.834		0.664	0.330	0.617		0.231	
Adjusted R Square	0.484	0.845	0.201	0.070	0.479	–0.418	–0.315	0.558	0.751		0.497	–0.006	0.425		–0.153	
Manufacturing: Wood & Wooden Products																
Multiple R	0.633	0.530		0.670	0.438				0.591	0.407					0.742	0.593
R Square	0.400	0.281		0.448	0.192				0.349	0.166					0.551	0.352
Adjusted R Square	0.100	–0.078		0.172	–0.212				0.024	–0.252					0.326	0.028
Electricity, gas and water supply																
Multiple R	0.449					0.603	0.874		0.286	0.090	0.737	0.605	0.157	0.651	0.456	0.217
R Square	0.201					0.363	0.764		0.082	0.008	0.544	0.365	0.025	0.423	0.208	0.047
Adjusted R Square	–0.198					0.045	0.647		–0.377	–0.488	0.315	0.048	–0.463	0.135	–0.188	–0.429

Construction																
Multiple R			0.724			0.346	0.878				0.810	0.435	0.477		0.976	
R Square			0.524			0.119	0.770				0.657	0.189	0.227		0.953	
Adjusted R Square			0.286			–0.321	0.656				0.485	–0.216	–0.159		0.929	
Trade and repair																
Multiple R	0.828	0.744	0.418	0.921	0.636	0.955	0.951	0.799		0.569		0.729	0.860		0.463	0.632
R Square	0.686	0.553	0.174	0.849	0.405	0.911	0.904	0.639		0.324		0.532	0.739		0.214	0.399
Adjusted R Square	0.528	0.330	–0.238	0.773	0.107	0.867	0.856	0.458		–0.014		0.297	0.608		–0.179	0.099
Hotels and restaurants																
Multiple R	0.388			0.932	0.724		0.955				0.945	0.890			0.461	0.781
R Square	0.151			0.868	0.525		0.912				0.893	0.793			0.212	0.610
Adjusted R Square	–0.274			0.803	0.287		0.867				0.840	0.689			–0.182	0.415
Transport, storage and communication* (2004–2006)																
Multiple R	1.000		1.000		1.000		1.000		1.000		1.000	1.000		1.000	1.000	1.000
R Square	1.000		1.000		1.000		1.000		1.000		1.000	1.000		1.000	1.000	1.000
Financial intermediation																
Multiple R	0.781	0.889	0.663		0.833		0.649				0.775	0.407			0.941	
R Square	0.609	0.790	0.439		0.694		0.422				0.600	0.166			0.885	
Adjusted R Square	0.414	0.686	0.159		0.541		0.133				0.401	–0.251			0.828	
Real estate, rental and business activities																
Multiple R	0.643		0.267			0.431	0.832	0.616			0.971	0.676			0.604	0.215
R Square	0.413		0.072			0.185	0.692	0.379			0.943	0.457			0.365	0.046
Adjusted R Square	0.120		–0.393			–0.222	0.538	0.069			0.914	0.185			0.048	–0.431
Other community, social and personal service activities																
Multiple R	0.476		0.794			0.893	0.627				0.741	0.893		0.466	0.869	
R Square	0.227		0.631			0.798	0.393				0.549	0.798		0.217	0.756	
Adjusted R Square	–0.160		0.446			0.697	0.090				0.323	0.697		–0.174	0.633	

Source: Based on data obtained from the Polish Information and Foreign Investment Agency (PAIIZ) and the author's own analysis.

Appendix 3a1 Results of regression – RLAis and amount of total regional investment in select industries (H3a) control

Investment per Industry (2000–2006)	DOLNOŚLĄSKIE	KUJAWSKO-POMORSKIE	ŁÓDZKIE	LUBELSKIE	LUBUSKIE	MAŁOPOLSKIE	MAZOWIECKIE	OPOLSKIE	PODKARPACKIE	PODLASKIE	POMORSKIE	ŚLĄSKIE	ŚWIĘTOKRZYSKIE	WARMIŃSKO-MAZURSKIE	WIELKOPOLSKIE	ZACHODNIOPOMORSKIE
Agriculture, hunting, and forestry																
Multiple R				0.192							0.067			0.776	0.481	
R square				0.037							0.004			0.602	0.232	
Mining and quarrying																
Multiple R	0.971					0.478	0.476	0.164				0.052				
R square	0.942					0.228	0.226	0.027				0.003				
Manufacturing: Chemicals and Chemical Products																
Multiple R	0.653	0.088	0.240	0.339	0.329	0.496	0.084	0.047	0.832		0.381	0.431	0.425		0.666	0.063
R square	0.427	0.008	0.057	0.115	0.108	0.246	0.007	0.002	0.692		0.145	0.186	0.180		0.443	0.004
Manufacturing: Consumer Products																
Multiple R	0.742		0.366				0.643								0.588	1.000
R square	0.550		0.134				0.413								0.345	1.000
Manufacturing: Electrical Machinery and Apparatus																
Multiple R	0.809	0.525	0.586				0.175		0.392		0.039	0.730			0.451	0.232
R Square	0.655	0.276	0.344				0.031		0.154		0.001	0.532			0.203	0.054
Manufacturing: Fabrics and Textiles																
Multiple R	0.551	0.688	0.173		0.112	0.874	0.892	0.857		0.446		0.508	0.470	0.538	0.851	
R square	0.303	0.473	0.030		0.013	0.764	0.796	0.735		0.199		0.258	0.221	0.289	0.724	

Manufacturing: Food, Drinks, and Tobacco Products																
Multiple R	0.114	0.163	0.385	0.467	0.435	0.404	0.769	0.587	0.086	0.776	0.094	0.073	0.773	0.926	0.109	0.655
R square	0.013	0.027	0.148	0.218	0.189	0.163	0.591	0.344	0.007	0.602	0.009	0.005	0.598	0.857	0.012	0.429
Manufacturing: Furniture ND Consumer Goods																
Multiple R	0.565	0.290		0.262			0.265				0.357	0.204		0.734	0.447	0.076
R square	0.319	0.084		0.069			0.070				0.128	0.042		0.539	0.200	0.006
Manufacturing: Glass																
Multiple R									0.900							
R square									0.810							
Manufacturing: Leather and Leather Products																
Multiple R		0.748	0.887		0.148		0.926		0.309							0.517
R square		0.559	0.787		0.022		0.858		0.095							0.267
Manufacturing: Machinery and Equipment																
Multiple R	0.101		0.647	0.419			0.372	0.478				0.408	0.781	0.752	0.876	0.680
R square	0.010		0.419	0.176			0.138	0.228				0.166	0.611	0.565	0.768	0.463
Manufacturing: Metals and Metal Products																
Multiple R	0.694	0.082	0.527	0.299	0.337	0.244	0.646	0.058	0.583	0.777	0.218	0.243	0.246		0.639	0.784
R square	0.481	0.007	0.278	0.089	0.113	0.060	0.417	0.003	0.339	0.603	0.047	0.059	0.061		0.408	0.615
Manufacturing: Other Non-Metal Goods																
Multiple R	0.757	0.609	0.563	0.498	0.299	0.494	0.296	0.599	0.501		0.475	0.077	0.489	0.182	0.101	0.692
R square	0.572	0.371	0.317	0.248	0.089	0.244	0.087	0.359	0.251		0.225	0.006	0.239	0.033	0.010	0.479
Manufacturing: Pharmaceuticals																
Multiple R				0.250			0.566								0.599	
R square				0.062			0.320								0.359	
Manufacturing: Pulp and Paper / Publishing and Printing																
Multiple R	0.891	0.261	0.918	0.272	0.635	0.724	0.061			0.360	0.575	0.638	0.335	0.549	0.029	0.756
R square	0.793	0.068	0.843	0.074	0.404	0.524	0.004			0.130	0.330	0.406	0.112	0.301	0.001	0.571

Continued

Appendix 3a1 Continued

Investment per Industry (2000–2006)	DOLNOŚLĄSKIE	KUJAWSKO-POMORSKIE	ŁÓDZKIE	LUBELSKIE	LUBUSKIE	MAŁOPOLSKIE	MAZOWIECKIE	OPOLSKIE	PODKARPACKIE	PODLASKIE	POMORSKIE	ŚLĄSKIE	ŚWIĘTOKRZYSKIE	WARMIŃSKO-MAZURSKIE	WIELKOPOLSKIE	ZACHODNIOPOMORSKIE
Manufacturing: Radio, Television, Communication Equipment, and Apparatus																
Multiple R		0.525					0.883								0.850	
R square		0.276					0.780								0.723	
Manufacturing: Rubber and Plastics																
Multiple R	0.045	0.414	0.452	0.304	0.488	0.520	0.018		0.462	0.681	0.723	0.490		0.636	0.639	0.504
R square	0.002	0.171	0.204	0.092	0.238	0.270	0.000		0.213	0.464	0.523	0.240		0.404	0.409	0.254
Manufacturing: Transport Equipment																
Multiple R	0.809	0.903	0.481	0.429	0.114	0.034	0.246	0.722	0.913		0.799	0.433	0.578		0.481	
R square	0.655	0.815	0.232	0.184	0.013	0.001	0.061	0.521	0.834		0.639	0.187	0.334		0.231	
Manufacturing: Wood and Wooden Products																
Multiple R	0.537	0.382		0.177	0.301				0.031	0.280					0.517	0.484
R square	0.288	0.146		0.031	0.090				0.001	0.079					0.267	0.234
Electricity, gas, and water supply																
Multiple R	0.080					0.558	0.328		0.196	0.085	0.621	0.020	0.085	0.585	0.037	0.209
R square	0.006					0.311	0.107		0.038	0.007	0.386	0.000	0.007	0.342	0.001	0.044

Construction																
Multiple R			0.723			0.070	0.877				0.353	0.079	0.477		0.935	
R square			0.523			0.005	0.768				0.125	0.006	0.227		0.874	
Trade and repair																
Multiple R	0.519	0.171	0.383	0.376	0.174	0.828	0.901	0.297		0.569		0.661	0.771		0.436	0.121
R square	0.269	0.029	0.146	0.141	0.030	0.685	0.812	0.088		0.324		0.437	0.594		0.190	0.015
Hotels and restaurants																
Multiple R	0.156			0.894	0.474		0.275				0.690	0.748			0.160	0.780
R square	0.024			0.798	0.225		0.076				0.476	0.560			0.025	0.608
Transport, storage, and communication* (2004–2006)																
Multiple R	0.064		0.584		0.534		0.778		0.492		0.962	0.800		1.000	0.194	0.297
R square	0.004		0.341		0.285		0.605		0.242		0.925	0.641		1.000	0.037	0.088
Financial intermediation																
Multiple R	0.455	0.605	0.659		0.828		0.366				0.335	0.386			0.938	
R square	0.207	0.366	0.435		0.686		0.134				0.112	0.149			0.879	
Real estate, rental, and business activities																
Multiple R	0.614		0.202			0.299	0.610	0.055			0.840	0.513			0.603	0.184
R square	0.377		0.041			0.090	0.372	0.003			0.705	0.263			0.364	0.034
Other community, social, and personal service activities																
Multiple R	0.330		0.034			0.680	0.255				0.188	0.872		0.461	0.274	
R square	0.109		0.001			0.462	0.065				0.035	0.761		0.212	0.075	

Source: Based on data obtained from the Polish Information and Foreign Investment Agency (PAIIZ) and the author's own analysis.

Appendix 3b Ratio for value added in years 2000 and 2006 in Millions Pln. (H3b)

PKD sections	2000	2006	Ratio
POLAND	662,224	931,179	1.406
Mean			1.308
Agriculture, hunting, and forestry	32,649	39,353	1.205
fishing	241	237	0.983
Mining and quarrying	13,572	16,860	1.242
Manufacturing	121942	182029	1.493
Electricity, gas, and water supply	18,688	26,751	1.431
construction	46954	55337	1.179
Trade and repair	134,411	186,798	1.390
Hotels and restaurants	8,562	10,576	1.235
Transport, storage, and communication	48,055	65,541	1.364
Financial intermediation	32,808	42,602	1.299
Real estate, rental, and business activities	83,700	130,305	1.557
other community, social, and personal service activities	25,669	33,963	1.323
DOLNOŚLĄSKIE	52,434	75,348	1.437
Mean			1.395
Agriculture, hunting, and forestry	1,829	1,653	0.904
fishing	6	13	2.167
Mining and quarrying	1,656	2,446	1.477
Manufacturing	10,458	19,576	1.872
Electricity, gas, and water supply	1383	2057	1.487
construction	3,744	4,451	1.189
Trade and repair	10189	13662	1.341
Hotels and restaurants	691	862	1.247
Transport, storage, and communication	3518	3949	1.123
Financial intermediation	3,011	2,735	0.908
Real estate, rental, and business activities	6663	10287	1.544
other community, social, and personal service activities	1,719	2,560	1.489
KUJAWSKO-POMORSKIE	32,772	44,113	1.346
Mean			1.375
Agriculture, hunting, and forestry	2,292	2,721	1.187
fishing	4	8	2.000
Mining and quarrying	37	41	1.108
Manufacturing	7418	9700	1.308
Electricity, gas, and water supply	501	910	1.816
construction	2344	2741	1.169
Trade and repair	6,848	9,847	1.438
Hotels and restaurants	334	465	1.392
Transport, storage, and communication	2,092	2,214	1.058

Continued

Appendix 3b Continued

PKD sections	2000	2006	Ratio
Financial intermediation	1129	1338	1.185
Real estate, rental, and business activities	3,677	5,407	1.470
other community, social, and personal service activities	1176	1678	1.4237
LUBELSKIE	26747	35884	1.342
Mean			1.258
Agriculture, hunting, and forestry	1178	2491	1.144
fishing	17	12	0.706
Mining and quarrying	406	431	1.062
Manufacturing	4234	5604	1.324
Electricity, gas, and water supply	433	752	1.737
construction	1700	2121	1.248
Trade and repair	5583	7544	1.351
Hotels and restaurants	308	392	1.273
Transport, storage, and communication	1896	2223	1.172
Financial intermediation	1187	1279	1.078
Real estate, rental, and business activities	2737	4215	1.540
other community, social, and personal service activities	757	1110	1.466
LUBUSKIE	15723	21910	1.393
Mean			1.469
Agriculture, hunting, and forestry	755	839	1.111
fishing	6	7	1.167
Mining and quarrying	267	915	3.427
Manufacturing	3030	4879	1.61
Electricity, gas, and water supply	296	437	1.476
construction	1025	1230	1.200
Trade and repair	3331	4446	1.335
Hotels and restaurants	198	287	1.449
Transport, storage, and communication	1246	1417	1.137
Financial intermediation	549	566	1.031
Real estate, rental, and business activities	1858	2623	1.412
other community, social, and personal service activities	592	754	1.274
ŁÓDZKIE	41006	57651	1.406
Mean			1.326
Agriculture, hunting, and forestry	2426	3526	1.453
fishing	3	2	0.667
Mining and quarrying	647	899	1.389
Manufacturing	8318	12012	1.444
Electricity, gas, and water supply	1560	1979	1.269
construction	2295	3284	1.431

Continued

Appendix 3b Continued

PKD sections	2000	2006	Ratio
Trade and repair	8796	12326	1.401
Hotels and restaurants	433	642	1.483
Transport, storage, and communication	2489	2789	1.121
Financial intermediation	1253	1946	1.553
Real estate, rental, and business activities	5159	7657	1.484
other community, social, and personal service activities	1344	1641	1.221
MAŁOPOLSKIE	48444	69212	1.429
Mean			1.316
Agriculture, hunting, and forestry	1694	1930	1.139
fishing	4	4	1.000
Mining and quarrying	770	836	1.086
Manufacturing	9409	14188	1.508
Electricity, gas, and water supply	1183	1596	1.349
construction	3800	4673	1.23
Trade and repair	10540	14663	1.391
Hotels and restaurants	832	1115	1.34
Transport, storage, and communication	3398	3865	1.137
Financial intermediation	1556	2337	1.502
Real estate, rental, and business activities	5893	9900	1.68
other community, social, and personal service activities	1669	2395	1.435
MAZOWIECKIE	133607	201350	1.507
Mean			1.386
Agriculture, hunting, and forestry	5411	7579	1.401
fishing	7	7	1.000
Mining and quarrying	73	87	1.192
Manufacturing	19629	25558	1.302
Electricity, gas, and water supply	4593	7679	1.672
construction	8335	9772	1.172
Trade and repair	25653	38663	1.507
Hotels and restaurants	1909	1939	1.016
Transport, storage, and communication	11776	23283	1.977
Financial intermediation	12154	18836	1.550
Real estate, rental, and business activities	20039	34183	1.706
other community, social, and personal service activities	8547	9725	1.138
OPOLSKIE	15677	20501	1.308
Mean			1.206
Agriculture, hunting, and forestry	1055	1074	1.018
fishing	3	4	1.333
Mining and quarrying	90	85	0.944
Manufacturing	3125	4530	1.45
Electricity, gas, and water supply	925	1058	1.144

Continued

Appendix 3b Continued

PKD sections	2000	2006	Ratio
construction	1255	1266	1.009
Trade and repair	2707	3806	1.406
Hotels and restaurants	168	199	1.185
Transport, storage, and communication	1129	1079	0.956
Financial intermediation	582	552	0.948
Real estate, rental, and business activities	1645	2527	1.536
other community, social, and personal service activities	449	698	1.555
PODKARPACKIE	25367	35044	1.381
Mean			1.228
Agriculture, hunting, and forestry	1134	1080	0.952
fishing	6	4	0.667
Mining and quarrying	309	187	0.605
Manufacturing	5925	8378	1.414
Electricity, gas, and water supply	529	823	1.556
construction	1846	2159	1.17
Trade and repair	5164	7341	1.422
Hotels and restaurants	262	336	1.282
Transport, storage, and communication	1514	1919	1.268
Financial intermediation	758	976	1.288
Real estate, rental, and business activities	2523	3847	1.525
other community, social, and personal service activities	733	1171	1.598
PODLASKIE	15782	21457	1.36
Mean			1.316
Agriculture, hunting, and forestry	1565	2484	1.587
fishing	3	4	1.333
Mining and quarrying	30	27	0.900
Manufacturing	2571	3362	1.308
Electricity, gas, and water supply	298	425	1.426
construction	1015	1217	1.199
Trade and repair	3114	4173	1.34
Hotels and restaurants	182	234	1.286
Transport, storage, and communication	1127	1156	1.026
Financial intermediation	459	657	1.431
Real estate, rental, and business activities	1813	2557	1.41
other community, social, and personal service activities	480	747	1.556
POMORSKIE	37296	52927	1.419
Mean			1.333
Agriculture, hunting, and forestry	1165	1319	1.132
fishing	67	78	1.164
Mining and quarrying	250	331	1.324
Manufacturing	7843	11160	1.423

Continued

Appendix 3b Continued

PKD sections	2000	2006	Ratio
Electricity, gas, and water supply	657	1017	1.548
construction	2918	3526	1.208
Trade and repair	6814	10106	1.483
Hotels and restaurants	499	591	1.184
Transport, storage, and communication	3189	4322	1.355
Financial intermediation	2012	2565	1.275
Real estate, rental, and business activities	5008	7802	1.558
other community, social, and personal service activities	1435	1929	1.344
ŚLĄSKIE	89070	121189	1.361
Mean			1.185
Agriculture, hunting, and forestry	1776	1263	0.711
fishing	7	4	0.571
Mining and quarrying	8363	9684	1.158
Manufacturing	15270	26129	1.711
Electricity, gas, and water supply	3186	3962	1.244
construction	6851	7497	1.094
Trade and repair	18703	23763	1.271
Hotels and restaurants	1065	1353	1.271
Transport, storage, and communication	5707	7271	1.274
Financial intermediation	3147	3370	1.071
Real estate, rental, and business activities	12040	17385	1.444
other community, social, and personal service activities	2782	3908	1.405
ŚWIĘTOKRZYSKIE	17491	23792	1.36
Mean			1.206
Agriculture, hunting, and forestry	1226	1474	1.202
fishing	4	2	1.500
Mining and quarrying	145	199	1.372
Manufacturing	3165	4886	1.544
Electricity, gas, and water supply	643	670	1.042
construction	1492	1547	1.037
Trade and repair	3767	5493	1.458
Hotels and restaurants	190	277	1.458
Transport, storage, and communication	1150	1274	1.108
Financial intermediation	539	525	0.974
Real estate, rental, and business activities	1709	2510	1.469
other community, social, and personal service activities	460	604	1.313
WARMIŃSKO-MAZURSKIE	19324	26333	1.363
Mean			1.348
Agriculture, hunting, and forestry	1974	2146	1.087
fishing	22	21	0.955

Continued

Appendix 3b Continued

PKD sections	2000	2006	Ratio
Mining and quarrying	31	58	1.871
Manufacturing	3447	5163	1.498
Electricity, gas, and water supply	374	528	1.412
construction	1323	1527	1.154
Trade and repair	3704	5029	1.358
Hotels and restaurants	281	350	1.246
Transport, storage, and communication	1236	1346	1.089
Financial intermediation	538	819	1.522
Real estate, rental, and business activities	2130	3314	1.556
other community, social, and personal service activities	666	957	1.437
WIELKOPOLSKIE	61593	86795	1.409
Mean			1.314
Agriculture, hunting, and forestry	4724	6140	1.300
fishing	10	12	1.200
Mining and quarrying	451	579	1.284
Manufacturing	13196	21438	1.625
Electricity, gas, and water supply	1257	1651	1.313
construction	4886	5809	1.189
Trade and repair	13178	17708	1.344
Hotels and restaurants	697	894	1.283
Transport, storage, and communication	3860	4799	1.243
Financial intermediation	2874	2919	1.016
Real estate, rental, and business activities	6659	10278	1.543
other community, social, and personal service activities	1777	2556	1.438
ZACHODNIOPOMORSKIE	29891	37674	1.26
Mean			1.189
Agriculture, hunting, and forestry	1445	1635	1.131
fishing	69	56	0.812
Mining and quarrying	45	54	1.200
Manufacturing	4905	55464	1.114
Electricity, gas, and water supply	868	1206	1.389
construction	2126	2517	1.184
Trade and repair	6320	8229	1.302
Hotels and restaurants	512	640	1.250
Transport, storage, and communication	2727	2636	0.967
Financial intermediation	1059	1181	1.115
Real estate, rental, and business activities	4147	5813	1.402
other community, social, and personal service activities	1083	1531	1.414

Source: Based on data obtained from the Central Statistical Office (GUS) and the Polish Information and Foreign Investment Agency (PAIIZ) and the author's own analysis.

Appendix 3c Results of regression between RLAis and labor cost (H3c)

Wage 2002–2006	DOLNOŚLĄSKIE	KUJAWSKO-POMORSKIE	ŁÓDZKIE	LUBELSKIE	LUBUSKIE	MAŁOPOLSKIE	MAZOWIECKIE	OPOLSKIE	PODKARPACKIE	PODLASKIE	POMORSKIE	ŚLĄSKIE	ŚWIĘTOKRZYSKIE	WARMIŃSKO-MAZURSKIE	WIELKOPOLSKIE	ZACHODNIOPOMORSKIE
Agriculture, hunting and forestry																
Multiple R				1.000							0.931			0.779	0.193	
R Square				1.000							0.867			0.607	0.037	
Construction																
Multiple R			1.000			0.336	0.013				0.835	0.054	0.548		0.694	
R Square			1.000			0.113	0.000				0.696	0.003	0.300		0.481	
Electricity, gas and water supply																
Multiple R	0.515					0.779	0.109		0.747	0.603	0.846	0.811	0.514	0.692	0.797	0.236
R Square	0.266					0.607	0.012		0.558	0.363	0.716	0.657	0.264	0.479	0.635	0.056
Financial intermediation																
Multiple R	0.449	0.148	0.471		0.656		0.292				0.844	0.447			0.387	
R Square	0.202	0.022	0.222		0.430		0.085				0.712	0.200			0.150	
Hotels and restaurants																
Multiple R	0.930			1.000	0.733		0.477				0.974	0.884			0.937	0.724
R Square	0.865			1.000	0.538		0.228				0.948	0.781			0.878	0.524

Manufacturing: Chemicals & Chemical Products																
Multiple R	0.790	0.743	0.229	0.170	0.929	0.927	0.773	0.876	0.773		0.667	0.984	1.000		0.142	0.062
R Square	0.624	0.552	0.053	0.029	0.864	0.860	0.598	0.767	0.598		0.445	0.968	1.000		0.020	0.004
Manufacturing: Consumer Products																
Multiple R	0.957		0.173				0.782								0.381	1.000
R Square	0.915		0.030				0.611								0.145	1.000
Manufacturing: Electrical Machinery and Apparatus																
Multiple R	0.841	0.450	0.339				0.507		0.911		0.852	0.583			0.609	0.177
R Square	0.707	0.203	0.115				0.257		0.830		0.725	0.340			0.370	0.031
Manufacturing: Fabrics & Textiles																
Multiple R	0.661	0.757	0.313		0.105	0.807	0.427	0.313		0.431		0.285	0.704	0.755	0.364	
R Square	0.437	0.572	0.098		0.011	0.651	0.182	0.098		0.185		0.081	0.495	0.569	0.132	
Manufacturing: Food, Drinks & Tobacco Products																
Multiple R	0.903	0.078	0.671	0.655	0.888	0.493	0.135	0.414	0.625	0.477	0.516	0.366	0.903	0.932	0.902	0.376
R Square	0.816	0.006	0.450	0.429	0.788	0.243	0.018	0.172	0.390	0.227	0.266	0.134	0.815	0.869	0.813	0.141
Manufacturing: Furniture & Consumer Goods																
Multiple R	0.604	0.883		0.574			0.607				0.510	0.078		0.861	0.964	0.756
R Square	0.365	0.780		0.329			0.369				0.260	0.006		0.741	0.930	0.571
Manufacturing: Glass																
Multiple R									0.200							
R Square									0.040							
Manufacturing: Leather & Leather Products																
Multiple R		0.922	0.404		0.574		0.263		0.202							0.730
R Square		0.850	0.163		0.330		0.069		0.041							0.533
Manufacturing: Machinery & Equipment																
Multiple R	0.682		0.247	0.437			0.270	0.393				0.857	0.703	0.489	0.697	0.743
R Square	0.465		0.061	0.191			0.073	0.154				0.735	0.494	0.240	0.486	0.552

Continued

Appendix 3c Continued

Wage 2002–2006	DOLNOŚLĄSKIE	KUJAWSKO-POMORSKIE	ŁÓDZKIE	LUBELSKIE	LUBUSKIE	MAŁOPOLSKIE	MAZOWIECKIE	OPOLSKIE	PODKARPACKIE	PODLASKIE	POMORSKIE	ŚLĄSKIE	ŚWIĘTOKRZYSKIE	WARMIŃSKO-MAZURSKIE	WIELKOPOLSKIE	ZACHODNIOPOMORSKIE
Manufacturing: Metals & Metal Products																
Multiple R	0.686	0.757	0.404	0.336	0.071	0.411	0.660	0.130	0.475	0.186	0.770	0.177	0.626		0.067	0.646
R Square	0.470	0.574	0.163	0.113	0.005	0.169	0.436	0.017	0.225	0.035	0.594	0.031	0.392		0.004	0.417
Manufacturing: Other Non-Metal Goods																
Multiple R	0.826	0.021	0.465	0.304	0.132	0.114	0.806	0.143	0.324		0.547	0.111	0.437	0.341	0.901	0.359
R Square	0.683	0.000	0.216	0.092	0.017	0.013	0.650	0.020	0.105		0.299	0.012	0.191	0.117	0.812	0.129
Manufacturing: Pharmaceuticals																
Multiple R				0.525			0.284								0.193	
R Square				0.275			0.081								0.037	
Manufacturing: Pulp & Paper / Publishing & Printing																
Multiple R	0.947	0.866	0.418	0.837	0.814	0.017	0.825			1.000	0.906	0.881	0.114	0.735	0.751	0.878
R Square	0.897	0.751	0.174	0.700	0.662	0.000	0.681			1.000	0.820	0.776	0.013	0.540	0.564	0.771
Manufacturing: Radio, Television, Communication Equipment & Apparatus																
Multiple R		0.450					0.138								0.193	
R Square		0.203					0.019								0.037	

Manufacturing: Rubber & Plastics																
Multiple R	0.478	0.925	0.218	0.280	0.775	0.147	0.101		0.692	0.698	0.486	0.852		0.866	0.021	0.709
R Square	0.228	0.856	0.047	0.079	0.600	0.022	0.010		0.479	0.487	0.236	0.727		0.750	0.000	0.503
Manufacturing: Transport Equipment																
Multiple R	0.968	0.368	0.315	0.348	0.563	0.513	0.736	0.464	0.633		0.824	0.051	0.708		0.897	
R Square	0.936	0.136	0.099	0.121	0.317	0.263	0.542	0.215	0.401		0.679	0.003	0.501		0.804	
Manufacturing: Wood & Wooden Products																
Multiple R	0.611	0.070		0.894	0.263				0.402	0.881					0.798	0.887
R Square	0.373	0.005		0.799	0.069				0.161	0.776					0.636	0.786
Mining and quarrying																
Multiple R	0.997					0.614	0.972	0.550				0.917				
R Square	0.993					0.377	0.945	0.303				0.840				
Other community, social and personal service activities																
Multiple R	0.789		0.561			0.320	0.450				0.679	0.897		0.474	0.248	
R Square	0.622		0.315			0.103	0.203				0.461	0.804		0.224	0.061	
Real estate, rental and business activities																
Multiple R	0.294		0.423			0.498	0.540	0.106			0.741	0.659			0.179	0.751
R Square	0.087		0.179			0.248	0.291	0.011			0.549	0.435			0.032	0.565
Trade and repair																
Multiple R	0.427	0.603	0.387	0.487	1.000	0.456	0.781	0.724		0.715		0.826	0.650		0.853	0.745
R Square	0.182	0.364	0.150	0.237	1.000	0.208	0.610	0.524		0.511		0.682	0.422		0.728	0.554

Source: Based on data obtained from the Polish Information and Foreign Investment Agency (PAIIZ) and the author's own analysis.

Appendix 3d Results of regression between RLAis and labor and skilled labor availability (H3d)

2000–2006 Total available workforce (including skilled)	DOLNOŚLĄSKIE	KUJAWSKO-POMORSKIE	ŁÓDZKIE	LUBELSKIE	LUBUSKIE	MAŁOPOLSKIE	MAZOWIECKIE	OPOLSKIE	PODKARPACKIE	PODLASKIE	POMORSKIE	ŚLĄSKIE	ŚWIĘTOKRZYSKIE	WARMIŃSKO-MAZURSKIE	WIELKOPOLSKIE	ZACHODNIOPOMORSKIE
Agriculture, hunting and forestry																
Multiple R				0.463							0.610			0.917	0.999	
R Square				0.215							0.372			0.842	0.998	
Construction																
Multiple R			0.667			0.672	0.897				0.481	0.566	0.719		0.143	
R Square			0.445			0.451	0.805				0.231	0.321	0.517		0.020	
Financial intermediation																
Multiple R	0.175	0.822	0.481		0.332		0.186				0.735	0.740			0.441	
R Square	0.031	0.675	0.232		0.110		0.035				0.540	0.548			0.195	
Hotels and restaurants																
Multiple R	0.533			0.117	0.494		0.050				0.556	0.226			0.863	0.130
R Square	0.284			0.014	0.244		0.002				0.309	0.051			0.745	0.017
Manufacturing: Chemicals & Chemical Products																
Multiple R	0.673	0.143	0.388	0.175	0.747	0.297	0.354	0.895	0.288		0.151	0.042	0.667		0.512	0.053
R Square	0.453	0.020	0.151	0.031	0.558	0.088	0.126	0.801	0.083		0.023	0.002	0.445		0.262	0.003
Manufacturing: Consumer Products																
Multiple R	0.675		0.220				0.715								0.451	1.000
R Square	0.456		0.049				0.512								0.203	1.000

Manufacturing: Electrical Machinery and Apparatus																
Multiple R	0.278	0.143	0.530				0.524		0.222		0.085	0.552			0.505	0.787
R Square	0.077	0.020	0.281				0.274		0.049		0.007	0.305			0.255	0.619
Manufacturing: Fabrics & Textiles																
Multiple R	0.401	0.222	0.202		0.775	0.112	0.800	0.183		0.053		0.491	0.187	0.689	0.827	
R Square	0.160	0.049	0.041		0.601	0.013	0.640	0.034		0.003		0.241	0.035	0.474	0.685	
Manufacturing: Food, Drinks & Tobacco Products																
Multiple R	0.660	0.888	0.579	0.885	0.410	0.314	0.634	0.879	0.846	0.728	0.225	0.170	0.456	0.722	0.049	0.589
R Square	0.435	0.789	0.335	0.784	0.168	0.099	0.401	0.772	0.716	0.530	0.050	0.029	0.208	0.521	0.002	0.347
Manufacturing: Furniture & Consumer Goods																
Multiple R	0.127	0.318		0.779			0.235				0.486	0.628		0.650	0.600	0.872
R Square	0.016	0.101		0.607			0.055				0.236	0.395		0.422	0.360	0.761
Manufacturing: Glass																
Multiple R									0.204							
R Square									0.041							
Manufacturing: Leather & Leather Products																
Multiple R		0.035	0.053		0.558		0.753		0.240							0.078
R Square		0.001	0.003		0.311		0.566		0.058							0.006
Manufacturing: Machinery & Equipment																
Multiple R	0.210		0.312	0.489			0.835	0.200				0.195	0.599	0.718	0.937	0.298
R Square	0.044		0.097	0.239			0.698	0.040				0.038	0.359	0.515	0.878	0.089
Manufacturing: Metals & Metal Products																
Multiple R	0.507	0.243	0.538	0.128	0.057	0.491	0.759	0.475	0.589	0.494	0.102	0.664	0.596		0.653	0.152
R Square	0.257	0.059	0.290	0.016	0.003	0.241	0.577	0.226	0.347	0.244	0.010	0.441	0.356		0.427	0.023
Manufacturing: Other Non-Metal Goods																
Multiple R	0.534	0.331	0.722	0.272	0.082	0.303	0.723	0.508	0.148		0.576	0.053	0.016	0.220	0.161	0.496
R Square	0.285	0.110	0.521	0.074	0.007	0.092	0.522	0.258	0.022		0.332	0.003	0.000	0.048	0.026	0.246
Manufacturing: Pharmaceuticals																
Multiple R				0.669			0.053								0.570	
R Square				0.448			0.003								0.325	

Continued

Appendix 3d Continued

2000–2006 Total available workforce (including skilled)	DOLNOŚLĄSKIE	KUJAWSKO-POMORSKIE	ŁÓDZKIE	LUBELSKIE	LUBUSKIE	MAŁOPOLSKIE	MAZOWIECKIE	OPOLSKIE	PODKARPACKIE	PODLASKIE	POMORSKIE	ŚLĄSKIE	ŚWIĘTOKRZYSKIE	WARMIŃSKO-MAZURSKIE	WIELKOPOLSKIE	ZACHODNIOPOMORSKIE
Manufacturing: Pulp & Paper / Publishing & Printing																
Multiple R	0.423	0.094	0.084	0.820	0.646	0.355	0.088			0.849	0.282	0.157	0.060	0.621	0.105	0.147
R Square	0.179	0.009	0.007	0.672	0.418	0.126	0.008			0.721	0.080	0.025	0.004	0.385	0.011	0.021
Manufacturing: Radio, Television, Communication Equipment & Apparatus																
Multiple R		0.143					0.134								0.737	
R Square		0.020					0.018								0.544	
Manufacturing: Rubber & Plastics																
Multiple R	0.724	0.247	0.316	0.334	0.298	0.328	0.814		0.192	0.383	0.300	0.229		0.791	0.331	0.083
R Square	0.525	0.061	0.100	0.111	0.089	0.108	0.663		0.037	0.146	0.090	0.052		0.626	0.110	0.007
Manufacturing: Transport Equipment																
Multiple R	0.847	0.080	0.717	0.474	0.785	0.180	0.236	0.066	0.301		0.677	0.257	0.724		0.703	
R Square	0.717	0.006	0.514	0.225	0.617	0.032	0.056	0.004	0.090		0.458	0.066	0.523		0.494	

Manufacturing: Wood & Wooden Products																
Multiple R	0.327	0.544		0.367	0.168				0.117	0.332					0.765	0.770
R Square	0.107	0.296		0.134	0.028				0.014	0.110					0.585	0.593
Other community, social and personal service activities																
Multiple R	0.610		0.505			0.721	0.399				0.366	0.921		0.058	0.327	
R Square	0.372		0.255			0.520	0.159				0.134	0.849		0.003	0.107	
Real estate, rental and business activities																
Multiple R	0.654		0.857			0.409	0.871	0.404			0.859	0.734			0.598	0.758
R Square	0.428		0.734			0.167	0.759	0.164			0.738	0.539			0.357	0.574
Trade and repair																
Multiple R	0.799	0.059	0.302	0.736	0.513	0.983	0.560	0.871		0.631		0.544	0.617		0.616	0.063
R Square	0.639	0.004	0.091	0.542	0.263	0.965	0.313	0.759		0.399		0.296	0.381		0.380	0.004
Transport, storage and communication* (2004–2006)																
Multiple R	0.541		0.972		0.359		0.718		0.665		0.830	0.424		1.000	0.321	0.245
R Square	0.293		0.944		0.129		0.515		0.442		0.689	0.180		1.000	0.103	0.060

Source: Based on data obtained from the Polish Information and Foreign Investment Agency (PAIIZ) and the author's own analysis.

Appendix 3d1 Results of regression between RLAis and skilled labor availability (H3d)

Secondary Unemployment (2000–2006)	DOLNOŚLĄSKIE	KUJAWSKO-POMORSKIE	ŁÓDZKIE	LUBELSKIE	LUBUSKIE	MAŁOPOLSKIE	MAZOWIECKIE	OPOLSKIE	PODKARPACKIE	PODLASKIE	POMORSKIE	ŚLĄSKIE	ŚWIĘTOKRZYSKIE	WARMIŃSKO-MAZURSKIE	WIELKOPOLSKIE	ZACHODNIOPOMORSKIE
Agriculture, hunting and forestry																
Multiple R				0.491							0.557			0.549	0.122	
R Square				0.242							0.310			0.301	0.015	
Mining and quarrying																
Multiple R	0.886					0.538	0.063	0.380				0.125				
R Square	0.785					0.290	0.004	0.144				0.016				
Manufacturing: Chemicals& Chemical Products																
Multiple R	0.791	0.495	0.303	0.223	0.823	0.527	0.069	0.574	0.329		0.308	0.326	0.343		0.197	0.220
R Square	0.626	0.245	0.092	0.050	0.677	0.277	0.005	0.329	0.109		0.095	0.106	0.118		0.039	0.048
Manufacturing: Consumer Products																
Multiple R	0.736		0.379				0.127								0.146	1.000
R Square	0.541		0.143				0.016								0.021	1.000
Manufacturing: Electrical Machinery and Apparatus																
Multiple R	0.415	0.641	0.401				0.125		0.558		0.319	0.874			0.015	0.406
R Square	0.172	0.411	0.161				0.016		0.312		0.102	0.764			0.000	0.165
Manufacturing: Fabrics & Textiles																
Multiple R	0.256	0.322	0.001		0.439	0.754	0.144	0.571		0.530		0.114	0.455	0.631	0.194	
R Square	0.065	0.104	0.000		0.193	0.569	0.021	0.326		0.281		0.013	0.207	0.398	0.038	

Manufacturing: Food, Drinks & Tobacco Products																
Multiple R	0.625	0.505	0.470	0.779	0.171	0.415	0.285	0.100	0.521	0.565	0.137	0.142	0.701	0.595	0.090	0.179
R Square	0.391	0.255	0.221	0.606	0.029	0.172	0.081	0.010	0.272	0.319	0.019	0.020	0.491	0.354	0.008	0.032
Manufacturing: Furniture & Consumer Goods																
Multiple R	0.088	0.226		0.619			0.836				0.425	0.448		0.743	0.488	0.762
R Square	0.008	0.051		0.383			0.700				0.181	0.201		0.552	0.238	0.581
Manufacturing: Glass																
Multiple R									0.491							
R Square									0.241							
Manufacturing: Leather & Leather Products																
Multiple R		0.618	0.804		0.450		0.108		0.137							0.478
R Square		0.382	0.647		0.202		0.012		0.019							0.229
Manufacturing: Machinery & Equipment																
Multiple R	0.300		0.527	0.541			0.584	0.378				0.134	0.573	0.817	0.522	0.250
R Square	0.090		0.278	0.292			0.341	0.143				0.018	0.328	0.667	0.272	0.062
Manufacturing: Metals & Metal Products																
Multiple R	0.348	0.480	0.510	0.095	0.249	0.387	0.646	0.290	0.053	0.711	0.224	0.423	0.204		0.005	0.289
R Square	0.121	0.230	0.260	0.009	0.062	0.149	0.417	0.084	0.003	0.506	0.050	0.179	0.042		0.000	0.083
Manufacturing: Other Non-Metal Goods																
Multiple R	0.388	0.101	0.234	0.279	0.371	0.225	0.005	0.068	0.474		0.534	0.009	0.343	0.293	0.449	0.152
R Square	0.150	0.010	0.055	0.078	0.137	0.051	0.000	0.005	0.225		0.285	0.000	0.118	0.086	0.202	0.023
Manufacturing: Pharmaceuticals																
Multiple R				0.709			0.427								0.395	
R Square				0.503			0.183								0.156	
Manufacturing: Pulp & Paper / Publishing & Printing																
Multiple R	0.492	0.590	0.784	0.705	0.896	0.720	0.475			0.019	0.477	0.305	0.037	0.396	0.510	0.382
R Square	0.242	0.348	0.615	0.498	0.802	0.519	0.225			0.000	0.227	0.093	0.001	0.157	0.260	0.146

Continued

Appendix 3d1 Continued

Secondary Unemployment (2000–2006)	DOLNOŚLĄSKIE	KUJAWSKO-POMORSKIE	ŁÓDZKIE	LUBELSKIE	LUBUSKIE	MAŁOPOLSKIE	MAZOWIECKIE	OPOLSKIE	PODKARPACKIE	PODLASKIE	POMORSKIE	ŚLĄSKIE	ŚWIĘTOKRZYSKIE	WARMIŃSKO-MAZURSKIE	WIELKOPOLSKIE	ZACHODNIOPOMORSKIE
Manufacturing: Radio, Television, Communication Equipment & Apparatus																
Multiple R		0.641					0.313								0.142	
R Square		0.411					0.098								0.020	
Manufacturing: Rubber & Plastics																
Multiple R	0.518	0.373	0.368	0.254	0.279	0.400	0.532		0.563	0.598	0.443	0.516		0.788	0.243	0.466
R Square	0.269	0.139	0.136	0.065	0.078	0.160	0.283		0.317	0.357	0.196	0.266		0.620	0.059	0.217
Manufacturing: Transport Equipment																
Multiple R	0.876	0.276	0.579	0.536	0.523	0.332	0.554	0.645	0.681		0.661	0.142	0.380		0.703	
R Square	0.767	0.076	0.335	0.287	0.273	0.110	0.307	0.416	0.464		0.437	0.020	0.145		0.494	
Manufacturing: Wood & Wooden Products																
Multiple R	0.369	0.503		0.306	0.139				0.375	0.238					0.431	0.962
R Square	0.136	0.253		0.094	0.019				0.141	0.057					0.186	0.926
Electricity, gas and water supply																
Multiple R	0.436					0.443	0.312		0.235	0.331	0.495	0.176	0.354	0.250	0.384	0.306
R Square	0.190					0.196	0.097		0.055	0.109	0.245	0.031	0.125	0.062	0.147	0.093

Construction																
Multiple R			0.249			0.068	0.613				0.174	0.225	0.208		0.478	
R Square			0.062			0.005	0.376				0.030	0.050	0.043		0.229	
Trade and repair																
Multiple R	0.472	0.011	0.352	0.784	0.204	0.769	0.685	0.812		0.517		0.746	0.654		0.748	0.487
R Square	0.223	0.000	0.124	0.614	0.041	0.591	0.470	0.659		0.267		0.557	0.428		0.560	0.238
Hotels and restaurants																
Multiple R	0.196			0.198	0.447		0.708				0.388	0.609			0.560	0.339
R Square	0.038			0.039	0.200		0.501				0.150	0.371			0.314	0.115
Transport, storage and communication* (2004–2006)																
Multiple R	0.174		0.707		0.810		0.946		0.548		0.952	0.996		1.000	0.719	0.762
R Square	0.030		0.499		0.656		0.895		0.300		0.907	0.992		1.000	0.517	0.581
Financial intermediation																
Multiple R	0.380	0.539	0.341		0.069		0.263				0.328	0.015			0.253	
R Square	0.144	0.290	0.116		0.005		0.069				0.108	0.000			0.064	
Real estate, rental and business activities																
Multiple R	0.263		0.309			0.282	0.008	0.214			0.015	0.648			0.013	0.547
R Square	0.069		0.095			0.079	0.000	0.046			0.000	0.420			0.000	0.299
Other community, social and personal service activities																
Multiple R	0.499		0.644			0.152	0.254				0.153	0.182		0.052	0.431	
R Square	0.249		0.414			0.023	0.065				0.023	0.033		0.003	0.186	

Source: Based on data obtained from the Polish Information and Foreign Investment Agency (PAIIZ) and the author's own analysis.

Appendix 3d2 Results of regression between RLAis and skilled labor availability (H3d)

Teritary Unemployment (2000–2006)	DOLNOŚLĄSKIE	KUJAWSKO-POMORSKIE	ŁÓDZKIE	LUBELSKIE	LUBUSKIE	MAŁOPOLSKIE	MAZOWIECKIE	OPOLSKIE	PODKARPACKIE	PODLASKIE	POMORSKIE	ŚLĄSKIE	ŚWIĘTOKRZYSKIE	WARMIŃSKO-MAZURSKIE	WIELKOPOLSKIE	ZACHODNIOPOMORSKIE
Agriculture, hunting and forestry																
Multiple R				0.354							0.301			0.633	0.822	
R Square				0.125							0.091			0.400	0.676	
Mining and quarrying																
Multiple R	0.071					0.717	0.837	0.785				0.140				
R Square	0.005					0.513	0.701	0.616				0.020				
Manufacturing: Chemicals& Chemical Products																
Multiple R	0.078	0.277	0.333	0.734	0.359	0.478	0.493	0.646	0.892		0.222	0.596	0.806		0.925	0.094
R Square	0.006	0.077	0.111	0.538	0.129	0.229	0.243	0.418	0.796		0.049	0.355	0.650		0.855	0.009
Manufacturing: Consumer Products																
Multiple R	0.073		0.321				0.805								0.758	1.000
R Square	0.005		0.103				0.648								0.575	1.000
Manufacturing: Electrical Machinery and Apparatus																
Multiple R	0.433	0.186	0.760				0.534		0.173		0.385	0.021			0.707	0.864
R Square	0.188	0.035	0.577				0.285		0.030		0.148	0.000			0.500	0.747
Manufacturing: Fabrics & Textiles																
Multiple R	0.523	0.577	0.288		0.879	0.591	0.899	0.506		0.021		0.916	0.707	0.345	0.825	
R Square	0.273	0.333	0.083		0.773	0.349	0.808	0.256		0.000		0.839	0.499	0.119	0.681	

Manufacturing: Food, Drinks & Tobacco Products																
Multiple R	0.624	0.924	0.633	0.219	0.936	0.529	0.771	0.976	0.300	0.694	0.306	0.501	0.404	0.808	0.048	0.858
R Square	0.389	0.854	0.400	0.048	0.877	0.279	0.594	0.952	0.090	0.482	0.093	0.251	0.163	0.653	0.002	0.735
Manufacturing: Furniture & Consumer Goods																
Multiple R	0.898	0.512		0.066			0.145				0.217	0.816		0.415	0.499	0.709
R Square	0.806	0.262		0.004			0.021				0.047	0.666		0.172	0.249	0.502
Manufacturing: Glass																
Multiple R									0.836							
R Square									0.700							
Manufacturing: Leather & Leather Products																
Multiple R		0.311	0.277		0.304		0.838		0.243							0.401
R Square		0.096	0.077		0.092		0.702		0.059							0.161
Manufacturing: Machinery & Equipment																
Multiple R	0.506		0.326	0.859			0.888	0.049				0.817	0.168	0.282	0.645	0.664
R Square	0.256		0.106	0.738			0.789	0.002				0.668	0.028	0.080	0.416	0.441
Manufacturing: Metals & Metal Products																
Multiple R	0.683	0.082	0.590	0.440	0.334	0.599	0.765	0.506	0.893	0.815	0.533	0.933	0.651		0.580	0.566
R Square	0.467	0.007	0.348	0.193	0.112	0.359	0.585	0.256	0.797	0.663	0.284	0.871	0.424		0.337	0.320
Manufacturing: Other Non-Metal Goods																
Multiple R	0.748	0.619	0.677	0.112	0.099	0.761	0.756	0.791	0.563		0.187	0.356	0.353	0.699	0.489	0.805
R Square	0.559	0.383	0.458	0.013	0.010	0.579	0.571	0.625	0.317		0.035	0.127	0.125	0.488	0.239	0.648
Manufacturing: Pharmaceuticals																
Multiple R				0.597			0.006								0.007	
R Square				0.356			0.000								0.000	
Manufacturing: Pulp & Paper / Publishing & Printing																
Multiple R	0.648	0.220	0.175	0.278	0.079	0.243	0.160			0.771	0.139	0.778	0.189	0.651	0.454	0.524
R Square	0.420	0.049	0.031	0.077	0.006	0.059	0.026			0.595	0.019	0.606	0.036	0.423	0.206	0.274

Continued

Appendix 3d2 Cont nued

Teritary Unemployment (2000–2006)	DOLNOŚLĄSKIE	KUJAWSKO-POMORSKIE	ŁÓDZKIE	LUBELSKIE	LUBUSKIE	MAŁOPOLSKIE	MAZOWIECKIE	OPOLSKIE	PODKARPACKIE	PODLASKIE	POMORSKIE	ŚLĄSKIE	ŚWIĘTOKRZYSKIE	WARMIŃSKO-MAZURSKIE	WIELKOPOLSKIE	ZACHODNIOPOMORSKIE
Manufacturing: Radio, Television, Communication Equipment & Apparatus																
Multiple R		0.186					0.267								0.818	
R Square		0.035					0.071								0.669	
Manufacturing: Rubber & Plastics																
Multiple R	0.351	0.556	0.476	0.675	0.848	0.746	0.683		0.468	0.790	0.159	0.435		0.031	0.255	0.404
R Square	0.123	0.309	0.227	0.456	0.719	0.556	0.466		0.219	0.624	0.025	0.189		0.001	0.065	0.163
Manufacturing: Transport Equipment																
Multiple R	0.160	0.181	0.437	0.860	0.731	0.385	0.296	0.136	0.769		0.378	0.341	0.460		0.065	
R Square	0.026	0.033	0.191	0.740	0.534	0.149	0.088	0.018	0.591		0.143	0.116	0.212		0.004	
Manufacturing: Wood & Wooden Products																
Multiple R	0.059	0.325		0.075	0.093				0.228	0.236					0.408	0.471
R Square	0.003	0.106		0.006	0.009				0.052	0.056					0.166	0.222
Electricity, gas and water supply																
Multiple R	0.563					0.079	0.562		0.251	0.296	0.207	0.135	0.720	0.967	0.367	0.415
R Square	0.317					0.006	0.316		0.063	0.087	0.043	0.018	0.518	0.935	0.135	0.172

Construction																
Multiple R			0.689			0.773	0.907				0.492	0.501	0.821		0.424	
R Square			0.474			0.598	0.822				0.242	0.251	0.674		0.180	
Trade and repair																
Multiple R	0.315	0.860	0.438	0.500	0.934	0.621	0.618	0.282		0.345		0.277	0.160		0.149	0.398
R Square	0.099	0.740	0.192	0.250	0.872	0.385	0.382	0.080		0.119		0.077	0.026		0.022	0.159
Hotels and restaurants																
Multiple R	0.867			0.877	0.745		0.701				0.424	0.463			0.485	0.578
R Square	0.752			0.770	0.555		0.491				0.180	0.215			0.235	0.335
Transport, storage and communication* (2004–2006)																
Multiple R	0.512		0.897		0.979		0.254		0.567		0.974	0.989		1.000	0.482	0.346
R Square	0.262		0.804		0.958		0.065		0.322		0.948	0.978		1.000	0.232	0.120
Financial intermediation																
Multiple R	0.548	0.452	0.856		0.992		0.481				0.478	0.430			0.933	
R Square	0.301	0.204	0.732		0.984		0.232				0.228	0.185			0.871	
Real estate, rental and business activities																
Multiple R	0.900		0.585			0.430	0.806	0.450			0.784	0.406			0.497	0.921
R Square	0.811		0.343			0.185	0.65	0.203			0.614	0.165			0.247	0.848
Other community social and personal service activities																
Multiple R	0.626		0.059			0.812	0.577				0.505	0.818		0.546	0.256	
R Square	0.392		0.003			0.659	0.333				0.255	0.668		0.298	0.065	

Source: Based on data obtained from the Polish Information and Foreign Investment Agency (PAIIZ) and the author's own analysis.

Appendix 3e Results of regression between RLAis and market size and wages (H3e)

Wage and Population = Market size (2002–2006)	DOLNOŚLĄSKIE	KUJAWSKO-POMORSKIE	ŁÓDZKIE	LUBELSKIE	LUBUSKIE	MAŁOPOLSKIE	MAZOWIECKIE	OPOLSKIE	PODKARPACKIE	PODLASKIE	POMORSKIE	ŚLĄSKIE	ŚWIĘTOKRZYSKIE	WARMIŃSKO-MAZURSKIE	WIELKOPOLSKIE	ZACHODNIOPOMORSKIE
Agriculture, hunting and forestry																
Multiple R				1.00							0.93			0.88	0.84	
R Square				1.00							0.87			0.77	0.71	
Construction																
Multiple R			1.00			0.80	0.64				0.83	0.80	0.76		0.88	
R Square			1.00			0.63	0.41				0.70	0.64	0.58		0.78	
Electricity, gas and water supply																
Multiple R	0.91					0.78	0.47		0.99	0.77	0.96	0.84	0.79	0.73	0.90	0.43
R Square	0.84					0.61	0.22		0.99	0.59	0.92	0.70	0.62	0.53	0.80	0.19
Financial intermediation																
Multiple R	0.68	0.16	0.74		0.89		0.73				0.98	0.49			0.65	
R Square	0.46	0.03	0.55		0.79		0.53				0.95	0.24			0.42	
Hotels and restaurants																
Multiple R	0.95			1.00	0.88		0.63				0.99	0.92			0.97	0.94
R Square	0.90			1.00	0.78		0.40				0.98	0.84			0.94	0.88
Manufacturing: Chemicals & Chemical Products																
Multiple R	0.83	0.81	0.24	0.37	0.95	0.93	0.83	0.88	0.84		0.89	0.98	1.00		0.65	0.51
R Square	0.70	0.66	0.06	0.14	0.91	0.86	0.68	0.77	0.71		0.79	0.97	1.00		0.42	0.26

Manufacturing: Consumer Products																
Multiple R	0.97		0.38				0.96								0.60	1.00
R Square	0.95		0.15				0.91								0.36	1.00
Manufacturing: Electrical Machinery and Apparatus																
Multiple R	0.93	0.96	0.74				0.85		0.94		0.87	0.98			0.63	0.35
R Square	0.87	0.91	0.55				0.73		0.88		0.75	0.96			0.40	0.12
Manufacturing: Fabrics & Textiles																
Multiple R	0.66	0.76	0.57		0.55	1.00	0.73	0.80		0.94		0.35	0.95	0.77	0.82	
R Square	0.44	0.58	0.33		0.30	0.99	0.53	0.65		0.88		0.12	0.90	0.59	0.68	
Manufacturing: Food, Drinks & Tobacco Products																
Multiple R	0.93	0.95	0.71	0.95	0.92	0.73	0.15	0.92	0.80	0.86	0.90	0.76	0.91	0.95	0.90	0.75
R Square	0.86	0.91	0.50	0.91	0.85	0.53	0.02	0.85	0.63	0.73	0.81	0.57	0.83	0.89	0.81	0.56
Manufacturing: Furniture & Consumer Goods																
Multiple R	0.62	0.88		0.89			0.88				0.66	0.73		0.90	0.97	0.84
R Square	0.38	0.78		0.79			0.77				0.44	0.54		0.80	0.93	0.71
Manufacturing: Glass																
Multiple R									0.99							
R Square									0.99							
Manufacturing: Leather & Leather Products																
Multiple R		0.93	0.99		0.82		0.70		0.90							0.81
R Square		0.86	0.98		0.68		0.49		0.82							0.65
Manufacturing: Machinery & Equipment																
Multiple R	0.99		0.53	0.86			0.95	0.69				0.90	0.86	0.98	0.96	0.94
R Square	0.97		0.28	0.74			0.90	0.48				0.80	0.73	0.96	0.92	0.89
Manufacturing: Metals & Metal Products																
Multiple R	0.79	0.81	0.91	0.38	0.56	0.41	0.66	0.80	0.49	0.76	0.82	0.90	0.90		0.38	0.94
R Square	0.63	0.66	0.83	0.15	0.31	0.17	0.44	0.63	0.24	0.57	0.67	0.80	0.80		0.14	0.88

Continued

Wage and Population = Market size (2002–2006)	DOLNOŚLĄSKIE	KUJAWSKO-POMORSKIE	ŁÓDZKIE	LUBELSKIE	LUBUSKIE	MAŁOPOLSKIE	MAZOWIECKIE	OPOLSKIE	PODKARPACKIE	PODLASKIE	POMORSKIE	ŚLĄSKIE	ŚWIĘTOKRZYSKIE	WARMIŃSKO-MAZURSKIE	WIELKOPOLSKIE	ZACHODNIOPOMORSKIE
Manufacturing: Other Non-Metal Goods																
Multiple R	0.86	0.10	0.76	0.30	0.29	0.62	0.90	0.45	0.55		0.55	0.51	0.82	0.42	0.91	0.77
R Square	0.75	0.01	0.58	0.09	0.09	0.38	0.81	0.20	0.30		0.31	0.26	0.68	0.18	0.83	0.59
Manufacturing: Pharmaceuticals																
Multiple R				0.83			0.72								0.84	
R Square				0.68			0.52								0.71	
Manufacturing: Pulp & Paper / Publishing & Printing																
Multiple R	0.98	0.94	0.88	0.97	0.82	0.98	0.83			1.00	0.91	0.96	0.15	0.76	0.87	0.94
R Square	0.95	0.89	0.77	0.93	0.68	0.96	0.69			1.00	0.83	0.91	0.02	0.58	0.76	0.88
Manufacturing: Radio, Television, Communication Equipment & Apparatus																
Multiple R		0.96					0.58								0.84	
R Square		0.91					0.34								0.71	
Manufacturing: Rubber & Plastics																
Multiple R	0.99	0.97	0.58	0.57	1.00	0.95	0.61		0.86	0.95	0.76	0.85		0.87	0.93	0.80
R Square	0.99	0.94	0.34	0.32	0.99	0.91	0.38		0.74	0.91	0.58	0.73		0.76	0.86	0.63

Manufacturing: Transport Equipment																
Multiple R	0.97	0.52	0.97	0.87	0.57	0.55	0.89	0.87	0.87		0.83	0.72	0.95		0.98	
R Square	0.94	0.27	0.94	0.75	0.33	0.31	0.78	0.76	0.76		0.69	0.52	0.90		0.96	
Manufacturing: Wood & Wooden Products																
Multiple R	0.90	0.45		0.94	0.26				0.78	0.91					0.81	0.89
R Square	0.82	0.20		0.87	0.07				0.61	0.82					0.66	0.79
Mining and quarrying																
Multiple R	1.00					0.91	0.98	0.72				0.92				
R Square	1.00					0.83	0.97	0.52				0.85				
Other community, social and personal service activities																
Multiple R	0.90		0.86			0.93	0.72				0.90	0.90		0.50	0.84	
R Square	0.81		0.75			0.86	0.51				0.82	0.80		0.25	0.71	
Real estate, rental and business activities																
Multiple R	0.92		0.90			0.96	0.80	0.85			0.89	0.95			0.34	0.82
R Square	0.85		0.81			0.93	0.64	0.73			0.79	0.90			0.12	0.67
Trade and repair																
Multiple R	0.86	0.60	0.43	0.96	1.00	0.90	0.80	0.95		0.86		0.89	0.98		0.90	0.82
R Square	0.75	0.36	0.19	0.91	1.00	0.81	0.64	0.91		0.73		0.79	0.95		0.81	0.66
Transport, storage and communication* (2004–2006)																
Multiple R	1.00															
R Square	1.00															

Source: Based on data obtained from the Polish Information and Foreign Investment Agency (PAIIZ) and the author's own analysis.

Appendix 3f Results of regression between RLAis and regional private amount of R&D spending (H3f).

Private R&D per Region & Industry (2000–2005)	DOLNOŚLĄSKIE	KUJAWSKO-POMORSKIE	ŁÓDZKIE	LUBELSKIE	LUBUSKIE	MAŁOPOLSKIE	MAZOWIECKIE	OPOLSKIE	PODKARPACKIE	PODLASKIE	POMORSKIE	ŚLĄSKIE	ŚWIĘTOKRZYSKIE	WARMIŃSKO-MAZURSKIE	WIELKOPOLSKIE	ZACHODNIOPOMORSKIE
Agriculture, hunting and forestry																
Multiple R				0.075							0.904			0.263	0.625	
R Square				0.006							0.816			0.069	0.391	
Mining and quarrying																
Multiple R	0.614					0.809	0.392	0.597				0.652				
R Square	0.377					0.654	0.153	0.357				0.424				
Manufacturing: Chemicals& Chemical Products																
Multiple R	0.485	0.424	0.498	0.261	0.700	0.487	0.549	0.635	0.457		0.056	0.144	0.383		0.267	0.782
R Square	0.235	0.180	0.248	0.068	0.490	0.237	0.302	0.403	0.209		0.003	0.021	0.146		0.071	0.612
Manufacturing: Consumer Products																
Multiple R	0.812		0.376				0.034								0.256	1.000
R Square	0.659		0.141				0.001								0.066	1.000
Manufacturing: Electrical Machinery and Apparatus																
Multiple R	0.164	1.000	0.423				0.161		0.351		0.715	0.357			0.634	0.383
R Square	0.027	1.000	0.179				0.026		0.123		0.511	0.128			0.403	0.147
Manufacturing: Fabrics & Textiles																
Multiple R	0.364	0.631	0.466		0.419	0.824	0.086	0.629		0.324		0.706	0.509	0.233	0.589	
R Square	0.132	0.398	0.217		0.176	0.679	0.007	0.396		0.105		0.498	0.259	0.054	0.347	

Manufacturing: Food, Drinks & Tobacco Products																
Multiple R	0.873	0.932	0.630	0.841	0.096	0.740	0.399	0.825	0.996	0.801	0.356	0.295	0.465	0.055	0.232	0.711
R Square	0.763	0.868	0.396	0.708	0.009	0.548	0.159	0.680	0.991	0.641	0.127	0.087	0.217	0.003	0.054	0.505
Manufacturing: Furniture & Consumer Goods																
Multiple R	0.553	0.450		0.816			0.538				0.482	0.758		0.209	0.305	0.080
R Square	0.306	0.202		0.666			0.289				0.232	0.575		0.044	0.093	0.006
Manufacturing: Glass																
Multiple R									0.045							
R Square									0.002							
Manufacturing: Leather & Leather Products																
Multiple R		0.300	0.163		0.303		0.021		0.310							0.907
R Square		0.090	0.027		0.092		0.000		0.096							0.823
Manufacturing: Machinery & Equipment																
Multiple R	0.791		0.132	0.031			0.717	0.206				0.316	0.916	1.000	0.836	0.930
R Square	0.626		0.017	0.001			0.515	0.042				0.100	0.839	1.000	0.700	0.865
Manufacturing: Metals & Metal Products																
Multiple R	0.047	0.047	0.888	0.612	0.029	0.734	0.472	0.468	0.631	0.882	0.407	0.717	0.452		0.393	0.969
R Square	0.002	0.002	0.789	0.375	0.001	0.539	0.222	0.219	0.398	0.778	0.166	0.514	0.204		0.154	0.938
Manufacturing: Other Non-Metal Goods																
Multiple R	0.289	0.741	0.063	0.143	0.639	0.598	0.165	0.831	0.310		0.154	0.583	0.225	0.572	0.513	0.557
R Square	0.084	0.549	0.004	0.020	0.408	0.358	0.027	0.690	0.096		0.024	0.340	0.050	0.327	0.264	0.310
Manufacturing: Pharmaceuticals																
Multiple R				0.652			0.859								0.842	
R Square				0.425			0.737								0.709	

Continued

Appendix 3f Continued

Private R&D per Region & Industry (2000–2005)	DOLNOŚLĄSKIE	KUJAWSKO-POMORSKIE	ŁÓDZKIE	LUBELSKIE	LUBUSKIE	MAŁOPOLSKIE	MAZOWIECKIE	OPOLSKIE	PODKARPACKIE	PODLASKIE	POMORSKIE	ŚLĄSKIE	ŚWIĘTOKRZYSKIE	WARMIŃSKO-MAZURSKIE	WIELKOPOLSKIE	ZACHODNIOPOMORSKIE
Manufacturing: Pulp & Paper / Publishing & Printing																
Multiple R	0.212	0.216	0.254	0.942	0.966	0.560	0.221			0.380	0.441	0.279	0.305	0.284	0.136	0.725
R Square	0.045	0.047	0.064	0.888	0.934	0.314	0.049			0.145	0.194	0.078	0.093	0.081	0.018	0.526
Manufacturing: Radio, Television, Communication Equipment & Apparatus																
Multiple R		1.000					0.329								0.606	
R Square		1.000					0.108								0.367	
Manufacturing: Rubber & Plastics																
Multiple R	0.147	0.601	0.096	0.147	0.229	0.866	0.335		0.243	0.757	0.125	0.078		0.388	0.391	0.907
R Square	0.022	0.361	0.009	0.022	0.052	0.751	0.113		0.059	0.573	0.016	0.006		0.150	0.153	0.823
Manufacturing: Transport Equipment																
Multiple R	0.438	0.174	0.425	0.029	0.482	0.156	0.432	0.009	0.130		0.302	0.054	0.749		0.809	
R Square	0.192	0.030	0.181	0.001	0.232	0.024	0.187	0.000	0.017		0.091	0.003	0.560		0.655	
Manufacturing: Wood & Wooden Products																
Multiple R	0.307	0.304		0.801	0.394				0.676	0.268					0.578	0.101
R Square	0.094	0.092		0.641	0.155				0.457	0.072					0.334	0.010

Electricity, gas and water supply																
Multiple R	0.567					0.231	0.394		0.280	0.055	0.728	0.566	0.737	0.327	0.171	0.194
R Square	0.321					0.053	0.156		0.078	0.003	0.530	0.320	0.543	0.107	0.029	0.038
Construction																
Multiple R			0.848			0.415	0.410				0.611	0.313	0.501		0.912	
R Square			0.720			0.172	0.168				0.373	0.098	0.251		0.832	
Trade and repair																
Multiple R	0.000	0.911	0.307	0.547	0.361	0.952	0.664	0.102		0.441		0.308	0.676		0.494	0.907
R Square	0.000	0.829	0.094	0.299	0.130	0.905	0.441	0.010		0.194		0.095	0.457		0.244	0.823
Hotels and restaurants																
Multiple R	0.401			0.253	0.414		0.499				0.553	0.135			0.559	0.889
R Square	0.161			0.064	0.171		0.249				0.306	0.018			0.313	0.790
Transport, storage and communication* (2004–2006)																
Multiple R	1.000		1.000		1.000		1.000		1.000		1.000	1.000		1.000	1.000	1.000
R Square	1.000		1.000		1.000		1.000		1.000		1.000	1.000		1.000	1.000	1.000
Financial intermediation																
Multiple R	0.094	0.537	0.656		0.196		0.466				0.301	0.083			0.164	
R Square	0.009	0.289	0.430		0.039		0.217				0.091	0.007			0.027	
Real estate, rental and business activities																
Multiple R	0.561		0.958			0.408	0.220	0.528			0.435	0.048			0.389	0.309
R Square	0.315		0.917			0.166	0.049	0.279			0.190	0.002			0.151	0.095
Other community, social and personal service activities																
Multiple R	0.018		0.066			0.693	0.692				0.090	0.652		0.386	0.874	
R Square	0.000		0.004			0.481	0.478				0.008	0.425		0.149	0.764	

Source: Based on data obtained from the Polish Information and Foreign Investment Agency (PAIIZ) and the author's own analysis.

Appendix 4 H4a Fortune 500 2000 and 2006

Investor name	Fortune 500 – 2000	Fortune 500 – 2006	Fortune 500 – 2000 & 2006	Location	Powiat	Wojewodztwo	Country of registration	Country-of-origin	Activities (PKD)	Activities (class)	Comments
		increase since 2000	present since at least 2000								
Autoliv AB	0	1	0	Oława	Olawski	Dolnośląskie	Sweden	Sweden	Manufacture of transport equipment;	Manufacture of parts and accessories for motor vehicles and their engines;	Autoliv Polska Sp. z o. o. – Oława, Jelcz
General Mills	1	0	0	Torun	Torun	Kujawsko-Pomorskie		USA	food processing		stake in Toruń-Pacific Sp. z o. o. (Toruń)
Lucent Technologies Network Systems Netherlands BV	0	1	1	Bydgoszcz	Bydgoszcz	Kujawsko-Pomorskie	The Netherlands	USA	Manufacture of electrical machinery and apparatus;	Manufacture of television and radio transmitters and apparatus for line telephony and line telegraphy;	Lucent Technologies Poland Sp. z o. o. – Warsaw and Bydgoszcz
Harris	1	0	0	Lodz	Lodzki	Łódzkie		Austria	retail trade		Domar S.A. (Łódź)

PepsiCo	1	1	1	Łódź	Lodz	Łódzkie	USA	USA	Manufacture of food, drinks and tobacco products;	Manufacture of beverages;	PepsiCo General Bottlers Poland Sp. z o. o. – Bottling plants in Łódź, Białystok, Gdańsk, Kraków, Poznań, Szczecin, Wrocław, Żywiec and Pniewy. Salted snacks factory in Grodzisk Mazowiecki. Sale of "Delicja" confectionery to Danone
Caterpillar Inc.	1	1	1	Janów Lubelski	Janowski	Lubelskie	USA	USA	Manufacture of transport equipment;	Manufacture of parts and accessories for motor vehicles and their engines;	Caterpillar Poland Sp. z o. o. – Janów Lubelski
Sara Lee D/E N.V.	0	1	0	Gorzów Wielkopolski	Gorzów Wielkopolski	Lubuskie	The Netherlands	The Netherlands	Manufacture of leather and leather products;	Manufacture of footwear;	Bama Polska Sp. z o. o. – Gorzów Wielkopolski
Ballinger Holdings Ltd.	0	1	0	Warsaw	Warsaw	Mazowieckie	Cyprus	Cyprus	Financial intermediation;	Financial intermediation, except insurance and pension funding;	50% stake in Ballinger Capital Sp. z o. o.
PARKER HANNIFIN GmbH	0	1	0	Warsaw	Warsaw	Mazowieckie	Germany	Germany	Manufacture of machinery and equipment;	Manufacture of other general purpose machinery;	Parker Hannifin Sp. z o. o. – Warsaw, Wrocław, Świebodzice
Readymix Group	1	0	0	Ostroleka	Ostroleka	Mazowieckie		International	other non-metal goods		Ytong Ostrołęka Sp. z o. o., cement aggregates plant in Szczecin, plant in Ostrołęka

Continued

Appendix 4 H4a Cont nued

Investor name	Fortune 500 – 2000	Fortune 500 – 2006	Fortune 500 – 2000 & 2006	Location	Powiat	Wojewodztwo	Country of registration	Country-of-origin	Activities (PKD)	Activities (class)	Comments
		increase since 2000	present since at least 2000								
Lucent Technologies Network Systems Netherlands BV	1	0	0	Warsaw	Warsaw	Mazowieckie		The Netherlands	electrical machinery and apparatus		Lucent Technologies Poland S.A. (Warsaw and Bydgoszcz) – production of equipment for telecommunications
3M Nederland B.V.	1	1	1	Warsaw	Warsaw	Mazowieckie	The Netherlands	The Netherlands	Manufacture of chemicals and chemical products; wholesale and retail trade; repair of motor vehicles, motorcycles and personal and household goods;	Manufacture of pharmaceuticals, medicinal chemicals and botanical products; other wholesale;	3M Poland Sp. z o. o. – Kajetany near Warsaw, 3M Poland Sp. z o. o. – Wroclaw
Levi Strauss	0	1	0	Plock	Płock	Mazowieckie	The Netherlands	The Netherlands	Manufacture of fabrics and textiles;	Manufacture of other wearing apparel and accessories;	Levi Strauss Poland Sp. z o. o. – Office in Warsaw. Factory in Płock
Eli Lilly Nederland	0	1	0	Warsaw	Warsaw	Mazowieckie	The Netherlands	The Netherlands	Wholesale and retail trade; repair of motor vehicles, motorcycles and personal and household goods;	Wholesale of household goods;	Eli Lilly Polska Sp. z o. o. – Warsaw

Merrill Lynch Investment Ltd.	1	0	0	Warsaw	Warsaw	Mazowieckie		United Kingdom	capital investment		stake in Mostostal Export (Warsaw)
Xerox Ltd.	1	1	1	Warsaw	Warsaw	Mazowieckie	United Kingdom	United Kingdom	Wholesale and retail trade; repair of motor vehicles, motorcycles and personal and household goods;	Other retail sale of new goods in specialized stores;	Xerox Polska Sp. z o. o. – Warsaw
Ford	1	0	0	Plonsk	Plonski	Mazowieckie		USA	automotive		Ford Poland S.A. – car assembly plant (Płońsk), Purchasing Center Europe (Warsaw)
J.P. Morgan	1	0	0	Warsaw	Warsaw	Mazowieckie		USA	banking		J.P. Morgan Polska Sp. z o. o., shares in Bank Handlowy w Warszawie S.A.
GTECH Corporation	1	0	0	Warsaw	Warsaw	Mazowieckie		USA	business activities		Grytek Sp. z o. o. (Warsaw)
Gillette	1	0	0	Warsaw	Warsaw	Mazowieckie		USA	consumer products		Gillette Poland S.A. (Warsaw), Wizamet S.A. Łódź – razor production, distribution of toiletries
Cigna Global Holdings Inc	1	1	1	Warsaw	Warsaw	Mazowieckie	USA	USA	Financial intermediation;	Insurance and pension funding, except compulsory social security;	Towarzystwo Ubezpieczeń i Reasekuracji Cigna Stu S.A., Cigna Stu Życie
Nationwide Global Holdings Inc	0	1	0	Warsaw	Warsaw	Mazowieckie	USA	USA	Financial intermediation;	Insurance and pension funding, except compulsory social security;	Nationwide Towarzystwo Ubezpieczeń na Życie S.A. – Warsaw

Continued

Appendix 4 H4a Continued

Investor name	Fortune 500 – 2000	Fortune 500 – 2006	Fortune 500 – 2000 & 2006	Location	Powiat	Wojewodztwo	Country of registration	Country-of-origin	Activities (PKD)	Activities (class)	Comments
		increase since 2000	present since at least 2000								
Citigroup	0	1	0	Warsaw	Warsaw	Mazowieckie	USA	USA	Financial intermediation;	Monetary intermediation; other financial intermediation;	Citibank Handlowy S.A. – Warsaw
General Electric Corporation (GE)	1	1	1	Warsaw	Warsaw	Mazowieckie	USA	USA	Financial intermediation; manufacture of electrical machinery and apparatus;	Monetary intermediation; manufacture of instruments and appliances for measuring, checking, testing, navigating and other purposes, except industrial process control equipment;	Representative Office in Poland – Representative Office in Poland – Warsaw, GE Capital Bank – Gdańsk, GE Bank Mieszkaniowy – Warsaw, GE Power Controls – factories in Bielsko – Biała, Kłodzko, Łódź, GE Medical Systems Polska Sp. z o. o. – Warsaw, GE Aircra
AmRest Holding BV	1	0	0	Warsaw	Warsaw	Mazowieckie		USA	hotels and restaurants, property management		AmRest Sp. z o. o., American Retail Systems Sp. z o. o. – 14 Pizza Hut, KFC and Taco Bell restaurants (Warsaw, Wrocław, Poznań, Szczecin, Leszno, Jelenia Góra, Gorzów Wielkopolski

Colgate-Palmolive America INC	1	1	1	Halinów	Warsaw	Mazowieckie	USA	USA	Manufacture of chemicals and chemical products;	Manufacture of soap and detergents, cleaning and polishing preparations, perfumes and toilet preparations;	55% stake in Colgate – Palmolive Poland Sp. z o. o. – Office in Halinów near Warsaw
Praxair Inc.	1	1	1	Warsaw	Warsaw	Mazowieckie	USA	USA	Manufacture of chemicals and chemical products;	Manufacture of basic chemicals;	Praxair Polska Sp. z o. o. – Plants in Warsaw, Gliwice, Poznań, Siewierz and Wrocław
Procter & Gamble Mexico Holding	1	1	1	Warsaw	Warsaw	Mazowieckie	The Netherlands	USA	Manufacture of chemicals and chemical products; manufacture of pulp and paper, publishing and printing;	Manufacture of soap and detergents, cleaning and polishing preparations, perfumes and toilet preparations; manufacture of articles of paper and paperboard;	Procter & Gamble Operations Polska Sp. z o. o.
Motorola Inc.	1	1	1	Warsaw	Warsaw	Mazowieckie	USA	USA	Manufacture of electrical machinery and apparatus;	Manufacture of television and radio transmitters and apparatus for line telephony and line telegraphy;	Motorola Polska Sp. z o. o. – Warsaw, Motorola Polska Electronics Sp. z o. o. – Kraków, Motorola Polska Software Center in Kraków

Continued

Appendix 4 H4a Continued

Investor name	Fortune 500 – 2000	Fortune 500 – 2006	Fortune 500 – 2000 & 2006	Location	Powiat	Wojewodztwo	Country of registration	Country-of-origin	Activities (PKD)	Activities (class)	Comments
		increase since 2000	present since at least 2000								
Smithfield Foods	1	1	1	Warsaw	Warsaw	Mazowieckie	USA	USA	Manufacture of food, drinks and tobacco products;	Production, processing and preserving of meat and meat products;	Animex – Krakowskie Zakłady Pierzarskie Sp. z o.o. – Kraków, ANIMEX Grupa Drobiarska Sp. z o.o. – Suwałki, Animex Sp. z o. o. – Warsaw, Animex-Pasze Sp. z o.o. – Zamość, Contipasz S.A. – Grodków, Grupa Animex S.A. – Ostróda, Iławskie Zakłady Drobiarskie E
Whirlpool Europe Srl	0	1	0	Warsaw	Warsaw	Mazowieckie	Italy	USA	Manufacture of machinery and equipment;	Manufacture of domestic appliances n.e.c.;	Whirlpool Polska Sp. z o. o. – Warsaw Polar S.A. – Wrocław
Delphi Automotive Systems	0	1	0	Błonie	Warszawski Zachodni	Mazowieckie	USA	USA	Manufacture of transport equipment;	Manufacture of parts and accessories for motor vehicles and their engines;	Delphi Poland S.A. – Office in Kraków. Factories in Błonie, Ostrów Wielkopolski, Jeleśnia, Gdańsk, Krosno. Delphi Polska Automotive Systems Poland Sp. z o. o. – factory in Tychy, R&D – Center in Kraków

Apache Corporation	0	1	0	Warsaw	Warsaw	Mazowieckie	USA	USA	Mining and quarrying;	Extraction of crude petroleum and natural gas;	Apache Poland Sp. z o. o. – Warsaw
Oracle Corporation	1	1	1	Warsaw	Warsaw	Mazowieckie	USA	USA	Real estate, rental and business activities;	Software consultancy and supply; Database activities;	Oracle Polska Sp. z o. o. – Warsaw
United Parcel Service Inc. (UPS)	0	1	0	Warsaw	Warsaw	Mazowieckie	USA	USA	Transport, storage and communication;	Post and courier activities;	UPS Polska Sp. z o. o. – Warsaw
Unisys Corporation	1	1	1	Warsaw	Warsaw	Mazowieckie	USA	USA	Wholesale and retail trade; repair of motor vehicles, motorcycles and personal and household goods;	Other retail sale of new goods in specialized stores;	Unisys Polska Sp. z o. o. – Warsaw
Visteon Automotive Systems	0	1	0	Praszka	Oleski	Opolskie	USA	USA	Manufacture of transport equipment;	Manufacture of parts and accessories for motor vehicles and their engines;	Visteon Poland S.A. – Praszka, Polmot ZEM – Duszniki
United Technologies Automotive	1	1	1	Mielec	Mielecki	Podkarpackie		USA	electrical machinery and apparatus		UT Automotive Poland Sp. z o. o. (EURO-PARK Mielec SEZ) – cable and wiring manufacturer
Owens-Illinois Inc.	1	1	1	Jarosław	Jarosławski	Podkarpackie	USA	USA	Manufacture of other non-metal goods;	Manufacture of glass and glass products;	Owens – Illionois Polska S.A., Huta Szkła – Activity in Jarosław (Podkarpackie Voivodship), Huta Szkła Antoninek – Poznań

Continued

Appendix 4 H4a Continued

Investor name	Fortune 500 – 2000	Fortune 500 2006	Fortune 500 – 2000 & 2006	Location	Powiat	Wojewodztwo	Country of registration	Country-of-origin	Activities (PKD)	Activities (class)	Comments
		increase since 2000	present since at least 2000								
Goodrich Aerospace Canada LTD	0	1	0	Krosno	Krosno	Podkarpackie	Canada	USA	Manufacture of transport equipment;	Manufacture of aircraft and spacecraft;	Goodrich Krosno Sp. z o. o. – Krosno
Lear Corporation	1	1	1	Mielec	Mielecki	Podkarpackie	USA	USA	Manufacture of transport equipment;	Manufacture of parts and accessories for motor vehicles and their engines;	Lear Automotive (EEDS) Poland Sp. z o. o. – Mielec Lear Corporation Poland Sp. z o. o. – Tychy, Gliwice, Warsaw
Enron International	1	0	0	Nowa Sarzyna	Lezajsk	Podkarpackie		USA	power, gas and water supply		Elektrociepłownia Nowa Sarzyna Sp. z o. o. – combined heat plant
Eaton	0	1	0	Tczew	Tczewski	Pomorskie	USA	USA	Manufacture of transport equipment;	Manufacture of parts and accessories for motor vehicles and their engines;	98% stake in Eaton Truck Components S.A. – Activity in Tczew Eaton Automotive Systems Sp. z o. o. – Bielsko-Biała
Intel Europe Inc.		1		Gdańsk	Gdańsk	Pomorskie	USA	USA	Real estate, rental and business activities;	Computer and related activities;	Intel Technology Poland Sp. z o. o. – Gdańsk
Foster Wheeler Energy	1	0	0	Sosnowiec	Sosnowiec	Śląskie		Finland	metal products		Foster Wheeler Energy Fakop Sp. z o. o. (Sosnowiec)

TRW	1	0	0	Czechowice-Dziedzice	Bielski	Śląskie		USA	Manufacture of transport equipment;		TRW Steering Systems Poland Sp. z o. o. – car components production
Timken Company	0	1	0	Sosnowiec	Sosnowiec	Śląskie	USA	USA	Manufacture of machinery and equipment;	Manufacture of machinery for the production and use of mechanical power, except aircraft, vehicle and cycle engines;	Timken Polska Sp. z o. o. – Sosnowiec
General Motors Corporation	1	1	1	Gliwice	Gliwice	Śląskie	USA	USA	Manufacture of transport equipment;	Manufacture of motor vehicles;	General Motors Manufacturing Poland Sp. z o. o. – car production in Gliwice, General Motors Poland Sp. z o. o. – Office in Warsaw, GMAC Commercial Finance Sp. z o. o. – Office in Warsaw, Isuzu Motors Polska Sp. z o. o.
Tenneco Global Holding Inc	0	1	0	Rybnik	Rybnik	Śląskie	USA	USA	Manufacture of transport equipment;	Manufacture of parts and accessories for motor vehicles and their engines;	Tenneco Automotive Polska Sp. z o. o. – Office in Warsaw. Factories in Rybnik and Gliwice
Aesculap AG	1	1	1	Nowy Tomyśl	Tomyski	Wielkopolskie	Germany	Germany	Manufacture of electrical machinery and apparatus;	Manufacture of medical and surgical equipment and orthopaedic appliances;	98.73% stake in Aesculap Chifa Sp. z o. o. – Nowy Tomyśl (Wielkopolskie Voivodship)

Continued

Appendix 4 H4a Continued

Investor name	Fortune 500 – 2000	Fortune 500 – 2006	Fortune 500 – 2000 & 2006	Location	Powiat	Wojewodztwo	Country of registration	Country-of-origin	Activities (PKD)	Activities (class)	Comments
		increase since 2000	present since at least 2000								
Dana Corporation	1	0	0	Gostyn	Gostynski	Wielkopolskie		USA	Manufacture of transport equipment;		WIX-FILTRON Sp. z o. o. (Gostyń) – car components production
H.J. Heinz Company	0	1	0	Pudliszki	Gostyński	Wielkopolskie	USA	USA	Manufacture of food, drinks and tobacco products;	Processing and preserving of fruit and vegetables;	H.J. Heinz Polska S.A. – Pudliszki
Wm. Wrigley Jr. Company	0	1	0	Poznań	Poznań	Wielkopolskie	USA	USA	Manufacture of food, drinks and tobacco products;	Manufacture of other food products;	99.96% stake in Wrigley Poland Sp. z o. o. – Office in Poznań
ArvinMeritor	0	1	0	Swarzędz	Poznanski	Wielkopolskie	USA	USA	Manufacture of transport equipment;	Manufacture of parts and accessories for motor vehicles and their engines;	ArvinMeritor Sp. z o. o. – Swarzędz

Conoco Central Europe Inc	1	0	0	chain	USA	distribution of petroleum products, retail trade	Conoco Poland Sp. z o. o.- gas station network
US West	1	0	0	chain	USA	telecommunications	22.5% of shares of Polska Telefonia Cyfrowa – GSM system operator
Total	34	40	19				
Increase since year 2000		18%					
Present in both year 2000 & 2006			48%				

Source: Based on data obtained from the Polish Information and Foreign Investment Agency (PAIIZ) and the author's own analysis.

Appendix 4 H4b Fortune 500 firms in Mazowieckie

Investor name	Fortune 500 – 2000	Fortune 500 – 2006	Fortune 500 – 2000 & 2006	% change of the 2000 RLAic	change of the 2000 RLAic	change in the presence of F500 firms	Location	Wojewodztwo	Country of origin	Activities (PKD)
GTECH Corporation	1	0	0	0	–	–	Warsaw	Mazowieckie	USA	Capital investment/ business activities
Merrill Lynch Investment Ltd.	1	0	0	0	–	–	Warsaw	Mazowieckie	United Kingdom	Capital investment
Ballinger Holdings Ltd.	0	1	0	0.48	–	+	Warsaw	Mazowieckie	Cyprus	Financial intermediation;
Cigna Global Holdings Inc	1	1	1	0.48	–	=	Warsaw	Mazowieckie	USA	Financial intermediation;
Nationwide Global Holdings Inc	0	1	0	0.48	–	+	Warsaw	Mazowieckie	USA	Financial intermediation;
J.P. Morgan	1	0	0	0.48	–	–	Warsaw	Mazowieckie	USA	Financial intermediation;
Citigroup	0	1	0	0.48	–	+	Warsaw	Mazowieckie	USA	Financial intermediation;
General Electric Corporation (GE)	1	1	1	0.48	–	=	Warsaw	Mazowieckie	USA	Financial intermediation; manufacture of electrical machinery and apparatus;
AmRest Holding BV	1	0	0	1.04	+	–	Warsaw	Mazowieckie	USA	Hotels and restaurants, property management

Praxair Inc.	1	1	1	0.73	–	=	Warsaw	Mazowieckie	USA	Manufacture of chemicals and chemical products;
Colgate-Palmolive America INC	1	1	1	0.73	–	=	Halinów	Mazowieckie	USA	Manufacture of chemicals and chemical products;
Procter & Gamble Mexico Holding	1	1	1	0.73	–	=	Warsaw	Mazowieckie	USA	Manufacture of chemicals and chemical products; manufacture of pulp and paper, publishing and printing;
3M Nederland B.V.	1	1	1	0.73	–	=	Warsaw	Mazowieckie	The Netherlands	Manufacture of chemicals and chemical products; wholesale and retail trade; repair of motor vehicles, motorcycles and personal and household goods;
Gillette	1	0	0	0.00	–	–	Warsaw	Mazowieckie	USA	Manufacture of consumer products
Lucent Technologies Network Systems Netherlands BV	1	0	0	0.67	–	–	warsaw	Mazowieckie	The Netherlands	Manufacture of electrical machinery and apparatus

Continued

Appendix 4 H4b Continued

Investor name	Fortune 500 – 2000	Fortune 500 – 2006	Fortune 500 – 2000 & 2006	% change of the 2000 RLAic	change of the 2000 RLAic	change in the presence of F500 firms	Location	Wojewodztwo	Country of origin	Activities (PKD)
Motorola Inc.	1	1	1	0.67	–	=	Warsaw	Mazowieckie	USA	Manufacture of electrical machinery and apparatus;
Levi Strauss	0	1	0	0.37	–	+	Plock	Mazowieckie	The Netherlands	Manufacture of fabrics and textiles;
Smithfield Foods	1	1	1	0.76	–	=	Warsaw	Mazowieckie	USA	Manufacture of food, drinks and tobacco products;
Whirlpool Europe Srl	0	1	0	0.64	–	+	Warsaw	Mazowieckie	USA	Manufacture of machinery and equipment;
PARKER HANNIFIN GmbH	0	1	0	0.64	–	+	Warsaw	Mazowieckie	Germany	Manufacture of machinery and equipment;
Readymix Group	1	0	0	0.56	–	–	Ostroleka	Mazowieckie	International	Manufacture of other non-metal goods
Delphi Automotive Systems	0	1	0	1.91	+	+	Błonie	Mazowieckie	USA	Manufacture of transport equipment;
Ford	1	0	0	1.91	+	–	Plonsk	Mazowieckie	USA	Manufacture of transport equipment;
Apache Corporation	0	1	0	0.64	–	+	Warsaw	Mazowieckie	USA	Mining and quarrying;

Oracle Corporation	1	1	1	1.39	+	=	Warsaw	Mazowieckie	USA	Real estate, renting and business activities;
United Parcel Service Inc. (UPS)	0	1	0	1.07	+	+	Warsaw	Mazowieckie	USA	Transport, storage and communication;
Xerox Ltd.	1	1	1	0.87	–	=	Warsaw	Mazowieckie	United Kingdom	Wholesale and retail trade; repair of motor vehicles, motorcycles and personal and household goods;
Unisys Corporation	1	1	1	0.87	–	=	Warsaw	Mazowieckie	USA	Wholesale and retail trade; repair of motor vehicles, motorcycles and personal and household goods;
Eli Lilly Nederland	0	1	0	0.87	–	+	Warsaw	Mazowieckie	The Netherlands	Wholesale and retail trade; repair of motor vehicles, motorcycles and personal and household goods;
Total	19	21	11							
increase since year 2000		11%								
present in both year 2000 & 2006			52%							

Source: Based on data obtained from the Polish Information and Foreign Investment Agency (PAIIZ) and the author's own analysis.

Appendix 4a Fortune 500 firms and other leading foreign firms in Poland

Investor name	Fortune 500-until year 2006*	Large firms entered in years 2007 and 2008	Location	Wojewodztwo	Country-of-origin	Activities(PKD)	Activities
Dolnośląskie							
Nokia-Siemens		1	Wroclaw	Dolnośląskie	Finland	Telecommunications	R&D
Copengemini		1	Wroclaw	Dolnośląskie	France	Services-Business services	R&D
Siemens		1	Wroclaw	Dolnośląskie	Germany	Manufacture of electrical machinery	R&D
KPIT		1	Wroclaw	Dolnośląskie	India	Services-Business services	IT
Wipro technologies			Wroclaw	Dolnośląskie	India	Services-Business services	IT
Autoliv AB	0		Olawa	Dolnośląskie	Sweden	Manufacture of transport	Manufacture of parts
HP		1	Wroclaw	Dolnośląskie	USA	Services-Business services	R&D
Remy International		1	Wroclaw	Dolnośląskie	USA	Manufacture of transport	R&D
CSS		1	Wroclaw	Dolnośląskie	USA	Services-Business services	IT
Google		1	Wroclaw	Dolnośląskie	USA	Services-Business services	IT
	1	9					
	Increase	900%					
				Łódzkie			
Harris	0		Lodz	Łódzkie	Austria	Wholesale and retail trade	
Bosch-Siemens		1	Lodz	Łódzkie	Germany	Manufacture of transport	R&D
Atos Origin		1	Lodz	Łódzkie	Netherlands	Services-Business services	IT
PepsiCo	1		Lodz	Łódzkie	USA	Manufacture of food and drinks	
Manufacture of beverages;							
	2	2					
	Increase	100%					
		Lubuskie					

Sara Lee D/E	0		Gorzów Wielkopo	Lubuskie	The Netherlands	Manufacture of leather	
Manufacture of foot wear							
N.V		1	Zielona Gora	Lubuskie	Philippines	Manufacture of electrical machinery	R&D
	1 Increase	1 100%					

* Firms annotated with 0 entered Poland after year 2000 and before 2006

				Małopolskie			
Pliva		1	Krakow	Małopolskie	Croatia	Power, gas, and water supply	R&D
Lurgi		1	Krakow	Małopolskie	Germany	Power, gas, and water supply	R&D
Fatro SpA		1	Krakow	Małopolskie	Italy	Manufacture of pharmaceuticals	Biotech/Pharma
HSL		1	Krakow	Małopolskie	Netherlands	Services-Business services	IT
ABB		1	Krakow	Małopolskie	Switzerland	Manufacture of electrical machinery	R&D
IBM		1	Krakow	Małopolskie	USA	Services-Business services	R&D
Sabre		1	Krakow	Małopolskie	USA	Services-Business services-travel	R&D
CH2M Hill		1	Krakow	Małopolskie	USA	Power, gas, and water supply	R&D
	0 Increase	8					
				Mazowieckie			
Balinger Holdings Ltd	0		Warsaw	Mazowieckie	Cyprus	Financial intermediation	Financial Intermediation
TopGan		1	Warsaw	Mazowieckie	France	Nanotechnology	R&D

Continued

Appendix 4a Continued

Investor name	Fortune 500-until year 2006*	Large firms entered in years 2007 and 2008	Location	Wojewodztwo	Country-of-origin	Activities(PKD)	Activities
Bayer AG		1	Warsaw	Mazowieckie	Germany	Manufacture of chemicals	
Biotech/pharma							
PARKER HANNIFIN	0		Warsaw	Mazowieckie	Germany	Manufacture of machinery	Manufacture of
Hexal AG		1	Warsaw	Mazowieckie	Germany	Manufacture of Pharmaceuticals	Biotech/pharma
Egis Pharmaceutical		1	Warsaw	Mazowieckie	Hungary	Manufacture of Pharmaceuticals	Biotech/pharma
Readymix Group	0		Warsaw	Mazowieckie	International	Manufacture of other non-metal	
LG Electronic		1	Clechanow	Mazowieckie	So. Korea	Manufacture of electrical machinery	R&D
Samsung Electronic		1	Warsaw	Mazowieckie	So. Korea	Telecommunications	R&D
Cederrath		1	Radzymin	Mazowieckie	Sweden	Manufacture of chemicals	R&D
Lucent technologies	0		Warsaw	Mazowieckie	The Netherlands	Manufacture of electrical machinery	
3M Netherland B.V	1		Warsaw	Mazowieckie	The Netherlands	Manufacture of chemicals	Manufacture of
*-Firms annotated with 0 entered Poland after year 2000 and before 2006							
Levi strauss	0		Plock	Mazowieckie	The Netherlands	Manufacture of fabrics and textiles	Manufacture of
Boxter Healthcare		1	Warsaw	Mazowieckie	The Netherlands	Manufacture of Pharmaceuticals	Biotech/pharma
Eli Lilly Netherland	0		Warsaw	Mazowieckie	The Netherlands	Wholesale and retail trade; repair	Wholesale of household

Glaxo smithkine		1	Warsaw	Mazowieckie	United Kingdom	Manufacture of Pharmaceuticals	Biotech/pharma
Merrill Lynch Investment Ltd	0		Warsaw	Mazowieckie	United Kingdom	Financial intermediation;	
Xerox Ltd	1		Warsaw	Mazowieckie	United Kingdom	Wholesale and retail trade; repair	Other retail sale of new
Ford	0		Plonsk	Mazowieckie	USA	Automotive	
J.P. Morgan	0		Warsaw	Mazowieckie	USA	Financial intermediation	
Gillette	0		Warsaw	Mazowieckie	USA	Manufacture of consumer products	
Cigna Global Holdings Inc	1		Warsaw	Mazowieckie	USA	Financial intermediation	Insurance and pension
Nationwide Global Holdings	0		Warsaw	Mazowieckie	USA	Financial intermediation	Insurance and pension
Citigroup	0		Warsaw	Mazowieckie	USA	Financial intermediation	Monetary Intermediation
General Electric Corporation	1		Warsaw	Mazowieckie	USA	Financial intermediation	Monetary Intermediation
AmRest Holding BV	0		Garwoli	Mazowieckie	USA	Hotels and restaurants	
Avon		1	Garwoli	Mazowieckie	USA	Manufacture of chemicals	R&D
Colgate-Palmolive	1		Halinów	Mazowieckie	USA	Manufacture of chemicals	Manufacture of soap
Praxair Inc	1		Warsaw	Mazowieckie	USA	Manufacture of chemicals	Manufacture of basic
Procter &Gamble Mexico	1		Warsaw	Mazowieckie	USA	Manufacture of chemicals	Manufacture of soap
Motorola Inc	1		Warsaw	Mazowieckie	USA	Manufacture of electrical machinery	Manufacture of television
Smith field Foods	0		Warsaw	Mazowieckie	USA	Manufacture of food and drinks	Production, Processing

Continued

Appendix 4a Continued

Investor name	Fortune 500-until year 2006*	Large firms entered in years 2007 and 2008	Location	Wojewodztwo	Country-of-origin	Activities(PKD)	Activities
Whirlpool Europe Srl		1	Warsaw	Mazowieckie	USA	Manufacture of machinery	Manufacture
IVAX Corporation	0		Warsaw	Mazowieckie	USA	Manufacture of Pharmaceuticals	Biotech/pharma
Delphi Automotive	0		Blonie	Mazowieckie	USA	Manufacture of transport equipment	Manufacture of Parts
Apache Corporation	0		Warsaw	Mazowieckie	USA	Mining and quarrying	Extraction of crude
Oracle Corporation	1		Warsaw	Mazowieckie	USA	Real estate, renting, and business	Software consultancy
GTECH corporation	0		Warsaw	Mazowieckie	USA	Service -Business services	
Microsoft		1	Warsaw	Mazowieckie	USA	Service -Business services	R&D
SAS Institutes		1	Warsaw	Mazowieckie	USA	Service -Business services	R&D
vantyx systems		1	Warsaw	Mazowieckie	USA	Service -Business services	IT
United Parcel Service Inc	0		Warsaw	Mazowieckie	USA	Transport, storage and communication	Post and courier
Unisys Corporation	1		Warsaw	Mazowieckie	USA	Wholesale and retail trade; repair	Other retail sale
	29 Increase	15 52%					
Podkarpackie							
East Springs International NV		1	Iwonicz Zdrój	Podkarpackie	France	Manufacture of chemicals	
Biotech/Pharma							

*-Firms annotated with 0 entered Poland after year 2000 and before 2006

United Technologies	1		Mielec	Podkarpackie	USA	Electrical machinery and apparatus	
Owens-Illinois Inc	1		Jarosla	Podkarpackie	USA	Manufacture of other non-metal	Manufacture of glass
Goodrich Aerospace	0		Krosno	Podkarpackie	USA	Manufacture of transport equipment	Manufacture of aircraft
Lear Corporation	1		Mielec	Podkarpackie	USA	Manufacture of transport equipment	Manufacture of parts and
Pratt&Whitney		1	Rzeszow	Podkarpackie	USA	Manufacture of transport equipment	R&D
Enron International	0		Nowa Sarzyna	Podkarpackie	USA	Power, gas and water supply	
	5 Increase	2 40%					
Pomorskie							
Alstom		1	Elblag	Pomorskie	France	Power, gas and water supply	R&D
ZenSar Technology		1	Gdansk	Pomorskie	India	Service-Business services	IT
Compuware		1	Gdansk	Pomorskie	USA	Manufacture of electrical machinery	R&D
Eaton	0		Tczew	Pomorskie	USA	Manufacture of transport equipment	Manufacture of parts
Intel Europe Inc			Gdansk	Pomorskie	USA	Real estate, renting, and business	Computer and related
GeInterlogix		1	Gdansk	Pomorskie	USA	Service-Business services	R&D

*-Firms annotated with 0 entered Poland after year 2000 and before 2006

Continued

Appendix 4a Continued

Investor name	Fortune 500-until year 2006*	Large firms entered in years 2007 and 2008	Location	Wojewodztwo	Country-of-origin	Activities(PKD)	Activities
First Data Corporation		1	Gdansk	Pomorskie	USA	Service-Business services	IT
	2 Increase	5 250%					
Śląskie							
Bombardier		1	Katowice	Śląskie	Canada	Manufacture of transport equipment	R&D
Foster Wheeler Energy	0		Sosnowiec	Śląskie	Finland	Manufacture of metal products	
Ontrack		1	Katowice	Śląskie	Netherland	Services-Business services	R&D
Timken Company	0		Sosnowiec	Śląskie	USA	Manufacture of machinery	Manufacture of machinery
TRW	0		Czechowice	Śląskie	USA	Manufacture of transport equipment	
General Motors corporation	1		Gliwice	Śląskie	USA	Manufacture of transport equipment	Manufacture of motor
Tenneco Global Holding Inc	0		Rybnik	Śląskie	USA	Manufacture of transport equipment	Manufacture of parts
TRW Automotive		1	Czestochowa	Śląskie	USA	Manufacture of transport equipment	R&D
Emtex Pitney Bowes		1	Bielsko Biala	Śląskie	USA	Services-Business services	IT
	5 Increase	4 80%					

*-Firms annotated with 0 entered Poland after year 2000 and before 2006

				Wielkopolskie			
Biofarma		1	Poznań	Wielkopolskie	France	Manufacture of pharmaceuticals	Biotech/Pharma
Aesculap AG	1		Nowy Tomyśl	Wielkopolskie	Germany	Manufacture of electrical machinery	Manufacture of medical equipment
Philips		1	Pila	Wielkopolskie	Netherlands	Manufacture of electrical machinery	R&D
ICN Switzerland AG		1	Poznań	Wielkopolskie	Switzerland	Manufacture of pharmaceuticals	Biotech/Pharma
H.J. Heinz Company	0		Pudliszki	Wielkopolskie	USA	Manufacture of food and drinks	Processing
Wm. Wrigley Jr. Comapny	0		Poznań	Wielkopolskie	USA	Manufacture of food and drinks	Manufacture of other foods
Dana Corporation	0		Gostyn	Wielkopolskie	USA	Manufacture of transport	
ArvinMeritor	0	1	Swarzędz	Wielkopolskie	USA	Manufacture of transport	Manufacture of parts
	5	3					
	Increase	60%					

*-Firms annotated with [illegible] entered Poland after year 2000 and before 2006

Notes

1 Location Choice and Clustering of Foreign Subsidiaries on the Economic Sustainability and Competitiveness of the Host Regions

1. The amount of FDI on a per capita basis in Poland is lower than in many of its neighbors. However, due to the country's large population size, total FDI amount is significant and exceeds that of its Central European neighbors.
2. As collected from industry annual white papers by Frost and Sullivan and the Polish. Information and Foreign Investment Agency (PAIIZ) for the year 2008.

2 Heterogeneity of Economic Space: Introduction of the Problem

1. A powiat is a sub-region of a voivodship within the present, new, administrative division of Poland.
2. *Polska Klasyfikacja Dzialalnosci (PKD).*
3. The phrase "flying geese pattern of development" was coined originally by Kaname Akamatsu in 1930s articles in Japanese. The late Saburo Okita (1914–1993), well-known Japanese economist and a foreign minister in the 1980s, greatly contributed to introducing the FG pattern of development to wider audiences, including the political and business world. Thus, the regional transmission of FG industrialization, driven by the catching-up process through diversification/rationalization of industries, has become famous as an engine of Asian economic growth (Kojima, 2000).
4. Originally, articles were published in Japanese and presented to world academia after World War II, in 1961; and in 1962 the articles were available in English.
5. Polska Agencja Infirmacji i Investycji Zagranicznych (PAIIZ). A Guide to Special Economic Zones in Poland in 2008.
6. EU membership requires adoption of EU legislation across a range of commercial and civil law, including trade rules, financial regulation, and competition policy (Bevan ans Estrin, 2004.

3 Local Strengths and Foreign Firms' Location Choice: The Research Design, Data, and Methodology

1. *Powiat* is a region type, a number of which comprise a *wojewodztwo*, a main division unit of the country.
2. Secondary panel data.
3. The RDB data describe voivodships, *powiats*, and *gminas* as elements of social and administrative organization of the country, as well as regions

and sub-regions that are part of territorial units nomenclature, for statistical purposes. It collects, systematically completes, and updates statistical information on specific territorial division units.

4. Since 1975 the territorial administration of Poland consisted of 49 regions (voivodships, województwo), and 2,450 municipalities (*gminas*). In the 1990s a process of political and economic reform led to a new territorial administration, and in 2000, 16 regions (*województwo*, NUTS 2), 308 provinces or districts (*powiats*, NUTS 3), and 2,459 municipalities (NUTS 4) were constituted. At the same time, 50 Regional Development Agencies were created at regional and large city levels. http://www.west-east-id.net/download/marzo2006/WEID_Policy%20Options_%20Report_.pdf
5. As compared to other European countries, Poland is homogeneous in regards to nationality. It is estimated that no more than 3 percent of the total population is made up of national minorities. http://www.development.wne.uw.edu.pl/index.php/Main/Students#Jobs
6. 2000–2002 PKD categories; 2003 and on new (EU) PKD categories. Adjustments were made so that measures remain intact and accurately reflect the actual results. In 2003 the PKD categories have changed in preparation for transition to Poland's accession to the EU. The categories were adjusted to reflect continuity.
7. The sub-unit level analysis will be applied only in cases in which particular specialization of regions will need to be examined. In general, no particular analysis will be conducted as to up-stream and down-stream relationships between industries and firms.
8. Introduction of a new code classification, the PKD system, was induced by the merging of earlier PKD statistical code systems operational in the United Nations (ISIC/CPC), the European Union, (NACE/CPA) and in the countries of North America (NAICS). http://msp.money.pl/zakladam_firme/pkd2007/ (last accessed November 16, 2009).
9. The method used by Cantwell (1989) will be adopted here. "One of the main drawbacks of using absolute numbers of patents is the difficulty associated with then making comparisons between the activities of heterogeneous areas of technological endeavor. Since the propensity to patent is higher in certain fields of activity (for example, pharmaceuticals), this poses potential problems when undertaking comparative analyses" (Cantwell, 1989). Relatively, here, using this index, strengths between industries and countries of origin will be equalized.
10. The results of the analysis are presented in Appendix 1.
11. A *powiat* is a sub-region of a voivodship within the present administrative division of Poland.
12. Due to the problem of having only a single measure of value added in the manufacturing class, this research will test only a few, most represented, manufacturing RLA industrial classes to establish the relationship between the industrial concentration of foreign firms and value-added in those selected industries.
13. As found in: http://www.paiz.gov.pl/prawo/prawo_konkurencji/artykuly/szczegolna_pozycja_msp. Act of WE (Wspólnota Europejska) related to small and medium firms (Dz.U. WE L 10 of January 13, 2001: p. 33).

4 Concentration of Foreign Firms in Poland based on Industrial Specialization and Country-of-Origin Criteria: The Results and Summary of the Evidence

1. *The Chemical and Plastic Industries in Poland.* PAIIZ Report 2008.
2. Ibid.
3. White Paper: "The Biotechnology Sector in Poland." Published by Frost and Sullivan and the Polish Information and Foreign Investment Agency (PAIIZ). October 2008.
4. Ibid.
5. Ibid. The park is expected to have been realized in the years 2007–2015. Phase I of the project was to have been completed by the year 2010. It consists of creating a technology incubator and a research centre financed by public funds.
6. PAIIZ Sectoral Study Report 2013. *Pharmaceutical and Biotechnological Sector in Poland.* February 19, 2013
7. Frost and Sullivan and the Polish Information and Foreign Investment Agency (PAIIZ). October 2008.
8. Although outside of the time frame of this study, Dell Ireland moved to Poland in 2008. Dell moved production of computer systems for customers in Europe, the Middle East and Africa (EMEA) from Limerick to its Polish facility. (last accessed September 27, 2010: http://www.dell.com/content/topics/global.aspx/corp/pressoffice/en/2009/2009_01_08_rr_000?c=us&l=en).
9. PAIIZ Sectoral Study Report 2013. *Information Technology Sector in Poland.* February 19, 2013.
10. *Poland Electrical Industry.* PAIIZ Report 2008.
11. PAIIZ Sectoral Report for 2008. http://www.paiz.gov.pl/publications/sectoral_studies; (last accessed December 17, 2008).
12. Ibid.
13. The reclassification of the old PKD categories took place in 2003 to reflect the EU PKD categories which were implemented and took effect on data in 2004 when Poland joined the EU.
14. *The Aviation Sector in Poland.* PAIIZ Report, 2008.
15. Ibid.
16. As of May 1, 2004, foreign residents and investors from the member states of the European Economic Community are not required to obtain a license/permit from the Ministry of Internal Affairs for purchase of property, with the exception of: agricultural and forest properties for the period of 12 years from the date of accession of the Republic of Poland to the European Union. (author's translation) http://www.cudzoziemcy.pl/index.php?l_prawo_artid=article3214&l_prawo_ct=cat333&s=prawo&lang=pl
17. As presented in Farnoux et al. (2004), with the original source being Banque de France calculations, based on NBP data.
18. *ECB Monthly Bulletin,* July 2002. "The Eurosystem's dialogue with accession countries."
19. Polish Information and Foreign Investment Agency. *Poland's Construction Industry.* http://www.paiz.gov.pl/files/?id_plik=10558 (last accessed June 20, 2013).

20. PAIIZ data – description of PKD class and sub-class.
21. A single investor in a class in the whole country would give a region an RLAis advantage measure. Therefore, for the purposes of this research, this will be discounted as a term of a relative strength.
22. That was the case only throughout the period of this study. In 2009, the foreign investor withdrew in light of the global economic decline and low demand for the products in foreign markets. The firm itself was bought back by the employees.
23. Campos and Kinoshita (2006). *Foreign Direct Investment in Sub-Saharan Africa: Origins, Targets, Impact and Potential.* Edited by S. Ibi Ajayi. Published by African Economic Research Consortium.
24. Represented as average monthly gross wages and salary in relation to the average domestic – Poland = 100.

6 Final Analysis of FDI Patterns Across Regions in Poland and Policy Recommendations

1. Campos and Kinoshita, (2006). *Foreign Direct Investment in Sub-Saharan Africa: Origins, Targets, Impact and Potential.* Edited by S. Ibi Ajayi. Published by: African Economic Research Consortium.

7 Afterword

1. Adekoya, R. (2013). "Poland a European leader in FDI job creation." http://www.wbj.pl/article-62974-poland-a-european-leader-in-fdi-job-creation.html (last accessed July 5, 2013)
2. Ibid.

References

Acs, Z. J., Morck, R., Shaver, J. M., and Yeung, B. (1996). "The internationalization of small and medium-sized enterprises: a policy perspective." *Small Business Economics*, Vol. 9: 7–20.

Acs, Z. J., Morck, R., Shaver, J. M., and Yeung, B. (1997). "The internationalization of small and medium-sized enterprises: a policy perspective." *Small Business Economics*, Vol. 9, No. 1, (February).

Aitken, B. and Harrison, A. (1999). "Do domestic firms benefit from direct foreign investment? Evidence from Venezuela." *The American Economic Review*, Vol. 89, No. 3, (June): 605–618.

Alcácer, J. and Chung, W. (2007). "Location strategies and knowledge spillovers." *Management Science*, Vol. 53, No. 5: 760–776.

Ambos, B. (2005). "Foreign direct investment in industrial research and development: a study of German MNCs." *Research Policy*, Vol. 34, No. 4: 395–410.

Arthur, B. (1986). "Industry location patterns and the importance of history." CEPR Paper No. 84, Stanford.

—— (1989). "Competing technologies, increasing returns, and lock-in by historical events." *The Economic Journal*, Vol. 99, No. 394: 116–131.

Athreye, S. and Cantwell, J. (2007). "Creating competition? Globalisation and the emergence of new technology producers." *Research Policy*, Vol. 36, No. 2: 209–226.

Audretsch, D. B. and Feldman, M. P. (1994). "External economies and spatial clustering," in P. Krugman and A. Venables (eds), *The Location of Economic Activity: New theories and Evidence*. London: Center of Economic Policy Research.

Audretsch, D. B. and Stephan, P. E. (1996). "Company-scientist locational links: the case of biotechnology." *The American Economic Review*, Vol. 86, No. 3: 641–652.

Bandera, V. N. and White, J. T. (1968). "U.S. direct investments and domestic markets in Europe." *Economia Internationale*, Vol. 21, (February): 117–133.

Baptista R. and Swann, G. M. P. (1998). "Do firms in clusters innovate more?" *Research Policy*, 27: 525–540.

Barrios, S., Bertinelli, L., and Strobl, E. (2006). "Coagglomeration and spillovers." *Regional Science and Urban* Economics, Vol. 36, No. (4): 467–481.

Barro, R. and Martin, S. I. (1995). *Economic Growth*. New York: McGraw-Hill.

Bartik, T. J. (1985). "Business location decisions in the United States: estimates of the effects of unionization, taxes, and other characteristics of states." *Journal of Business & Economic Statistics*, Vol. 3, No. 1: 14–22.

Berry, H. (2006). "Leaders, laggards, and the pursuit of foreign knowledge." *Strategic Management Journal*, Vol. 27: 151–168.

Bevan, A. A. and Estrin, S. (2004). "The determinants of foreign direct investment into European transition economies." *Journal of Comparative Economics*, Vol. 32, No. 4: 775–787.

Birkinshaw, J. and Hood, N. (1998). "Multinational subsidiary evolution: Capability and charter change in foreign-owned subsidiary companies." *The Academy of Management Review* Vol. 23, No. 4: 773–795.

Blomstrom, M. (1991). "Host country benefits of foreign investment." NBER Working Paper No. W3615 (February), Available at SSRN: http://ssrn.com/abstract=268197.

Borensztein, E., De Gregorio, J., and Lee, J–W. (1993). "How does foreign direct investment affect economic growth?" *Journal of International Economics*, Vol. 45 (1998): 115–135.

Blomström, M. and Kokko, A. (1997). *How Foreign Investment Affects Host Countries*. World Bank, International Economics Department, International Trade Division.

Boudier-Bensebaa, F. (2005). "Agglomeration economies and location choice: foreign direct investment in Hungary." *Economics of Transition*, Vol. 13, No. 4: 605–628.

Braunerhjelm, P. (2008). "Specialization of regions and universities: the new versus the old." *Industry and Innovation*, Vol. 15, No. 3: 253–275.

Brülhart, M. (1998). "Trading places: industrial specialization in the European Union." *JCMS: Journal of Common Market Studies*, Vol. 36, No. 3: 319–346.

Campos, N. and Kinoshita, Y. (2003). "Why does FDI go where it goes? New evidence from the transition economies." IMF Working Paper.

—— (2006). *Foreign Direct Investment in Sub-Saharan Africa: Origins, Targets, Impact and Potential*, edited by Ibi Ajayi. African Economic Research Consortium.

Cantwell, J. A. (1989). *Technological Innovation and Multinational Corporations*. Oxford: Blackwell.

—— (1991a). "The international agglomeration of R&D," in M. Casson (ed.), *Global Research Strategy and International Competitiveness*. Oxford: Blackwell.

—— (1991b). "The theory of technological competence and its application to international production," in D. McFetridge (ed.), *Foreign Investment, Technology and Economic Growth*. Calgary: University of Calgary Press.

—— (ed.) (1994). *Transnational Corporations and Innovatory Activities. United Nations Library on Transnational Corporations*. London: Routledge.

—— (2000). "Technological lock-in of large firms since the interwar period." *European Review of Economic History*, Vol. 4: 147–174.

—— (2009). "Location and the multinational enterprise." *Journal of International Business Studies*, Vol. 40: 35–41.

Cantwell, J. A. and Iammarino, S. (1998). "MNCs, technological innovation and regional systems in the EU: some evidence in the Italian case." *International Journal of the Economics of Business*, Vol. 5, No. 3: 383–408.

—— (2000). "Multinational corporations and the location of technological innovation in the UK regions." *Regional Studies*, Vol. 34: 317–332.

—— (2001). "EU regions and multinational corporations." *Industrial and Corporate Change*, Vol. 10, No. 4.

—— (2003). *Multinational Corporations and European Regional System of Innovation*. New York: Routledge.

Cantwell, J. A., Iammarino, S., and Noonan, C. A. (2000). "Sticky places in slippery space – the location of innovation by MNCs in the European regions," in N. Pain (ed.), *Inward Investment, Technological Change and Growth: The impact of MNCs on the UK economy*. Oxford: Pergamon, 210–239.

Cantwell J. A. and Janne, O. (1999). "Technological globalisation and innovative centres: the role of corporate technological leadership and locational hierarchy." *Research Policy*, Vol. 28: 119–144.

Cantwell, J. A. and Mudambi, R. (2000). "The location of MNE R&D activity: the role of investment incentives." *Management International Review*, Vol. 40, No. 1: 127–148.

—— (2005). "MNE competence-creating subsidiary mandates." *Strategic Management Journal*, Vol. 26: 1109–1128.

—— (2011). "Physical attraction and the geography of knowledge sourcing in multinational enterprises." *Global Strategy Journal*, Vol. 1, No. (3–4): 206–232.

Cantwell, J. A. and Piscitello, L. (1997). *The Emergence of Corporate International Networks for Accumulation of Dispersed Technological Competences*. Whiteknights: University of Reading.

—— (2002). "Agglomeration and location of foreign R&D activities in the European regions," proceedings of the 28th Annual Conference of the European International Business Academy, Athens (December).

Cantwell, J. A. and Vertova, G. (2004). "Historical evolution of technological diversification." *Research Policy*, Vol. 33, No. 3: 511–529.

Carter, F. and Turnock, D. (2005). *Foreign direct investment and regional development in East Central Europe and the Former Soviet Union: A Collection of Essays*. Ashgate Publishing.

Caves, R. (1971). "International corporations: the industrial economics of foreign investment." *Economica*, Vol. 56: 279–293.

Chen, H. and Chen, T.-J. (1998). "Network linkages and location choice in foreign direct investment." *Journal of International Business Studies*, Vol. 29, No. 3: 445–468.

Cheng, L. K. and Kwan, Y. K. (1999). "FDI stock and its determinants," in Y. Wu (ed.), *Foreign Direct Investment and Economic Growth in China*. Cheltenham: Edward Elgar, 42–56.

—— (2000). "What are the determinants of the location of foreign direct investment? The Chinese experience." *Journal of International Economics*, Vol. 51, No. 2: 379–400.

Cheng, Y. (2009). "Determinants of FDI mode choice: acquisition, brownfield, and greenfield entry in foreign markets." *Canadian Journal of Administrative Sciences*, Vol. 23, No. 3: 202–220.

Chidlow, A., Salciuviene, L., and Young, S. (2009). "Regional determinants of inward FDI distribution in Poland." *International Business Review*, Vol. 18, No. 2: 119–133.

Chung, W. and Alcácer, J. (2002). "Knowledge seeking and location choice of foreign direct investment in the United States." *Management Science*, Vol. 48, No. 12: 1534–1554.

Cieślik, A. (2004). *Location of multinational firms and national border effects: The Case of Poland*. Warsaw: Warsaw University.

Crozet, M., Mayer, T., and Mucchielli, J.-L. (2003). "How do firms agglomerate? A study of FDI in France." CEPR Discussion Papers, International Trade No. 3873. London: Centre for Economic Policy Research.

Coughlin, C. C., Terza, J. V., and Arromdee, V. (1991). "State characteristics and the location of foreign direct investment within the United States." *The Review of Economics and Statistics*, Vol. 65: 675–683.

Culem, C. G. (1988). "The locational determinants of direct investments among industrialized countries." *European Economic Review*, Vol. 32, No. 4: 885–904.

David, P. and Rosenbloom, J. (1990). "Marshallian factor market externalities and the dynamics of industrial localization." *Journal of Urban Economics*, Vol. 28: 349–370.

de Mello Jr, L. R. (1997). "Foreign direct investment in developing countries and growth: a selective survey." *The Journal of Development Studies*, Vol. 34, No. 1: 1–34.

De Propris, L., Driffield, N., and Menghinello, S. (2005). "Local industrial systems and the location of FDI in Italy." *International Journal of the Economics of Business*, Vol. 12, No. 1, (February): 105–121.

Despiney-Zochowska, B. A. (2001). "The Marshallian district – an attempt to interpret regional development in Poland." Paper presented at Regional Studies Association International conference, Regional Transitions European Regions and the Challenges of Development, Integration and Enlargement. Gdańsk.

Devereux, M. P., Griffith, R., and Simpson, H. (2004). "The geographic distribution of production activity in the UK.." *Regional Science and Urban Economics*, Vol. 34, No. 5: 533–564.

Dunning, J. H. (1977). "Trade, location of economic activity and the multinational enterprise: the search for an eclectic approach," in B. Ohlin, P. O. Hessleborn, and P. M. Wijkman (eds), *The International Location of Economic Activity*. London: Macmillan.

—— (1981). *International Production and the Multinational Enterprise*. London: Allen & Unwin.

—— (1993). *Multinational Enterprises in the Global Economy*. Wokingham, Berks: Addison–Wesley.

—— (1995). "Reappraising the eclectic paradigm in an age of alliance capitalism." *Journal of International Business Studies*, Vol. 26.

—— (1997). *Alliance Capitalism and Global Business*. London: Routledge.

Dunning, J. H. (2002). *Regions, Globalization, and the Knowledge-Based Economy*. Oxford: Oxford University Press.

Ellison, G. and Glaeser, E. L. (1997). "Geographic concentration in U.S. manufacturing industries: a dartboard approach." *Journal of Political Economy*, Vol. 105, No. 5, 879–927.

Ergas, H. (1986). "Does technology policy matter?" CEPR Conference, London.

European Central Bank (2002). "The Eurosystem's dialogue with accession countries." *ECB Monthly Bulletin*, (July).

Evans, C. (2003). "The economic significance of national border effects." *American Economic Review*, Vol. 93: 1291–1312.

Farnoux, L. et al. (2004). "Foreign direct investment in the Polish financial sector." Case study prepared for the CGFS Working Group on Financial Sector FDI.

Feenstra, R. C. and Hanson, G. (1997). "Foreign direct investment and relative wages: evidence from Mexico's maquiladoras." *Journal of International Economics*, Vol. 42, No. 3–4: 371–393.

Feenstra, R. C. and Markusen, J. R. (1994). "Accounting for growth with new inputs." *International Economic Review*, 429–447.

Florida, R. (1995). "'Toward the learning region." *Futures*, Vol. 27, No. 5, 527–536.

—— (1997). "The globalization of R&D: results of a survey of foreign-affiliated R&D laboratories in the USA." *Research policy*, Vol. 26, No. 1: 85–103.

Ford, S. and Strange, R. (1999). "Where do Japanese manufacturing firms invest within Europe, and why?" *Transnational Corporation*, Vol. 8, No. 1: 117–142.

Frost and Sullivan and the Polish Information and Foreign Investment Agency (PAIIZ) (2008). "The Biotechnology Sector in Poland." White Paper, (October).

—— (2008). "The Renewable Energy Sector in Poland." White Paper, (October).

Fujita, M. and Krugman, P. (2004). "The new economic geography: past, present and the future." *Papers in Regional Science*, Vol. 83: 139–164.

Fujita, M. and Thisse, J. F. (1996). "Economics of agglomeration." *Journal of the Japanese and International Economies*, Vol. 10, No. 4: 339–378.

Glaeser, E. L. and Kohlhase, J. E. (2003). "Cities, regions and the decline of transport costs." NBER Working Paper No. 9886.

Globerman, S. (2001). "The location of higher value added activities." Occasional Paper No. 27, Western Washington University.

Główny Urząd Statystyczny (GUS). Report: *Value Added Activity 2000–2006*.

—— Report: *Dzialalnosc gospodarcza spolek z udzialem 2005*.

—— Report: *Dzialalnosc innowacyjna przedsiebiorstw 2002–2004*.

Guimarães, P., Figueiredo, O., and Woodward, D. (2000). "Agglomeration and the location of foreign direct investment in Portugal." *Journal of Urban Economics*, Vol. 47, No. 1: 115–135.

Harrison, B. (1994). *Lean and mean: The Changing Landscape of Power in the Age of Flexibility*. New York: Basic Books.

He, C. (2002). "Information costs, agglomeration economies and the location of foreign direct investment in China." *Regional Studies*, Vol. 36, No. 9: 1029–1036.

Head, K., Ries, J., and Swenson, D. (1995). "Agglomeration benefits and location choice: evidence from Japanese investment in the United States." *Journal of International Economics*, Vol. 38, No. 3/4: 223–247.

—— (1999). "Attracting foreign manufacturing: investment promotion and agglomeration." *Regional Science and Urban Economics*, Vol. 29, No. 2: 197–218.

Index Mundi (2013).*Poland Economy Profile 2013*. Report, http://www.indexmundi.com/poland/economy_profile.html Last accessed August 15, 2013.

Jaffe, A. B. (1989). "Real Effects of Academic Research." *The American Economic Review*, Vol. 79, No. 5 (December): 957–970.

Jaffe, A. B., Trajtenberg, M., and Henderson, R. (1993). "Geographic localization of knowledge spillovers as evidence by patent citations." *Quarterly Journal of Economics*, Vol. 108, No. 3: 577–98.

Javorcik, B. S. and Spatareanu, M. (2003). "To share or not to share: does local participation matter for spillovers from foreign direct investment?" World Bank, Working Paper No. 3118.

—— (2008). "To share or not to share: does local participation matter for spillovers from foreign direct investment?" *Journal of Development Economics*, Vol. 85, No. 1, 194–217.

Javorcik, B. S. (2004). "Does foreign direct investment increase the productivity of domestic firms? In search of spillovers through backward linkages." *The American Economic Review*, Vol. 94, No. 3: 605–627.

Kaldor, N. (1955–1956). "Alternative theories of distribution." *The Review of Economic Studies* Vol. 23, No. 2: 83–100.

Ketels, M. and Memedovic, O. (2008). "From clusters to cluster-based economic development." *International Journal of Technological Learning, Innovation and Development*, Vol. 1, No. 3.

Kindleberger-Audretsch. (1983). *Multinational Corporation in the 1980*. Mit Press. Chapter 2 by Kogut, B.

Kojima, K. (2000). "The 'flying geese' model of Asian economic development: origin, theoretical extensions, and regional policy implications." *Journal of Asian Economics*, Vol. 11: 375–401.

Knickerbocker, F. T. (1973). *Oligopolistic Reaction and Multinational Enterprise*. Boston: Harvard University.

Kogut, B. and Chang, S. J. (1991). "Technological capabilities and Japanese foreign direct investment in the United States." *Review of Economics and Statistics*, Vol. 73: 401–413.

—— (2010). "Urbanization, agglomeration, and coagglomeration of service industries," in *Agglomeration Economics*. University of Chicago Press, (151–180).

Kuemmerle, W. (1999a). "The drivers of foreign direct investment into research and development – an empirical investigation." *Journal of International Business Studies*, Vol. 30: 1–24.

—— (1999b). "Foreign direct investment in industrial research in the pharmaceutical and electronics industries – results from a survey of multinational firms." *Research Policy*, Vol. 28, No. 2: 179–193.

Krugman, P. (1991). "Increasing returns and economic geography." *Journal of Political Economy*, Vol. 99: 483–499.

—— (1998). "What's new about the new economic geography?" *Oxford Review of Economic Policy*, Vol. 14: 7–17.

Langhorne, R. (2001). *The Coming of Globalization: Its Evolution and Contemporary Consequences*. Palgrave MacMillan.

Lansbury, M., Pain, N., and Smidkova, K. (1996). "Foreign direct investment in Central Europe since 1990: an econometric study." *National Institute Economic Review*, No. 156.

Leahy, D. and Pavelin, S. (2003). "Follow-my-leader FDI and tacit collusion." *International Journal of Industrial Organization*, Vol. 21, No. 3: 439–453.

—— (2008). "Playing away to win at home." *Journal of Economics and Business*, Vol. 60, No. 5: 455–468.

Lin, P. and Saggi, K. (1999). "Incentives for foreign investment under imitation." *The Canadian Journal of Economics*, Vol. 32, No. 5, (November): 1275–1298.

—— (2002). "Timing of entry under externalities." *Journal of Economics*, Vol. 75, No. 3: 211–225.

Lipsey, R. E. (2002). "Home and host country effects of FDI." NBER Working Paper No. 9293. Cambridge, MA: National Bureau of Economic Research.

Lipsey, R. E. and Kravis, I. B. (1985). "The competitive position of U.S. manufacturing firms." NBER Working Paper Series, January 1985.

Little, J. S. (1978). "Location decision of foreign direct investment in the United States." *New England Economic Review*, Vol. 4, No. 4: 43–63.

Lundvall, B. A. (1986). *Technological Unemployment in a Small Open Economy*. Institute of Production, Aalborg University.

Malecki, E. (1997). "Technology and economic development: the dynamics of local, regional, and national change." University of Illinois at Urbana-Champaign's Academy for Entrepreneurial Leadership Historical Research Reference in Entrepreneurship.

—— (1980) "Dimensions of R&D location in the United States." *Research Policy*, Vol. 9: 2–22.

Mariotti, S. and Piscitello, L. (1995). "Information costs and location of FDIs within the host country: empirical evidence from Italy." *Journal of International Business Studies*, Vol. 26, No. 4.

Marshall, A. (1920). *Principles of Economics* (8th edn.). London: Macmillan.
Marshall, A. and Marshall, M. P. (1920). *The Economics of Industry*. London: Macmillan.
Martin, R. and Sunlay, P. (2003). "Deconstructing clusters: chaotic concept or policy panacea?" *Journal of Economic Geography*, Vol. 3: 5–35.
Mutinelli, M. and Piscitello, L. (1998). "The entry mode choice of MNEs: an evolutionary approach." *Research Policy*, Vol. 27, No. 5: 491–506.
Nachum, L. and Keeble, D. (2003). "Neo-Marshallian clusters and global networks: the linkages of media firms in Central London." *Long Range Planning*, Vol. 36, No. 5, (October): 459–480.
Nelson, R. R. (ed.) (1993). *National Innovation Systems: A comparative analysis*. Oxford: Oxford University Press.
Pavlínek, P. (2004). "Regional development implications of foreign direct investment in Central Europe." *European Urban and Regional Studies*, Vol. 11, No. 1: 47–70.
Polska Agencja Infirmacji i Investycji Zagranicznych (PAIIZ). Annual reports. Data tables years 2000–2006.
—— A Guide to Special Economic Zones in Poland in 2008.
Pitelis, N. Ch. (2010). "Foreign direct investment and economic integration." MPRA Paper No. 23938, posted 17 July.
Polish Information and Foreign Investment Agency. "Poland's Construction Industry." http://www.paiz.gov.pl/files/?id_plik=10558 Last Accessed November 20, 2009.
—— (2008a). *The Aviation Sector in Poland*. PAIIZ Report.
—— (2008b). *Poland's Electrical Industry*. PAIIZ Report.
—— (2008c). *Poland's Agribusiness Industry*. PAIIZ Report.
Porter, M. (1985). *Competitive Advantage*. New York: Free Press.
—— (1990). *The Competitive Advantage of Nations*. New York: Free Press.
—— (1996). "What is strategy?" *Harvard Business Review*, Vol. 74, No. 6: 61–78.
—— (1998a). "Clusters and competition: new agendas for companies, governments, and institutions," in M. Porter, *On Competition*. Boston: Harvard Business School Press, 19–287).
—— (1998b). "The microeconomic foundations of economic development." *The Global Competitiveness Report 1998*. Geneva: World Economic Forum, 38–63.
—— (2000). "Location, competition, and economic development: local clusters in a global economy." *Economic Development Quarterly*, Vol. 14, No. 1, (February): 15–34.
Porter, M., Ketels, Ch., and Delgado, M. (2006). "The microeconomic foundations of prosperity: findings from the Business Competitiveness Index." *The Global Competitiveness Report 2007–2008*, World Economic Forum.
Porter, M. and Stern, S. (2001). "Location matters." *Sloan Management Review*, Vol. 42, No. 4: 28–36.
Rugman, A. and Verbeke, A. (2001). "Subsidiary-specific advantages in multinational enterprises." *Strategic Management Journal*, Vol. 22, No. 3: 237–250.
Sampson, R. C. (2004). "Organizational choice in R&D alliances: Knowledge-based and transaction cost perspectives." *Managerial and Decision Economics*, Vol. 25, No. 6–7: 421–436.
Saxenian, A., (1994). *Regional Advantage*. Cambridge: Harvard University Press.
Scaperlanda, A. and Mauer, L. J. (1969). "The determinants of U.S. direct investment in the EEC." *American Economic Review*, Vol. 59, (September): 558–568.

Schumpeter, J. A. (1942). *Capitalism, Socialism, and Democracy*. New York: Harper & Bros.

—— (1954). *History of Economic Analysis*. Routledge. (First edition by New York: Oxford University Press).

—— (1994). *History of Economic Analysis*. Routledge. (First edition, New York: Oxford University Press, 1954).

Shaver, J. M. (1998a). "Accounting for endogeneity when assessing strategy performance: does entry mode choice affect FDI survival?" *Management Science*, Vol. 44, No. 4: 571–585.

—— (1998b). "Do foreign-owned and U.S.-owned establishments exhibit the same location pattern in U.S. manufacturing industries?" *Journal of International Business Studies* 3rd Quarter, Vol. 29, No. 3.

Shaver, J. M. and Flyer, F. (2000). "Agglomeration economies, firm heterogeneity, and foreign direct investment in the United States." *Strategic Management Journal*, Vol. 21: 1175–1193.

Smith, A. (1776). *An Inquiry into the Nature and Causes of the Wealth of Nations*. Dunwoody, GA: Norman S. Berg.

Smith, D. F. and Florida, R. (1994). "Agglomeration and industrial location: an econometric analysis of Japanese-affiliated manufacturing establishments in automotive-related industries." *Journal of Urban Economics*, Vol. 36, No. 1, (July): 23–41.

Soete, L. (1987). "The impact of technological innovation on international trade patterns: the evidence reconsidered." *Research Policy*, Vol. 16, No. 2–4, (August): 101–130.

Storper, M. (1992). "The limits to globalization: technology districts and international trade." *Economic Geography*, Vol. 68, No. 1: 60–93.

—— (1995). "The resurgence of regional economies, ten years later. The region as a nexus of untraded interdependencies." *European Urban and Regional Studies*, Vol. 2, No. 3: 191–221.

Tang, H., Zoli, E., and Klytchnikova, I. (2000). "Banking crises in transition countries: fiscal costs and related issues." World Bank Policy Research Paper No. 2484, Washington, D.C.

—— (1826, trans. 1966) *Von Thünen's Isolated State: An English Edition of Der Isolie STaat*, trans. C. M. Wartenberg, edited and with an introduction by P. Hall. Oxford: Pergamon.

Venables, A. J. (1996). "Equilibrium locations of vertically linked industries." *International Economic Review*, Vol. 37, No. 2.

—— (1999). "But why does geography matter, and which geography matters?" *International Regional Science Review*, Vol. 22, No. 2: 238–241.

Vernon, R. (1966). "International investment and international trade in the product cycle." *Quarterly Journal of Economics*, Vol. 80: 190–207.

—— (1974). "The location of economic activity," in J. H. Dunning (ed.), *Economic Analysis and the Multinational Enterprise*. London: Allen & Unwin.

Webber, M. J. (1972) *Impact of Uncertainty on Location*. London: MIT Press.

—— (1984) *Industrial Location*. London: Sage.

Weber, A. (1909, reprinted 1929). *Theory of the Location of Industries*, trans. C. J. Friedrich. Chicago: University of Chicago Press.

Wells, L. T. (ed.) (1972). *The Product Life Cycle and International Trade*. Cambridge, MA: Harvard University Press.

Wheeler, D. and Mody, A. (1992). "International investment location decisions. The case of U.S. firms." *Journal of International Economics*, Vol. 33, No. 1–2, (August): 57–76.
Woodward, D. P., (1992). "Locational determinants of Japanese manufacturing start-ups in the United States." *Southern Economic Journal*, Vol. 58, No. 3: 690–708.
Zhao, C. (2009). *Global Knowledge Linkages and the Innovativeness of Local Clusters: Evidence from the Guangzhou Software Cluster in China*. IBIMA Business Review.

Index

Printed and bound by CPI Group (UK) Ltd, Croydon, CR0 4YY